Voyages, the Age of Sail

NEW PERSPECTIVES ON MARITIME HISTORY AND NAUTICAL ARCHAEOLOGY

UNIVERSITY PRESS OF FLORIDA

Florida A&M University, Tallahassee
Florida Atlantic University, Boca Raton
Florida Gulf Coast University, Ft. Myers
Florida International University, Miami
Florida State University, Tallahassee
New College of Florida, Sarasota
University of Central Florida, Orlando
University of Florida, Gainesville
University of North Florida, Jacksonville
University of South Florida, Tampa
University of West Florida, Pensacola

Voyages, the Age of Sail

Documents in American Maritime History,

Volume I,

1492–1865

EDITED BY JOSHUA M. SMITH AND

THE NATIONAL MARITIME HISTORICAL SOCIETY

University Press of Florida

Gainesville/Tallahassee/Tampa/Boca Raton

Pensacola/Orlando/Miami/Jacksonville/Ft. Myers/Sarasota

Library of Congress Cataloging-in-Publication Data
Voyages, The age of sail : documents in American maritime history,
Volume I, 1492–1865 / edited by Joshua M. Smith and the National
Maritime Historical Society.
p. cm.—(New perspectives on maritime history and nautical
archaeology)
Collection of edited historical documents, and companion volume to
Voyages, The age of engines.
Includes bibliographical references.
ISBN 978-0-8130-3304-4 (alk. paper)
1. Navigation—United States—History—Sources. 2. United States—
History, Naval—Sources. 3. Sailing ships—United States—History—
Sources. 4. Merchant marine—United States—History—Sources.
5. Voyages and travels—History—Sources. I. Smith, Joshua M.
II. National Maritime Historical Society (U.S.)
VK23.V69 2009
387.50973'0903—dc22   2008033948

The University Press of Florida is the scholarly publishing agency for the
State University System of Florida, comprising Florida A&M University,
Florida Atlantic University, Florida Gulf Coast University, Florida In-
ternational University, Florida State University, New College of Florida,
University of Central Florida, University of Florida, University of North
Florida, University of South Florida, and University of West Florida.

University Press of Florida
15 Northwest 15th Street
Gainesville, FL 32611-2079
www.upf.com

Dedicated to the Midshipmen
of the United States Merchant Marine Academy

He who commands the sea has command of everything.
THEMISTOCLES

CONTENTS

PREFACE

Why study maritime history? Consider that more than half the U.S. population lives in coastal counties. The resident population in this area is expected to increase by twenty-five million people by 2015. The world ocean, covering more than two-thirds of the earth's surface, is the engine that drives the planet's environment. The Great Lakes possess about 20 percent of the earth's surface freshwater. Ocean shipping carries 90 percent of the nation's commerce. The United States Navy is the largest and most powerful in the world by far. There are many institutes of higher learning dedicated entirely to working with or on the nation's waters, including three of the five federal service academies and five state-run merchant marine academies. Yet Americans cannot be said to have a firm grasp of the importance of the oceans, Great Lakes, and major rivers. *Voyages* is part of an effort by the National Maritime Historical Society and the David M. Milton Charitable Trust to remind Americans just how large a role our nation's waterways have played in our history.

There are few events in American history that cannot be said to have a maritime element. But maritime history has suffered as a field for decades because it has had no textbook or standardized curricular resources, such as a published document collection. *Voyages* is an attempt to establish a usable, portable, and interesting set of documents on America's maritime past that revolve around historically significant themes. The impetus behind this collection is that documents and images stir students to think more deeply about the impact of all things marine on American society. By providing a body of documents that they themselves analyze, *Voyages* enables students to move beyond being passive participants and to become active learners, putting together patterns from the clues left in these documents and images. Whenever possible, maritime events are linked with larger trends impacting American history.

Voyages consists of almost one hundred and fifty sources divided into two volumes, of which this is the first. Each chapter is broken down into historically significant themes based on three to four items arranged in chronological order. Furthermore, each item is accompanied by three "questions for discussion" that serve to further focus student learning and possibly to form the basis of student assignments. Most of these documents are edited from versions found in published sources, although a few are the result of archival research or the loan of personal papers. Numerous alterations have been made to enrich their educational value. Spelling has been modified in many instances for clarity, and sections have been cut out for the sake of brevity. Footnotes have been added, removed, or altered to better inform students with background information. All ship names have been italicized. Items should in no way be considered accurate duplications of the originals, but are excerpts edited for educational value. In all cases, the source used has been cited.

DOCUMENT-BASED LEARNING

Historians are often compared to detectives because they must reconstruct past events out of evidence that is often difficult to put together. Typically, historians rely on written documents such as letters, diaries, government reports, and the like. More recently, historians have reassessed maps and images as primary documents, too; this is a particularly useful discovery given that about half of all students are more visually oriented, while the other half is more comfortable with text. But not all documents are created equal. While some evidence is reliable, some is less trustworthy but may have value nonetheless. While evaluating the evidence and interpreting its meaning is difficult, most historians relish this task as a complex riddle that, when solved, will reveal new insights into the human experience. In maritime terms, think of it as a hunt for buried treasure.

Interpreting historical documents is a basic skill that hones students' analytical skills. It is not a new idea; Harvard history professor Albert Bushnell Hart began publishing collections of documents for student interpretation over a century ago. But in the twenty-first century, with American textual literacy apparently declining, the skills gained through document-based research remain more important than ever. Ideally, after reading the document closely, students will respond constructively and analytically to the ideas advanced in the text. Many students may find it useful to ask themselves a series of analytical questions in order to assess a historical document. The following list is but a sample of how these questions might be conceived:

1. Who was the author of the document? How did their position, rank, or viewpoint influence how they saw events?

2. When was the document created? What other events occurred around the same time that may have influenced the author?

3. Why was the document or image created? What sort of evidence did the document's author present to support their views?

4. How reliable is the document as a source of factual information? Does its author have any sort of bias?

5. What is the document's historical significance? How does it reflect on major themes in American history?

6. What questions does this document leave unanswered?

Instructors and students reading the documents in *Voyages* should realize that four major themes run through this collection. These themes have slowly evolved in teaching a course called *History of American Sea Power* at the United States Merchant Marine Academy in Kings Point, New York. This is a mandatory course taken by all first-year students in order to awaken them to the importance of maritime matters in shaping the nation's history. While obviously this is important knowledge for future ship's officers, groups such as the National Maritime Historical Society believe this is important for all Americans to understand.

THEMES

The first theme is that maritime trade was a crucial element in the historical development of the United States. Columbus sailed across the Atlantic in search of a trade route. Most European settlements came into existence for commercial purposes. The African slave trade has many ramifications for American history, but it must be recognized that economic demands and desires lay at its root. Differences over maritime trade contributed to the American Revolution, and spilled over into the political debates that shaped the Constitution and early American politics. Maritime developments shaped westward movement and the industrial and transportation revolutions. America is a commercial nation, and seaborne commerce has played a significant role in our economic development. Male and female merchants and entrepreneurs, such as Keziah Coffin, Robert Fulton, Robert Dollar, Henry J. Kaiser, and Malcolm McLean represent the aggressive commercial spirit that has made this nation wealthy.

Wealth, however, needs protection, and American writers such as Alfred Thayer Mahan remind us that navies are inextricably linked with commercial development. To paraphrase Admiral Stephen B. Luce (founder of the

Naval War College in Newport, Rhode Island), military sea power is the off-spring of commerce, not its parent. John Paul Jones was a great naval leader not because he captured HMS *Serapis*, but because he brought confusion and destruction to Britain's merchant fleets. When Oliver Hazard Perry defeated a British fleet on Lake Erie, it was important because it opened the Great Lakes to American enterprise, first agricultural and later industrial. In World War II, German U-boats threatened to isolate this industrial nation from supplying its Allies and receiving raw materials. More recently, threats to American security include attacking oil tankers or planting a nuclear bomb in a container ship. Securing seaborne shipping thus remains a crucial element in protecting American business interests, our standard of living, and even the lives of ordinary citizens in our commercial centers, many of which are ports, whether on the ocean, Great Lakes, or western rivers.

The second theme found in this book is power and authority versus degradation, slavery, or powerlessness. Indeed, few scenarios evoke the arbitrary power of one human being over another as much as the often-brutal relationship between the master of a ship in the age of sail and the vessel's crew, or more pointedly, a human cargo of enslaved Africans. The reaction against this power imbalance was often violent, including mutiny, piracy, and militant labor union unrest.

Slavery is one of the most shameful and contentious episodes in American history and is arguably the best example of a power imbalance. Several documents in this collection relate to slavery, including the important memoirs of Olaudah Equiano, an African enslaved on the Guinea coast who endured the hellish "middle passage" to America and later became a sailor. Other documents relate to South Carolina's controversial decision to imprison "colored" seamen while in port, still others relate to the efforts of abolitionists to free slaves by using a coastal schooner to transport them northward.

While African slavery was an important element of race relations, they are far more complex than a dichotomy between black and white. All races and many ethnic groups faced discrimination at some point. On the West Coast, Chinese faced legalized discrimination for many decades under the Chinese Exclusion Act of 1882. It was only with the advent of radical labor unions like Joe Curran's National Maritime Union (NMU) that discrimination began to decline on merchant ships, albeit slowly. The U.S. Navy also struggled with racial integration well into the 1970s.

The third theme revolves around the complex relationship of human

communities to the environment. From the early days of European exploration of the Americas, the natural bounty of its lands and waters has been
viewed with an eye toward exploitation. As a result of over-harvesting, fish
stocks and whale populations have plummeted. Understanding the use of
marine resources reveals a great deal about human society. For example,
whaling in the early nineteenth century was often seen as a metaphor for
the struggle between American civilization and nature. So, too, knowing
who claimed the right to act as the arbiter of the use of natural resources
can inform us about racial inequalities. In California in the late 1800s, for
example, the legislature created laws ostensibly to conserve valuable fisheries, but in reality they were meant to exclude Chinese immigrants from the
West Coast.

In the late twentieth and early twenty-first century these debates became
more heated as fish stocks shrank and environmental awareness grew. But
questions remain. For example, can American efforts to regulate offshore
fisheries during the Cold War be best understood as an environmental concern, or was it just another episode in U.S.-Soviet competition? Do nine-
teenth-century treaties with Native Americans give them the right to hunt
whales in the 1990s, and is it racist for environmental groups to oppose
those whale hunts? How are the Great Lakes supposed to deal with invasive
species brought in by commercial shipping? These are the sort of questions
that will continue to haunt the American relationship with its marine environment.

The fourth theme is one of the basic underpinnings of all historical approaches to interpretation, acknowledging persistence or change in human
society. In terms of persistence, Native Americans have consistently asserted their separate identity from the rest of American society, despite five
hundred years of effort to eradicate or assimilate them. In terms of change,
maritime labor unions have fought for society to accept seafarers as first-
class citizens, with the same rights and privileges as land-based workers.

Some of the most powerful recent historical scholarship has focused on
gender and sexuality in American society. In many ways these studies focus
on power imbalances, but another powerful element in them is their focus
on change and continuity in gender roles. The relationship between men
and women continues to change and raises many questions. Should institutions such as the U.S. Naval Academy cling to its traditional culture, or
should it accept women as fully capable of combat roles?

Many of these documents incorporate elements from one or more of
these four themes. Indeed, the most powerful of these documents incor-

porate elements of all four. The questions at the end of each source often reflect the four themes outlined above.

ACKNOWLEDGMENTS

The genesis of this book began with discussions with Burchenal Green of the National Maritime Historical Society. Without her kind encouragement, this project (which has taken some curious twists and turns along the way) would never have gotten off the ground. So, too, the generosity of the David M. Milton Charitable Trust has made this project possible.

Librarians are the unsung heroes of any book, and this is no exception. The staff of the Schuyler Otis Bland Library at the United States Merchant Marine Academy in Kings Point, New York, provided stellar service. In particular, Dr. George Billy, Donald Gill, and Marion Stern gave significant contributions in terms of time and effort. So, too, the staff of the Naval Historical Center, especially Ed Marolda and Michael Crawford, proved enthusiastic supporters of this project, as did Bob Browning and Bill Thiesen of the Coast Guard Historian's Office. Colleagues and fellow scholars have played an important role in collecting these documents. John Hattendorf, Brian Payne, Mike Butler, Danny Vickers, Chris Magra, Kenneth Blume, Hans Carlson, Tim Lynch, Arthur Donovan, Walter Lewis, and Bill Bunting helped provide materials or constructive criticism. Scholars may not like to admit it, but administrators are important in the creation of any written work. Dean Warren Mazek and Dr. Gary Lombardo of the U.S. Merchant Marine Academy both provided encouragement. Historians rarely get to speak directly with their sources, but J. Robert Lunney and Keith Johnson were kind enough to permit me to use documents they authored. As usual, my wife Jea has been more than patient in enduring her husband's writing process, as has my daughter Dorothea.

Compiling a work such as this is fraught with peril, but the responsibility for all choices, errors, mistakes, and omissions in compiling *Voyages* are entirely mine.

1

AMERICA AND
THE ATLANTIC WORLD

From the European discovery through the end of the American Revolution, American communities remained closely connected with the sea. Indeed, virtually all American cities at the time of the Revolution were seaports. Even the rural South could not have thrived as it did without ships to carry tobacco and other crops across the Atlantic. Large numbers of colonial Americans made their living on the sea as fishermen, sailors, merchants, and shipbuilders. Nor was this experience confined to white men; Native Americans, African Americans (both slave and free), and women all participated in maritime affairs. Toward the end of the colonial period, maritime trade issues created enormous friction between colonists and Great Britain; seaport communities such as Boston were centers of resistance to Crown authority, and as such many suffered cruelly during the War of Independence.

Historians have conceptualized the remarkable intermingling of peoples from Europe, Africa, and North and South America during this period as the *Atlantic World*. The great European empires were connected by merchant and naval fleets in a web of trade and migrations (both voluntary and forced), bringing goods, animals, cultures, pathogens, and ideas together in new ways that changed all the societies that surrounded the Atlantic Ocean. For many Europeans, this interaction was positive, bringing them newfound wealth and power. For Native Americans, contact with diseases from Europe and Africa proved devastating, killing millions and disrupting cultures just as they faced invasion. For Africans the results were also harmful, as millions found themselves ripped from their native land and forced into chattel slavery to provide labor in the New World. Nor did all Europeans buy into the new European imperialism; outcasts, especially seafarers, sometimes responded by becoming pirates and rebelling against a social hierarchy stacked against them.

AGE OF RECONNAISSANCE

This chapter addresses a variety of issues important to historians of this period. The initial contact between European sailors and Native Americans during the "age of reconnaissance" is the first. And while this story is generally conceived of as a story of European mariners and land-bound Native peoples, European observers frequently noted the nautical abilities of the peoples they encountered. The economic basis for creating overseas colonies was also an important consideration for European nations. Staple goods such as fish could be found in abundance in the Americas, but the prohibitive cost of arranging a flow of these goods across the North Atlantic demanded that Europeans construct new ways of organizing their wealth, such as joint-stock companies and wideranging governmental regulations of seaborne commerce. The issue of crossing the Atlantic to found new societies was often a profoundly uncomfortable experience, so much so that a large portion of the peoples who crossed did so against their will, such as African slaves and European indentured servants.

Sailors were the key element to the shipping that connected Europe, America, and Africa, and to the economic and political growth and demographic changes that created a new Atlantic World. While often held in little esteem by society, the individuals who manned merchant ships and men o' war held themselves apart from the rest of society. By any reckoning, they were a remarkably diverse lot, reflecting the diversity and complexity of the Atlantic World that they connected. Closely related to the sailors were the merchants, the men and women who owned the commercial shipping. But the neat web of economic policies, sailors, and merchants faced a much-romanticized challenge in the pirates who plundered shipping and coastal communities. Readers can decide for themselves whether piracy represented an alternative society with egalitarian ideals or was merely crime conducted on a massive scale.

After Columbus and other European explorers encountered the Americas, other seafarers followed, curious about this "New World," anxious to define its shores and catalog its riches for their superiors in the "Old World." In the view of historian J. H. Parry, this was the "age of reconnaissance," a two-hundred-year period between 1450 and 1650 when European mariners reached out and began to discover the extent to which the sea connected the different parts of the globe.[1] Each of the documents below contributes

---

1   J. H. Parry, *The Age of Reconnaissance* (Cleveland: World Pub. Co., 1963).

to bigger ideas about the European interest in this New World. The Columbus letter is a fine example of the idea that the Spanish sought "gold, God, and glory" in the New World. The Barlow and Amadas piece is representative of the imperial competition for control of the world's sealanes between Spain and England in the 1580s. Thomas Hariot's 1588 account of his 1584 voyage to Virginia is a singularly important view of Native American society as it existed at the time of contact with Europeans, especially because Theodor de Bry produced a popular edition of Hariot's book with engravings based on the artwork of mapmaker John White. The account of the *Half Moon*'s voyage up what would become known as the Hudson River reflects the desire of some Europeans to get around North America; for them it was simply blocking the way to the riches of the East.

Christopher Columbus, "Islands of the Indian Sea" (1493)

The story of Christopher Columbus (1451–1506) is widely known. This Italian seaman finally persuaded the Spanish monarchy to fund a fleet of three vessels to sail westward across the Atlantic in search of a sea route to Asia. In October 1492, the tiny fleet chanced upon one of the Bahama Islands. While he did not know it, Columbus and his crew had happened upon the Americas.

Immediately on his return to Europe in March 1493, Columbus composed a letter to Luis de Santangel, the high steward or chancellor of the exchequer for the Spanish kingdom of Aragon, to report the findings of his first voyage across the Atlantic. The news spread rapidly across Europe that Columbus's westward voyage had succeeded in finding the islands of the "Indian sea." Columbus continued to believe he had found islands off the Asian mainland and was clearly disappointed when the islands he came across did not prove to be part of a larger continent.

In this letter Columbus describes the peoples and places he visited, clearly with the intention of claiming them for the Spanish crown. In particular, note how he describes the native peoples and his interactions with them, and how these peoples interacted with the sea.

Sir,

As I know that you will have pleasure from the great victory which our Lord hath given me in my voyage, I write you this, by which you shall know that in thirty-three days I passed over to the Indies with the fleet which the most illustrious King and Queen, our Lords, gave me; where I found very many islands peopled with inhabitants beyond

number. And, of them all, I have taken possession for their Highnesses, with proclamation and the royal standard displayed; and I was
not gainsaid. To the first which I found, I gave the name Sant Salvador,
in commemoration of His High Majesty, who marvelously hath given
all this: the Indians call it Guanahani. The second I named the Island
of Santa Maria de Concepcion, the third Ferrandina, the fourth, Isa-
bella, the fifth La Isla Juana; and so for each one a new name. When I
reached Juana, I followed its coast westwardly, and found it so large
that I thought it might be mainland, the province of Cathay.[1] And as I
did not thus find any towns and villages on the sea-coast, save small
hamlets with the people whereof I could not get speech, because they
all fled away forthwith, I went on further in the same direction, thinking I should not miss of great cities or towns. And at the end of many
leagues,[2] seeing that there was no change, and that the coast was bearing me northwards, whereunto my desire was contrary, since the winter was already confronting us, I formed the purpose of making from
thence to the South, and as the wind also blew against me, I determined not to wait for other weather and turned back as far as a port
agreed upon; from which I sent two men into the country to learn if
there were a king, or any great cities. They traveled for three days, and
found innumerable small villages and a numberless population, but
nought of ruling authority; wherefore they returned. I understood sufficiently from other Indians whom I had already taken, that this land,
in its continuousness, was an island; and so I followed its coast eastwardly for a hundred and seven leagues as far as where it terminated;
from which headland I saw another island to the east, eighteen leagues
distant from this, to which I at once gave the name La Spañola. And I
proceeded thither, and followed the northern coast, as with La Juana,
eastwardly for a hundred and eighty-eight great leagues in a direct
easterly course, as with La Juana. . . . In it, there are many havens on
the sea-coast, incomparable with any others that I know in Christendom, and plenty of rivers so good and great that it is a marvel. . . .
There could be no believing, without seeing, such harbors as are here,
as well as the many and great rivers, and excellent waters, most of
which contain gold. In the trees and fruits and plants, there are great
diversities from those of Juana. In this, there are many spiceries, and

---

1   Cathay: a European name for China.
2   Leagues: one league was roughly equivalent to three nautical miles.

great mines of gold and other metals. The people of this island, and of all the others that I have found and seen, or not seen, all go naked, men and women, just as their mothers bring them forth; although some women cover a single place with the leaf of a plant, or a cotton something which they make for that purpose. They have no iron or steel, nor any weapons; nor are they fit thereunto; not because they be not a well-formed people and of fair stature, but that they are most wondrously timorous. They have no other weapons than the stems of reeds in their seeding state, on the end of which they fix little sharpened stakes. Even these, they dare not use; for many times has it happened that I sent two or three men ashore to some village to parley, and countless numbers of them sallied forth, but as soon as they saw those approach, they fled away in such wise that even a father would not wait for his son. And this was not because any hurt had ever been done to any of them: on the contrary, at every headland where I have gone and been able to hold speech with them, I gave them of everything which I had, as well cloth as many other things, without accepting aught therefore; but such they are, incurably timid. It is true that since they have become more assured, and are losing that terror, they are artless and generous with what they have, to such a degree as no one would believe but him who had seen it. Of anything they have, if it be asked for, they never say no, but do rather invite the person to accept it, and show as much lovingness as though they would give their hearts. And whether it be a thing of value, or one of little worth, they are straightways content with whatsoever trifle of whatsoever kind may be given them in return for it. I forbade that anything so worthless as fragments of broken platters, and pieces of broken glass, and strap buckles, should be given them; although when they were able to get such things, they seemed to think they had the best jewel in the world, for it was the hap of a sailor to get, in exchange for a strap, gold to the weight of two and a half castellanos,[1] and others much more for other things of far less value; while for new blancas[2] they gave everything they had, even though it were [the worth of] two or three gold castellanos, or one or two arrobas[3] of spun cotton. They took even pieces of broken barrel-hoops, and gave whatever they had, like senseless brutes; insomuch that it seemed to me bad. I forbade it,

---

1   Castellanos: small gold coins.
2   Blancas: small coins worth about one-third of a cent.
3   Arroba: about 25 pounds.

and I gave gratuitously a thousand useful things that I carried, in order that they may conceive affection, and furthermore may become Christians; for they are inclined to the love and service of their Highnesses and of all the Castilian nation, and they strive to combine in giving us things which they have in abundance, and of which we are in need. And they knew no sect, nor idolatry; save that they all believe that power and goodness are in the sky, and they believed very firmly that I, with these ships and crews, came from the sky; and in such opinion, they received me at every place where I landed, after they had lost their terror. And this comes not because they are ignorant: on the contrary, they are men of very subtle wit, who navigate all those seas, and who give a marvelously good account of everything, but because they never saw men wearing clothes nor the like of our ships. And as soon as I arrived in the Indies, in the first island that I found, I took some of them by force, to the intent that they should learn [our speech] and give me information of what there was in those parts. And so it was, that very soon they understood [us] and we them, what by speech or what by signs; and those [Indians] have been of much service. To this day I carry them [with me] who are still of the opinion that I come from Heaven [as appears] from much conversation which they have had with me. And they were the first to proclaim it wherever I arrived; and the others went running from house to house and to the neighboring villages, with loud cries of "Come! Come to see the people from Heaven!" Then, as soon as their minds were reassured about us, every one came, men as well as women, so that there remained none behind, big or little; and they all brought something to eat and drink, which they gave with wondrous lovingness. They have in all the islands very many canoes,[1] after the manner of rowing-galleys, some larger, some smaller; and a good many are larger than a galley of eighteen benches. They are not so wide, because they are made of a single log of timber, but a galley could not keep up with them in rowing, for their motion is a thing beyond belief. And with these, they navigate through all those islands, which are numberless, and ply their traffic. I have seen some of those canoes with seventy and eighty men in them, each one with his oar. In all those islands, I saw not much diversity in the looks of the people, nor in their manners and language; but they all understand each other, which is a thing of singular advantage

---

1   Canoes: this is the first known appearance of this West Indian word in Europe.

for what I hope their Highnesses will decide upon for converting them to our holy faith, unto which they are well disposed. . . . This is [a land] to be desired, and once seen, never to be relinquished in which (although, indeed, I have taken possession of them all for their Highnesses, and all are more richly endowed than I have skill and power to say, and I hold them all in the name of their Highnesses who can dispose thereof as much and as completely as of the kingdoms of Castile) in this Española, in the place most suitable and best for its proximity to the gold mines, and for traffic with the mainland both on this side and with that over there belonging to the Great Khan,[1] where there will be great commerce and profit, I took possession of a large town which I named the city of Navidad.[2] And I have made fortification there, and a fort (which by this time will have been completely finished) and I have left therein men enough for such a purpose, with arms and artillery, and provisions for more than a year, and a boat, and a [man who is] master of all seacraft for making others; and great friendship with the king of that land, to such a degree that he prided himself on calling and holding me as his brother. And even though his mind might change towards attacking those men, neither he nor his people know what arms are, and go naked. As I have already said, they are the most timorous creatures there are in the world, so that the men who remain there are alone sufficient to destroy all that land, and the island is without personal danger for them if they know how to behave themselves. It seems to me that in all those islands, the men are all content with a single wife; and to their chief or king they give as many as twenty. The women, it appears to me, do more work than the men. Nor have I been able to learn whether they held personal property, for it seemed to me that whatever one had, they all took share of, especially of eatable things. . . . Thus I have not found, nor had any information of monsters, except of an island which is here the second in the approach to the Indies, which is inhabited by a people whom, in all the islands, they regard as very ferocious, who eat human flesh. These have many canoes with which they run through all the islands of India, and plunder and take as much as they can. They are no more ill shapen than the others, but have the custom of wearing

---

1   Great Khan: i.e., belonging to China.
2   Navidad: meaning Nativity or Christmas, because the *Santa Maria* accidentally grounded on that day. As a result, Columbus decided to leave some men behind in a partially finished fort.

their hair long, like women; and they use bows and arrows of the same reed stems, with a point of wood at the top, for lack of iron which they have not. Amongst those other tribes who are excessively cowardly, these are ferocious; but I hold them as nothing more than the others. These are they who have to do with the women of Matinino which is the first island that is encountered in the passage from Spain to the Indies in which there are no men. Those women practice no female usages, but have bows and arrows of reed such as above mentioned; and they arm and cover themselves with plates of copper of which they have much. In another island, which they assure me is larger than Española, the people have no hair. In this there is incalculable gold; and concerning these and the rest I bring Indians with me as witnesses. And in conclusion, to speak only of what has been done in this voyage, which has been so hastily performed, their Highnesses may see that I shall give them as much gold as they may need, with very little aid which their Highnesses will give me; spices and cotton at once, as much as their Highnesses will order to be shipped . . . and aloe-wood as much as they shall order to be shipped; and slaves as many as they shall order to be shipped, and these shall be from idolaters. And I believe that I have discovered rhubarb and cinnamon, and I shall find that the men whom I am leaving there will have discovered a thousand other things of value; as I made no delay at any point, so long as the wind gave me an opportunity of sailing, except only in the town of Navidad till I had left things safely arranged and well established. And in truth I should have done much more if the ships had served me as well as might reasonably have been expected. This is enough; and [thanks to] Eternal God our Lord who gives to all those who walk His way, victory over things which seem impossible; and this was signally one such, for although men have talked or written of those lands, it was all by conjecture, without confirmation from eyesight, amounting only to this much that the hearers for the most part listened and judged that there was more fable in it than anything actual, however trifling. Since thus our Redeemer has given to our most illustrious King and Queen, and to their famous kingdoms, this victory in so high a matter, Christendom should have rejoicing therein and make great festivals, and give solemn thanks to the Holy Trinity for the great exaltation they shall have by the conversion of so many peoples to our holy faith; and next for the temporal benefit which will bring hither refreshment and profit, not only to Spain, but to all Christians. This briefly, in accordance with the facts. Dated, on the caravel, off the Canary Islands, the 15 February of the year 1493.

At your command,
THE ADMIRAL.

Questions for Discussion:
1. What does this letter reveal about what Columbus sought in this voyage?
2. How did Columbus interact with the native peoples of these islands?
3. How did Columbus formulate this letter for its intended audience?

Bernard Quaritch, *The Spanish Letter of Columbus to Luis de San' Angel* (London: G. Norman & Son, 1893), 11–18.

Arthur Barlow and Philip Amadas, "The Abundant New World" (1584)

The English were relatively late in exploring the Americas and, while they occasionally reconnoitered the Americas for navigation or raiding, did not make serious efforts to scout North America for settlement purposes until the 1580s. The renewed interest in America came about as part of the imperial competition between England and Spain. As detailed by Kenneth R. Andrews in *Trade, Plunder and Settlement*, Sir Walter Raleigh financed the expedition in order to establish a colony in North America to serve as a privateering base to harass Spanish galleons returning to Spain laden with New World gold and silver.[1] He sent Arthur Barlow (1550–1620) and Philip Amadas (1550–1618) across the ocean in two ships to determine an appropriate location.

On their return, Barlow and Amadas submitted this report, one of the very earliest accounts in English of the southern coast. Like Columbus, the Englishmen found the native inhabitants to be able boatmen and also engaged in trade with them. They were obviously impressed with the bounty of the land they discovered. Their recommendations would lead to Raleigh's attempt to colonize Roanoke Island the following year. The ruler of England, Queen Elizabeth I, would name the English territories in America

---

1   Kenneth R. Andrews, *Trade, Plunder and Settlement: Maritime Enterprise and the Genesis of the British Empire, 1480–1630* (Cambridge: Cambridge University Press, 1984).

Virginia as a memorial to her status as the "virgin queen," and perhaps as a statement on its presumed pristine state.

The 27 day of Aprill, in the yeere of our redemption, 1584 we departed the West of England, with two barkes[1] well furnished with men and victuals, having received our last and perfect direcions by your letters, confirming the former instructions, and commandements delivered by your selfe at our leaving the river of Thames. And I thinke it a matter both unnecessary for the manifest discoverie of the Country, as also for tediousnesse sake, to remember unto you the diurnall of our course, sayling thither and returning: onely I have presumed to present unto you this briefe discourse, by which you may judge how profitable this land is likely to succeede, as well to your selfe, (by whose direction and charge, and by whose servantes this our discoverie hath beene performed) as also to her Highnesse, and the Common wealth, in which we hope your wisedome will be satisfied, considering that as much as by us hath bene brought to light, as by those smal meanes, and number of men we had, could any way have bene expected or hoped for. . . .

The second of July, we found shole water, wher we smelt so sweet, and so strong a smell, as if we had bene in the midst of some delicate garden abounding with all kinde of odoriferous flowers, by which we were assured, that the land could not be farre distant: and keeping good watch, and bearing but slacke saile, the fourth of the same moneth we arrived upon the coast, which we supposed to be a continent and firme lande, and we sayled along the same a hundred and twentie English miles before we could finde any entrance, or river issuing into the Sea. The first that appeared unto us, we entered, though not without some difficultie, & cast anker about three harquebuz-shot[2] within the havens mouth, on the left hand of the same: and after thankes given to God for our safe arrivall thither, we manned our boats, and went to view the land next adjoyning, and to take possession of the same, in the right of the Queenes most excellent Majestie, as rightful Queene, and Princesse of the same, and after delivered the same over to your use, according to her Majesties grant, and letters patents, under her Highnesse great Seale. Which being performed, according

---

1   Barkes: sometimes spelled barques, a word almost interchangeable with ships.
2   Harquebuz-shot: within gunshot.

to the ceremonies used in such enterprises, we viewed the land about us, being, whereas we first landed, very sandie and low towards the waters side, but so full of grapes, as the very beating and surge of the Sea overflowed them, of which we found such plentie, as well there as in all places else, both on the sand and on the greene soile on the hills, as in the plains, as well on every little shrubbe, as also climbing towards the tops of high Cedars, that I think in all the world the like abundance is not to be found: and my self having seen those parts of Europe that most abound, find such difference as were incredible to be written.

We passed from the Sea side towards the tops of those hills next adjoyning, being but of meane height and from thence wee beheld the Sea on both sides to the North, and to the South, finding no end any of both ways. This land lay stretching itself to the West, which after wee found to bee but an Island of twenty miles long, and not above six miles broad. Under the bank or hill whereon we stood, we beheld the vallyes replenished with goodly Cedar trees, and having discharged our harquebuz-shot, such a flocke of Cranes (the most part white) arose under us, with such a cry redoubled by many ecchoes, as if an armie of men had showted all together. . . .

We remained by the side of this Island two whole days before we saw any people of the Countrey: the third day we espied one small boat rowing towardes us having in it three persons: this boat came to the Island side, foure harquebuz-shot from our shippes, and there two of the people remaining, the third came along the shoreside towards us, and wee being then all within boord, he walked up and downe upon the point of the land next unto us: then the Master and the Pilot of the Admiral, Simon Fernandino, and the Captaine Philip Amadas, my self, and others rowed to the land, whose comming this fellow attended, never making any shew of fear or doubt. And after he had spoken of many things not understood by us, we brought him with his owne good liking, aboord the ships, and gave him a shirt, a hat & some other things, and made him taste of our wine, and our meat, which he liked very well: and after having viewed both barks, he departed, and went to his own boat again, which hee had left in a little Cove or Creeke adjoyning: as soon as hee was two bow shoot into the water, he fell to fishing, and in less then half an hour, he had laden his boat as deep, as it could swimme, with which hee came again to the point of the land, and there he divided his fish into two parts, pointing one part to the ship, and the other to the pinnesse: which, after he had (as much as he might) requited the former benefits received, departed out of our sight.

The next day there came unto us divers boats, and in one of them the King's brother, accompanied with fortie or fiftie men, very handsome and goodly people, and in their behaviour as mannerly and civil as any of Europe. His name was Granganimeo, and the king is called Wingina, the country Wingandacoa, and now by her Majestie Virginia. The manner of his coming was in this sort: hee left his boats altogether as the first man did a little from the shippes by the shore, and came along to the place over against the ships, followed with fortie men. When he came to the place over against the ships, followed with fortie men. When he came to the place, his servants spread a long matte upon the ground, on which he sat down, and at the other end of the matte four others of his companie did the like, the rest of his men stood round about him, somewhat a farre off: when we came to the shore to him with our weapons, hee never moved from his place, nor any of the other four, nor never mistrusted any harm to be offered from us, but sitting still he beckoned us to come and sit by him, which we performed: and being set hee made all signes of joy and welcome, striking on his head and his breast and afterwards on ours, to shew wee were all one, smiling and making shew the best he could of all love, and familiaritie. After hee had made a long speech unto us, wee presented him with divers things, which hee received very joyfully, and thankfully. None of the company durst speake one worde all the time: onely the four which were at the other end, spake one in the others ear very softly.

The King is greatly obeyed, and his brothers and children reverenced: the King himself in person was at our being there, sore wounded in a fight which hee had with the King of the next country, called Wingina, and was shot in two places through the body, and once clean through the thigh, but yet he recovered: by reason whereof and for that hee lay at the chief towne of the country, being six dayes journey off, we saw him not at all.

After we had presented this his brother with such things as we thought he liked, wee likewise gave somewhat to the other that sat with him on the matte: but presently he arose and took all from them and put it into his own basket, making signs and tokens, that all things ought to bee delivered unto him, and the rest were but his servants, and followers. A day or two after this we fell to trading with them, exchanging some things that we had, for Chamoys, Buffe, and Deere skinnes: when we shewed him all our packet of merchandize, of all things that he saw, a bright tin dish most pleased him, which hee presently took up and clapt it before his breast, and after made a hole in the brim thereof and hung it about his neck, making signs that it would defend him against his enemies arrows: for those people maintain a deadly and terrible war, with the people and King adjoyning. We exchanged our tin dish for twenty skinnes, worth twentie Crowns, or twenty Nobles: and a copper kettle for fifty skins worth fifty Crowns. They offered us good exchange for our hatchets, and axes, and for knives, and would have given any thing for swords: but wee would not depart with any. After two or three days the King's brother came aboard the shippes, and drank wine, and eat of our meat and of our bread, and liked exceedingly thereof: and after a few days overpassed, he brought his wife with him to the ships, his daughter and two or three children: his wife was very well favoured, of meane stature and very bashfull: shee had on her back a long cloak of leather, with the furre side next to her body, and before her a piece of the same: about her forehead she had a bande of white Corall, and so had her husband many times: in her eares she had bracelets of pearls hanging down to her middle, (whereof wee delivered your worship a little bracelet) and those were of the bigness of good pease. The rest of her women of the better sort had pendants of copper hanging in either ear, and some of the children of the king's brother and other noble men, have five or six in either ear: he himself had upon his head a broad plate of gold, or copper for being unpolished we knew not what metal it should be, neither would he by any means suffer us to take it off his head, but feeling it, would bow very easily. His apparel was as his wives, onely the women wear their hair long on both sides, and the men but on one. They are of colour yellowish, and their hair black for the most part, and yet we saw children that had very fine aburne, and chestnut coloured hair.

After that these women had bene there, there came down from all parts great store of people, bringing with them leather, corall, divers kinds of dies very excellent, and exchanged with us: but when Granganimeo the king's brother was present, none durst trade but himself: except such as wear red pieces of copper on their heads like himselfe: for that is the difference between the noble men, and the governours

of the countreys, and you have understood since by these men, which
we brought home, that no people in the world carry more respect
to their King, Nobility, and Governours, then these doe. The King's
brother's wife, when she came to us (as she did many times) was followed with forty or fifty women always: and when she came into the
shippe, she left them all on land, saving her two daughters, her nurse
and one or two more. The King's brother always kept this order, as
many boats as he would come withall to the shippes, so many fires
would hee make on the shore a farre off, to the end we might understand with what strength and company he approached. Their boats
are made of one tree, either of Pine or of Pitch trees: a wood not commonly known to our people, nor found growing in England. They have
no edge-tools to make them withall: if they have any they are very few,
and those it seems they had twentie yeres since, which, as those two
men declared, was out of a wreck which happened upon their coast of
some Christian ship, being beaten that way by some storme and out-
ragious weather, whereof none of the people were saved, but only the
ship, or some part of her being cast upon the sand, out of whose sides
they drew the nayles and the spikes, and with those they made their
best instruments. The manner of making their boats is thus: they burn
down some great tree, or take such as are wind fallen, and putting
gum and rosen[1] upon one side thereof, they set fire into it, and when
it hath burnt it hollow, they cut out the coal with their shells, and ever
where they would burn it deeper or wider they lay on gums, which
burn away the timber, and by this means they fashion very fine boats,
and such as will transport twenty men. Their oars are like scoopes,
and many times they set with long poles, as the depth serveth.

The King's brother had great liking of our armour, a sword, and divers other things which we had: and offered to lay a great box of pearl
in gage for them: but we refused it for this time, because we would not
make them know, that we esteemed thereof, until we had understood
in what places of the country the pearl grew: which now your Worship doeth very well understand. He was very just of his promise: for
many times we delivered him merchandize upon his word, but ever
he came within the day and performed his promise. He sent us every
day a brase[2] or two of fat Bucks, Conies, Hares, Fish the best of the

---

1   Rosen: rosin, a by-product of turpentine used in making varnish and for other pur-
    poses.
2   Brase: a brace, or pair.

world. He sent us diverse kinds of fruits, Melons, Walnuts, Cucumbers, Gourds, Pease, and divers roots, and fruits very excellent good, and of their Country corn, which is very white, faire and well tasted, and groweth three times in five months.

Questions for Discussion:
1. What evidence is provided regarding Native Americans and their relationship to the marine environment?
2. What role did trade play in the relationship between the English sailors and the native peoples they met?
3. How does this report relate to Sir Walter Raleigh's plans for the creation of a base from which to attack Spanish shipping?

Henry S. Burrage, ed., *Early English and French Voyages, Chiefly from Hakluyt, 1534–1608* (New York: Charles Scribner's Sons, 1906), 227–34.

Thomas Hariot and Theodor de Bry, "Visualizing Virginia" (ca. 1588–1595)

As Karen Kupperman reminds us in *Indians and English: Facing Off in Early America*,[1] the interactions between Europeans and Native Americans were remarkably complex, inspiring a great deal of curiosity among both groups. But for the English interaction always had a purpose, because they viewed Indians as the key to English economic success in North America.

Although relative latecomers to the New World, the English were anxious for reports on its potential, and scientists such as Thomas Hariot (1560–1621) obliged by visiting Virginia in 1584 with Sir Walter Raleigh's expedition and recording his observations in his 1588 book with a telling title, *Report of the New found land of Virginia, of the commodities and of the nature and manners of the naturall inhabitants*. Europeans had a huge thirst for knowledge about the New World, and in 1595 Flemish engraver Theodor de Bry (1528–1598) produced a popular book lavishly illustrated with engravings based upon Hariot's writings and the watercolor paintings of cartographer John White (c. 1540–1606), who also went to Virginia in 1584. Taken together, Hariot's observations and White's paintings remain one of the best sources available on Native American society as it existed at the time of contact with Europeans. So too, it is a record of Native Americans' interactions with the maritime environment, and Europeans were

---

1   Karen Ordahl Kupperman, *Indians and English: Facing Off in Early America* (Ithaca, N.Y.: Cornell University Press, 2000).

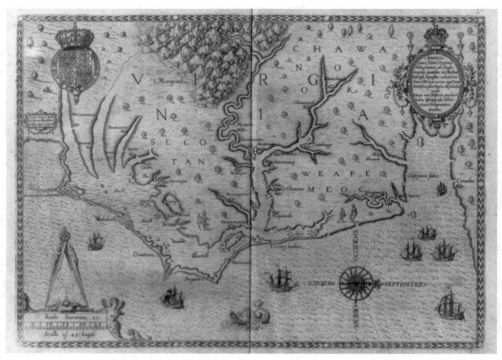

"The Englishmen's arrival in Virginia," 1585. Engraving by Theodor de Bry, courtesy of the Library of Congress # LC-USZ62-5402002.

quick to admire the indigenous peoples' boats, boathandling, and knowledge of fishing, aspects admirably recorded by Hariot and De Bry.

> The sea coasts of Virginia arre full of Islands, wher by the entrance into the mayne land is hard to finde. For although they bee separated with divers and sundrie large Division, which seeme to yeeld convenient entrance, yet to our great perill we proved that they wear shallowe, and full of dangerous flatts, and could never perce opp into the mayne land, until wee made trialls in many places with or small pinness.[1] At lengthe wee fownd an entrance uppon our mens diligent serche therof. After that wee had passed opp, and sayled ther in for a short space we discovered a mightye river fallinge downe in to the

---

1   Pinness: pinnace, an open rowing boat, such as the one pictured in the middle of the above image.

sownde[1] over against those Islands, which nevertheless wee could not saile opp any thinge far by Reason of the shallewness, the mouth ther of beinge annoyed with sands driven in with the tyde therfore saylinge further, wee came unto a Good bigg island, the Inhabitants therof as soone as they saw us began to make a great and horrible crye, as people which never befoer had seene men apparelled like us, and camme a way makinge out crys like wild beasts or men out of their wits. But beeng gentlye called backe, wee offered them of our wares, as glasses, knives, babies,[2] and other trifles, which wee thought they deligted in. Soe they stood still, and percevinge our Good will and courtesie came fawning upon us, and bade us welcome. Then they brought us to their village in the island called, Roanoac,[3] and unto their Weroans or Prince, which entertained us with Reasonable curtesie, although they wear amased at the first sight of us. Suche was our arrival into the parte of the world, which we call Virginia, the stature of bodye of which people, theyr attire, and maneer of lyvinge, their feasts, and banketts, I will particullerlye declare unto you.

The manner of makinge their boates in Virginia is verye wonderful. For wheras they want Instruments of iron, or other like unto ours, yet they knowe howe to make them as handsomelye, to saile with whear they liste in their Rivers, and to fishe withall, as ours. First they choose some longe, and thicke tree, accordinge to the bignes of the boate which they would frame, and make a fire on the grownd abowt the Roote therof, kindlinge the same by little, and little with drie mosse of trees, and chipps of woode that the flame should not mounte opp too highe, and burne to muche of the lengte of the tree. When it is almost burnt thorough, and readye to fall they make a new fire, which they suffer to burne untill the tree fall of its owne accord. Then burninge of the topp, and boughs of the tree in suche wise that the bodie of the same may Retayne his just lengthe, they raise it uppon potes laid over cross wise upon forked posts, at such a reasonable heighte as they may handsomlye worke uppon it. Then take they of the barke with certayne shells: they reserve the innermost parte of the lennke,[4] for the nethermost parte of the boate. On the other side they make a fire accordinge to the lengthe of the bodye of the tree, savinge at bothe the endes. That

---

1   Sound: a large open bay.
2   Babies: dolls, puppets, or carved images.
3   Roanoac: Roanoke.
4   Lennke: this is unclear, but may be a typographical error for "bark."

Lintrium conficiendorum ratio.   XII.

Ea est in VIRGINIA cymbas fabricandi ratio: nam cum ferreis instrumentu aut aliis nostris similibus careant, eas tamen parare nerunt nostris non minus commodas ad nauigandum quo lubet per flumina & ad piscandum. Primum arbore aliqua crassa & alta delecta, pro cymba quam parare volunt magnitudine, ignem circa eius radices summa tellure in ambitu struunt ex arborum musco bene resiccato, & ligni assulis paulatim ignem excitantes, ne flamma altius ascendat, & arboru longitudinem minuat. Pane adusta & ruinam minante arbore, nouum suscitant ignem, quem flagrare sinunt donec arbor sponte cadat. Adustis deinde arboris fastigio & ramis, vt truncus iustam longitudinem retineat, lignis transuersis supra furcas positis imponunt, ea altitudine vt commode laborare possint, tunc cortice conchis quibusdam adempto, integriorem trunci partem pro cymba inferiore parte seruant, in altera parte ignem secundum trunci longitudinem struunt, praterquam extremis, quod satis adustum illis videtur, restincto igne conchis scabunt, & nouo suscitato igne denuo adurunt, atque ita deinceps pergunt, subinde vrentes & scabentes, donec cymba necessarium alueum nacta sit. Sic Domini spiritus rudibus hominibus suggerit rationem, qua res in suum vsum necessarias conficere queant.

B 4

which they thinke is sufficientlye burned they quenche and scrape away with shells, and makinge a new fire they burne it agayne, and soe they continue somtimes burninge and sometimes scrapinge, until the boate have sufficient bothowmes. Thus God indueth thise savage people with sufficient reason to make thinges necessarie to serve their turnes.

They have likewise a notable way to catche fishe in their Rivers, for whear as they lacke both iron, and steele, they fasten unto their

"How they catch fish," 1590. Engraving by Theodor de Bry, courtesy of the Library of Congress # LC-USZ62-54016.

Reedes or longe Rodds, the hollowe tayle of a certaine fishe like to a
sea crabb in steede of a poynte, wherwith by nighte or day they stricke
fishes, and take them opp into their boates. They also know how to
use the prickles, and pricks of other fishes. They also make weares,[1]
with settinge opp reedes or twigges in the water, which they soe plant
one with another, that they growe still narrower, and narrower, as ap-
peareth by this figure. There was never seene amonge us soe cunninge
a way to take fish withall, wherof sondrie sortes as they fownde in
their Rivers unlike unto ours, which are also of a verye good taste.
Doubtless it is a pleasant sighte to see the people, somtimes wadinge,
and goinge sometimes sailinge in those Rivers, which are shallowe
and not deepe, free from all care of heapinge opp Riches for their pos-
terite, content with their state, and livinge frendlye together of those
thinges which god of his bountye hath given unto them, yet without
givinge him any thankes according to his desarte.

So savage is this people, and deprived of the true knowledge of god.
For they have none other then is mentioned before in this worke.

Questions for Discussion:
1. What do these images and text suggest about the Native American relationship with the sea?
2. What strengths and weaknesses do these images and texts have in understanding European attitudes toward the New World?
3. What do these texts and images reveal about how Europeans attempted
to understand this New World?

Thomas Hariot, *Narrative of the English Plantations of Virginia* (London: Bernard Quaritch, 1893).

Robert Juet, "Hudson Explores a River" (1609)

Henry Hudson (1565–1611) was an experienced English seaman and explorer who made several efforts to discover a Northwest Passage through
or around North America so that Europeans could sail to Asia more easily.
Sometimes he sailed in the hire of the English, as when the London-based
Muscovy Company hired him to find a northwest route to the Spice Islands,
and sometimes in the pay of the Dutch East India Company. In 1609 the
Dutch East India Company supplied Hudson with a small eighty-ton ves-

---

1   Weares: weirs, fences, often made of brush, used for catching fish.

sel, the *Half Moon*, with a crew composed of both Dutch and English sailors to find a northern route to Asia.

The North American leg of his voyage took him from Maine to Chesapeake Bay, but he had no luck in finding a potential passage until September, when he entered the Hudson River in modern-day New York. Like Columbus and the Englishmen Barlow and Amadas, the keeper of this chronicle, Robert Juet, chief mate of the *Half Moon*, carefully describes the Native Americans he encountered, and found they were proficient both in and on the water.

The first of September, faire weather, the wind variable betweene east and south; we steered away north northwest. At noone we found our height to bee 39 degrees, 3 minutes.[1] The second, in the morning, close weather, the winde at south in the morning; from twelve untill two of the clocke we steered north northwest, and had sounding one and twentie fathoms: and in running one glasse we had but sixteene fathoms, then seventeene, and so shoalder and shoalder[2] untill it came to twelve fathoms. We saw a great fire, but could not see the land; then we came to ten fathoms, whereupon we brought our tackes aboord, and stood to the eastward east south-east, foure glasses. Then the sunne arose, and wee steered away north againe, and saw the land from the west by north to the northwest by north, all like broken islands, and our soundings were eleven and ten fathoms. Then wee looft in for the shoare, and faire by the shoare we had seven fathoms. The course along the land we found to be northeast by north. From the land which we had first sight of, untill we came to a great lake of water, as wee could judge it to bee, being drowned land, which made it to rise like islands, which was in length ten leagues.[3] The mouth of that land hath many shoalds, and the sea breaketh on them as it is cast out of the mouth of it. And from that lake or bay the land lyeth north by east, and wee had a great streame out of the bay; and from thence our sounding was ten fathoms two leagues from the land. At five of the clocke we anchored, being little winde, and rode in eight fathoms water; the night was faire. This night I found the land to hail the compasse 8 degrees. For to the northward off us we saw high hills. For the

---

1   39 degrees, 3 minutes: 39° 3' North latitude.
2   Shoalder: shallower.
3   League: roughly three nautical miles.

day before we found not above 2 degrees of variation.[1] This is a very good land to fall with, and a pleasant land to see.

The third, the morning mystie, untill ten of the clocke; then it cleered, and the wind came to the south south-east, so wee weighed and stood to the northward. The land is very pleasant and high, and bold to fall withall. At three of the clock in the after-noone, wee came to three great rivers. So we stood along to the northermost, thinking to have gone into it, but we found it to have a very shoald barre before it, for we had but ten foot water. Then we cast about to the southward, and found two fathoms, three fathoms, and three and a quarter, till we came to the souther side of them; then we had five and six fathoms, and anchored.

The fourth, in the morning, as soone as the day was light, wee saw that it was good riding farther up. So we sent out boate to sound, and found that it was a very good harbour, and foure and five fathomes, two cables length from the shoare. Then we weighed and went in with our ship. Then our boate went on land with our net to fish, and caught ten great mullets, of a foote and a halfe long a peese, and a ray as great as foure men could hale into the ship. So wee trimmed our boate and rode still all day. At night the wind blew hard at the north-west, and our anchor came home, and we drove on shoare, but took no hurt, thanked bee God, for the ground is soft sand and ooze. This day the people of the countrey came aboord of us, seeming very glad of our comming, and brought greene tobacco, and gave us of it for knives and beads. They goe in deere skins loose, well dressed. They have yellow copper. They desire cloathes, and are very civill. They have great store of maize, or Indian wheate, whereof they make good bread. The countrey is full of great and tall oake.

The fifth, in the morning, as soone as the day was light, the wind ceased and the flood came. So we heaved off our ship againe into five fathoms water, and sent our boate to sound the bay, and we found that there was three fathoms hard by the souther shoare. Our men went on land there, and saw great store of men, women, and children, who gave them tabacco at their comming on land. So they went up into the woods, and saw great store of very goodly oakes and some currants. For one of them came aboord and brought some dryed, and gave me some, which were sweet and good. This day many of the people came

---

1   Variation: how much a compass varied from pointing to magnetic north.

aboard, some in mantles of feathers, and some in skinnes of divers sorts of good furres. Some women also came to us with hempe. They had red copper tabacco pipes, and other things of copper they did weare about their neckes. At night they went on land againe, so wee rode very quiet, but durst not trust them.

The sixth, in the morning, was faire weather, and our master sent John Colman, with foure other men in our boate, over to the north-side to sound the other river, being foure leagues from us. They found by the day shoald water, two fathoms; but at the north of the river eighteen, and twentie fathoms, and very good riding for ships; and a narrow river to the westward, between two ilands. The lands, they told us, were as pleasant with grasse and flowers and goodly trees as ever they had seene, and very sweet smells came from them. . . .

The tenth, faire weather, we rode still till twelve of the clocke. Then we weighed and went over, and found it shoald all the middle of the river, for wee could finde but two fathoms and a halfe and three fathomes for the space of a league; then wee came to three fathomes and foure fathomes, and so to seven fathomes, and anchored, and rode all night in soft ozie ground. The banke is sand.

The eleventh was faire and very hot weather. At one of the clocke in the after-noone wee weighed and went into the river, the wind at south south-west, little winde. Our soundings were seven, sixe, five, sixe, seven, eight, nine, ten, twelve, thirteene, and fourteene fathomes. Then it shoalded againe, and came to five fathomes. Then wee anchored, and saw that it was a very good harbour for all windes, and rode all night. The people of the country came aboord of us, making shew of love, and gave us tabacco and Indian wheat, and departed for that night, but we durst not trust them.

The twelfth, very faire and hot. In the afternoone, at two of the clocke, wee weighed, the winde being variable betweene the north and the north-west. So we turned into the river two leagues and anchored. This morning, at our first rode in the river, there came eight and twentie canoes full of men, women and children to betray us: but we saw their intent, and suffered none of them to come aboord of us. At twelve of the clocke they departed. They brought with them oysters and beanes, whereof wee bought some. They have great tabacco pipes of yellow copper, and pots of earth to dresse their meate in. It floweth south-east by south within.

The thirteenth, faire weather, the wind northerly. At seven of the clocke in the morning, as the floud came we weighed, and turned foure miles into the river. The tide being done wee anchored. Then there came foure canoes aboord: but we suffered none of them to come into our ship. They brought great store of very good oysters aboord, which we bought for trifles. In the night I set the variation of the compasse, and found it to be 13 degrees. In the after-noone we weighed, and turned in with the floud, two leagues and a halfe further, and anchored all night; and had five fathoms soft ozie ground; and had an high point of land, which shewed out to us, bearing north by east five leagues off us.

The fourteenth, in the morning, being very faire weather, the wind south-east, we sayled up the river twelve leagues, and had five fathoms, and five fathoms and a quarter lesse; and came to a streight betweene two points, and had eight, nine, and ten fathoms; and it attended north-east by north, one league: and wee had twelve, thirteene, and fourteene fathomes. The river is a mile broad: there is very high land on both sides. Then we went up north-west, a league and an halfe deepe water. Then north-east by north, five miles; then north-west by north, two leagues, and anchored. The land grew very high and mountainous. The river is full of fish.

The fifteenth, in the morning, was misty, untill the sunne arose: then it cleered. So wee weighed with the wind at south, and ran up into the river twentie leagues, passing by high mountaines. Wee had a very good depth, as sixe, seven, eight, nine, ten, twelve, and thirteene fathomes, and great store of salmons in the river. This morning our two savages got out of a port and swam away. After wee were under sayle, they called to us in scorne. At night we came to other mountaines, which lie from the rivers side. There wee found very loving people, and very old men: where wee were well used. Our boat went to fish, and caught great store of very good fish. . . .

The seventeenth, faire sun-shining weather, and very hot. In the morning, as soone as the sun was up, we set sayle, and ran up sixe leagues higher, and found shoalds in the middle of the channell, and small ilands, but seven fathoms water on both sides. Toward night we borrowed so neere the shoare, that we grounded: so layed out our small anchor, and heaved off againe. Then we borrowed on the banke in the channell, and came aground againe; while the floud ran we heaved off againe, and anchored all night.

The eighteenth, in the morning, was faire weather, and we rode still. In the after-noone our masters mate went on land with an old savage, a governor of the countrey; who carried him to his house, and made him good cheere. The nineteenth, was faire and hot weather: at the floud, being neere eleven of the clocke, wee weighed, and ran higher up two leagues above the shoalds, and had no lesse water then five fathoms; we anchored, and rode in eight fathomes. The people of the countrie came flocking aboord, and brought us grapes and pompions, which wee bought for trifles. And many brought us bevers skinnes and otters skinnes, which wee bought for beades, knives, and hatchets. So we rode there all night.

The twentieth, in the morning, was faire weather. Our masters mate with foure men more went up with our boat to sound the river, and found two leagues above us but two fathomes water, and the channell very narrow; and above that place, seven or eight fathomes. Toward night they returned: and we rode still all night. The one and twentieth was faire weather, and the wind all southerly: we determined yet once more to go farther up into the river, to trie what depth and breadth it did beare; but much people resorted aboord, so wee went not this day. Our carpenter went on land, and made a fore-yard. And our master and his mate determined to trie some of the chiefe men of the countrey, whether they had any treacherie in them. So they tooke them downe into the cabin, and gave them so much wine and aqua vita,[1] that they were all merrie: and one of them had his wife with them, which sate so modestly, as any of our countrey women would doe in a strange place. In the ende one of them was drunke, which had beene aboord of our ship all the time that we had beene there: and that was strange to them; for they could not tell how to take it. The canoes and folke went all on shoare: but some of them came againe, and brought stropes of beades: some had sixe, seven, eight, nine, ten; and gave him. So he slept all night quietly.

The two and twentieth was faire weather: in the morning our masters mate and foure more of the companie went up with our boat to sound the river higher up. The people of the countrey came not aboord till noone: but when they came, and saw the savages well, they were glad. So at three of the clocke in the afternoone they came aboord, and brought tabacco, and more beades, and gave them to our master, and made an oration, and shewed him all the countrey round about. Then

---

1 Aqua vitae: strong liquor.

they sent one of their companie on land, who presently returned, and brought a great platter full of venison dressed by themselves; and they caused him to eate with them: then they made him reverence and departed, all save the old man that lay aboord. This night, at ten of the clocke our boat returned in a showre of raine from sounding of the river; and found it to bee at an end for shipping to goe in. For they had beene up eight or nine leagues, and found but seven foot water, and unconstant soundings.

The three and twentieth, faire weather. At twelve of the clocke wee weighed, and went downe two leagues to a shoald that had two channels, one on the one side, and another on the other, and had little wind, whereby the tyde layed us upon it. So there wee sate on ground the space of an houre till the floud came. Then we had a little gale of wind at the west. So wee got our ship into deepe water, and rode all night very well.

The foure and twentieth was faire weather: the winde at the north-west, wee weighed, and went downe the river seven or eight leagues; and at halfe ebbe wee came on ground on a banke of oze in the middle of the river, and sate there till the floud. Then wee went on land, and gathered, good store of chest-nuts. At ten of the clocke wee came off into deepe water, and anchored. . . .

The second, faire weather. At break of day wee weighed, the winde being at north-west, and got downe seven leagues; then the floud was come strong, so we anchored. Then came one of the savages that swamme away from us at our going up the river with many other, thinking to betray us. But we perceived their intent, and suffered none of them to enter our ship. Whereupon two canoes full of men, with their bowes and arrowes shot at us after our sterne: in recompence whereof we discharged six muskets, and killed two or three of them. Then above an hundred of them came to a point of land to shoot at us. There I shot a falcon[1] at them, and killed two of them: whereupon the rest fled into the woods. Yet they manned off another canoe with nine or ten men, which came to meet us. So I shot at it also a falcon, and shot it through, and killed one of them. Then our men with their muskets killed three or foure more of them. So they went their way; within a mile after wee got downe two leagues beyond that place, and anchored in a bay, cleere from all danger of them on the other side

---

1 Falcon: a small cannon.

of the river, where we saw a very good piece of ground: and hard by it there was a cliffe, that looked of the colour of a white greene, as though it were either copper or silver myne: and I thinke it to be one of them, by the trees that grow upon it. For they be all burned, and the other places are greene as grasse; it is on that side of the river that is called Mannahata. There we saw no people to trouble us: and rode quietly all night; but had much wind and raine. . . .

We continued our course toward England, without seeing any land by the way, all the rest of this month of October: and on the seventh day of November, stilo novo, being Saturday, by the grace of God we safely arrived in the range of Dartmouth, in Devonshire, in the yeere 1609.

Questions for Discussion:
1. How does Juet's writings reflect a mariner's relationship to the environment?
2. What role did trade play in the relations between Hudson's sailors and the Native Americans they met?
3. What strengths or weaknesses does this sort of account have for historians studying this period?

Robert Juet, "Hudson's discovery of Hudson River," in *Great Epochs in American History*, vol. 1, *Voyages Of Discovery And Early Explorations: 1000 A.D.–1682*, ed. Francis W. Halsey, (New York: Funk & Wagnalls, 1912), 168–78.

MERCANTILISM IN THE 1600s

The impulse of European nations to colonize America and other parts of the globe was an important part of a new conception of economics later labeled *mercantilism*. While feudal society emphasized land ownership and agriculture as the basis of wealth, mercantilism emphasized trade and maritime commerce. As outlined in McCusker and Menard's *The Economy of British America*,[1] mercantilism was the idea that foreign trade could enrich a nation and beggar its neighbors. Colonies produced raw materials for the nations that owned them, stimulating the mother nation's exports, and giving it a positive balance of trade that presumably enriched its rulers.

The wealth of the New World was not necessarily gold and silver; as

---

1   John J. McCusker and Russell R. Menard, *The Economy of British America, 1607–1789* (Chapel Hill: University of North Carolina Press, 1985).

Captain John Smith relates, fish could be the foundation for creating a prosperous and powerful nation, and fish were in abundance in the waters of the New World. In mercantilist terms, the North American fisheries were important not only for the fish that fed the hungry European populace, but also as a "nursery of seamen" that produced skilled seamen who would serve in navies in time of war.

Mercantilism's goal of beggaring one's neighbors meant that European nations were almost constantly at war as they attempted to seize other nation's colonies or plunder their merchant fleets. The Netherlands was a mercantilist nation that used its navy to capture the colonial wealth of its rivals. The Dutch West India Company was a powerful joint-stock company that possessed its own fleet and founded colonies like Nieuw-Nederland, or modern-day New York. The account below details the success of one such operation against a Spanish fleet.

Thomas Mun, a merchant himself, lays down the ideal qualities of a merchant in his essay and connects them with enriching England itself. Many economists deem it the first clear statement of the idea of a balance of trade. Mercantilists generally believed that a nation must sell more goods than it imported, because the balance would be received in specie or credit, strengthening the nation. If a nation had a negative trade balance, that nation's specie drained out, weakening it. This is one reason why international trade, and therefore shipping, was so central to mercantilism.

Perhaps the most significant portion of the English vision of mercantilism was the body of laws known as the "Navigation Acts." These laws controlled virtually every aspect of shipping: from the time of day ships could be loaded to where cargoes could be shipped and what goods could be shipped where. Most importantly, the laws reserved shipping to and from British colonies for British and colonial shipping, effectively shutting out foreign merchants and ships. Reproduced below is a portion of the Navigation Act of 1660, which became the basis for British shipping policy for almost two hundred years.

John Smith, "New England Fisheries" (1614)

Few individuals stand out so boldly in the early English colonization of America as Captain John Smith (1580–1631). Smith was an adventurer; a sailor and soldier who had fought in eastern Europe against the Turks, eventually suffering capture and enslavement before being released and returning to England via North Africa. He was one of the leaders of the Jamestown colony, the first permanent English settlement in North America, founded in 1607. After a few years he left Jamestown but returned to the New World in 1614, this time to the waters of coastal New England in what was originally intended to be a whaling expedition.

In this account, Smith extols the potential wealth of New England's fisheries in what would come to be known as the Gulf of Maine. A large portion of his treatise on New England argues that the English should found a permanent colony there, with Smith as its leader. Smith believed that the true wealth of New England lay not in gold and silver, but in its rich fisheries. Indeed, North American fishing grounds were the scene of intense competition between European nations as they scrambled to control the natural resources of the New World.

In the moneth of April, 1614, with two Ships from *London*, of a few Marchants, I chanced to arive in *New-England*, a parte of *Ameryca*, at the Ile of *Monahiggan*,[1] in 43½ of Northerly latitude: our plot was there to take Whales and make tryalls of a Myne of Gold and Copper. If those failed, Fish and Furres was then our refuge, to make our selves savers howsoever we found this Whalefishing a costly conclusion: we saw many, and spent much time in chasing them; but we could not kill any: They being a kinde of Jubartes,[2] and not the Whale that yields Finnes and Oyle as wee expected. For our Golde, it was rather the Masters device to get a voyage that protected it, then any knowledge hee had at all of any such matter. Fish and Furres was now our guard, and by our fate arrival and long lingering about the Whale. The prime of both those seasons were past ere wee perceived it; we thinking that their seasons served at all times: but wee found it otherwise; for by the midst of June, the fishing failed. Yet in July and August some was taken, but not sufficient to defray so great a charge as our stay required. Of dry fish we made about 40000, of Cor fish[3] about 7000. Whilest the sailers fished, my selfe with eight or nine other of them might best bee spared; Ranging the coast in a small boat, wee got for trifles neer 1100 Bever skinnes, 100 Martins, and neer as many Otters; and the most of them within the distance of twenty leagues. We ranged the Coast both East and West much furder; but Eastwards

---

1   Monahiggan: Monhegan Island, off the Maine coast.
2   Jubartes: humpback whales, which were not considered commercially valuable in
     1614.
3   Cor fish: a form of salted codfish.

our commodities were not esteemed, they were so neare the French who affords them better and right against us in the Main was a Ship of Sir *Frances Popphames*,[1] that had there such acquaintance, having many yeares used onely that porte, that the most parte there was had by him. And 40 leagues westwards were two French Ships, that had made there a great voyage by trade, during the time wee tried those conclusions, not knowing the Coast, nor Salvages habitation. With these furres, the Traine,[2] and Cor-fish I returned for *England* in the Bark; where within six monthes after our departure from the *Downes*, we safe arrived back. The best of this fish was solde for five pound the hundreth, the rest by ill usage betwixt three pound and fifty shillings. The other Ship staied to fit herself for *Spaine* with the dry fish which was sould, by the Sailers reporte that returned, at forty ryalls[3] the quintal, each hundred weighing two quintals and a half. . . .[4]

The maine Staple, from hence to bee extracted for the present to produce the rest, is fish; which however it may seeme a mean and base commoditie: yet who will but truly take the pains and consider the sequell, I thinke will allow it well worth the labour. It is strange to see what great adventures the hopes of setting forth men of war to rob industrious innocent, would procure; or such massie promises in grosse: though more are choked then well fedde with such hastie hopes. But who doth not know that the poore Hollanders, chiefly by fishing, at a great charge and labour in all weathers in the open Sea, are made a people so hardy, and industrious? and by venting this poore commodity to the Easterlings for as meane, which is Wood, Flax, Pitch, Tarre, Rosin, Cordage, and such like (which they exchange againe, to the French, Spaniards, Portugales, and English, &c. for what they want) are made so mighty, strong and rich, as no State but *Venice*, of twice their magnitude, is so well furnished with so many faire shipping and all sorts of marchandize, as well of Golde, Silver, Pearles, Diamonds, Pretious stones, Silkes, Velvets, and Cloth of golde; as Fish, Pitch, Wood, or such grosse commodities? What Voyages and Discoveries, East and West, North and South, yea about the world, make they? What an Army by Sea and Land, have they long maintained in

---

1   Sir Frances Popphames: Sir Francis Popham (1572–1644), a wealthy English investor in early fishing ventures in New England.
2   Traine: oil derived from codfish livers.
3   Ryalls: reals, or Spanish silver coins.
4   Quintal: roughly one hundred and twelve pounds.

despite of one of the greatest Princes of the world? And never could the Spaniard with all his Mynes of golde and Silver, pay his debts, his friends, and army, halfe so truly, as the Hollanders stil have done by this contemptible trade of fish. Divers (I know) may alledge, many other assistances. But this is their Myne; and the Sea the source of those silvered streames of all their vertue; which hath made them now the very miracle of industrie, the pattern of perfection for these affaires; and the benefit of fishing is that *Primum mobile*[1] that turnes all their *Spheres* to this height of plenty, strength, honour and admiration.

Herring, Cod, and Ling,[2] is that triplicitie that makes their wealth and shippings multiplicities, such as it is, and from which a halfe of pounds starling; yet it is most certaine (if records be true:) and in this faculty they are so naturalized, and of their vents so certainly acquainted, as there is no likelihood they will ever bee paralleld having 2 or 3000 Busses, Flat bottomes, Sword pinks, Todes, and such like, that breedes them Saylers, Mariners, Souldiers and Merchants, never to be wrought out of that trade, and fit for any other. I will not deny but others may gaine as well as they, that will use it, though not so certainly, nor so much in quantity; for want of experience. And this Herring they take upon the Coast of *Scotland* and *England*; their Cod and Ling, upon the Coast of *Izeland* and the North Sea.

Hamborough, and the *East Countries*,[3] for Sturgion and Caviare, gets many thousands of pounds from *England*, and the *Straites*; *Portugale*, and the *Biskaines*, and the *Spaniards*, make 40 or 50 Saile yearly to *Cape-blank*, to hooke for Porgos, Mullet, and make *Puttardo*:[4] and *New Found Land*, doth yearly fraught neere 800 sayle of Ships with a sillie leane skinny Poore-John,[5] and Cornfish,[6] which at least yearly amounts to 3 or 400000 pound. If from all those parts such paines is taken from this poore gaine of fish, and by them hath neither meate, drinke, nor clothes, wood, iron, nor steele, pitch, tarre, nets, leades, salt, hookes, nor lines, for shipping, fishing, nor provision, but at the second, third, fourth, or fifth hand, drawne from so many severall

---

1   Primum mobile: prime mover, and also a term from Ptolemaic astronomy.
2   Ling: a kind of edible fish.
3   Hamborough: Hamburgh, Germany, and the countries as far east as Russia.
4   Puttardo: sometimes *puttargo*, a paste made out of salted fish.
5   Poore-John: a European fish similar to cod, but considered inferior.
6   Cornfish: corfish, cured fish ready for sale in Europe.

parts of the world ere they come together to be used in this voyage: If these I say can gaine, and Saylers line going for shares, lesse then the third part of their labours, and yet spend as much time in going and coming, as in staying there, so short is the season of fishing; why should wee more doubt then *Holland, Portugale, Spaniards, French,* or other, but to doe much better then they, where there is victual to feede us, wood of all sorts, to build Boats, Ships, or Barks; they fish at our doores, pitch, tarre, masts, yards, and most of other necessaries onely for making? And here are no hard Landlords to rackle us with high rents, or extorted fines to consume us, no tedious pleas in law to consume us with their many years disputations for Justice: no maltitudes to occasion such impediments to good orders, as in popular States. So freely hath God and his Majesty bestowed those blessings on them that will attempt to obtaine them, as here every man may be master and owne labour and land; or the greatest part in a small time. If hee have nothing but his hands, he may set up this trade; and by industrie quickly grow rich; spending but halfe the time wel, which in *England* we abuse in idlenes, worse or as ill. Here is ground also as good as any lyeth in the height of forty one, forty two, forty three, &c.[1] which is as temperate and as fruitfull as any other paralell in the world. . . .

In March, April, May, and halfe June, here is Cod in abundance; in May, June, July, and August Mullet and Sturgion; whose roes doe make Caviare and Puttargo. Herring if any desire them, I have taken many out of the bellies of Cods, some in nets; but the Salvages compare their store in the Sea, to the haires on their heads: and surely there are an incredible abundance upon this Coast. In the end of August, September, October, and November, you have Cod againe to make Cor fish, or Poore John: and each hundred is as good as two or three hundred is as good as tow or three hundred in the *New-Found Land.* So that halfe the labour in hooking, splitting, and turning, is saved: and you may have your fish at what Market you will, before they have any in *New-Found Land*; where their fishing is chiefly but in June and July: whereas it is here in March, April, May, September, October, and November, as is said. So that by reason of this plantation, the Marchants may have fraught both out and home: which yields an advantage worth consideration.

---

1   Forty one . . . : Between forty-one and forty-three degrees north of the equator.

Your Cor-fish you may in like manner transport as you see cause, to serve the Ports in *Portugale* (as *Lisbon, Auera, Porta port,* and divers others, or what market you please) before your *Ilanders* returne: They being typed to the season in the open sea; you having a double season, and fishing before your doors, may every night sleep quietly a shore with good cheare and what fires you will, or when you please with your wives and familie: they onely, their ships in the maine Ocean.

The Mullets heere are in that abundance, you may take them with nets, sometimes by hundred, where at *Cape blank* they hooke them; yet those but one foot and a halfe in length; these two, three, or foure, as oft I have measured: much Salmon some have found up the Rivers, as they have passed: and heer the ayre is so temperate, as all these at any time may well be preserved.

Now, young boyes and girles Salvages, or any other, be they never such idlers, may turne, carry, and return fish, without either shame, or any great paine: hee is very idle that is past twelve yeares of age and cannot doe so much: and she is very olde, that cannot spin a thred to make engines to catch them.

Questions for Discussion:

1. What does this document reveal about the European seafarers who came to the New World in this period?

2. What riches did Smith originally plan on finding in New England, and why did he have to change his plans once there?

3. What was Smith's attitude toward the marine environment he found in the waters off New England?

John Smith, "A Description of New England: or The Observations, and Discoveries of Captain John Smith (Admirall of that Country) in the North of America, in the year of our Lord 1614," in *Old South Leaflets, Volume V* (Boston: Directors of the Old South Work, 1902), 417–28.

Dutch West India Company, "Preservation and Prosperity" (1629)

The Dutch West India Company received a charter from the Dutch government in 1621 giving it a monopoly over all trade with North America, including the African slave trade, and a license to attack Spanish shipping. In 1614 the company established the colony of Nieuw-Nederland, in modern-day New York, only five years after Henry Hudson's exploration of the river named after him. Like its larger and wealthier counterpart, the Dutch East

India Company, the Dutch West India Company was a joint-stock company owned by shareholders but operated under a charter from the States-General of the United Netherlands. This charter permitted the company to found colonies and establish what amounted to their own armed forces, both armies and navies. The Dutch were not alone in this type of arrangement; the Virginia Company established the first successful English colony in North America, and the Honourable East India Company not only established trade with India, but eventually came to rule much of the Indian subcontinent.

For modern eyes, it may be difficult to separate this company's search for profit from the national goals of the Netherlands government—but in a mercantilist system the company's search for profit was a crucial function of enriching the state. The best example of this was when the Dutch West India Company's Admiral Piet Hein (1577–1629) successfully waged war on the Spanish American colonies, plundering cities and seizing a treasure fleet—all for the profit of the company's shareholders and the benefit of the Dutch national treasury. With this enormous victory in mind, the directors of the company took the opportunity to remind the Dutch government of the services it had rendered.

High and Mighty Lords,

ALTHOUGH we are confident that you, High and Mighty, can in your usual wisdom, and will, pursuant to your special regard and favor for us, consider that the security and welfare of our beloved Fatherland is most intimately connected with the preservation and prosperity of our Company, yet we have deemed it our duty to lay, with all submission, before you, High and Mighty, in a summary manner, the principal points which, in these parts, ought to be taken into consideration.

First: it is to be considered with what longing the Company has been expected, for many years, by all good Patriots at home, and all good wishers of our state abroad; and how slowly it has been brought to maturity, against numerous contradictions and countermines on the part of others.

Secondly: that you, High and Mighty, have, of your own motion and unasked, incorporated your subjects, and promised, in the form of a mutual contract and reciprocal connection, to afford them every help in case of war, and to maintain, in their integrity, all their contracts with foreigners.

Thirdly: that thereupon, the Capital of this Company was wholly subscribed and sufficiently paid in, through the several efforts of the Directors appointed thereunto by you, High and Mighty, by such as you yourselves consider have most at heart the maintenance of the true Reformed religion[1] and the liberties of our beloved Fatherland; so that many have contributed abundantly thereunto even out of their poverty.

Fourthly: that by means of this Company, even from its very incipiency, a great number of ships were partly purchased and partly chartered, which otherwise must have lain idle in consequence of the dullness of trade.

Fifthly: that by means of the same, many large and small vessels, and especially, very fine and fast sailing yachts have been built, to the great increase of Navigation.

Sixthly: that the number of our vessels has, from time to time, so much increased, that we have at present over one hundred full rigged ships, of various burthens, at sea, mostly fitted for war.

Seventhly: that we have employed, from time to time, in said ships, a great number of seamen and soldiers, so that we had last year 9,000 men, and now, at present, full 15,000 in our service; whereby the people were wonderfully benefited; many experienced pilots formed, and so many educated, that the country can always find fit persons to be employed on board its ships as chief and subordinate officers.

Eighthly: that we have victualled the aforesaid ships, some for 12, some for 15, and even many for 18 months and more.

Ninthly: that we have provided our ships so well with heavy guns, that we had, last year, on board our marine, full 264 metal pieces, amongst which were many demi-carthouns;[2] and nearly 1400 heavy swivels,[3] which number is much increased this year, so that we have at present over 400 metal pieces on board of our ships, and over 2000 swivels, besides pedereros[4] to the number of far beyond 600.

And finally: that we have provided them with a great quantity of powder, mostly manufactured in this country, so that we have expended, this year, on board our ships, over one hundred thousand

---

1   Reformed religion: Protestant faith.
2   Demi-carthouns: cannons firing a twenty-four-pound ball.
3   Swivels: swivel cannons, small cannons that pivoted easily.
4   Pedereros: small swivel cannons.

pounds of powder. From all which it must at once be seen, what trade our equipments have created in this country; how many people we have employed, and with what a remarkable force we have increased Your High Mightinesses' navy, of which Your High Mightinesses can make use in time of need, as the Company's aid, without boasting, was particularly well timed in the last public difficulties.

It is now to be further considered what wealth these, our ships, have brought into this country.

First: omitting what has been imported these previous years in course of trade in gold, elephants' teeth, pepper, hides, peltries, timber, salt and such like; the silver, coined and in bars, received in the beginning of this year, in consequence of the capture of the fleet from New Spain, amounted to so great a treasure, that never did any fleet bring such a prize to this, or any other country.

Secondly: we have now, during some consecutive years, plundered the enemy and enriched this country with many large parcels of Indigo, so that over 4000 cases have been received at the close of the last, and the beginning of this year.

Thirdly: a large quantity of Sugar, so that we have brought in, this year alone, three thousand chests.

Fourthly: a wonderful large quantity of Raw hides, and have taken 36[ml1] principally this year from the enemy.

Fifthly: the handsomest lot of Cochineal[2] that was ever brought into this country.

Sixthly: a considerable quantity of Tobacco, which is now an important article of commerce.

And finally, a vast amount of wealth in all sorts of precious stones, silk and silk goods, musk, amber, all sorts of drugs, Brazil and Log Wood[3] and other wares, too numerous to mention here; so that we have already brought several millions into this country. All which wares, sold and distributed among the good inhabitants, were consumed here and conveyed elsewhere, and therefore enriched your High Mightinesses' subjects, and increased the revenue.

The damage done thereby to our enemies, is easily estimated. We have, moreover, captured some even of the King of Spain's galleons,

---

1   M: millennia, or thousands.
2   Cochineal: a valuable red dye from Central America made from insects.
3   Log Wood: a valuable type of wood from the West Indies and Central America used in making dye.

hitherto considered invincible, besides some other of his men of War, exclusive of more than two hundred ships and barks which we have taken from his subjects, and partly appropriated to our own use, and partly destroyed.

Our ships and fleets also reduced, and for a time kept possession of, the rich and mighty city of St. Salvador, in Brazil; sacked Porto Rico; pointed out the way to seize its exceedingly enclosed harbors, and have destroyed the castle of Margrita.[1]

By all which acts have we not only drained the King of Spain's treasury, but also further pursued him at considerable expense.

We say, exhausted his treasury—

First, by depriving him of so much silver, which was as blood from one of the arteries of his heart. . . .

Your High Mightinesses'
Humble Servants,
The Deputies of the Chartered West India Company

Questions for Discussion:
1. How does this document relate to the concept of mercantilism?
2. What economic advantage did the Dutch West India Company's ships bring to the Netherlands?
3. What does this document reveal about the power of joint-stock companies in the 1600s?

E. B. O'Callaghan, ed., *Documents Relative to the Colonial History of the State of New York*, vol. 1 (Albany, N.Y.: Weed, Parsons, and Co., 1856), 40–42.

Thomas Mun, "England's Treasure by Forraign Trade" (ca. 1630s)

Thomas Mun (1571–1641) was a wealthy London merchant who was involved with trade in the Mediterranean early in his career and later with the East India Company's trade with Asia. He was also one of Britain's foremost economic writers and an early advocate of mercantilism. Mun believed that England's wealth was not merely the sum of the gold bullion it possessed, but lay in the nation's extensive foreign commerce. This piece, written by Mun for his son in the 1630s, was not published until 1664. In it, he catalogs the ideal qualities of a merchant and urges England to export more than it imports, cultivate its wastelands, minimize the import of foreign goods, and use only English ships to transport its goods. Colonial mer-

---

1   Margrita: probably Isla Margrita, an island in the Caribbean.

chants would have recognized the value of Mun's ideas, especially his ideas on the qualities of a merchant.

Chapter I: The Qualities which are required in a perfect Merchant of Forraign Trade.

The love and service of our Country consisteth not so much in the knowledge of those duties which are to be performed by others, as in the skilful practice of that which is done our selves; and therefore (my Son) it is now fit that I say something of the Merchant, which I hope in due time shall be thy Vocation: Yet herein are my thoughts free from all Ambition, although I rank thee in a place of so high esteem; for the Merchant is worthily called The Steward of the Kingdoms Stock, by way of Commerce with other Nations; a work of no less Reputation than Trust, which ought to be performed with great skill and conscience, that so the private gain may ever accompany the publique good. And because the nobleness of this profession may the better stir up thy desires and endeavours to obtain those abilities which may effect it worthily, I will briefly set down the excellent qualities which are required in a perfect Merchant.

1. He ought to be a good Penman, a good Arithmetician, and a good Accomptant, by that noble order of Debtor and Creditor, which is used onely amongst Merchants; also to be expert in the order and form of Charter-parties, Bills of Lading, Invoyces, Contracts, Bills of Exchange, and policies of Ensurance.

2. He ought to know the Measures, Weights and Monies of all forraign Countries, especially where we have Trade, & the Monies not onely by their several denominations, but also by their intrinsique values in weight & fineness, compared with the Standard of this Kingdome, without which he cannot well direct his affaires.

3. He ought to know the Customs, Tolls, Taxes, Impositions, Conducts and other charges upon all matters of Merchandize exported or imported to and from the said Forraign Countries.

4. He ought to know in what several commodities each Country abounds, and what be the wares which they want, and how and from whence they are furnished with the same.

5. He ought to understand, and to be a diligent observer of the rates of Exchanges by Bills, from one State to another, whereby he may the

better direct his affairs, and remit over and receive home his Monies to the most advantage possible.

6. He ought to know what goods are prohibited to be exported or imported in the said forraign Countreys, lest otherwise he should incur great danger and loss in the ordering of his affairs.

7. He ought to know upon what rates and conditions to fraight his Ships, and ensure his adventures from one Countrey to another, and to be well acquainted with the laws, orders and customes of the Ensurance office both here and beyond the Seas, in the many accidents which may happen upon the damage or loss of Ships or goods, or both these.

8. He ought to have knowledge in the goodness and in the prices of all the several materials which are required for the building and repairing of Ships, and the divers workmanships of the same, as also for the Masts, Tackling, Cordage, Ordnance, Victuals, Munition and Provisions of many kinds; together with the ordinary wages of Commanders, Officers and Mariners, all which concern the Merchant as he is an Owner of Ships.

9. He ought (by the divers occasions which happen sometime in the buying and selling of one commodity and sometimes in another) to have indifferent if not perfect knowledge in all manner of Merchandize or wares, which is to be as it were a man of all occupations and trades.

10. He ought by his voyaging on the Seas to become skilful in the Art of Navigation.

11. He ought as he is a Traveller, and sometimes abiding in forraign Countreys to attain to the speaking of divers Languages, and to be a diligent observer of the ordinary Revenues and expences of forraign Princes, together with their strength both by Sea and Land, their laws, customes, policies, manners, religions, arts, and the like; to be able to give account thereof in all occasions for the good of his Countrey.

12. Lastly, although there be no necessity that such a Merchant should be a great Scholar; yet is it (at least) required, that in his youth he learn the Latine tongue, which will the better enable him in all the rest of his endeavours.

Thus have I briefly shewed thee a pattern for thy diligence, the Merchant in his qualities; which in truth are such and so many, that I find no other profession which leadeth into more worldly knowledge. And it cannot be denied but that their sufficiency doth appear likewise in the excellent government of State at Venice, Luca, Genoa, Florence, the low Countreys, and divers other places of Christendom. And in those States also where they are least esteemed, yet is their skill and knowledge often used by those who sit in the highest places of Authority: It is therefore an act beyond rashness in some, who do disenable their Counsel and judgment (even in books printed) making them uncapable of those ways and means which do either enrich or empoverish a Common-wealth, when in truth this is only effected by the mystery of their trade, as I shall plainly shew in that which followeth. It is true indeed that many Merchants here in England finding less encouragement given to their profession than in other Countreys, and seeing themselves not so well esteemed as their Noble Vocation requireth, and according to the great consequence of the same, doe not therefore labour to attain unto the excellencie of their profession, neither is it practised by the Nobility of this Kingdom as it is in other States from the Father to the Son throughout their generations, to the great encrease of their wealth, and maintenance of their names and families: Whereas the memory of our richest Merchants is suddenly extinguished; the Son being left rich, scorneth the profession of his Father, conceiving more honor to be a Gentleman (although but in name) to consume his estate in dark ignorance and excess, than to follow the steps of his Father as an Industrious Merchant to maintain and advance his Fortunes. But now leaving the Merchants praise we will come to his practice, or at least to so much thereof as concerns the bringing of Treasure into the Kingdom.

Chapter II: The Means to enrich this Kingdom, and to encrease our Treasure.

Although a Kingdom may be enriched by gifts received, or by purchase taken from some other Nations, yet these are things uncertain and of small consideration when they happen. The ordinary means therefore to encrease our wealth and treasure is by Forraign Trade, wherein wee must ever observe this rule; to sell more to strangers yearly than wee consume of theirs in value. For suppose that when this Kingdom is plentifully served with the Cloth, Lead, Tinn, Iron, Fish and other native commodities, we doe yearly export the overplus to forraign Countries to the value of twenty two hundred thousand pounds; by which means we are enabled beyond the Seas to buy and bring in forraign wares for our use and Consumption, to the value of twenty hundred thousand pounds; By this order duly kept in our trading, we may rest assured that the Kingdom shall be enriched yearly two hundred thousand pounds, which must be brought to us in so much Treasure; because that part of our stock which is not returned to us in wares must necessarily be brought home in treasure.

For in this case it cometh to pass in the stock of a Kingdom, as in the estate of a private man; who is supposed to have one thousand pounds yearly revenue and two thousand pounds of ready money in his Chest: If such a man through excess shall spend one thousand five hundred pounds per annum, all his ready money will be gone in four years; and in the like time his said money will be doubled if he take a Frugal course to spend but five hundred pounds per annum; which rule never faileth likewise in the Commonwealth, but in some cases (of no great moment) which I will hereafter declare, when I shall shew by whom and in what manner this ballance of the Kingdoms account ought to be drawn up yearly, or so often as it shall please the State to discover how much we gain or lose by trade with forraign Nations. But first I will say something concerning those ways and means which will encrease our exportations and diminish our importations of wares; which being done, I will then set down some other arguments both affirmative and negative to strengthen that which is here declared, and thereby to shew that all the other means which are commonly supposed to enrich the Kingdom with Treasure are altogether insufficient and meer fallacies.

Chapter III: The particular ways and means to encrease the exportation of our commodities, and to decrease our Consumption of forraign wares.

The revenue or stock of a Kingdom by which it is provided of forraign wares is either Natural or Artificial. The Natural wealth is so much only as can be spared from our own use and necessities to be exported unto strangers. The Artificial consists in our manufactures and industrious trading with forraign commodities, concerning which I will set down such particulars as may serve for the cause we have in hand.

1. First, although this Realm be already exceeding rich by nature, yet might it be much encreased by laying the waste grounds (which are infinite) into such employments as should no way hinder the pres-

ent revenues of other manufactured lands, but hereby to supply our selves and prevent the importations of Hemp, Flax, Cordage, Tobacco, and divers other things which now we fetch from strangers to our great impoverishing.

2. We may likewise diminish our importations, if we would soberly refrain from excessive consumption of forraign wares in our diet and rayment, with such often change of fashions as is used, so much the more to encrease the waste and charge; which vices at this present are more notorious amongst us than in former ages. Yet might they easily be amended by enforcing the observation of such good laws as are strictly practised in other Countries against the said excesses; where likewise by commanding their own manufactures to be used, they prevent the coming in of others, without prohibition, or offence to strangers in their mutual commerce.

3. In our exportations we must not only regard our own super-fluities, but also we must consider our neighbours necessities, that so upon the wares which they cannot want, nor yet be furnished thereof elsewhere, we may (besides the vent of the Materials) gain so much of the manufacture as we can, and also endeavour to sell them dear, so far forth as the high price cause not a less vent in the quantity. But the superfluity of our commodities which strangers use, and may also have the same from other Nations, or may abate their vent by the use of some such like wares from other places, and with little inconve-nience; we must in this case strive to sell as cheap as possible we can, rather than to lose the utterance of such wares. For we have found of late years by good experience, that being able to sell our Cloth cheap in Turkey, we have greatly encreased the vent thereof, and the Vene-tians have lost as much in the utterance of theirs in those Countreys, because it is dearer. And on the other side a few years past, when by excessive price of Wools our Cloth was exceeding dear, we lost at the least half our clothing for forraign parts, which since is no otherwise (well neer) recovered again than by the great fall of price for Wools and Cloth. We find that twenty five in the hundred less in the price of these and some other Wares, to the loss of private mens revenues, may raise above fifty upon the hundred in the quantity vented to the benefit of the publique. For when Cloth is dear, other Nations doe presently practise clothing, and we know they want neither art nor materials to this performance. But when by cheapness we drive them from this employment, and so in time obtain our dear price again,

then do they also use their former remedy. So that by these alterations we learn, that it is in vain to expect a greater revenue of our wares than their condition will afford, but rather it concerns us to apply our endeavours to the times with care and diligence to help our selves the best we may, by making our cloth and other manufactures without deceit, which will encrease their estimation and use.

4. The value of our exportations likewise may be much advanced when we perform it our selves in our own Ships, for then we get only not the price of our wares as they are worth here, but also the Merchants gains, the changes of ensurance, and fraight to carry them beyond the seas. As for example, if the Italian Merchants should come hither in their own shipping to fetch our Corn, our red Herrings or the like, in the case the Kingdom should have ordinarily but 25s[1] for a quarter of Wheat, and 20s for a barrel of red herrings, whereas if we carry these wares our selves into Italy upon the said rates, it is likely that wee shall obtain fifty shillings for the first, and forty shillings for the last, which is a great difference in the utterance or vent of the Kingdoms stock. And although it is true that the commerce ought to be free to strangers to bring in and carry out at their pleasure, yet nevertheless in many places the exportation of victuals and munition are either prohibited, or at least limited to be done onely by the people and Shipping of those places where they abound.

5. The frugal expending likewise of our own natural wealth might advance much yearly to be exported unto strangers; and if in our rayment we will be prodigal, yet let this be done with our own materials and manufactures, as Cloth, Lace, Imbroderies, Cutworks and the like, where the excess of the rich may be the employment of the poor, whose labours notwithstanding of this kind, would be more profitable for the Commonwealth, if they were done to the use of strangers.

6. The Fishing in his Majesties seas of England, Scotland and Ireland is our natural wealth, and would cost nothing but labour, which the Dutch bestow willingly, and thereby draw yearly a very great profit to themselves by serving many places of Christendom with our Fish, for which they return and supply their wants both of forraign Wares and Mony, besides the multitude of Mariners and Shipping, which hereby are maintain'd, whereof a long discourse might be made to

---

1   25s: twenty-five shillings. In old English currency there were twelve pennies to a shilling and twenty shillings to one pound sterling.

shew the particular manage of this important business. Our Fishing plantation likewise in New England, Virginia, Groenland, the Summer Islands and the New-found-land, are of the like nature, affording much wealth and employments to maintain a great number of poor, and to encrease our decaying trade.

7. A Staple or Magazin for forraign Corn, Indigo, Spices, Raw-silks, Cotton wool or any other commodity whatsoever, to be imported will encrease Shipping, Trade, Treasure, and the Kings customes, by exporting them again where need shall require, which course of Trading, hath been the chief means to raise Venice, Genoa, the low-Countreys, with some others; and for such a purpose England stands most commodiously, wanting nothing to this performance but our own diligence and endeavour.

8. Also wee ought to esteem and cherish those trades which we have in remote or far Countreys, for besides the encrease of Shipping and Mariners thereby, the wares also sent thither and receiv'd from thence are far more profitable unto the kingdom than by our trades neer at hand: As for example; suppose Pepper to be worth here two Shillings the pound constantly, if then it be brought from the Dutch at Amsterdam, the Merchant may give there twenty pence the pound, and gain well by the bargain; but if he fetch this Pepper from the East-indies, he must not give above three pence the pound at the most, which is a mighty advantage, not only in that part which serveth for our own use, but also for that great quantity which (from hence) we transport yearly unto divers other Nations to be sold at a higher price: whereby it is plain, that we make a far greater stock by gain upon these Indian Commodities, than those Nations doe where they grow, and to whom they properly appertain, being the natural wealth of their Countries. But for the better understanding of this particular, we must ever distinguish between the gain of the Kingdom, and the profit of the Merchant; for although the Kingdom payeth no more for this Pepper than is before supposed, nor for any other commodity bought in forraign parts more than the stranger receiveth from us for the same, yet the Merchant payeth not only that price, but also the fraight, ensurance, customes and other charges which are exceeding great in these long voyages; but yet all these in the Kingdoms accompt are but commutations among our selves, and no Privation of the Kingdoms stock, which being duly considered, together with the support

also of our other trades in our best Shipping to Italy, France, Turkey, and East Countreys and other places, by transporting and venting the wares which we bring yearly from the East Indies; It may well stir up our utmost endeavours to maintain and enlarge this great and noble business, so much importing the Publique wealth, Strength, and Happiness. Neither is there less honour and judgment by growing rich (in this manner) upon the stock of other Nations, than by an industrious encrease of our own means, especially when this later is advanced by the benefit of the former, as we have found in the East Indies by sale of much of our Tin, Cloth, Lead and other Commodities, the vent whereof doth daily encrease in those Countreys which formerly had no use of our wares.

9. It would be very beneficial to export money as well as wares, being done in trade only, it would encrease our Treasure; but of this I write more largely in the next Chapter to prove it plainly.

10. It were policie and profit for the State to suffer manufactures made of forraign Materials to be exported custome-free, as Velvets and all other wrought Silks, Fustians, thrown Silks and the like, it would employ very many poor people, and much encrease the value of our stock yearly issued into other Countreys, and it would (for this purpose) cause the more forraign Materials to be brought in, to the improvement of His Majesties Customes. I will here remember a notable increase in our manufacture of winding and twisting only of forraign raw Silk, which within 35 years to my knowledge did not employ more than 300 people in the City and suburbs of London, where at this present time it doth set on work above fourteen thousand souls, as upon diligent enquiry hath been credibly reported unto His Majesties Commissioners for Trade, and it is certain, that if the said forraign Commodities might be exported from hence, free of custome, this manufacture would yet encrease very much, and decrease as fast in Italy and in the Netherlands. But if any man allege the Dutch proverb, "Live and let others live;" I answer, that the Dutchmen notwithstanding their own Proverb, doe not onely in these Kingdoms, encroach upon our livings, but also in other forraign parts of our trade (where they have power) they do hinder and destroy us in our lawful course of living, hereby taking the bread out of our mouth, which we shall never prevent by plucking the pot from their nose, as of late years too many of us do practise to the great hurt and dishonour of this fa-

mous Nation; We ought rather to imitate former times in taking sober and worthy courses more pleasing to God and suitable to our ancient reputation.

11. It is needful also not to charge the native commodities with too great customes,[1] lest by indearing them to the strangers use, it hinder their vent. And especially forraign wares brought in to be transported again should be favoured, for otherwise that manner of trading (so much importing the good of the Commonwealth) cannot prosper nor subsist. But the Consumption of such forraign wares in the Realm may be the more charged, which will turn to the profit of the kingdom in the Ballance of the Trade, and thereby also enable the King to lay up the more Treasure out of his yearly incomes. . . .

12. Lastly, in all things we must endeavour to make the most we can of our own, whether it be Natural or Artificial, And forasmuch as the people which live by the Arts are far more in number than they who are masters of the fruits, we ought the more carefully to maintain those endeavours of the multitude, in whom doth consist the greatest strength and riches both of the King and Kingdom: for where the people are many, and the arts good, there the traffique must be great, and the Countrey rich. . . . But what need we fetch the example so far, when we know that our own natural wares doe not yeild us so much profit as our industry? For Iron ore in the Mines is of no great worth, when it is compared with the employment and advantage it yields being digged, tried, transported, brought, sold, cast into Ordnance, Muskets, and many other instruments of war for offence and defence, wrought into Anchors, bolts, spikes, nayles and the like, for the use of Ships, Houses, Carts, Coaches, Ploughs, and other instruments for Tillage. Compare our Fleece-wools with our Cloth, which requires shearing, washing, carding, spinning, Weaving, fulling, dying, dressing and other trimmings, and we shall find these Arts more profitable than the natural wealth, whereof I might instance other examples, but I will not be more tedious, for if I would amplify upon this and the other particulars before written, I might find matter sufficient to make a large volume, but my desire in all is only to prove what I propound with brevity and plainness.

---

1   Customes: customs taxes. Mun is warning that high taxes will drive away customers.

Questions for Discussion:

1. What relationship did Mun see between merchants and maritime activity?

2. According to Mun, how is foreign trade related to the wealth of the nation?

3. How does Mun fit English colonies into his economic vision?

Thomas Mun, *England's Treasure by Forraign Trade* (New York: Macmillan, 1895), 2–18.

Parliament, "Encourageing and Increasing of Shipping and Navigation" (1660)

The Navigation Acts were a body of laws designed to protect English and colonial shipping and exploit colonial trade for the benefit of the mother country. Initially passed by Parliament during the Commonwealth period when Oliver Cromwell ruled England, King Charles II confirmed the legislation after the restoration of the British monarchy.

The Navigation Acts of 1660 were in large part a reaction to the success of Dutch maritime commerce, which threatened the prosperity of England's own budding empire. The Navigation Acts as a whole protected colonial shipping from foreign competition and endowed colonists with almost all the privileges that English merchants and seafarers possessed. In fact, English political economists such as Sir Josiah Child warned that the Navigation Acts were too generous to colonists and that colonial shipping was both dangerous and prejudicial to the "Mother Kingdom." But the Navigation Acts also imposed restrictions on colonial maritime trade. Some of the more notable aspects were a requirement that three-fourths of any ship's crew had to be English subjects and the prohibition of colonial vessels' trading beyond the Cape of Good Hope in Africa. The acts banned all foreign shipping from colonial ports and forbade the colonies from exporting certain goods, including tobacco, wool, wood, sugar, and cotton, directly to nations other than England and Ireland. The penalties for violating the acts were severe, often resulting in the confiscation of the entire ship and cargo. The Navigation Acts thus remain a matter of debate for historians who cannot agree if they were a blessing or a curse to colonial shipping and seaborne commerce.

I. For the increase of Shiping and incouragement of the Navigation of this Nation, wherin under the good providence and protection of God the Wealth Safety and Strength of this Kingdome is soe much concerned Bee it Enacted by the Kings most Excellent Majesty and by the Lords and Commons in this present Parliament assembled and the Authoritie therof That from and after the First day of December One thousand six hundred and sixty and from thence forward noe Goods or Commodities whatsoever shall be Imported into or Exported out of any Lands Islelands Plantations or Territories to his Majesty belonging or in his possession or which may hereafter belong unto or be in the possession of His Majesty His Heires and Successors in Asia Africa or America in any other Ship or Ships Vessell or Vessells whatsoever but in such Ships or Vessells as doe truely and without fraude belong onely to the people of England or Ireland Dominion of Wales or Towne of Berwicke upon Tweede, or are of the built of, and belonging to any of the said Lands Islands Plantations or Territories as the Proprietors and right Owners therof and wherof the Master and three fourthes of the Marriners at least are English under the penalty of the Forfeiture and Losse of all the Goods and Commodityes which shall be Imported into, or Exported out of, any the aforesaid places in any other Ship or Vessell, as alsoe of the Ship or Vessell with all its Guns Furniture Tackle Ammunition and Apparell, one third part thereof to his Majesty his Heires and Successors, one third part to the Governour of such Land Plantation Island or Territory where such default shall be commited in case the said Ship or Goods be there seised, or otherwise that third part alsoe to his Majesty his Heires and Successors, and the other third part to him or them who shall Seize Informe or sue for the same in any Court of Record by Bill Information Plaint or other Action wherein noe Essoigne Protection or Wager of Law shall be allowed, And all Admiralls and other Commanders at Sea of any the Ships of War or other Ship haveing Commission from His Majesty or from his Heires or Successors are hereby authorized and strictly required to seize and bring in as prize all such Ships or Vessells as shall have offended contrary hereunto and deliver them to the Court of Admiralty there to be proceeded against and in case of condemnation one moyety of such Forfeitures shall be to the use of such Admiralls or Commanders and their Companies to be divided and proportioned amongst them according to the Rules and Orders of the Sea in cases of Ships taken prize, and the other moyety to the use of his Majesty his Heires and Successors. . . .

III. And it is further Enacted . . . that noe Goods or Commodityes whatsoever of the growth production or manufacture of Africa Asia or

America or of any part thereof, or which are discribed or laid downe in the usuall Maps or Cards of those places be Imported into England Ireland or Wales Islands of Guernsey or Jersey or Towne of Berwicke upon Tweede in any other Ship or Ships Vessell or Vessels whatsoever, but in such as doe truly and without fraude belong onely to the people of England or Ireland, Dominion of Wales or Towne of Berwicke upon Tweede or of the Lands Islands Plantations or Territories in Asia Africa or America to his Majesty belonging as the proprietors and right owners therof, and wherof the Master and three fourthes at least of the Mariners are English under the penalty of the forfeiture of all such Goods and Commodityes, and of the Ship or Vessell in which they were Imported with all her Guns Tackle Furniture Ammunition and Apparell, one moyety to his Majesty his Heires and Successors, and the other moyety to him or them whoe shall Seize Inform or Sue for the same. . . .

IV. And it is further Enacted . . . that noe Goods or Commodityes that are of forraigne growth production or manufacture and which are to be brought into England Ireland Wales, the Islands of Guernsey & Jersey or Towne of Berwicke upon Tweede in English built shiping, or other shiping belonging to some of the aforesaid places, and navigated by English Mariners as abovesaid shall be shiped or brought from any other place or Places, Country or Countries but onely from those of their said Growth Production or Manufacture, or from those Ports where the said Goods and Commodityes can onely or are or usually have beene first shiped for transportation and from none other Places or Countryes under the penalty of the forfeiture of all such of the aforesaid Goods as shall be Imported from any other place or Country contrary to the true intent and meaning hereof, as alsoe of the ship in which they were imported with all her Guns Furniture Ammunition Tackle and Apparel, one Moyety to His Majesty His Heires and Successors and the other Moyety to him or them that shall seize informe or sue for the same in any Court of Record to be recovered as is before exprest.

V. And it is further Enacted by the Authority aforesaid That any sort of Ling Stockefish Pilchard, or any other kinde of dryed or salted fish usually fished for and caught by the people of England Ireland Wales or Towne of Berwicke upon Tweede, or any sort of Codfish or Herring, or any Oyle or Blubber made or that shall be made of any kinde of Fish whatsoever, or any Whale fines or Whale bones which shall be imported into England Ireland Wales or Towne of Berwicke upon Tweede not haveing beene caught in Vessels truely and properly belonging thereunto as Proprietors and right Owners thereof and the said Fish cured saved or dryed, and the Oyle and Blubber aforesaid (which shall be accompted and pay as oyle) not made by the people thereof, and shall be imported into England Ireland or Wales or Towne of Berwicke upon Tweede shall pay double Aliens custome.

VI. And be it further Enacted by the Authority aforesaid That from henceforth it shall not be lawfull to any person or persons whatsoever to Load or cause to be Loaden and carryed in any Bottome or Bottomes Ship or Ships Vessell or Vessels whatsoever wherof any Stranger or Strangers borne (unlesse such as bee Denizens or Naturalized) be Owners part Owners or Master and wherof three Fourthes of the Mariners at least shall not be English any Fish Victuall Wares Goods Commodityes or things of what kinde or Nature soever the same shall be from one Port or Creeke of England Ireland Wales Islands of Guernsey or Jersey or Towne of Berwicke upon Tweede to another Port or Creeke of the same or of any of them under penalty for every one that shall offend contrary to the true meaning of this branch of this present Act to forfeit all such goods. . . .

XVIII. And it is further Enacted . . . noe Sugars Tobaccho Cotton Wool Indicoes Ginger Fustick or other dyeing wood of the Growth Production or Manufacture of any English Plantations in America Asia or Africa shall be shiped carryed conveyed or transported from any of the said English Plantations to any Land Island Territory Dominion Port or place whatsoever other then to such other English Plantations as doe belong to His Majesty His Heires and Successors or to the Kingdome of England or Ireland or Principallity of Wales or Towne of Berwicke upon Tweede there to be laid on shore under the penalty of the Forfeiture of the said Goods or the full value thereof, as alsoe of the Ship. . . .

XIX. And be it further Enacted . . . That for every Ship or Vessel which from and after . . . [December 25, 1660] . . . shall set saile out of, or from England Ireland Wales or Towne of Berwicke upon Tweede for any English Plantation in America Asia [or] Africa sufficient bond shall be given with one surety to the cheife Officers of the Custome house, of Such Port or place from whence the said Ship shall set saile to the value of one thousand pounds if the ship be of lesse burthen then one hundred Tuns, and of the summe of two thousand pounds if the Ship shall be of greater burthen, That in case the said Ship or Vessel shall loade any of the said Commodityes at any of the said English Plantations, that the same Commodityes shall be by the said ship brought to some Port of England Ireland Wales, or to the Port or Towne of Berwicke upon Tweede and shall there unload and put on shore the same, the danger of the Seas onely excepted, And for all ships coming from any other Port or Place to any of the aforesaid plantations who by this Act are permitted to trade there, that the Governour of such English plantation shall before the said Ship or Vessel be permitted to loade on board any of the said Commodityes take Bond in manner and to the value aforesaid for each respective Ship or Vessel, That such Ship or Vessell shall carry all the aforesaid Goods that shall be laden on board in the said ship to some other of His Majestyes English plantations, or to England Ireland Wales or Towne of Berwicke upon Tweede, And that every ship or vessel which shall loade or take on board any of the aforesaid Goods until such Bond given to the said Governour or Certificate produced from the Officers of any Custome house of England Ireland Wales or of the Towne of Berwicke that such bond have beene there duely given, shall be forfeited with all her Guns Tackle Apparel and Furniture. . . .

Questions for Discussion:
1. Why might a colonial merchant welcome or dislike the Navigation Acts?
2. What does this document reveal about the power relationship between the British monarchy and those engaged in trade?
3. What provisions do these acts make to ensure colonial officials and others want to see the Act enforced?

William MacDonald, ed., *Select Charters and Other Documents Illustrative of American History, 1606–1775* (New York: Macmillan, 1899), 110–15.

COLONIAL MERCHANTS AND TRADE

Colonial merchants were the business leaders of colonial America and in the northern colonies were often the political leaders, too. Merchants had far-flung trading networks that stretched across the ocean to Africa, Europe, and southward to the West Indies. Primarily concentrated in port communities like Boston, New York, Philadelphia, and Charleston, merchants took charge of exporting American products like fish, flour, tobacco, and rice, and importing cloth, tea, wine, and African slaves in complex transactions that often took years to complete.

Given its importance to the colonial economy, it should hardly be surprising that scholars have written a great deal about this group. One of the more influential recent works is Cathy Matson's *Merchants and Empire*,[1] a study of New York's middling merchants, who frequently broke with mercantilist ideals and regulations in order to pursue their own dissenting economic ideas. Matson and other scholars understand that shipping was central to the merchant's trade. Merchants had to know their captains' abilities, recognize the strengths and weaknesses of their ships, trust their crews, and acknowledge the power of the sea to make or break their fortunes. Little wonder then that merchants spent much of their time at the waterfront, conversing with ship officers and other merchants, trying to determine which ventures might prove lucrative and which might end in bankruptcy.

The pursuit of profit, however, could be callous and cruel. The African slave trade—the largest involuntary movement of humans from one part of the globe to another—devastated African societies and families even as it enriched others, including American merchants and seafarers involved in the notorious Middle Passage.

Samuel Mulford, "Navigation Discourag'd" (1714)

One of the frustrating aspects of the Navigation Acts was the arbitrary manner in which Crown customs officials enforced them. In some colonies they were widely ignored; in others they were harshly enforced. In this instance, greedy customs officers in New York City victimized colonists on eastern Long Island, seizing their coasting vessels on the least pretext. The problem was exacerbated by geographical remoteness. Eastern Long Island, while a part of New York colony, was over a hundred miles from the nearest customhouse in New York City, yet most of its trade was with nearby New England. Customs regulations demanded that vessels from eastern Long Island proceed to New York before continuing their voyage outside the colony, even if Connecticut and Rhode Island were only a few dozen miles away. To obey the law was thus both inconvenient and expensive, but

---

1   Cathy Matson, *Merchants and Empire: Trading in Colonial New York* (Baltimore: Johns Hopkins University Press, 1997).

to ignore it invited disaster: the seizure of the vessel and all its cargo and furnishings.

Samuel Mulford (1644–1725) was an East Hampton merchant involved in the local whale fishery, employing both colonists and Native Americans on his vessels. He was an outspoken advocate of his locality who did his best to reduce taxes on whaling, once even traveling to London in a successful effort to have the unpopular taxes revoked. This document is a speech Mulford made while a member of New York's provincial assembly. The speech was controversial, and New York's royal governor threw Mulford in jail when it was published and distributed publicly.

Gentlemen;

The ill Measures that have been taken, and the Foundation laid within this Colony, which may bring the Subjects within the same to be Tenants at Will, both Persons and Estates, causeth me to make this Speech to this House; Requesting them to Consider well what they do: and not Sell a Birth-right Privilege for Fear, Favour, Affection or Lucre of Gain; but prove true to the Trust reposed in them: not to make ill Presidents and Laws, pernicious to the Publick: But to endeavour the Government may be carried on, for Her Majesties Benefit, and the Good of the Subjects; according to the Laws and Constitutions of *English* Government.

It is not unnecessary to mention the ill Circumstances the Colony was under in the time when a Duty was settled on the importation of Goods, for the Support of Government; there was not any Port or Officers appointed, where to make Entry of their Vessels, and get Clearing when Outward Bound, except at *New-York*; where there was so many Officers and Subtil Fellows to Inspect into every nice Point in the Law, and if they were not fulfilled and observed in every particular, their Vessels were Seised: So that not any man was fit for Master of a Vessel to go to New-York, except he were a Lawyer; and then they should not escape, except it was by Favour. As I was informed, several were made Sufferers, as followeth; One Vessel coming from the *West Indies*, had some Barrels of Pomento[1] on Board, in which, one Barrel had some Prohibited Goods in it, unknown to the Master: A Sailor makes Information,[2] the Vessel was Seised; altho' the Master proffer'd

---

1   Pomento: pimento, a mild red pepper.

2   Makes Information: informs officials of a breach of the law in order to secure a reward.

to make Oath he knew not any thing of it, yet the Vessel and Cargo was Condemned. A Coaster coming to *New-York*, made Entry at the Office, amongst other Goods Twelve Bridles;[1] but afterwards there was but Eleven of them, for which his Vessel was Seised: but he was favoured so much, that for the Sum of *Twenty* or *Thirty* Pounds, he got his Sloop Clear. Another Coaster coming to *New-York*; it seems a Woman sent a Hat by the Master, a Present to a Boy Related to her, Living in *New-York*; the Sloop was Seised about bringing of that Hat: But (as I was informed) was Favoured, that for the value of about *Twenty Pounds* got Clear. These and several other such like Measures being taken, much discouraged men to come to New-York. But in this time, we of the County of *Suffolk*, Namely *Southold, South Hampton* and *East Hampton*, were the greatest Sufferers; we not having an Office to Enter and Clear at: we having some small Coasting Vessels, not suffered to Load and Unload, except they went to *New-York* to Enter and Clear. And Three Sloops, Namely *Benjamin Horton, James Petty* and *Joseph Petty* Masters, coming from *Boston* to *New-York*, there made Entry of their Vessels and Cargo, was detained Thirteen Days before they could procure a Clearing to go home to *Southold*. Such hard Measures discouraged Men to go to *New-York*. And part of the Money granted Their Majesties for Support of Government, was improved to hire Men & Vessels to come down under a pretence of hindering *Indian*-Trade with *Boston*; and to Search our Houses. They Seised *Edward Petty*'s Sloop, that had not been out of the Countrey in about Four Months before (lay at the Oyster Pond all Winter) in *March* fitted to Load for New-York, was Seised, carried to *New-York*, there Condemned, because he presumed to take Mr. *Nathaniel Silvester*'s Family and Houshold Goods on Board his Sloop, and carry them to *Rhoad-Island* the Fall before; and so the Poor Man was destroyed, because he did not go 120 Miles for a Permit, to carry him and his 60 Miles. Another Sloop, Namely *John Paine* Master, coming from *Boston* with a Clearing for *New-Haven*, being near Plumgut, the Officer went on Board him, Seised his Sloop, carried her to *New-York*, where she was Condemned because he had a Pillow of Six Pounds of Cotton Wool for his Bolster in his Cabbin, which he did not make it appear he had given Bond for. Another Sloop, *James Rogers* Master, (which he upon Terms had of Capt. *Cyprian Southack*) coming from

---

1   Bridles: presumably horse tack.

Boston to *Shelter-Island*, was Boarded by the Officer from *New-York*, Seised, Carried away and Condemned, for having no Register.[1] (It seems Capt. *Southack* had a Register when went in her himself and when he put a Master in and went not himself, that Register would pass; but when *Rogers* hath it at *New-York*, it is called no Register).[2] Another small Sloop, Built up *Connecticut-River*, belonging to *John Davis* of *East Hampton*, took in the River a Load of Boards, went to *Rhoad-Island*, there took in Two Barrels of Molasses, and a Remnant in a Hogshead, went to the Custom-House for a Clearing to go to *New-York*, spake to the Officer to do it Authentick; *Davis* depending it was so, never looked into it until the Officer came on Board him, in or near Plumgut, demanding his Clearing, and read Two Barrels of Sugar and a Remnant in a Hogshead; the Master made answer, Not so; it is Molasses; there was never any Sugar on Board: It seems the Officer of *Rhoad-Island* mistook, and put in Sugar when it was Molasses; and sent under his Hand to *New-York* that it was his mistake; but all would not do, the Vessel was Condemned. So that almost all the Vessels belonging to our Towns were either Seised or Drove out of the Colony. There came a Boat from *Fairfield*,[3] which a Young Man hired to bring him over to be Married; to carry his Wife and Portion home: the Boat was Seised, carried to *New-York*, there lies and rots, as I am informed: The Young Man went up the Island, so got home with his Wife; and was compelled to Pay the Owner of the Boat *Thirty Pounds* for it. Our Vessels being thus carried and drove away, we had not Vessels to carry the Growth of the Countrey to a Market; nor bring us such Goods as we wanted: And if any come from *New-York* with Vessel and Goods, and the People would deal with them, the Trader would set the Price on his Goods, and also on what the People had of the Growth of the Countrey: And if the People would have sent their Effects to *New-York*, to have got Money to have Paid their Taxes, or Bought Goods, they were denied to have Fraight carried to *New-York*, or Goods brought from thence in their Vessels: So that they were Compelled to take what they were proffered or keep their Goods by

---

1   Register: a document issued by the customs house that permitted a vessel to engage in trade.

2   No Register: the register was the document proving ownership of a vessel. In this case New York authorities refused to recognize the validity of a register issued in Massachusetts.

3   Fairfield: a town in southeastern Connecticut.

them. *Southold* People being much Oppressed, as they informed me: Wheat then being at *Boston Five Shillings* and *Six-pence* per Bushel, and at *New-York* but *Three Shillings* and *Four-pence*; they had not liberty to carry or send it to *Boston*: Nor any Vessel suffer'd to come at them from thence; and not any coming to them from *New-York*, their Wheat and Grain lay by them, until the Vermin Eat and Spoil'd it; and they were much Impoverished thereby. So that by these and several other severe Measures being taken, whereby several were Destroyed, and much Impoverishing others: to the great Grievance of Their Majesties Liege People; Discouragement to the Inhabitants to Manure their Land, and causing several to Sell their Land, Move out of the Government; because they could not see how they should Live within the same. For where Trade is so Clogg'd, Navigation Discourag'd, Strangers Deter'd to come, causeth Goods Imported to be Scarce and Dear, and the Growth of the Countrey Low; which was the Misery of many in this Colony.

Questions for Discussion:
1. What does this document reveal about the impact of the Navigation Acts on colonists?
2. What does this document reveal about the power relationship between Crown customs officials and the people of eastern Long Island?
3. What impact did customhouse harassment of Long Island coasting vessels have on that area's development?

Samuel Mulford, *Samuel Mulford's Speech to the Assembly at New York*, (New York: William Bradford, 1714), Library of Congress, Printed Ephemera Collection, Portfolio 102, Folder 35a.

Robert Champlin, "Accounting for the Slave Trade" (1774)

In the eighteenth century, the transatlantic slave trade was big business, and as such it required a strict accounting of expenses and credits. Robert Champlin, master of the sloop *Adventure*, kept this account book of engaging in the slave trade in 1774 for the vessel's owners, who also happened to be his brothers, Christopher and George Champlin, of Newport, Rhode Island, a major port involved in the slave trade. Slavery was the engine that generated the wealth that made the British Empire the wealthiest and most powerful empire in the eighteenth century. Scholars such as Marcus Rediker in his book *The Slave Ship*[1] remind us that this gruesome trade was fundamental to the creation of European and American wealth and posits that it was even central to the rise of capitalism.

The British colonists in North America shared in this wealth; New England shipping families profited from it as well as southern plantation owners. As historian Philip D. Curtin reminds us, seeing the slave trade as an economic enterprise is one step toward understanding the cruel trade known dismissively in colonial society as "blackbirding." Viewed with disgust in the twenty-first century, only a scant handful of both black and white reformers opposed African chattel slavery in the eighteenth century.

New England slave ships paid for their cargoes of enslaved Africans with rum. In this trade book, every expense is laid out on the left hand side of the page, and the means of payment on the right side, with each transaction translated into the local units of currency. It is a chillingly exact process; there is no accounting for the Africans' humanity, they are simply live cargo assigned a number rather than a name. Few details are given about their care, other than a few expenses. Nonetheless, a surprising number of the Africans survived the dreaded Middle Passage between Africa and the West Indies on this voyage; only four died out of a total of sixty-three on board the *Adventure*, less than the average of about ten percent.

Verner W. Crane first published this account book as a pamphlet in 1922 based on a manuscript found in the Shepley Library in Providence, Rhode Island. The following abbreviated version has been modified for clarity of use by students. (*See pp. 58–63.*)

Questions for Discussion:
1. What patterns does this account book reveal about the African slave trade?
2. What evidence does this document reveal about the lives of the enslaved Africans taken on board the *Adventure*?
3. What strengths and weaknesses does a document like this trade book have in revealing the history of slave ships?

Verner W. Crane, *A Rhode Island Slaver: Trade Book of the Sloop Adventure, 1773–1774* (Providence, R.I.: Shepley Library, 1922), 1–6.

---

1   Marcus Rediker, *The Slave Ship: A Human History* (New York: Viking, 2007).

Sloop adventure & owners, Dr. | Contra - - - - - - - Cr.

	bars[1]	S	d			Bars	s	d
Sirelone[2] *December 28, 1773*				*Sirelone December 28, 1773*				
To Kings toms Costom[3]	15	00		By 15 gall of Rum	15	15		
To 100 gall of Rice	12			By 12 gall Do	12	12		
	27	00	00			27	00	00
29 To 3 Tun of Rice	270	00	00	29 By 360 gall of Rum	360	270		
To 1 Cag of Tallow	2	00	00	By 2 gall Do	2	2		
To 1 Hat	2	00		By 2 gall Do	2	2		
	274	00	00			274	00	00

	oz	ack	T[5]			oz	ack	T
the Dutch mines[4] *Janaory the 30, 1774*				*Dutch mine, Jane 30, 1774*				
To 1 woman Slave No 1	9	00	00	By 1 Tun of Rice		9	00	
To 6 oz 6 ackeys of gold	6	6		By 250 gall of Rum	250	6	6	
To Connoa hire		1		By 1 gall Do	1		1	
To Rum Expended		6		By 6 gall Do	6		6	
	15	13				15	13	00
Cape Cost[6] *31*				*cape Cost Jen 21*				
To Coneoa Hire		1		By 1 gall of Rum	1	00	1	
To 2 oz of gold	2	00		By 80 gall Do	80	2	00	
To large fish		1		By 1 gall Do	1		1	
To 4 fouls		2	00	By 2 gall Do	2		2	
	2	4	00			2	4	00
annamoboe[7] *Feby the 3*				*Annamboe Feb: 3*				
To 200 billets of wood		4		By 4 gall of Rum	4		4	
To 700 Billets of wood		14		By 14 gall of Rum	14		14	
-	1	2	00			1	2	00
4 To 1 Woman Slave N 2	9	6		4 By 140 gall of Rum &				
To 4 Emty Cask		12		10 ackeys of gold	140	9	6	
To Rum Expended		6	00	By 12 gall of Rum	12		12	
				By 6 gall Do	6		6	
	10	8	00			10	8	

---

1 On the Windward Coast a bar of iron of about forty pounds in weight was the unit of value. Francis Moore, *Travels in Africa* (1738), p. 45.

2 Sierra Leone.

3 Bryan Edwards, *History of the British Colonies in the West Indies* (1793), II. 53: "In some parts of the coast there is a duty paid on each ship, to the king or chief man of the country; which is called his customs. In other parts this is not exacted; but it is only in such places as have but little trade."

4 Elmina, most ancient of the Gold Coast stations. In 1482 the Portuguese built the fort of San Jarge D'Elmina. In 1637 the Dutch secured possession by conquest, and in the eighteenth century this was the principal Dutch post.

5 On the Gold Coast values were measured in ounces of gold and in fractions of an ounce called "ackeys" and "tacoes". The former was one sixteenth of an ounce (the equivalent of an "angel");

the latter a variable measure, but here used as one-eighth of an ackey. A Dutch factor wrote: "We use here another kind of weights, which are a sort of beans, the least of which are red, spotted with black, and are called Dambas; twenty-four of them amounting to an angel, and each of them reckoned two stiver weights; the white beans, with black spots, or those entirely black, are heavier, and accounted four stiver weights; these they usually call Tacoes; but there are some which weigh half or a whole gilder; but these are not esteemed certain weights, but used at pleasure, and often become instruments of fraud". William Bosman, *A New and Accurate Description of the Coast of Guinea* (1705), reprinted in Pinkerton, *Voyages and Travels* (1814), XVI. 374.

6 Cape Coast Castle. English fort about seven miles east of Elmina.

7 Anamaboe, an English fort ten miles east of the principal station at Cape Coast.

Sloop adventure & owners, Dr.				Contra - - - - - - - Cr.			
winebe[8] *5 Day*				*winebe the 5*			
To 6 Emty Hohh	9			By 9 gall of Rum	9	9	
To 3 Emty Hohh	6			By 6 gall Do	6	6	
To Caring the mate of	1			By 1 gall Do	1	1	
	1	00	00			1	00
				Rum 924 gall			
Quittrau[9] *7*				*Quittra 7*			
To 720 gall of Corn	4	8		By 72 gall of Rum	72	4	8
To 4 Hogs	8			By 8 gall Do	8	8	
To 4 Douzen fouls	4			By 4 gall Do	4	4	
	5	4	00			5	4	00
whydah[10] *Feb 17*				*whydah the 17*			
To a Canoa for Caring me ashore	1	00		By 1 gall of Rum	1	1	
To Rum Expended	2			By 2 gall Do	2	2	
to 1 Bag of limes	4			By ½ gall Do	½	4	
	3	4				3	4
21 To 2 Santagoes Cloaths[11]	11			21 By 11 gall of Rum	11	11	
To 2 trips of water	2			By 2 gall Do	2	2	
	00	13	00			00	13	00
Quittrau 26				*Quittrau 26 Feb*			
To 480 gall of Corn	2	00	00	By 32 gall of Rum	32	2	
To 6 Small Pigs	8			By 8 gall Do	8	8	
To 3 goats	4			By 4 gall Do	4	4	
To 1 Douzen of fouls	1			By 1 gall Do	1	1	
To 6 Small shots	4			By 4 gall Do	4	4	
	3	1	00			3	1	00
Winnebe march the 10				*Winnebe march the 10*			
To 1 Man Slave No 3	12	8		By 200 gall of Rum	200	12	8
To 4 Emty Hoghh	8			By 8 gall Do	8	8	
To Carring the mate of	1			By 1 gall Do	1	1	
	13	1				13	1	00
annamboe 17				*annamboe*			
To 2 women Slaves No 4 & 5	25	00		By 400 gall of Rum	400	25	00
	25					25	00	00
Cape Cost 21				*Cape Cost 21*			
To 7 Emty Hoghh	14			By 14 gall of Rum	14	14	
To wom slave No 6	4	6	00	By 4 oz 6 ackeys of gold	4	6	
	5	4				5	4	
				Rum Brot Down 1696			

---

8 Winnebah (Simpa), on the Gold Coast, about fifty miles east of Cape Coast Castle.

9 Quitta (Keta), on a sandy isthmus just east of the mouth of the Volta River, which divides the Gold Coast from the Slave Coast, and about one hundred and seventy-five miles east of Cape Coast Castle. "On the densely populated Slave Coast, the factories were few and the trade virtually open to all comers." U. B. Phillips, *American Negro Slavery* (1918), p. 26.

10 On the Slave Coast (Dahomey), ninety miles from the Volta. This was the eastern limit of the *Adventure's* cruise; from Sierra Leone she had followed the coast southward and eastward some twelve hundred and fifty miles.

11 Probably slave cloths. St. Jago was a hill, north-east of Elmina, where Fort Conradsburg was built by the Dutch in 1638.

Sloop adventure & owners,   Dr. | Contra - - - - - - - Cr.

Sloop adventure & owners,   Dr. | **Contra - - - - - - - Cr.**

			Rum Brot over 1696		
Cape Cost march the 22			*Cape Cost march the 22*		
To 1 wom Slave N 7	12 13		By 205 gall of Rum	205	12 13
To 1 woman slave N 8	12 13		By 205 gall Do	205	12 13
To 1 woman slave No 9	12 13		By 205 gall Do	205	12 13
To 1 woman Slave No 10	12 13		By 205 gall Do	205	12 13
To 1 woman Do No 11	12 13		By 205 gall Do	205	12 13
To 1 woman Do No 12	12 13		By 205 gall Do	205	12 13
To 1 woman Do No 13	12 13		By 205 gall Do	205	12 13
To 1 woman Do No 15	12 13		By 205 gall Do	205	12 13
To 1 woman Do No 16	12 13		By 205 gall Do	205	12 13
To 1 woman Do No 17	12 13		By 205 gall Do	205	12 13
To 1 woman Do No 18	12 13		By 205 gall Do	205	12 13
To 1 woman Do No 14	12 13		By 205 gall Do	205	12 13
	153 12				153 12 00
23 To 1 man Slave No 19	14 1		*23* By 225 gall of Rum	225	14 1
To 2 Men Do No 20 & 21	28 2 00		By 450 gall Do	450	28 2
To 2 Men Do No 22 & 23	28 2 00		By 450 gall Do	450	28 2
To 2 Men Do No 24 & 25	28 2		By 450 gall Do	450	28 2
To 2 Men Do No 26 & 27	28 2		By 450 gall Do	450	28 2
To 2 Men Do No 28 & 29	28 2		By 450 gall Do	450	28 2
To 2 Men Do No 31 & 30	28 2		By 450 gall Do	450	28 2
To 2 Men Do No 32 & 33	28 2		By 450 gall Do	450	28 2
	210 15 00				210 15
24 To 9 trips of water	9		*24* By 9 gall of Rum	9	9
To 40 Conkeys[12]		4	By 4 Tackcoes of gold		4
To 2 Douzen of fouls	4		By 4 ackeys of gold		4
To 1 Basket of limes	1		By 1 gall of Rum	1	1
	00 14 00				00 14 00
			Rum Brought Down 7512		
25 To 1 woman slave No 34	6 00 00		*25* By 96 gall of Rum	96	6 00 00
To Beef and Tobaco &[c.]	1 00		By 3 p of beef & do tobaco	00 1	
To Rum Expend.	4		By 4 gall of Rum	4	4
	6 5 00				6 5 00
26 To 7 Emty Hoghh	1 00 00		*26* By 16 gall of Rum	16	1 00 00
To 80 Conkeys	1		By 1 ackey of gold		1
To 30 Do		3	By 3 Tackcoes of gold		3
To fouls	3		By 3 ackeys of gold	00 3 00	
To 1 oz of gold	1 00 00		By 32 gall of Rum	32	1 00 00
	2 4 3				2 4 3
28 To 9 gall Pomoile[13]	9 00		*28* By 9 gall of Rum	9	9 00
To Ducks	1 00		By 1 gall Do	1	1
To 80 Conkeys	1		By 1 ackeys of gold		1
To 11 Trips of Water	11		By 11 gall of Rum	11	11
	1 6				1 6

12 Conchas or conchs: shell fish.
13 Palm oil: with slaves and gold a principal   commodity of West Africa in the eighteenth century, and today the chief export.

Sloop adventure & owners, Dr. | Contra - - - - - - - Cr.

Dr.				Cr.			
29	To 3 oz of gold		3 00 00	29	By 120 gall of Rum	120	3 00
	To 1 man slave No 35		12 8 00		By 200 gall Do	200	12 8
	To Beef and Tobaco		1		By 1 ackey of gold		1
	To 3 Bottles of mustard		1		By 4 p tobaco & 2 Do beef		1
	To Caring me a shore		1		By 1 gall of Rum	1	1
			15 11 00				15 11 00

annomoboe 31 | *annomoboe 31*

Dr.			Cr.			
To 7 felts		14	By 14 gall of Rum	14	14	
To 1 Canvis frock		2	By 2 gall Do	2	2 00	
To 300 Planting [14]		1 4	By 1 ackey 4 Tackcoes gold		1 4	
To Billets of wood		6 00	By 6 gall of Rum	6	6	
		1 7 00			1 7 00	

Rum Brought Down 8022

April the 1 Day | *april the 1 Day*

Dr.			Cr.			
To 12 gall of Pomoil		12	By 12 gall of Rum	12	12	
To 660 Billets of wood		13	By 13 gall Do	13	13	
To 6 Emty Cask		15	By 15 gall Do	15	15	
To 6 Emty Hoghh		1 8	By 24 gall Do	24	1 8	
		4 00 00			4 00 00	

2	To 1000 phramfros [15]	4	2	By 4 gall of Rum	4	4
	To 400 Plantings	4 00		By 4 gall Do	4	4
	To 600 Do	3 00		By 1 gall Do	1	1
	To 1 Basket of Peper	1		By 1 gall Do	1	1
	To 60 Billets of wood	1		By 3 ackeys of gold		3 00
	To 6 Emty Hoghh	1 8		By 24 gall of Rum	24	1 8
	To Rum Expend	4		By 4 gall of Rum	4	4
		2 9 00				2 9 00

3	To 1 man slave No 36	12 8	3	By 200 gall of Rum	200	12 8
	To 100 Billets of wood	2		By 2 gall Do	2	2
	To 1000 Phramfroes	4 00		By 4 gall Do	4	4
	To 2 Basket of Peper	1		By 1 gall Do	1	1
		12 15				12 15

4	To 300 Planting	1 4	4	By 1 ack & 4 Tackcoes		1 4
	To 4 gall Pomoile	4		By 4 gall of Rum	4	4
	To 1 man slave No 37	13 8		By 216 gall of Rum	216	13 8
		13 13 4				13 13 4

5	To 200 Planting	1	5	By 1 ack of gold		1
	To 300 Do	3		By 3 gall of Rum	3	3
	To Costoms payd agartown [16]	6 00		By 6 gall Do	6	6
	To 2 Not[e]s that Cap tuell [17] left Not Payd	6		By 6 gall Do	6	6
		1 00 00				1 00 00
					8565 gall	

---

[14] Plantains.
[15] Unidentified, but apparently provisions.
[16] Agah is a village on the coast, about a mile east of Anamaboe.
[17] Captain Samuel Tuell commanded the *Adventure* in 1772-1773 on a voyage to Africa and the West Indies. He made a successful voyage, purchasing slaves at from 140 to 160 gallons, and losing none of them in the Middle Passage. He sold his cargo in Barbadoes at £35 a head, round. See *Commerce of Rhode Island, 1726-1800*, I. (Massachusetts Historical Society *Collections*, LXIX), p. 397-429 *passim*.

Sloop adventure & owners, **Dr.**	Contra - - - - - - - - **Cr.**

<table>
<tr><td></td><td colspan="3" style="text-align:right">Rum Brought over   8565</td></tr>
<tr><td>april 9 Day</td><td colspan="3">april the 9</td></tr>
<tr><td>To 300 Plantings   1   4</td><td>By 1 ackey & 4 Tackcoes gold</td><td></td><td>1   4</td></tr>
<tr><td>To ½ gall of Pomoil   4</td><td>By ½ gall of Rum</td><td>½</td><td>4</td></tr>
<tr><td style="text-align:right">2   00</td><td></td><td></td><td>2   00</td></tr>
<tr><td>13 To 3000 Phramfroes   12</td><td>13 By 12 gall of Rum</td><td>12</td><td>12</td></tr>
<tr><td>To large Turtle   5</td><td>By 5 gall   Do</td><td>5</td><td>5</td></tr>
<tr><td>To the long Boats Expences   13</td><td>By 13 gall   Do</td><td>13</td><td>13</td></tr>
<tr><td style="text-align:right">1   14   00</td><td></td><td></td><td>1   14   00</td></tr>
</table>

Debit side (Dr.):

april 9 Day
- To 300 Plantings — 1   4
- To ½ gall of Pomoil — 4
  - 2 00

13
- To 3000 Phramfroes — 12
- To large Turtle — 5
- To the long Boats Expences — 13
  - 1 14 00

16
- To 4 Trips of water — 4
- To 2 Baskets of Peper — 1
- To 1 Basket of limes — 4
- To 1 Cag of Tallow — 1   4
  - 00   7   00

17
- To 8 Trips of water — 8
- To 1 Basket of limes — 4
  - 8   4

18
- To 400 Billets of wood — 8
- To 4 Trips of water — 4
- To Basket of Peper — 1
  - 00   13   00

19
- To 5 Trips of water — 5
- To Pay for the Pond — 8
- To 1 Basket of limes — 4
- To Rum Expended — 3
  - 1   00   4

23
- To 100 wood & 8 trips of water — 10
- To 4 Trips of water — 4
- To Canoa Hire — 3

annamaboe april 25
- To 100 Billets of wood — 2
- To 5 trips of water — 5
- To 30 p of shugar — 5
- To 1 Guinea Stuf — 4
- To 4 Remols [18] — 1   4
- To 2 guinea stufs — 8
  - 2   12   00

26
- To 1 man Slave No 38 — 14   1
- To 2 men Slaves No 39 & 40 — 28   2
- To 1 man Slave No 41 — 14   2
  - 56   4

Credit side (Cr.):

Rum Brought over   8565

april the 9
- By 1 ackey & 4 Tackcoes gold — 1   4
- By ½ gall of Rum   ½ — 4
  - 2 00

13
- By 12 gall of Rum   12 — 12
- By 5 gall   Do   5 — 5
- By 13 gall   Do   13 — 13
  - 1 14 00

16
- By 4 gall of Rum   4 — 4 00
- By 1 gall   Do   1 — 1
- By ½ gall   Do   ½ — 4
- By 1 akey & 4 Tack of gold   00   1   4
  - 7 00

17
- By 8 gall of Rum   8 — 8
- By ½ gall of Rum   ½ — 4
  - 8   4

18
- By 8 gallons of Rum   8 — 8
- By 4 gall   Do   4 — 4
- By 1 gall   Do   1 — 1
  - 00   13   00

19
- By 5 gall of Rum   5 — 5
- By 8 gall   Do   8 — 8
- By ½ gall   Do   ½ — 4
- By 3 gall   Do   3 — 3
  - 1   00   4

23
- By 10 gall of Rum   10 — 10
- By 4 gall   Do   4 — 4
- By 3 gall   Do   3 — 3
  - 8654

April 25
- By 2 gall of Rum   2 — 2
- By 5 gall   Do   5 — 5
- By 5 ackeys of gold — 5
- By 4 gall Do Rum   4 — 4
- By 20 gall   Do   20 — 1   4
- By 8 gall   Do   8 — 8
  - 2   12   00

26
- By 225 gall of Rum   225 — 14   1
- By 450 gall   Do   450 — 28   2
- By 225 gall   Do   225 — 14   1
  - 56   4

---

18   Romals, or "sea handkerchiefs".

Sloop adventure & owners, Dr.				Contra - - - - - - - Cr.			

27 To 1 man Slave No 42		14	1	27 By 225 gall of Rum	225	14	1
To 1 man Slave No 43		14	1	By 225 gall Do	225	14	1
To 1 man Slave No 44		14	1	By 225 gall Do	225	14	1
To 1 man Slave No 45		14	1	By 225 gall Do	225	14	1
To 1 man Slave No 46		14	1	By 225 gall Do	225	14	1
To 600 Billets of wood		12		By 12 gall Do	12	12	
To 1 Basket of Peper		1		By 1 gall Do	1	1	
To Fish for the Slaves		5		By 5 gall Do	5	5	
To 1 Trip of water		1		By 1 gall Do	1	1	
	71	9	00		71	9	00
28 To 1 Emty Hoghh		1		28 By 1 ackey of gold		1	
To 200 of wood		4		By 4 gall of Rum	4	4	
To 2000 of wood	2	8		By 40 gall Do	40	2	8
To Bringing the wood to the Boat		2		By 2 gall Do	2	2	
To fish for the Slaves		1		By 1 gall Do	1	1	
					10784		
april the 29				*april 29*			
To Half firken of Boter	00	12	00	By 12 gall of Rum	12	12	
To 14 large Spikes		3		By 3 ackeys of gold		3	
To 4 trips of water		4		By 4 gall Do [i. e. rum]	4	4	
To 3 gall of Pomoile		3		By 4 Tackcoes of gold			4
To fis[h] for the Slaves			4	By 3 ackeys of gold		3	
	1	6	4		1	6	4
30 To 3 gall of Pomoil		2		30 By 2 gkeys of gall D (sic)		2	
To 4 Trips of water		4		By 1 gall of Rum	1	1	
To 1 quire of Paper		1		By 4 gall Do	4	4	
To 4 Baskets of limes		2		By 2 gall Do	2	2	
To fish		1		By 1 ackey of gold		1	
	00	10			00	10	
may the 1				*may the 1 Day*			
To 1 woman slave No 47	12	8		By 200 gall of Rum	200	12	8
To 1 woman Slave No 48	12	8		By 200 gall of Rum	200	12	8
To 1 woman Slave No 49	12	8		By 200 gall Do	200	12	8
To 1 woman Slave No 50	12	8		By 200 gall Do	200	12	8
To 1 woman Slave No 51	12	8		By 200 gall Do	200	12	8
To 1 woman Slave No 52	12	8		By 200 gall Do	200	12	8
To 1 woman Slave No 53	12	8		By 200 gall Do	200	12	8
To 1 woman Slave No 54	12	8		By 200 gall Do	200	12	8
To 1 woman Slave No 55	12	8		By 200 gall Do	200	12	8
To 1 woman slave No 56	12	8		By 200 gall Do	200	12	8
To 1 man Slave No 57	13	12		By 220 gall Do	220	13	12
To 1 man Do No 58	13	12		By 220 gall Do	220	13	12
To 2 men Boys No 59 60	26	8		By 440 gall Do	440	26	8
To 2 men Boys Do No 61/62	26	8		By 440 gall Do	440	26	8
	207	8			207	8	
				rum 14107 gall			

Benjamin Wright, "Never See Cash So Scarce" (1768)

Trade with the West Indies was an important aspect of seaborne commerce for New England merchants. The Caribbean islands were completely given over to sugar production on plantations, with the grueling labor performed by African slaves. New England ships furnished these islands with food-stuffs like flour and salted fish, as well as wood and timber for anything from barrel staves to shingles to prefabricated houses. These ships returned to New England with cargoes of sugar, or more especially, molasses to be distilled into rum. New England rum was a major commodity in the African slave trade, which provided the labor to grow the sugarcane that made the molasses that became rum.

One of the merchants involved in this trade was Aaron Lopez (1731–1782), who was born in Portugal but who moved to North America to freely prac-tice his Jewish faith. He established himself in the early 1740s as a merchant in Newport, Rhode Island, which had one of North America's first Jewish communities and synagogues. Lopez engaged in a variety of trades, includ-ing whaling, slaving voyages, and the West Indies trade, and owned or had interests in over eighty sailing vessels during his life. Typical of colonial merchants, he had a web of connections that spanned the Atlantic World, including his older brother Abraham, who lived in Jamaica.

In this letter, Lopez's agent in Jamaica, a Rhode Island sea captain named Benjamin Wright, explains some of the difficulties he encountered in doing business there. As was common, it proved difficult to receive payments for cargoes in cash. With no international banking system, the chronic short-age of gold or silver coins meant that merchants developed a complex sys-tem of personal credit, often based on family members or acquaintances scattered around the Atlantic basin.

BENJAMIN WRIGHT TO AARON LOPEZ AND CO.
Savanna Lamarr, Jamaica, 2d January, 1768.
Gentlemen,

This serves to advise and acquaint you of my safe Arrival. I made this Island in Nineteen days, and were Seven days in sight of the Land, before I got into this Harbour, being almost calm. Have the Pleasure of acquainting you of getting my Horses in safe, and in very good order, notwithstanding, the terrible Gales of Wind I met with, before I could well clear the Land, which destroy'd the greater part of my small Stock, and had enough to do to keep the Ship off the Land, were obliged to carry Sail 'till the Seas broke entirely over me in order to keep myself from driving on Shore. Our Schooner *Ranger* arriv'd safe, and by all accounts had a blowing time off our Coast, has damaged no Goods. Captain Bardin has raised me better than Two hundred Pounds Cash, and as many Goods remaining on board as may amount to Eighty Pounds. Captain Charles Cunningham arrivd here about Ten days before me, he disposed of all his Fish and Candles before I arriv'd, and in short almost all his Cargo, his Dry Fish at 23/9 per Ct.,[1] Spt'y Candles[2] from 2/6 to 2/9. I have disposed of all my Dry Fish except about 20 hhds.[3] have sold none under 25/per Ct. have disposed of about 34 barrels Lamp Oil f'm £6 to 7£ Spt'y Candles I have sold from 2/6 to 2/9, have about 25 Boxes on hand at present. Could have disposed of every Box the first day I arrived, if I would have taken 2/6 they seem determined here to go upon the prudent lay. I have been obliged to open two accounts for one box Candles, they are of opinion that Spt'y Candles will be plenty and cheap this latter part of the Crop, but for my part I see no likelihood of it, but the Reverse. My Shad[4] am selling at 18/9 per bll.,[5] Sup. flour[6] 35/, Tarr at 25/, Philadelphia Staves[7] at 12£ per M, Rh'd Isl'd Staves at 9£ per M, Egg harbour Shingles at 40/ M, Boston Boards f'm 6 to 7£ M. All the Ports on the North Side[8] are glutted with Northern Goods. I can't give any encouragement to send any more Vessels to this Island this Year, am afraid that Produce will break very high this Year, by the Accounts from Europe that Rum sold well last year in England, and if Rum should break high Molosses will be high likewise. In regard to Jno. Bours's order on Mr. Abraham Lopez in your favour, I have deliverd to said Lopez, and have received the Bonds to amount of said Order, which Bonds am sensible are very good. Shall not be able to raise any Cash or Bills with the Bonds, must take them in produce and glad to get that timely. I find the greatest part of those Bonds not payable 'till some time in May and some till June. I have taken the shortest Dates, I have bespoke good Bills to the amount of Five hundred Sterling, and can have Two hundred Pounds Sterling more, if I can raise Cash to purchase them; but never see Cash

---

1   23/9 per Ct.: twenty-three shillings, nine pence per hundred pounds of fish.
2   Spt'y Candles: spermaceti candles.
3   Hhds: hogsheads, a large cask or barrel.
4   Shad: a type of food fish caught in East Coast rivers.
5   bll: barrel.
6   Sup. flour: superfine flour.
7   Staves: probably barrel staves.
8   North Side: on the northern side of Jamaica.

so scarce in this Isl'd since I knew it. I cannot get Bills for any Part of Cargo. Shall be much put to it to raise five hundred Pounds sterling in Cash to purchase those Bills.

You depend I shall not let any Opportunity slip may turn to Advantage. Hope you'll not fail sending the Remainder the Ships Provisions, with the white Oak Staves and heading to make our Puncheons, and if you please to send per Captain Potter 40 Boxes Spt'y Candles, shall be able to dispose of them. Mr. Abraham Per: Mendez informs me he has acquainted you of my arrival which hope come safe to hand.

Nothing remarkable to acquaint you with. You may depend hearing from me per all opportunities. Hope I shall be better able to acquaint you in my next what Quantity of Bills I shall be able to purchase.

The Wine will not sell here at any Rate, my Dry Fish did not turn out to my expectation. Osburn did not give close Attention enough when they were putt up. If the Fish had been such as we desired him to get I should have sold them all before this Time. Am Gentlemen, with Great Esteem, Your most Obedient humble Servant,

BENJ. WRIGHT.

Questions for Discussion:
1. What does this document reveal about the problems merchants experienced in the colonial period?
2. What does this document reveal about trade between the mainland colonies and the West Indies?
3. What strengths or weaknesses does this document have in understanding colonial commerce?

Massachusetts Historical Society, *Commerce of Rhode Island, 1726–1800*, vol. 1, *1726–1774*, Collections of the Massachusetts Historical Society, 7th ser., vol. 9, (Boston: Massachusetts Historical Society, 1914), 216–18.

J. Hector St. John de Crèvecoeur, "A Nantucket She-Merchant" (1782)

Not all colonial merchants were men. There were a small number of women who engaged in international trade, women sometimes referred to as "she-merchants." J. Hector St. John de Crèvecoeur (1735–1813) was born in France and served in the French army in New France during the French and Indian War. After British victory in that conflict, he settled in New York, married an American woman, and took up writing. In 1782 he published a book entitled *Letters from an American Farmer*. In this series of essays, Crèvecoeur explored the meaning of what it meant to be American, idealizing the simple hardworking life of the colonists.

In this piece, Crèvecoeur examines the distinctive seafaring society of Nantucket, an island whaling community in Massachusetts. Crèvecoeur was clearly impressed by the independence of Nantucket's women, who learned business practices while their husbands were away at sea. The fact that many of Nantucket's families in the 1700s were Quakers, a religious sect with advanced ideas about the equality of women, played a role as well. One of the most famous of the she-merchants was Keziah Coffin (1723–1798), who shrewdly invested her small savings in shipping, ultimately making her family the wealthiest on the island.

As the sea excursions are often very long, their wives in their absence are necessarily obliged to transact business, to settle accounts, and in short, to rule and provide for their families. These circumstances being often repeated, give women the abilities as well as a taste for that kind of superintendency, to which, by their prudence and good management, they seem to be in general very equal. This employment ripens their judgment, and justly entitles them to a rank superior to that of other wives; and this is the principal reason why those of Nantucket as well as those of Montreal[1] are so fond of society, so affable, and so conversant with the affairs of the world. The men at their return, weary with the fatigues of the sea, full of confidence and love, cheerfully give their consent to every transaction that has happened during their absence, and all is joy and peace. "Wife, thee hast done well," is the general approbation they receive, for their application and industry. What would the men do without the agency of these faithful mates? The absence of so many of them at particular seasons, leaves the town quite desolate; and this mournful situation disposes the women to go to each other's house much oftener than when their husbands are at home: hence the custom of incessant visiting has infected every one, and even those whose husbands do not go abroad.

The house is always cleaned before they set out, and with peculiar alacrity they pursue their intended visit, which consists of a social

1   Crèvecoeur here notes "Most of the merchants and young men of Montreal spend the greatest part of their time in trading with the Indians, at an amazing distance from Canada; and it often happens that they are three years together absent from home."

chat, a dish of tea, and an hearty supper. When the good man of the house returns from his labour, he peaceably goes after his wife and brings her home; meanwhile the young fellows, equally vigilant, easily find out which is the most convenient house, and there they assemble with the girls of the neighbourhood. Instead of cards, musical instruments, or songs, they relate stories of their whaling voyages, their various sea adventures, and talk of the different coasts and people they have visited. "The island of Catharine in the Brazil," says one, "is a very droll island, it is inhabited by none but men; women are not permitted to come in sight of it; not a woman is there on the whole island. Who among us is not glad it is not so here? The Nantucket girls and boys beat the world." At this innocent sally the titter goes round, they whisper to one another their spontaneous reflections: puddings, pies, and custards never fail to be produced on such occasions; for I believe there never were any people in their circumstances, who live so well, even to superabundance. As inebriation is unknown, and music, singing, and dancing, are held in equal detestation, they never could fill all the vacant hours of their lives without the repast of the table. Thus these young people sit and talk, and divert themselves as well as they can; if any one has lately returned from a cruise, he is generally the speaker of the night; they often all laugh and talk together, but they are happy, and would not exchange their pleasures for those of the most brilliant assemblies in Europe. This lasts until the father and mother return; when all retire to their respective homes, the men re-conducting the partners of their affections.

Thus they spend many of the youthful evenings of their lives; no wonder therefore, that they marry so early. But no sooner have they undergone this ceremony than they cease to appear so cheerful and gay; the new rank they hold in the society impresses them with more serious ideas than were entertained before. The title of master of a family necessarily requires more solid behaviour and deportment; the new wife follows in the trammels of Custom, which are as powerful as the tyranny of fashion; she gradually advises and directs; the new husband soon goes to sea, he leaves her to learn and exercise the new government, in which she is entered. Those who stay at home are full as passive in general, at least with regard to the inferior departments of the family. But you must not imagine from this account that the Nantucket wives are turbulent, of high temper, and difficult to be ruled; on the contrary, the wives of Sherburn[1] in so doing, comply only with the prevailing custom of the island: the husbands, equally submissive to the ancient and respectable manners of their country, submit, without ever suspecting that there can be any impropriety. Were they to behave otherwise, they would be afraid of subverting the principles of their society by altering its ancient rules; thus both parties are perfectly satisfied, and all is peace and concord. The richest person now in the island owes all his present prosperity and success to the ingenuity of his wife: this is a known fact which is well recorded; for while he was performing his first cruises, she traded with pins and needles, and kept a school. Afterward she purchased more consider-able articles, which she sold with so much judgment, that she laid the foundation of a system of business, that she has ever since prosecuted with equal dexterity and success. She wrote to London, formed con-nections, and, in short, became the only ostensible instrument of that house, both at home and abroad. Who is he in this country, and who is a citizen of Nantucket or Boston, who does not know *Aunt Kesiah*? I must tell you that she is the wife of Mr. C—n, a very respectable man, who, well pleased with all her schemes, trusts to her judgment, and relies on her sagacity, with so entire a confidence, as to be altogether passive to the concerns of his family. They have the best country seat on the island, at Quayes, where they live with hospitality, and in per-fect union. He seems to be altogether the contemplative man.

Questions for Discussion:

1. According to the author, how were the women of French-speaking Mon-treal and English-speaking Nantucket similar?
2. How did Crèvecoeur explain the self-reliance of Nantucket's women?
3. What does this document reveal about the relationships between men and women in colonial North America?

J. Hector St. John de Crèvecoeur, *Letters from an American Farmer* (New York: Fox, Duffield & Company, 1904), 205–10.

---

1   Sherburn: the main settlement on Nantucket.

ATLANTIC CROSSINGS

Crossing the Atlantic Ocean in the colonial period was a dangerous and unpleasant undertaking. There were many perils: ships foundered in high seas, wrecked on uncharted rocks, and found themselves attacked by the ships of foreign nations or pirates. Even on voyages safely completed, conditions on shipboard were often vile. Overcrowding, poor food, disease, and unpleasant company could be expected on any voyage.

In this selection of readings, Captain Gabriel Archer recounts the disease and bad weather encountered on the ship *Blessing* on its voyage to Jamestown in 1609. Two Dutch clergymen document their crossing on the flute-ship *Charles* and the difficulties they encountered with the ship's crew and its female owner. The third piece details the passage of German indentured servants to Philadelphia. While a voluntary undertaking, the trip is painted in horrific terms, and on arrival in Pennsylvania the passengers faced a cruel process of negotiating the terms of their servitude. The fourth document concerns the forced deportation and dispersion of Acadian settlers at the hands of the British government.

Taken together, these accounts reveal the hardships of travel by sea. But they also reveal some of the ethnic diversity of the colonial settlers, who came from all over western Europe. Furthermore, many of these migrants came against their will, as indentured servants or refugees. A useful entry point for understanding the impact of these diverse groups coming to the New World is historian Bernard Bailyn's short work, *The Peopling of British North America*.[1]

Gabriel Archer, "Letter from James Town" (1609)

Captain Gabriel Archer (1575–c. 1611) was a well-educated gentleman, attorney, sailor, and explorer who was deeply involved in early English efforts to explore and settle North America. He sailed with Bartholomew Gosnold in 1602 to explore Cape Cod and environs. Archer was cocaptain of the ship *Godspeed* that brought the first English settlers to Virginia in 1607 but returned to England in 1608 and came back with another fleet of colonists in 1609.

In this report of his 1609 voyage on the *Blessing*, he details the effect of disease and bad weather on the fleet. The account is particularly strong in detailing the ravages of disease in the fleet, the effect of a hurricane, and the

---

1   Bernard Bailyn, *The Peopling of British North America: An Introduction* (New York: Knopf, 1986).

distress of the Jamestown settlement, which faced a severe food shortage. Indeed, Archer himself would die in the coming "starving time" along with the vast majority of other Jamestown settlers.

From *Woolwich* the fifteenth of May, 1609, seven saile weyed anchor; and came to *Plimmouth*[1] the twentieth day, where Sir *George Somers*, with two small Vessels, consorted with us. Here we tooke into the *Blessing* (being the ship wherein I went) six Mares and two Horses; and the Fleet layed in some necessaries belonging to the action: in which businesse we spent time till the second of June. And then wee set sayle to Sea, but crost by South-west windes, we put in to *Faulemouth*, and there staying till the eight of June, we then gate out.

Our Course was commanded to leave the *Canaries* one hundred leagues to the Eastward at least, and to steere away directly for *Virginia*, without touching at the West *Indies*, except the Fleet should chance to be separated, then they were to repaire to the *Bermuda*, there to stay seven dayes in expectation of the Admiral;[2] and if they found him not, then to take their course to *Virginia*.

Now thus it happened; about six dayes after we lost the sight of *England*, one of Sir *George Somers* Pinnasses left our company, and (as I take it) bare up for *England*; the rest of the ships, *viz.* The *Sea Adventure* Admirall, wherein was Sir *Thomas Gates*, Sir *George Somer*, and Captaine *Newport*: The *Diamond* Vice-admirall, wherein was Captaine *Ratcliffe*, and Captaine *King*. The *Falcon* Reare-admirall, in which was Captaine *Martin*, and Master *Nellson*: The *Blessing*, wherein I and Captaine *Adams* went: The *Unitie*, wherein Captaine *Wood*, and Master *Pett* were. The *Lion*, wherein Captaine *Webb* remained: And the *Swallow* of Sir *George Somers*, in which Captaine *Moone*, and Master *Somer* went. In the *Catch* went one *Matthew Fitch* Master: and in the Boat of Sir *George Somers*, called the *Virginia*, which was built in the North Colony,[3] went one Captaine *Davies*, and one Master *Davies*. These were the Captaines and Masters of our Fleet.

We ran a Southerly course from the Tropicke of *Cancer*,[4] where

---

1 Plimmouth: Plymouth, England, a major port.
2 Admiral: the flagship of the fleet.
3 *Virginia*: the *Virginia* was the first vessel built in an English colony in America, at the mouth of the Kennebec River in modern Maine.
4 Tropicke of Cancer: the parallel of latitude that marks the northern limits of the Earth's tropical zone.

having the Sun within sixe or seven degrees right over our head in July, we bore away West; so that by the fervent heat and loomes breezes, many of our men fell sicke of the *Calenture*,[1] and out of two ships was throwne over-board thirtie two persons. The Vice-admiral was said to have the plague in her; but in the *Blessing* we had not any sicke, albeit we had twenty women and children.

Upon Saint *James* day,[2] being about one hundred and fiftie leagues distant from the West *Indies*, in crossing the Gulf of *Bahoma*, there hapned a most terrible and vehement storme, which was a taile of the West *Indian Horacono*;[3] this tempest separated all our Fleet one from another; and it was so violent that men could scarce stand upon the Deckes, neither could any man heare another speake. Being thus divided, every man steered his owne course; and as it fell out, about five or sixe days after the storme ceased (which endure fortie foure houres in extremitie), the *Lion* first, and after the *Falcon* and the *Unitie*, got sight of our Shippe, and so we layaway directly for *Virginia*, finding neither current nor winde opposite, as some have reported, to the great charge of our Counsell and Adventurers.

The *Unity* was sore distressed when she came up with us, for of seventy landmen, she had not ten sound; and all her Sea men were downe but onely the Master and his Boy with one poore sailer: but we relieved them. And we foure consorting, fell into the Kings River[4] haply the eleventh of August. In the *Unity* were borne two children at Sea, but both died: being both Boyes.

When wee came to *James* Towne, we found a Ship which had bin there in the River a month before we came. This was sent out of *England* by our Counsels leave and authority, to fish for Sturgeon; and to goe the ready way, without tracing through the Torrid Zone, and shee performed it: her Commander was Captaine *Argoll* (a good Marriner, and a very civill Gentleman) and her Master one *Robert Tindall*.

The people of our Colonie were found all in health (for the most part). Howbeit when Captaine *Argoll* came in, they were in such distresse, for many were dispersed in the Savages townes, living upon their almes for an ounce of Copper a day; and fourescore lived twenty

---

1   Calenture: sunstroke, or any fever induced by heat.
2   Saint James day: August 5th.
3   West Indian Horacono: a hurricane.
4   Kings River: the James River in Virginia was named after King James.

miles from the Fort and fed upon nothing but Oysters eight weekes space, having no other allowance at all: neither were the people of the Country able to relieve them if they would. Whereupon Captaine *Newport* and others have beene much to blame to informe the Counsell of such plenty of victuall in this Country, by which meanes they have beene slacke in this supply to give convenient content. Upon this, you that be adventurers, must pardon us, if you finde not returne of Commodity so ample as you may expect, because the law of nature bids us seeke sustenance first, and then to labour to content you afterwards. But upon this point I shall be more large in my next Letter.

After our foure Ships had bin in harbour a fewe dayes, came in the Vice admirall, having cut her maine Mast over boord, and had many of her men very sicke and weake; but she could tell no newes of our Governour: and some three or foure dayes after her came in the *Swallow*, with her maine Mast overboord also; and had a shrewd leake, neither did she see our Admirall.

Questions for Discussion:
1. According to Archer, what impact did the marine environment have on the relief fleet and the settlers already in Virginia?
2. What does this document reveal about the dangers faced by seventeenth-century mariners?
3. What problem faced the Virginia colonists before the fleet arrived?

———————
Edward Arber, ed., *Travels and Works of Captain John Smith, President of Virginia and Admiral of New England, 1580–1631*, vol. 1, (Edinburgh: John Grant, 1910), xciv–xcvii.

Jasper Dankers, "Margaret's Ship" (1679)

This is a translation of a journal originally written by a Dutch clergymen of a evangelical sect known as *Labadists* while on a voyage on the fluteship *Charles* from England to New York. The writer of this account, Jasper Dankers, had apparently been a seaman himself at one time, and volunteered to help the crew run the vessel. In this account Dankers describes the crew of the *Charles* and its passengers. Perhaps more interesting than the crew are the women on board. At least two of the officers had their wives on board; the woman who owned the ship, Margaret Hardenbroeck, was also on board; and there were female passengers as well.

Like the other documents in this section, the author of this journal describes an intensely uncomfortable experience. Bad company, bad food, an unskilled crew, and Margaret's high freight fee for a small package ensured that this trip was a miserable one.

Although this is such a miserable subject, that I deliberated long whether it were worth while to take any notice of it, yet since one does not know when a matter can be serviceable, I will nevertheless say something.

The persons who belonged to the ship were:

The captain, Thomas Singleton, an Englishman, and a quaker, from London, I believe. He had his wife with him, who was quite young, about 24 or 26 years old, and he was a person of 40 or 45. He was not the best or most experienced seaman by a long distance. He was proud and very assiduous or officious to please men, especially Margaret[1] and her man; yet he had some amiable qualities, he was affable. He was stingy; for when many mackerel were caught, he would not give one to the poor sailors. He was even displeased if the sailors came with their fish lines to fish near the place, where he was, because the fish might come to their lines instead of his. His wife was a young, worldly creature, who had not the least appearance of quakerism, but entirely resembled an English lady fashioned somewhat, upon the Dutch model. She was proud, and wore much silver and gold; and when Margaret once spoke to him about it, he said, "I did not give it to her." Whereupon Margaret asked, "Why did you give her money to buy them?" To which he replied, "She wanted it."

The English mate, who afterwards became captain, was a passionate person, inwardly still more than he showed outwardly, a great manpleaser where his interest was to be promoted. He was very close, but was compelled to be much closer in order to please Margaret.

The Dutch mate, Evert, was a wicked, impious fellow, who also drank freely. He was very proud of his knowledge and experience, which were none of the greatest.

The boatswain, Abram, of Plymouth, was rough and wicked in his orders, but he was a strong and able seaman. Robyn was the best.

I cannot permit myself to go further; it is too unpleasant a subject.

---

1   Margaret: Margaret Hardenbroeck was a wealthy Dutch colonist in New York, which had only recently become an English colony. She owned many ships and participated in the slave trade amongst other trades.

The passengers and crew were a wretched set. There was no rest; night or day, especially among the wives a rabble I cannot describe. It was as if they were in the fish market or apple market, night and day, without cessation; where, indeed, some of them had obtained their living, and even in worse places. There were nine or ten of them always together. Among the men there were some persons who drank like beasts, yes, drank themselves dead drunk, as you may judge from the fact that two or three of them drank thirty-five gallons of brandy, besides wine from the time we left England or Holland. It is not to be told what miserable people Margaret and Jan[1] were, and especially their excessive covetousness. In fine, it was a Babel. I have never in my life heard of such a disorderly ship. It was confusion without end. I have never been in a ship where there was so much vermin, which were communicated to us, and especially not a few to me, because being in the cordage at night I particularly received them. There were some bunks and clothes as full as if they had been sown. But I must forbear.

When we first came on board the ship we eat where we were, and with those we found there, but afterwards the messes were regulated, and we were placed on deck with five or six uncouth youngsters; where, nevertheless, we continued. This so exercised the other passengers, seeing us submit so willingly, that they themselves could no longer endure it, and desired us to come with them, and make a mess of eight. We had been compelled to buy our stores in England, as what we had were spoiled, or not sufficient. There was not a bit of butter or vinegar on the food during the whole voyage, except what we had purchased at Falmouth. I do not know how long it was we had nothing to eat except heads of salt fish, and those spoiled for the most part. We had to eat them till they were thrown overboard. Most of the time we had white peas, which our cook was too lazy to clean, or were boiled in stinking water, and when they were brought on the table we had throw them away. The meat was old and tainted; the pork passable, but enormously thick, as much as six inches; and the bread was mouldy or wormy. We had a ration of beer three times a day to drink at table. The water smelt very bad, which was the fault of the captain. When we left England they called us to eat in the cabin, but it was only a change of place and nothing more. Each meal was dished up three times in the cabin, first for the eight passengers, then for the captain,

---

1   Jan: Margaret's male servant.

mate, and wife, who sometimes did not have as good as we had, and lastly for Margaret and Mr. Jan who had prepared for them hardly any thing else except poultry and the like. But this is enough.

After we left England, I took upon myself, out of love of the thing, and because there were so few persons to work the ship, namely, ten in all, including the captain, to watch and attend the rudder, as well as to make observations in navigation; but when I perceived the sailors, on this account, became lazy and depended upon me, I left the ruddergang. Nevertheless, when an English ship came near running us down in the watch off Cape Cod, causing thereby much uproar and confusion in our ship, I did my best to unfasten a rope which they could not make loose, at which the mate raved and swore, and for which he would have almost struck or killed me. When my comrade heard of it he wished me not to do any thing more, and that was my opinion. I could not, however, refrain from helping to the last, but I abandoned the watch, and so caused the mate to feel that we were not insensible, for there was nothing else to be done to him. He, nevertheless, invited us daily more than anyone else. Finally, when the voyage was completed, there was no one, either captain, or mate, or sailor, or Margaret, who said "We thank you," except our poor Robyn. We had a little package put in the ship at Falmouth, about a foot and a half square, on which the captain charged us four guilders freight, in the money of Holland.

We represented to Margaret how we had managed with only one chest between us, although each passenger was entitled to have one of his own, but it was all to no purpose. Four guilders it must be. It was not that we had any difficulty in giving it, but it was only to be convinced of her unblushing avarice. The mate's wife was the least evil-inclined, and listened most to what was said to her, which we hope will bear fruit. We have truly conducted ourselves towards all in general and each one in particular, so that not only has everyone reason to be edified and convinced, but, by the grace of God, everyone renders us testimony that we have edified and convinced them as well by our lives as our conversation. Let him alone who is the author of all grace, receive therefore all the glory, to all eternity. Amen.

Questions for Discussion:
1. What does this document reveal about crossing the Atlantic circa 1679?

2. What does this account reveal about relations between men and women on the ship *Charles*?

3. How did Dankers describe the personalities and abilities of the officers and crew of the *Charles*?

Jasper Dankers and Peter Sluyter, *Journal of a Voyage to New York* (Brooklyn, N.Y.: Long Island Historical Society, 1867), 102–6.

Gottlieb Mittelberger, "Journey to Pennsylvania" (1750)

Gottlieb Mittelberger traveled to Pennsylvania from Germany in 1750 on the ship *Osgood* along with about five hundred poor German immigrants who would become indentured servants upon arriving in Philadelphia. In the colonial period it was common for poor Europeans to serve a term of service before receiving their freedom in return for their passage across the Atlantic. Mittelberger was horrified by the conditions they faced on board the ship, and even more so by the treatment of these servants once they were in America. He wrote this book in order to warn other Germans about the expense of immigration and the horrors of indentured servitude.

Mittelberger's account is important because it is an important insight into the German immigrant experience, starting with the trip down the Rhine and including the long and harrowing voyage across the Atlantic.

From Würtemberg or Durlach to Holland and the open sea we count about 200 hours; from there across the sea to Old England as far as Kaupp,[1] where the ships generally cast Anchor before they start on the great sea-voyage, 150 hours; from there, till England is entirely lost sight of, above 100 hours; and then across the great ocean, that is from land to land, 1200 hours according to the statements of mariners; at length from the first land in Pennsylvania to Philadelphia over 40 hours. Which makes together a journey of 1700 hours or 1700 French miles.

This journey lasts from the beginning of May to the end of October, fully half a year, amid such hardships as no one is able to describe adequately with their misery.

The cause is because the Rhine-boats from Heilbronn to Holland have to pass by 36 custom-houses, at all of which the ships are exam-

1   Kaupp: Cowes, a seaport on the Isle of Wight off southern England.

ined, which is done when it suits the convenience of the custom-house officials. In the meantime the ships with the people are detained long, so that the passengers have to spend much money. The trip down the Rhine alone lasts therefore 4, 5 and even 6 weeks.

When the ships with the people come to Holland, they are detained there likewise 5 or 6 weeks. Because things are very dear there, the poor people have to spend nearly all they have during that time. Not to mention many sad accidents which occur here; having seen with my own eyes how a man, as he was about to to board the ship near Rotterdam, lost two children at once by drowning.

Both in Rotterdam and in Amsterdam the people are packed densely, like herrings so to say, in the large sea-vessels. One person receives a place of scarcely 2 feet width and 6 feet length in the bed-stead, while many a ship carries four to six hundred souls; not to mention the innumerable implements, tools, provisions, water-barrels and other things which likewise occupy much space.

On account of contrary winds it takes the ships sometimes 2, 3 and 4 weeks to make the trip from Holland to Kaupp in England. But when the wind is good, they get there in 8 days or even sooner. Every-thing is examined there and the custom-duties paid, whence it comes that the ships ride there 8, 10 to 14 days and even longer at anchor, till they have taken in their full cargoes. During that time everyone is compelled to spend his last remaining money and to consume his little stock of provisions which had been reserved for the sea; so that most passengers, finding themselves on the ocean where they would be in greater need of them, must greatly suffer from hunger and want. Many suffer want already on the water between Holland and Old England.

When the ships have for the last time weighed their anchors near the city of Kaupp in Old England, the real misery begins with the long voyage. For from there the ships, unless they have good wind, must often sail 8, 9, 10 to 12 weeks before they reach Philadelphia. But even with the best wind the voyage lasts 7 weeks.

But during the voyage there is on board these ships terrible misery, stench, fumes, horror, vomiting, many kinds of sea-sickness, fever, dysentery, headache, heat, constipation, boils, scurvy, cancer, mouth-rot, and the like, all of which come from old and sharply salted food and meat, also from very bad and foul water, so that many die miser-ably.

Add to this want of provisions, hunger, thirst, frost, heat, damp-ness, anxiety, want, afflictions and lamentations, together with other trouble, as the lice abound so frightfully, especially on sick people, that they can be scraped off the body. The misery reaches the climax when a gale rages for 2 or 3 nights and days, so that every one believes that the ship will go to the bottom with all human beings on board. In such a visitation the people cry and pray most piteously.

When in such a gale the sea rages and surges, so that the waves rise often like high mountains one above the other, and often tumble over the ship, so that one fears to go down with the ship; when the ship is constantly tossed from side to side by the storm and waves, so that no one can either walk, or sit, or lie, and the closely packed people in the berths are thereby tumbled over each other, both the sick and the well-it will be readily understood that many of these people, none of whom had been prepared for hardships, suffer so terribly from them that they do not survive it.

I myself had to pass through a severe illness at sea, and I best know how I felt at the time. These poor people often long for consolation, and I often entertained and comforted them with singing, praying and exhorting; and whenever it was possible and the winds and waves permitted it, I kept daily prayer-meetings with them on deck. Be-sides, I baptized five children in distress, because we had no ordained minister on board. I also held divine service every Sunday by reading sermons to the people; and when the dead were sunk in the water, I commended them and our souls to the mercy of God.

Among the healthy, impatience sometimes grows so great and cruel that one curses the other, or himself and the day of his birth, and sometimes come near killing each other. Misery and malice join each other, so that they cheat and rob one another. One always reproaches the other with having persuaded him to undertake the journey. Fre-quently children cry out against their parents, husbands against their wives and wives against their husbands, brothers and sisters, friends and acquaintances against each other. But most against the soul-traf-fickers.

Many sigh and cry: "Oh, that I were at home again, and if I had to lie in my pig-sty!" Or they say: "O God, if I only had a piece of good bread, or a good fresh drop of water." Many people whimper, sigh and cry piteously for their homes; most of them get home-sick. Many hun-dred people necessarily die and perish in such misery, and must be cast into the sea, which drives their relatives, or those who persuaded them to undertake the journey, to such despair that it is almost impossible to pacify and console them. In a word, the sighing and crying and lamenting on board the ship continues night and day, so as to cause the hearts even of the most hardened to bleed when they hear it.

No one can have an idea of the sufferings which women in confinement have to bear with their innocent children on board these ships. Few of this class escape with their lives; many a mother is cast into the water with her child as soon as she is dead. One day, just as we had a heavy gale, a woman in our ship, who was to give birth and could not give birth under the circumstances, was pushed through a loop-hole [port-hole] in the ship and dropped into the sea, because she was far in the rear of the ship she could not be brought forward.

Children from 1 to 7 years rarely survive the voyage; and many a time parents are compelled to see their children miserably suffer and die from hunger, thirst and sickness, and then to see them cast into the water. I witnessed such misery in no less than 32 children in our ship, all of whom were thrown into the sea. The parents grieve all the more since their children find no resting-place in the earth, but are devoured by the monsters of the sea. It is a notable fact that children, who have not yet had the measles or small-pocks, generally get them on board the ship, and mostly die of them.

Often a father is separated by death from his wife and children, or mothers from their little children, or even both parents from their children; and sometimes whole families die in quick succession; so that often many dead persons lie in the berths beside the living ones, especially when contagious diseases have broken out on board the ship.

Many other accidents happen on board these ships, especially by falling, whereby people are often made cripples and can never be set right again. Some have also fallen into the ocean.

That most of the people get sick is not surprising, because, in addition to all other trials and hardships, warm food is served only three times a week, the rations being very poor and very little. Such meals can hardly be eaten, on account of being so unclean. The water which is served out on the ships is often very black, thick and full of worms, so that one cannot drink it without loathing, even with the greatest thirst. O surely, one would often give much money at sea for a piece of good bread, or a drink of good water, not to say a drink of good wine, if it were only to be had. I myself experienced that sufficiently, I am sorry to say. Toward the end we were compelled to eat the ship's biscuit which had been spoiled long ago; though in a whole biscuit there was scarcely a piece the size of a dollar that had not been full of red worms and spiders' nests. Great hunger and thirst force us to eat and drink everything; but many a one does so at the risk of his life. The sea-water cannot be drunk, because it is salt and bitter as gall. If this were not so, such a voyage could be made with less expense and without so many hardships.

At length, when, after a long and tedious voyage, the ships come in sight of land, so that the promontories can be seen, which the people were so eager and anxious to see, all creep from below on deck to see the land from afar, and they weep for joy, and pray and sing, thanking and praising God. The sight of the land makes the people on board the ship, especially the sick and the half dead, alive again, so that their hearts leap within them; they shout and rejoice, and are content to bear their misery in patience, in the hope that they may soon reach the land in safety. But alas!

When the ships have landed at Philadelphia after their long voyage, no one is permitted to leave them except those who pay for their passage or can give good security; the others, who cannot pay, must remain on board the ships till they are purchased, and are released from the ships by their purchasers. The sick always fare the worst, for the healthy are naturally preferred and purchased first; and so the sick and wretched must often remain on board in front of the city for 2 or 3 weeks, and frequently die, whereas many a one, if he could pay his debt and were permitted to leave the ship immediately, might recover and remain alive.

Before I describe how this traffic in human flesh is conducted, I must mention how much the journey to Philadelphia or Pennsylvania costs.

A person over 10 years pays for the passage from Rotterdam to Philadelphia 10 pounds, or 60 florins. Children from 5 to 10 years pay half price, 5 pounds or 30 florins. All children under 5 years are free. For these prices the passengers are conveyed to Philadelphia, and, as long as they are at sea, provided with food, though with very poor, as has been shown above.

But this is only the sea-passage; the other costs on land, from home to Rotterdam, including the passage on the Rhine, are at least 40 florins, no matter how economically one may live. No account is here taken of extraordinary contingencies. I may safely assert that, with the greatest economy, many passengers have spent 200 florins from home to Philadelphia.

The sale of human beings in the market on board the ship is carried on thus: Every day Englishmen, Dutchmen and High-German people come from the city of Philadelphia and other places, in part from a great distance, say 20, 30, or 40 hours away, and go on board the newly arrived ship that has brought and offers for sale passengers from Europe, and select among the healthy persons such as they deem suitable for their business, and bargain with them how long they will serve for their passage-money, which most of them are still in debt for. When they have come to an agreement, it happens that adult persons bind themselves in writing to serve 3, 4, 5 or 6 years for the amount due by them, according to their age and strength. But very young people, from 10 to 15 years, must serve till they are 21 years old.

Many parents must sell and trade away their children like so many head of cattle; for if their children take the debt upon themselves, the parents can leave the ship free and unrestrained; but as the parents often do not know where and to what people their children are going, it often happens that such parents and children, after leaving the ship, do not see each other again for many years, perhaps no more in all their lives.

Questions for Discussion:
1. What were some of the reasons Mittelberger gave for the high expense of immigrating to America?
2. According to Mittelberger, for whom was the transatlantic voyage most dangerous?
3. How is this voyage both similar and different from that of a slave ship?

Gottlieb Mittelberger, *Gottlieb Mittelberger's journey to Pennsylvania in the year 1750 and return to Germany in the year 1754* (Philadelphia: J. J. McVey, 1898), 17–27.

Charles Lawrence, "Dispers'd Among His Majesty's Colonies" (1755)

The Acadians were the descendants of French colonists who settled in what is today known as Nova Scotia and New Brunswick, Canada, with the majority living on lands bordering the Bay of Fundy. The British overran Acadia in their wars with France, which ceded control of the region in 1713. The Acadians thus became French-speaking British subjects, sandwiched between French and British colonial possessions—a decidedly uncomfortable situation given the almost perennial warfare between Britain and France, and one treated at length by historian Naomi Griffiths, in *From Migrant to Acadian*.[1] Despite this they had a flourishing culture in the early eighteenth century, with a distinctive agriculture based on reclaiming marshlands from the Bay of Fundy with a system of sophisticated dikes.

The Acadian idyll ended in 1755 when Charles Lawrence (1709–1760), the British governor of Nova Scotia, decided that the Acadians were a security risk and had to be forcibly expelled from the colony. With no external approval and little planning, Lawrence ordered British and colonial troops to forcibly collect the Acadian population and put them on board ships and send them away. Initially this deportation, known to Acadians as the *Grand derangement*, was to other American colonies, but eventually they were sent as far afield as England, France, and ultimately Louisiana, where they formed the basis for the people known as Cajuns—a corruption of the word Acadian. Historians estimate that approximately half of the deported Acadians died in this deportation from shipwrecks, disease, and exposure. Yet some returned to Nova Scotia, where they reestablished their distinctive culture.

The following document is a copy of Lawrence's orders to John Winslow, a Massachusetts soldier in the provincial service. It gives detailed instructions on arranging to forcibly deport the Acadian people.

HALIFAX, 11th August, 1755.
Instructions for Lieutenant-Colonel Winslow, commanding his Majesty's Troops at Minas, in his absence, for Capt. Alexander Murray, commanding his Majesty's Troops at Pesiquid, in relation to the transportation of the inhabitants of the District of Minas and Pesiquid River, of Canard, Cobiquid, &c. in Nova-Scotia:
Sir—
Having in my letter of the 31st of July last acquainted Captain Murray with the reasons which induced his Majesty's Council to come to the resolution of sending away the French inhabitants, and clearing the whole country of such bad subjects (which letter he will com-

---

1   Naomi Griffiths, *From Migrant to Acadian: A North American Border People, 1604–1755* (Montreal: McGill-Queen's University Press, 2005).

municate to you together with the Instructions I have since that sent him): it only remains for me to give you the necessary orders and instructions for putting in practice what has been so solemnly determined.

That the inhabitants may not have it in their power to return to this Province, nor to join in strengthening the French of Canada[1] or Louisbourg:[2] it is resolved that they shall be dispers'd among his Majesty's Colonies upon the Continent of America.

For this purpose Transports are sent up the Bay to ship off those at Chignecto and Colonel Moncton will order those he cannot fill there into Minas Basin to carry off some part of the inhabitants of these districts. You will have also from Boston Vessels to transport one thousand persons, reckoning two persons to a ton.

Upon the arrival of these Vessels from Boston or Chignecto in the Basin of Minas, as many of the inhabitants of the Districts of Mines, Piziquid, Cobequid, and the River of Canard &ca., as can be collected by any means, particularly the heads of Families and young men, are to be shipped on board of them at the above rate of two persons to a ton or as near it as possible. The tonnage to be ascertained by the Charter Partys[3] of the several transport Vessels which you will be furnished with an account of from the masters.

And to give you all the ease possible respecting the victualling of these transports I have appointed Mr. George Saul to act as agent Victualler upon this occasion and have given him particular instructions for that effect which he has directions to communicate to you and to furnish you with a copy of upon his arrival from Chignecto with the provisions ordered for victualling the whole transports.

Destination of the Vessels appointed to rendezvous in the Bason of Mines.
To be sent to North Carolina
    Such a number as will transport Five hundred persons, or thereabout.
To be sent to Virginia

---

1   Canada: modern-day Quebec.
2   Louisbourg: a major French fortress and naval base on nearby Cape Breton.
3   Charter Partys: contracts for the leasing of vessels.

Such a number as will transport one thousand persons, & To
Maryland

Such a number as will transport Five hundred persons, of in
proportion, if the number to be shipped off should exceed two
thousand persons.

If the Transports from Boston should arrive in Minas Basin before
Mr. Saul the Agent Victualler shall arrive from Chignecto they must
remain there till he does arrive with the provisions. But in case you
shall have embarked any of the inhabitants before the Agent Victualler
be on the spot you will if necessary allow each person so embarked 5
pounds of flour and one pound of pork for 7 days which allowance Mr.
Saul has orders to replace.

When the people are embarked you will please to give the Master
of each Vessel one of the letters (of which you will receive a number
signed by me) which you will address to the Governor of the Province
or Commander in Chief for the time being where they are to be put
on shore, and enclose therein the printed form of the certificate to be
granted to the Masters of the Vessels, to entitle them to their hire as
agreed upon by Charter party, and with these you will give each of
the masters their sailing orders in writing to proceed according to the
above destination and upon their arrival immediately to wait upon the
Governors or Commanders in Chief of the provinces to which they
are bound with the said letters and to make all possible dispatch in
debarking their passengers and obtaining certificates thereof agreeable to the form aforesaid. And you will in these orders, make it a
particular injunction to the said masters to be as careful and watchful
as possible during the whole course of the passage, to prevent the passengers from making any attempt to seize upon the Vessel, by allowing only a small number to be upon the decks at a time and using all
other necessary precautions to prevent the bad consequences of such
attempts; and that they be particularly careful that the inhabitants
have carry'd no arms or other offensive weapons on board with them
at their embarkation as also that they see the provisions regularly issued to the people agreeable to the allowance proportioned in Mr.
George Saul's Instructions.

As Captain Murray is well acquainted with the people and with the
country I would have you to consult with him upon all occasions and

particularly with relation to the means necessary for collecting the people together so as to get them on board, and if you find that fair means will not do with them, you must proceed by the most vigorous measures possible not only in compelling them to embark but in depriving those who shall escape of all means of shelter or support by burning their houses, and by destroying every thing that may afford them the means of subsistence in the Country.

You will receive herewith a Copy of the Charter party, which the Masters of the transport Vessels, taken up here, have entered into with the Governmt. for your information as to the terms; those from Boston will be nearly the same; and as you see they are hired by the month, you will use all possible dispatch to save expence to the publick.

If it is not very inconvenient I would have you send the Sloop *Dove* to Annapolis to take on board part of the inhabitants there destined for Connecticut to which place that vessel belongs.

When you have executed the business of shipping off all that can be collected of the inhabitants in the districts about Minas Basin you will march yourself or send a strong Detachment to Annapolis Royal to assist Major Handfield in shipping off those of that River, and you will so order it as all the stragglers that may be met with by the way may be taken up and carried to Annapolis in order to their being shipped with the rest.

As soon as the Transports have received their people on board and are ready to sail you are to acquaint the Commander of his Majesty's Ship therewith that he may take them under convoy and put to sea without loss of time.

Questions for Discussion:
1. Can the *Grand derangement* be considered ethnic cleansing or genocide?
2. What are Winslow's primary concerns in deporting the Acadians?
3. What clues does this document reveal about the conditions the Acadians might face once on shipboard?

Charles Lawrence to John Winslow, August 11, 1755, in *Selections from the Public Documents of the Province of Nova Scotia*, ed. Thomas B. Atkins and Benjamin Curren (Halifax, N.S.: C. Annand, 1869), 271–74.

COLONIAL SEAFARERS

Colonial America had excellent harbors, shipbuilding materials abounded, and nearby waters teemed with fish like the valuable cod. Colonial ports teemed with seafarers from many nations, bringing with them exotic goods, exciting tales, and their specialized seafaring language. One of the more accessible works about a colonial sailor is maritime historian Daniel Vickers's treatment of Ashley Bowen.[1] Bowen's autobiography reveals a complex character with strong religious views and a career path that took him from ship to shore and back again.

The social relations of seafarers reveal some of the dynamics of colonial society. While Puritan communities like Boston loathed the rowdy behavior of mariners, they desperately needed them. Labor markets sometimes meant that sailors had a strong temptation to desert and remain ashore in places like the Chesapeake region, creating a shortage of sailors to carry the region's trade. Native peoples proved willing to teach the local settlers how to harvest the bounty of the sea, especially whales. Taken together, these documents explore some of these complexities, revealing colonial attitudes toward the maritime workforce that was so vital to its prosperity.

Edward Randolph, "Runaways and Deserters" (1695)

Sailors lay at the heart of the mercantile system, yet they had a streak of independence that prevented them from being mere cogs in the wheels of the British Empire. In this document, a Crown official expresses his dismay at sailor desertions in the Chesapeake and makes some suggestions to prevent it.

Edward Randolph (ca. 1632–1703) was an English colonial agent in America who spent decades there attempting to regulate trade. His relations with the colonials were extremely bitter: the people of Massachusetts especially reviled his strict adherence to English customs policies, and he returned their hatred with a wholehearted disdain for colonial society. This letter to his superiors in England reflects his place within an aristocratic society; colonials of course had little or no status within such a system.

---

1   Ashley Bowen and Daniel Vickers, *The Autobiography of Ashley Bowen, (1728–1813)* (Peterborough, Ont.: Broadview Eds, 2006).

To the R^t. Hon$^{ble.}$ the Lords of the Committee for Trade and Foreign Plantations.

The humble Representation of Edward Randolph Surveyor General of His Ma^{ts1} Customes in the Colonies and Plantations upon the coast of America.

May it please yor Lopps.[2]

His Ma^{ts} ships of War sent yearly to convoy the Vessels trading to Virginia and Maryland, come to an anchor upon their arrival at Point Comfort in Virginia, and there continue till ye return of the Fleet to England; which is about 80 leagues distant from some of the harbors and creeks in Maryland, where ships from London and other places do yearly load, and not one of them is sent in to that Province to assist the Masters in their loading in case their Sailors fall sick or run away from them, now much practised. They go those long voyages to avoid being press'd into His Ma^{ts} Service at home: some get ashore, and are harbour'd and conceald by the Planters in the Country; but the far greater number (in expectation of much higher wages) are incouraged and entertaind in Philadelphia in Pensilvania where ship themselves either abord the Privateers for shares, or upon vessels trading illegally to South Carolina, or Carasaw;[3] whereby His Ma^{ts} loses every year the service of many able Sailors, who seldom return to Engl^d. The homeward bound ships are weakly man'd, and not capable to defend themselves ag^t the Common enemy; neither can ye Mast^{rs} comply with the Condition in their bonds to return ye men to England.

Nigh a 100 Sailors ran away last year from the ships belonging to London and other places, loading tobacco in Maryland and Pensilvania, which with the Sailors sickness, and the extraordinary frost and snow, so obstructed the Masters in their loading that 25 vessels, of which some carried 7 or 800 hogsh^{ds} a peece, were left by the Convoy to shift for themselves, and might have bin lost; but Colon. Nicholson[4] stopd them til they were all loaden, and made one Commodore[5] for that voyage.

Great differences arise often between ye Masters and their men,

---

1 Ma^{ts}: an abbreviation of "Majesty's."
2 Lopps: an abbreviation for "Lordships."
3 Carasaw: probably Curaçao, a Dutch island colony in the southern Caribbean.
4 Colon. Nicholson: Francis Nicholson, the governor of Maryland.
5 Made one Commodore: Nicholson forced the tobacco ships to wait and form their own convoy rather than sailing individually for England.

and sometimes mutinies among the Sailors, not to be compos'd by the Civil Magistrate; which might effectually and speedily be suppressd, if a Man of war Orderd this station in Patuxant river in Maryland, (being the place where ships clear with the Officers of His Ma^{ts} Customs) and to continue there til the ships loaden in ye remoter parts of the Bay, come thither, and are ready to join ye Virginia fleet at the Comand^{rs} prefixed time of sailing home.

Now to the end that Masters of vessels trading in those Plantations may be (for the future) not delayed in their loading and dispatch,

It is humbly proposed,

1. That one of the Convoy ships now bound out with ye Merch^t men to those Plantations, may (upon her arrival) be Orderd to fail to Patuxant river in Maryland, and to be aiding & assisting to the Masters as just occasion may require.

2. That direction be given to ye Governors in Virginia & Maryland to make Law injoining a severe penalty upon any Planter or other person whatsoever, that shall hereafter allure or entice any Sailor [&c] from his service abord ship or otherwise in the voyage, or shall harbor and conceal any of them in their houses or elsewhere.

3. That strict Order be sent to ye Governor of Pensilvania, and ye three lower Counties on Delaware bay, to seize upon & apprehend all Sailors and Mariners coming into that Government by land or water from Virginia or Maryland, and to send them back again with a guard, to be delivered to one of the Members of His Ma^{ts} Council in either Government from whence they run away, to be put abord one of His Ma^{ts} ships of war, to be proceeded against as Runaways & deserters of His Ma^{ts} fervice.

And whereas tis a known & common practice of Masters & Owners of Merch^{ts} ships to hire & entertain abord, upon extraordinary wages, the Sailors belonging to, & in His Ma^{ts} Service in ye Ships of war in the Plantations (as in New England &c.) by which means those ships are rendered incapable to pursue & perform their Services as in duty bound, which obliges ye Cap^{ts} & Comman^{rs} of His Ma^{ts} ships of war to press Sailors out of vessels trading to and from those Plantations, to the utter ruine of their voyage also.

It is therefore humbly proposed That all Masters & Owners of vessels upon merch^t imploy, who shall hire for wages, or keep abord any such Sailor without ye license under ye hand & seal of the Capt or Command^{rs} of the ship of war to whom he did belong first had & obtained, shall, upon due proof & conviction thereof, forfeit ye sum of, the one moiety to His Ma^ty and the other to him who shall inform & prosecute for the same within - days after ye offence committed.

And that every Capt or Comand^r of any of His Ma^ts Ships of war coming into any His Ma^ts Plantations, shall not, upon the death or running away of his men, press or take from abord, any of the Sailors or other persons belonging to Merch^ts vessels, without having first made known to ye Governor of such Plantation, the cause, and also ye number of men wanting to make up ye Complement, with all due regard had to the encouragem^t and promoting the Plantation Trade. Such like methods will be less chargeable to Merchants, and render His Ma^ts Ships at all times ready for Service.

Questions for Discussion:

1. What does this document reveal about the social hierarchy in colonial society?

2. How does this document reflect the crucial position mariners had in sustaining the British Empire?

3. How did Randolph's position in colonial society impact how he viewed issues like sailor desertions?

Robert Noxon Toppan and Alfred Thomas Scrope Goodrick, ed., *Edward Randolph; Including His Letters and Official Papers from the New England, Middle, and Southern Colonies in America, with Other Documents Relating Chiefly to the Vacating of the Royal Charter of the Colony of Massachusetts Bay, 1676–1703* (Boston: John Wilson & Son, 1898), 125–29.

Cotton Mather, "The Sea Is a School of Vice" (1700)

Cotton Mather (1663–1728) was an influential cleric and scholar of Puritan Boston, but is perhaps best known for his role in the Salem witch trials and the controversial introduction of smallpox inoculation to colonial society. While an imposing figure with impressive academic and social credentials, Mather also had a fascination with seafarers and pirates; he was a port-town parson who liked to bandy about nautical terms and write about sea adventures.

He published this sermon in 1700 to address the sinful ways of mariners while at the same time acknowledging their usefulness. Mariners had long been associated with riotous living while ashore, and Mather paints a vivid picture of their behavior, which sets them apart from most Puritans.

Our *Marriners* are a Generation of men, greatly Serviceable to the *Commonwealth*.[1] Ordinarily they are men of stout and brave Spirits: They are under God, indeed the very Defence of our Nation: And we are beholden to them for a very great part of those Enjoyments, whereby our Lives are sweetened unto us. The *Invaluable Benefits*, by the means of our *Seafaring Friends* done unto us, oblige us to no little Value and Friendship for them. What a Trouble should it be, unto all that have the *Fear of God* in them, to see such a *Useful* sort of men, so much abandoned unto all sort of *Sinfulness* and *Wretchedness*!

It must be acknowledged unto the *Exceeding Praise* of God; There are many *Marriners*, that *Fear the Lord exceedingly*. We can find many *Seamen*, that are *First-rate Christians*, and exceed other men, for Piety, for Probity, for Charity. When our Lord Jesus Christ singled out his *Disciples*, He chose a company of *Sailors*. Truly, our Lord Jesus Christ, has no truer or greater *Disciples* under Heaven, than some that spend their Dayes, not upon the *Earth*, but upon the *Sea*. But can we say, *They are all such*. I would to God, we could. . . .

Let the *Fear of God* cause you to *Steer clear* of the *Sins*, which are the more frequent *Rocks* or *Shoals*, whereupon the Souls of *Sailors* are *Shipwrack'd*. What is the *Fear of God*? We are told, in Job 28.28. *The Fear of the Lord*, is *to Depart from Evil*. Let our *Sea Faring* People then be *Sin fearing* people; and count *Sin* the worst *Evil* in the World. Indulge not your selves in any *One Sin*. You may see one thing aboard, that may be liveley set home this Council upon you. If there be but *One Leak* aboard allowed and neglected, that *One Leak* may prove the Destruction of all. Man, A *Lust* is a *Leak* in thy Soul, if it be allowed, it will prove thy Damnation at the last, it will *Drown thee in Perdition*.

But there are some *Vices*, which are the *Special Vices* of the *Sea*. Against those *Vices* especially, be all of *you* warned that go to *Sea*. . . .

As now; Is not the Sin of profane *Swearing* and *Cursing*, become too notorious among our *Sailors*? Reform that Impiety, Ye presumptuous *Fighters against God*, Reform it; else you that now Sail in a vast *Sea* of *Waters*, must ere long have that blasphemous unruly *Tongue*, tortured in the *Every Ocean* of the Wrath of God, where you shall in

---

1   Commonwealth: the Commonwealth of Massachusetts.

vain cry, *Oh! For a Drop of Water to cool my Tongue!* Think on that word, in Jam. 5.12. *Above all things my Brethren, Swear not.*

Filthy Speaking, *Baudy* Speaking, Unclean and Obscene *Ribaldry*, is too commonly heard in the mouths of *Sailors*. Leave off this *Baseness*. 'Tis more loathsome, than all the stuff cast up in the *Vomit* of the *Sea Sick.* . . .

The Sins of *Unchastity*, are too often the Sins of *Sailors. Fornication* and *Adultery*, and other Diabolical practices do render many Vessels, horribly *foul. Sailors*, be prevailed withal, to *Abhor* that Vice, which will render you, the *Abhorred of the Lord.* It were better for you, to drink the nasty *Bildge-water*, than to taste the *stolen waters* of *Unchastity*. Think on that Word of God, in Heb. 13.4. *Whoremongers, and Adulterers God will Judge.*

'Tis a significant similitude, in Jam. 3.4, 5. *Behold the Ships, which though they be so great, and are driven of fierce winds, yet are they turned about with a very small Helm, whithersoever the Governour listeth: Even so the Tongue.* That Little *Helm* is thy mouth; Govern it, O man, and Restrain it, by the Rules in the *Word* of God; else thou wilt run upon some fatal mischief. Mind, even if it were hung up in the *Steerage*, that Command of Heaven, in Psal. 34.12, 13. WHAT MAN IS HE THAT DESIRETH LIFE? KEEP THY TONGUE FROM EVIL.

I will add; The First man that ever built a *Ship*, once fell into the Sin of *Drunkeness*. Are none of you that *Sail* in a *Ship*, too liable unto that *woeful Sin*? Oh, Beware of that *Beastly Vice. Beastly*, did I call it? I have wrong'd the *Beasts*, by so calling it: *Beasts* will not be *Drunk*: To be *Drunk*, turns *Men* into worse than *Beasts*: A *Drunken* man, is but *Old English* for, A *Drowned* man. Let our *Sailors* take heed of being *Drunkards*, lest God Almighty *Drown* them, yea, *Damn* them, for their being so. Think on that word, in 1 Cor. 6.10. *Drunkards shall not inherit the Kingdom of God.*

Briefly; Whatever *Lewdness* may be too frequently incident unto *Sailors*; I must give you the word, *Bear away*, Oh, *Bear away* from it. We read about the *Ships* of *Jehoshaphat*, in 2 Chron 20.37. *The Ships were Broken, that they were not able to go their Voyage. Ahaziahs* men were his Marriners; a Wicked, Horrid, Abominable crue, were the *Ships* of that King *Mann'd* withal. Syrs, You'll hazard the *Breaking* of your *Ships*, and which is infinitely worse, the *Breaking* of your *Souls*, if you don't *break off* your Ungodly Wayes, and *Shape another Course.*

When You are Solicited unto the doing of any *Ill Thing*, I wish you would fortify your selves, with the Thoughts of *One Thing*, which often occurs unto the *Marriner*. Don't you often Divert your selves with *Fishing*? In doing so, then think with your selves, *The Devil has cast out his Hook, to catch my precious and immortal Soul: His Hooks I am told, are Baited with the pleasures of Sin; or, perhaps with the Hopes of Riches: If I do any Sinful Thing, to obtain these Pleasures and Riches, the Hooks of the Devil have taken me. But if I am seized by the Hooks of Hell, what, ah what is like to become of me, throughout Eternal Ages!*

In fine; 'Tis a common thing, for *Sailors* when they have received their *Wages*, to be gone into Ill Houses, and there *Squander away* in a *few weeks* at Riotous Living, all that they have got, by *many months* of hard Service aboard and abroad. Would not any Considerate *Marriner*, call that *man*, a *Fool*, and a *Sot*, and not worthy to be called a *man*, who should so ridiculously, throw away what he hath Earned with so much Difficulty. But, O Silly Sailor, come to thy wits, and think, *In these Impious Courses, I not only throw away all my Earnings, in such an unaccountable manner, that all mankind will deride me, and I shall tear my own Hair for madness, when I reflect upon it, but I shall throw away my own SOUL also, and for the Shadow of some filthy Delight, which is but for a moment, I shall cast my self into the Burning Lake of the Wrath of God, where the Smoak of my Torment will ascend for ever and ever.*

Questions for Discussion:
1. How does Mather communicate the importance and value of sailors in both practical and religious terms?
2. How did Mather's "Special Vices of the Sea" set seafarers apart from the rest of society?
3. How does Mather's sermon reveal the social and religious ideals of Puritan Boston?

Cotton Mather, *The Religious Marriner* (Boston: B. Green and J. Allen, 1700), 5–18.

J. Hector St. John de Crèvecoeur, "Simple Whalemen" (1782)

J. Hector St. John de Crèvecoeur (1735–1813) was born in France and served in the French army in New France during the French and Indian War. After

British victory in that conflict, he settled in New York, married an American woman, and took up writing. In 1782 he published a book entitled *Letters from an American Farmer*. In this series of essays, Crèvecoeur explored the meaning of what it meant to be American, idealizing the simple hardworking life of the colonists.

One of the places Crèvecoeur idealized was Martha's Vineyard and its whaling industry. Whaling was an early occupation for colonists and one that they largely learned from the Native Americans of eastern Long Island, Martha's Vineyard, and Nantucket. Crèvecoeur highlights the island as a place of racial harmony and rural equality, both of which could be traced to the local whalefishery.

This island is twenty miles in length, and from seven to eight miles in breadth. It lies nine miles from the continent, and with the Elizabeth Islands forms one of the counties of Massachusetts Bay, known by the name of Duke's County. Those latter, which are six in number, are about nine miles distant from the Vineyard, and are all famous for excellent dairies. A good ferry is established between the Edgar Town, and Falmouth on the main, the distance being nine miles. Martha's Vineyard is divided into three townships, viz. Edgar, Chilmark, and Tisbury; the number of inhabitants is computed at about 4000, 300 of which are Indians. Edgar is the best seaport, and the shire town, and as its soil is light and sandy, many of its inhabitants follow the example of the people of Nantucket. The town of Chilmark has no good harbour, but the land is excellent and no way inferior to any on the continent: it contains excellent pastures, convenient brooks for mills, stone for fencing, etc. The town of Tisbury is remarkable for the excellence of its timber, and has a harbour where the water is deep enough for ships of the line. The stock of the island is 20,000 sheep, 2000 neat cattle, beside horses and goats; they have also some deer, and abundance of sea-fowls. This has been from the beginning, and is to this day, the principal seminary of the Indians; they live on that part of the island which is called Chapoquidick, and were very early christianised by the respectable family of the Mahews, the first proprietors of it. The first settler of that name conveyed by will to a favourite daughter a certain part of it, on which there grew many wild vines; thence it was called Martha's Vineyard, after her name, which in process of time extended to the whole island. The posterity of the ancient Aborigines remain here to this day, on lands which their forefathers reserved for themselves, and which are religiously kept from any encroachments. The New England people are remarkable for the honesty with which they have fulfilled, all over that province, those ancient covenants which in many others have been disregarded, to the scandal of those governments. The Indians there appeared, by the decency of their manners, their industry, and neatness, to be wholly Europeans, and nowise inferior to many of the inhabitants. Like them they are sober, laborious, and religious, which are the principal characteristics of the four New England provinces. They often go, like the young men of the Vineyard, to Nantucket, and hire themselves for whalemen or fishermen; and indeed their skill and dexterity in all sea affairs is nothing inferior to that of the whites. The latter are divided into two classes, the first occupy the land, which they till with admirable care and knowledge; the second, who are possessed of none, apply themselves to the sea, the general resource of mankind in this part of the world. This island therefore, like Nantucket, is become a great nursery which supplies with pilots and seamen the numerous coasters with which this extended part of America abounds. Go where you will from Nova Scotia to the Mississippi, you will find almost everywhere some natives of these two islands employed in seafaring occupations. Their climate is so favourable to population, that marriage is the object of every man's earliest wish; and it is a blessing so easily obtained, that great numbers are obliged to quit their native land and go to some other countries in quest of subsistence. The inhabitants are all Presbyterians, which is the established religion of Massachusetts; and here let me remember with gratitude the hospitable treatment I received from B. Norton, Esq., the colonel of the island, as well as from Dr. Mahew, the lineal descendant of the first proprietor. Here are to be found the most expert pilots, either for the great bay, their sound, Nantucket shoals, or the different ports in their neighbourhood. In stormy weather they are always at sea, looking out for vessels, which they board with singular dexterity, and hardly ever fail to bring safe to their intended harbour. Gay-Head, the western point of this island, abounds with a variety of ochres of different colours, with which the inhabitants paint their houses.

The vessels most proper for whale fishing are brigs of about 150 tons burthen, particularly when they are intended for distant latitudes; they always man them with thirteen hands, in order that they may row two whale-boats; the crews of which must necessarily consist of six, four at the oars, one standing on the bows with the harpoon, and the other at the helm. It is also necessary that there should be two of these boats, that if one should be destroyed in attacking the whale, the other, which is never engaged at the same time, may be ready to save the hands. Five of the thirteen are always Indians; the last of the complement remains on board to steer the vessel during the action. They have no wages; each draws a certain established share in partnership with the proprietor of the vessel; by which economy they are all proportionately concerned in the success of the enterprise, and all equally alert and vigilant. None of these whalemen ever exceed the age of forty: they look on those who are past that period not to be possessed of all that vigour and agility which so adventurous a business requires. Indeed if you attentively consider the immense disproportion between the object assailed and the assailants; if you think on the diminutive size, and weakness of their frail vehicle; if you recollect the treachery of the element on which this scene is transacted; the sudden and unforeseen accidents of winds, etc., you will readily acknowledge that it must require the most consummate exertion of all the strength, agility, and judgment, of which the bodies and minds of men are capable, to undertake these adventurous encounters.

As soon as they arrive in those latitudes where they expect to meet with whales, a man is sent up to the mast head; if he sees one, he immediately cries out AWAITE PAWANA, here is a whale: they all remain still and silent until he repeats PAWANA, a whale, when in less than six minutes the two boats are launched, filled with every implement necessary for the attack. They row toward the whale with astonishing velocity; and as the Indians early became their fellow-labourers in this new warfare, you can easily conceive how the Nattick expressions became familiar on board the whale-boats. Formerly it often happened that whale vessels were manned with none but Indians and the master; recollect also that the Nantucket people understand the Nattick, and that there are always five of these people on board. There are various ways of approaching the whale, according to their peculiar species; and this previous knowledge is of the utmost consequence. When these boats are arrived at a reasonable distance, one of them rests on its oars and stands off, as a witness of the approaching engagement; near the bows of the other the harpooner stands up, and on him principally depends the success of the enterprise. He wears a jacket closely buttoned, and round his head a handkerchief tightly bound: in his hands he holds the dreadful weapon, made of the best steel, marked sometimes with the name of their town, and sometimes with that of their vessel; to the shaft of which the end of a cord of due length, coiled up with the utmost care in the middle of the boat, is firmly tied; the other end is fastened to the bottom of the boat. Thus prepared they row in profound silence, leaving the whole conduct of the enterprise to the harpooner and to the steersman, attentively following their directions. When the former judges himself to be near enough to the whale, that is, at the distance of about fifteen feet, he bids them stop; perhaps she has a calf, whose safety attracts all the attention of the dam, which is a favourable circumstance; perhaps she is of a dangerous species, and it is safest to retire, though their ardour will seldom permit them; perhaps she is asleep, in that case he balances high the harpoon, trying in this important moment to collect all the energy of which he is capable. He launches it forth—she is struck: from her first movements they judge of her temper, as well as of their future success. Sometimes in the immediate impulse of rage, she will attack the boat and demolish it with one stroke of her tail; in an instant the frail vehicle disappears and the assailants are immersed in the dreadful element. Were the whale armed with the jaws of a shark, and as voracious, they never would return home to amuse their listening wives with the interesting tale of the adventure. At other times she will dive and disappear from human sight; and everything must give way to her velocity, or else all is lost. Sometimes she will swim away as if untouched, and draw the cord with such swiftness that it will set the edge of the boat on fire by the friction. If she rises before she has run out the whole length, she is looked upon as a sure prey. The blood she has lost in her flight, weakens her so much, that if she sinks again, it is but for a short time; the boat follows her course with almost equal speed. She soon re-appears; tired at last with convulsing the element; which she tinges with her blood, she dies, and floats on the surface. At other times it may happen that she is not dangerously wounded, though she carries the harpoon fast in her body; when she will alternately dive and rise, and swim on with unabated vigour. She then soon reaches beyond the length of the cord, and carries the boat along with amazing velocity: this sudden impediment sometimes will retard her speed, at other times it only serves to rouse her anger, and to accelerate her progress. The harpooner, with the axe in his hands, stands ready. When he observes that the bows of the boat are greatly pulled down by the diving whale, and that it begins to sink deep and to take much water, he brings the axe almost in contact with the cord; he pauses, still flattering himself that she will relax; but the moment grows critical, unavoidable danger approaches: sometimes men more intent on gain, than on the preservation of their lives, will run great risks; and it is wonderful how far these people have carried their daring courage at this awful moment! But it is vain to hope, their lives must be saved, the cord is cut, the boat rises again. If after thus getting loose, she re-appears, they will attack and wound her a second time. She soon dies, and when dead she is towed alongside of their vessel, where she is fastened.

The next operation is to cut with axes and spades, every part of her body which yields oil; the kettles are set a boiling, they fill their barrels as fast as it is made; but as this operation is much slower than that of cutting up, they fill the hold of their ship with those fragments, lest a storm should arise and oblige them to abandon their prize. It is astonishing what a quantity of oil some of these fish will yield, and what profit it affords to those who are fortunate enough to overtake them.
. . .

In 1769 they fitted out 125 whalemen; the first fifty that returned brought with them 11,000 barrels of oil. In 1770 they fitted out 135 vessels for the fisheries, at thirteen hands each; four West-Indiamen,[1] twelve hands; twenty-five wood vessels,[2] four hands; eighteen coasters, five hands; fifteen London traders, eleven hands. All these amount to 2158 hands, employed in 197 vessels. Trace their progressive steps between the possession of a few whale-boats, and that of such a fleet!

The moral conduct, prejudices, and customs of a people who live two-thirds of their time at sea, must naturally be very different from those of their neighbours, who live by cultivating the earth. That long abstemiousness to which the former are exposed, the breathing of saline air, the frequent repetitions of danger, the boldness acquired in surmounting them, the very impulse of the winds, to which they are exposed; all these, one would imagine must lead them, when on shore, to no small desire of inebriation, and a more eager pursuit of those pleasures, of which they have been so long deprived, and which they must soon forego. There are many appetites that may be gratified on

---

1   West-Indiamen: vessels engaged with the islands of the West Indies in the Caribbean.
2   Wood vessels: boats or small vessels engaged in hauling timber and cordwood.

shore, even by the poorest man, but which must remain unsatisfied at sea. Yet notwithstanding the powerful effects of all these causes, I observed here, at the return of their fleets, no material irregularities; no tumultuous drinking assemblies: whereas in our continental towns, the thoughtless seaman indulges himself in the coarsest pleasures; and vainly thinking that a week of debauchery can compensate for months of abstinence, foolishly lavishes in a few days of intoxication, the fruits of half a year's labour. On the contrary all was peace here, and a general decency prevailed throughout; the reason I believe is, that almost everybody here is married, for they get wives very young; and the pleasure of returning to their families absorbs every other desire. The motives that lead them to the sea, are very different from those of most other sea-faring men; it is neither idleness nor profligacy that sends them to that element; it is a settled plan of life, a well founded hope of earning a livelihood; it is because their soil is bad, that they are early initiated to this profession, and were they to stay at home, what could they do? The sea therefore becomes to them a kind of patrimony; they go to whaling with as much pleasure and tranquil indifference, with as strong an expectation of success, as a landsman undertakes to clear a piece of swamp. The first is obliged to advance his time, and labour, to procure oil on the surface of the sea; the second advances the same to procure himself grass from grounds that produced nothing before but hassocks and bogs. . . . All their houses are neat, convenient, and comfortable; some of them are filled with two families, for when the husbands are at sea, the wives require less house-room. They all abound with the most substantial furniture, more valuable from its usefulness than from any ornamental appearance. Wherever I went, I found good cheer, a welcome reception; and after the second visit I felt myself as much at my ease as if I had been an old acquaintance of the family. They had as great plenty of everything as if their island had been part of the golden quarter of Virginia (a valuable track of land on Cape Charles): I could hardly persuade myself that I had quitted the adjacent continent, where everything abounds, and that I was on a barren sand-bank, fertilised with whale oil only. . . . I have often, by their fire-sides, traveled with them the whole length of their career, from their earliest steps, from their first commercial adventure, from the possession of a single whale-boat, up to that of a dozen large vessels! This does not imply, however, that every one who began with a whale-boat, has ascended to a like pitch of fortune; by no means, the same casualty, the same combination of good and evil which attends human affairs in every other part of the globe, prevails here: a great prosperity is not the lot of every man, but there are many and various gradations; if they all do not attain riches, they all attain an easy subsistence. After all, is it not better to be possessed of a single whale-boat, or a few sheep pastures; to live free and independent under the mildest governments, in a healthy climate, in a land of charity and benevolence; than to be wretched as so many are in Europe, possessing nothing but their industry: tossed from one rough wave to another; engaged either in the most servile labours for the smallest pittance, or fettered with the links of the most irksome dependence, even without the hopes of rising?

The majority of those inferior hands which are employed in this fishery, many of the mechanics, such as coopers, smiths, caulkers, carpenters, etc., who do not belong to the society of Friends, are Presbyterians, and originally came from the main. Those who are possessed of the greatest fortunes at present belong to the former; but they all began as simple whalemen: it is even looked upon as honourable and necessary for the son of the wealthiest man to serve an apprenticeship to the same bold, adventurous business which has enriched his father; they go several voyages, and these early excursions never fail to harden their constitutions, and introduce them to the knowledge of their future means of subsistence.

Questions for Discussion:
1. What does this document reveal about colonial society?
2. What distinguishes Native Americans from colonists on board these whaling vessels?
3. How does Crèvecoeur idealize the maritime society of Martha's Vineyard?

J. Hector St. John de Crèvecoeur, *Letters from an American Farmer* (New York: Fox, Duffield & Company, 1904), 165–82.

PIRACY AND COLONIAL AMERICA

Pirates have long attracted American audiences, both as readers and viewers. In recent years, scholars, such as Marcus Rediker in his seminal *Between the Devil and the Deep Blue Sea*, have identified pirates as an egalitarian society, an alternative to the elite-dominated European society that dominated the Atlantic World.[1] Other scholars, such as David Cordingly in *Under the Black Flag*, put forth the more traditional view that pirates were simply violent criminals.[2] What is less controversial is that pirates were a menace to sea-going commerce, operated in loosely organized groups, and usually died young. While the Caribbean was the most likely place to find pirates, they also sailed in North American waters and frequently took refuge in the mainland colonies. This selection of readings allows students to determine for themselves the nature of piracy.

William Penn, "Piracy Proclamation" (1699)

William Penn (1644–1718) is best known as the Quaker founder of Pennsylvania. In this document, Penn attempts to root out pirates who retired to Pennsylvania to enjoy their ill-gotten gains. The British Parliament had moved strongly to stop piracy through the Piracy Act of 1698, which empowered colonial governments to bring pirates to trial and execute them and to prosecute those found aiding pirates ashore. The Board of Trade, which supervised maritime affairs, had heard reports that the Pennsylvania government during Penn's absence in England abetted pirate activities. Penn, the son of a Royal Navy admiral, had no use for pirates and moved quickly to suppress piracy through the following proclamation and the creation of laws that allowed Pennsylvania authorities to imprison suspected pirates, although some Quakers initially resisted the anti-piracy plan.

> Whereas several *Piracies* and *Robberies* at Sea and on Sea-Coasts have of late years been committed in Many parts of the World, to the great Injury of Trade, the Terror and Ruine of many peaceable honest People under Governments in Amity with the Crown of England, and to the horrid Scandal of the English Nation; And whereas divers Persons justly suspected to be guilty of having practiced the Aforesaid Crimes, as well as by the Nature and Quantity of the Treasure about them, as by their being unable to give any good Account of themselves, their Residence, or Commerce, have for some time been observed to land on, and scatter themselves through these Northern

1 Marcus Rediker, *Between the Devil and the Deep Blue Sea: Merchant Seamen, Pirates, and the Anglo-American Maritime World, 1700–1750* (Cambridge: Cambridge University Press, 1987).

2 David Cordingly, *Under the Black Flag: The Romance and the Reality of Life Among the Pirates* (New York: Random House, 1996).

English Colonies of *America*, with a manifest Design of enjoying with Impunity and safety their ill gotten Riches.

Now to the End that All such Persons may be effectually discouraged from taking shelter in this Province, and They that attempt it may be speedily detected, and no longer escape the hands of *Justice*; I have thought fit, and do hereby *strictly* Charge and Command all *Magistrates* and *Officers* within this *Province* and *Counties* annexed as they will answer the Contrary at their Peril, to use their utmost Diligence vigorously to *Pursue, Apprehend,* and *Secure* every such *Person*, that may be thus suspected; and not only such *Persons*, but also to prosecute all *Others*, who shall knowingly *Harbour* any of Them or their *Goods*, or by any means directly or indirectly *Protect* them, or shall be Aiding or Assisting to Them to make their Escape or to withdraw themselves from *Justice*. And more Especially I do hereby Require and Command All the *Kings* Loving Subjects the Inhabitants of this *Province* & Territories, & particularly all *Keepers* of *Public Houses*, to have a watchfull Eye over, and strictly to Observe all *Strangers* coming among them, and such to Apprehend, or cause to be Apprehended and Secured, as they find unable to give a Reasonable and Credible Account of their former Abode and Conversation, and about whom is found any such Quantity of *East-India, Arabian* or other Foreign *Goods* or *Coins* as may render them justly suspected as aforesaid: Whether they pretend to have got their wealth by Privateering against Ships under *French* Commissions, which for some time past has been happily at an End, or by an open Trade to *Madagascar*,[1] known to be the *Magazine* of Spoils and Plunders committed on the *East-India-Seas*: And to take care that the said Persons in safe custody be kept, till upon due Information thereof given to me, they shall receive my further Orders. And the better to Encourage a due Prosecution of these my Commands; It is hereby Promised that whosoever shall Discover, Secure and Deliver into the Hands of *Justice*, any such suspected Person, who shall be afterwards Convicted of the aforesaid Crime, shall receive the Sum of Ten Pounds, as a Reward of their good Service. Given under my Hand and Seal at *Philadelphia* the 23d. day of the Tenth Month, the Eleventh Year of the Reign of WILLIAM the Third of *Great Britain*,

---

1   Madagascar: a large island off the southeast coast of Africa that became a notorious pirate hangout in this period.

France and *Ireland* King &c. and the Nineteenth of This Government. *Anno Domini.* 1699.

W. Penn.

Questions for discussion:
1. What does this document reveal about how colonial society felt about pirates?
2. What does this document reveal about the pirates themselves?
3. Why did this proclamation put such an emphasis on prosecuting those who sheltered pirates?

William Penn, "Piracy Proclamation" (Philadelphia: Printed by Reinier Jansen, 1699), Broadside, Library of Congress, Rare Book and Special Collections Division.

Alexander Spotswood, "Pirates on the James River" (1720)

Pirates were a constant headache for colonial governments throughout the Atlantic World, and Virginia was no exception. In this letter, the colonial lieutenant governor of Virginia, Alexander Spotswood (1676–1740), reports his anti-pirate activities to the Commissioners of the Customs. Like William Penn's proclamation of 1699, this document reveals pirates attempting to settle in America to enjoy their ill-gotten gains ashore. Furthermore, it seems that at least some people were willing to take gifts or bribes from pirates and shelter them from the authorities.

More disturbingly, this item also describes the typical fate of pirates: execution by hanging at a shoreside gibbet. The King's justice could be harsh for those pirates who showed no remorse, but those deemed capable of reform might escape with their lives. Colonial officials also had an interest in recovering the pirate's booty, which was after all stolen goods.

I forgot in my last to informe y'r Lord'ps that one Capt. Knott, of the West River Merch't, *London*, being taken in his passage hither by one Callifax, a Pirate, eight of y'r Pirat's crew took their passage in Knott's Ship w'th an Intent to disperse themselves w'th the Booty they had gott, and, accordingly as soon as the Ship arrived within the Capes,[1] four of them went away in a boat w'ch the Pirate Commander

---

1   Within the Capes: inside Chesapeake Bay.

had given them for that purpose, designing for Maryland; The other four, who intended for North Carolina, came w'th ye ship into James River, Capt. Knott made what haste he could to discover to me what kind of passengers be had been obliged to bring w'th him and the first four being driven back by a Storm, were with ye others, happily taken, and at their Tryal, upon full Evidence, convicted of divers notorious Pyracys. Six of them appeared the most profligate Wretches I ever heard of, for, as they behaved themselves with the greatest impudence at the Bar,[1] they were no sooner taken from it than they vented their imprecations on their Judge and all concerned in their prosecution, and vow'd if they were again at liberty they would spare none alive that should fall into their hands. I thought it necessary for the greater Terrour to hang up four of them in Chains. Two others were executed at the same time, and Two who shew'd a just Abhorrence of their past Crimes I sent on board the Man of War on this station, being desirous to imitate his Maj'ty's Royal Example by mixing Mercy w'th Justice. The crew to which these Pirats belonged, had committed abundances of Piracys last year on the Coast of Guinea. The Ship they had last was called the *Maripus Del Campo*, which they took last Summer from the Emperor's Subjects on the Coast of Africa. In this Ship they took the Vice Adm'l of the Brazil Fleet richly laden, homeward bound for Lisbon, and afterwards took several English Ships and Vessels in the West Indies. The eight Pyrates brought in hither had for their share of the booty three Negro men and a boy, a quantity of Gold dust and Moyders[2] which I have now secured in my hands for his Ma'ty's use, but as they had found means before they were taken to Lodge a good part of their Effects in the hands of some planters here with whom they got acquainted with; and it is but lately that those Effects have been delivered up after a great deal of search and trouble, So that the final Sentence of the Court of Admiralty not being yet passed nor the Acco't of Charges adjusted I cannot by this Conveyance send a true State of what remains in my hands. . . .

There have been also bro't in hither last Month in the Ship *Callabar*, Merchant of Bristol, Tho. Kennedy, M'r, one and twenty Negro Slaves, w'ch he delivered up to me as Piratical Effects, and upon w'ch

---

1   At the Bar: in court.
2   Moyders: moidore, a Portuguese gold coin.

I am to await his Majesty's Commands. These Slaves were given to Capt. Kennedy by one Edward England, Comm'd'r of a Pirate Ship by whom Kennedy was taken on the Coast of Guinea last Winter and as the Pirats had detained him for some months and plundered him of sundry Goods, they pretended to give him these Negroes in recompense for his Losses. When Masters of Ships are so honest as to discover and Yield up what is thus given them in lieu of their own private losses I cannot but recommend them to his Maj'ty's favour that some consideration may be had of their sufferings and damages. And here I beg leave to do Justice to Capt. Knott, by whose prudent Conduct not only the aforementioned Pirats were brought to punishment, but the Lives of the Witnesses preserved, who served to Convict them on their Tryal, for two Jews and two Portuguese who had been prisoners among the Pirats were put on board Capt. Knott's Ship at the same time with the eight Pyrats, and had it not been for the good management of the Captain it is not to be supposed the Pyrats would have left any of them to Witness against them. And as he was thus Instrumental in bringing these Miscreants to punishment, he was no less faithful in a just discovery of such of their Effects as he had knowledge of; for he not only discovered and delivered up the Sugar, Tobacco, and Gold dust w'ch the Pirats presented him with as a Compensation for his Liquors, Stores and Goods wh'ch they had taken from him, and even some Moyders, w'ch they gave him in lieu of the Guineas and English money they plundered him of, but he likewise obliged his Men to deliver up everything the Pirates had given them. I, therefore, humbly recommend him to Yo'r Lords'ps' favor so far as to assist him in his Application to his Maj'ty for Reparations of his particular Losses out of the piratical Effects he has discovered and delivered up, w'ch are of much greater Value; And seeing Capt. Kennedy has in like manner acted so just a part in delivering up the Negroes given him by the Pirates, in consideration of the damages he and his Owners had sustained by their Means. I beg leave to recommend him, also, to Yo'r Lord'ps' assistance for obtaining Reparation out of the produce of the Slaves he has thus delivered up to his Maj'ty's use; And because it is a common practice among the Pirats to make presents to Masters of Ships and Seamen of such Commoditys they have less use of, in lieu of what they take away, and that without the voluntary confession of the persons themselves, it is impossible to discover such Piratical Effects,

I humbly offer to Yo'r Lo'ps' consideration whether it may not be for his Maj'ty's Service that as an Encouragement to those who shall faithfully discover any such Piratical Effects, their particular Losses may be repaired out of the Effects they so deliver up, where ye proper Owners are not like to make any Claim. And if his Majesty shall be pleased to notify such an Encouragement by Proclamation, I am persuaded it would be a means to discover abundance of Piratical Effects, w'ch otherwise may be concealed and converted to private use, many men being rather willing to run all risques in keeping what they have gott than to put themselves to the trouble of a discovery, when they have nothing to expect. . . .

Questions for Discussion:
1. What does this document reveal about how the British government maintained the authority of the law in its colonial seaports?
2. What does this document reveal about colonial society on Chesapeake Bay?
3. How does Spotswood's position in society influence what he reports in this letter?

R. A. Brock, ed., *The Official Letters of Alexander Spotswood*, vol. 1, (Richmond: Virginia Historical Society, 1882), 337–40.

Charles Johnson, "The Life of Mary Read" (1724)

Interest in the lives of pirates is not new; even in the early 1700s, when piracy was still common, the reading public was devouring a new book, *A General History of the Pirates*, first printed in 1724. The true author of this work remains unknown, although some suspect Daniel Defoe, author of *Robinson Crusoe*, wrote the book under a pseudonym. The book shaped popular notions of piracy and provided the standard account of the lives of many pirates.

Probably no section of the book is more famous than that on female pirates. One of these, Mary Read (ca. 1690–1721), is particularly intriguing in that she spent a major portion of her life pretending to be male. Unquestionably she was a brave woman: her service in the British Navy and Army, fighting a duel to defend her lover, and her fierceness as a pirate all indicate she was a capable and perhaps ruthless individual. Like many pirates, the authorities eventually captured her. Faced with execution, she "pled her belly" (pregnancy), giving her temporary reprieve from hanging, but soon after died of an illness while still in prison.

Mary Read was born in England, her Mother was married young, to a Man who used the Sea, who going a Voyage soon after their Marriage, left her with Child, which Child proved to be a Boy. As to the Husband, whether he was cast away, or died in the Voyage, Mary Read could not tell; but however, he never returned more; nevertheless, the Mother, who was young and airy, met with an Accident, which has often happened to Women who are young, and do not take a great deal of Care; which was, she soon proved with Child again, without a Husband to Father it, but how, or by whom, none but her self could tell, for she carry'd a pretty good Reputation among her Neighbours. Finding her Burthen grew, in order to conceal her Shame, she takes a formal Leave of her Husband's Relations, giving out, that she went to live with some Friends of her own, in the Country: Accordingly she went away, and carry'd with her her young Son, at this Time, not a Year old: Soon after her Departure her Son died, but Providence in Return, was pleased to give her a Girl in his Room, of which she was safely delivered, in her Retreat, and this was our Mary Read.

Here the Mother liv'd three or four Years, till what Money she had was almost gone; then she thought of returning to London, and considering that her Husband's Mother was in some Circumstances, she did not doubt but to prevail upon her, to provide for the Child, if she could but pass it upon her for the same, but the changing a Girl into a Boy, seem'd a difficult Piece of Work, and how to deceive an experienced old Woman, in such a Point, was altogether as impossible; however, she ventured to dress it up as a Boy, brought it to Town, and presented it to her Mother-in-Law, as her Husband's Son; the old Woman would have taken it, to have bred it up, but the Mother pretended it would break her Heart, to part with it; so it was agreed betwixt them, that the Child should live with the Mother, and the supposed Grandmother should allow a Crown a Week for its Maintainance.

Thus, the Mother gained her Point, she bred up her Daughter as a Boy, and when she grew up to some Sense, she thought proper to let her into the Secret of her Birth, to induce her to conceal her Sex. It happen'd that the Grandmother died, by which Means the Subsistance that came from that Quarter, ceas'd, and they were more and more reduced in their Circumstances; wherefore she was obliged to put her Daughter out, to wait on a French Lady, as a Foot-boy being now thirteen Years of Age: Here she did not live long, for growing bold and strong, and having also a roving Mind, she enter'd herself on board a Man of War, where she served some Time, then quitted it, went over into Flanders, and carry'd Arms in a Regiment of Foot, as a Cadet; and tho' upon all Actions, she behaved herself with a great deal of Bravery, yet she could not get a Commission, they being generally bought and sold; therefore she quitted the Service, and took on in a Regiment of Horse; she behaved so well in several Engagements, that she got the Esteem of all her Officers; but her Comrade, who was a Fleming, happening to be a handsome young Fellow, she falls in Love with him, and from that Time, grew a little more negligent in her Duty, so that, it seems, Mars and Venus could not be served at the same Time; her Arms and Accoutrements which were always kept in the best Order, were quite neglected: 'Tis true, when her Comrade was order'd out upon a Party, she used to go without being commanded, and frequently run herself into Danger, where she had no Business, only to be near him; the rest of the Troopers little suspecting the secret Cause which moved her to this Behaviour, fancy'd her to be mad, and her Comrade himself could not account for this strange Alteration in her, but Love is ingenious, and as they lay together in the same Tent, and were constantly together, she found a Way of letting him discover her Sex, without appearing that it was done with Design.

He was much surprized at what he found out, and not a little pleased, taking it for granted, that he should have a Mistress solely to himself, which is an unusual Thing in a Camp, since there is scarce one of those Campaign Ladies, that is ever true to a Troop or Company; so that he thought of nothing but gratifying his Passions with very little Ceremony; but he found himself strangely mistaken, for she proved very reserved and modest, and resisted all his Temptations, and at the same Time was so obliging and insinuating in her Carriage, that she quite changed his Purpose, so far from thinking of making her his Mistress, he now courted her for a Wife.

This was the utmost Wish of her Heart, in short, they exchanged Promises, and when the Campaign was over, and the Regiment marched into Winter Quarters, they bought Woman's Apparel for her, with such Money as they could make up betwixt them, and were publickly married.

The Story of two Troopers marrying each other, made a great Noise, so that several Officers were drawn by Curiosity to assist at the Ceremony, and they agreed among themselves that every one of them should make a small Present to the Bride, towards House-keeping, in Consideration of her having been their Fellow-Soldier. Thus being set up, they seemed to have a Desire of quitting the Service, and settling in the World; the Adventure of their Love and Marriage had gained them so much Favour, that they easily obtained their Discharge, and they immediately set up an Eating-House or Ordinary, which was the Sign of the Three Horse-Shoes, near the Castle of Breda, where they soon run into a good Trade, a great many Officers eating with them constantly.

But this Happiness lasted not long, for the Husband soon died, and the Peace of Ryswick being concluded, there was no Resort of Officers to Breda, as usual, so that the Widow having little or no Trade, was forced to give up House-keeping, and her Substance being by Degrees quite spent, she again assumes her Man's Apparel, and going into Holland, there takes on in a Regiment of Foot, quartered in one of the Frontier Towns: Here she did not remain long, there was no Likelihood of Preferment in Time of Peace, therefore she took a Resolution of seeking her Fortune another Way; and withdrawing from the Regiment, ships herself on board of a Vessel bound for the West Indies.

It happened this Ship was taken by English Pyrates, and Mary Read was the only English Person on board, they kept her amongst them, and having plundered the Ship, let it go again; after following this Trade for some Time, the King's Proclamation came out, and was published in all Parts of the West-Indies, for pardoning such Pyrates, who should voluntarily surrender themselves by a certain Day therein mentioned. The Crew of Mary Read took the Benefit of this Proclamation, and having surrender'd, liv'd quietly on Shore; but Money beginning to grow short, and hearing that Captain Woodes Rogers, Governor of the Island of Providence,[1] was fitting out some Privateers to cruise against the Spaniards, she, with several others, embark'd for that Island, in order to go upon the privateering Account, being resolved to make her Fortune one way or other.

These Privateers were no sooner sail'd out, but the Crews of some of them, who had been pardoned, rose against their Commanders,

---

1   Providence: a settlement on the Bahamas Islands.

and turned themselves to their old Trade: In this Number was Mary
Read. It is true, she often declared, that the Life of a Pyrate was what
she always abhor'd, and went into it only upon Compulsion, both this
Time, and before, intending to quit it, whenever a fair Opportunity
should offer it self; yet some of the Evidence against her, upon her
Tryal, who were forced Men, and had sail'd with her, deposed upon
Oath, that in Times of Action, no Person amongst them was more
resolute, or ready to board or undertake any Thing that was hazardous, than she and Anne Bonny; and particularly at the time they were
attack'd and taken, when they came to close Quarters, none kept the
Deck except Mary Read and Anne Bonny, and one more; upon which,
she, Mary Read, called to those under Deck, to come up and fight
like Men, and finding they did not stir, fired her Arms down the Hold
amongst them, killing one, and wounding others.

This was Part of the Evidence against her, which she denied; which,
whether true or no, thus much is certain, that she did not want Bravery, nor indeed was she less remarkable for her Modesty, according to
the Notions of Virtue: Her Sex was not so much as suspected by any
Person on board till Anne Bonny, who was not altogether so reserved
in Point of Chastity, took a particular Liking to her; in short, Anne
Bonny took her for a handsome young Fellow, and for some Reasons
best known to herself, first discovered her Sex to Mary Read; Mary
Read knowing what she would be at, and being very sensible of her
own Incapacity that Way, was forced to come to a right Understanding with her, and so to the great Disappointment of Anne Bonny, she
let her know she was a Woman also; but this Intimacy so disturb'd
Captain Rackam, who was the Lover and Gallant of Anne Bonny, that
he grew furiously jealous, so that he told Anne Bonny, he would cut
her new Lover's Throat, therefore, to quiet him, she let him into the
Secret also.

Captain Rackam (as he was enjoined) kept the Thing a Secret from
all the Ship's Company, yet, notwithstanding all her Cunning and
Reserve, Love found her out in this Disguise, and hinder'd her from
forgetting her Sex. In their Cruise they took a great Number of Ships
belonging to Jamaica, and other Parts of the West-Indies, bound to
and from England; and, when ever they met any good Artist, or other
Person that might be of any great Use to their Company, if he was not
willing to enter, it was their Custom to keep him by Force. Among
these was a young Fellow of a most engaging Behaviour, or, at least,

he was so in the Eyes of Mary Read, who became so smitten with his Person and Address, that she could neither rest Night or Day; but there is nothing more ingenious than Love, it was no hard Matter for her, who had before been practiced in these Wiles, to find a Way to let him discover her Sex: She first insinuated herself into his Liking, by talking against the Life of a Pyrate, which he was altogether averse to, so they became Mess-Mates and strict Companions: When she found he had a Friendship for her, as a Man, she suffered the Discovery to be made, by carelessly shewing her Breasts, which were very white.

The young Fellow, who was made of Flesh and Blood, had his Curiosity and Desire so rais'd by this Sight, that he never ceas'd importuning her, till she confessed what she was. Now begins the Scene of Love; as he had a Liking and Esteem for her, under her supposed Character, it was now turn'd into Fondness and Desire; her Passion was no less violent than his, and perhaps she express'd it, by one of the most generous Actions that ever Love inspired. It happened this young Fellow had a Quarrel with one of the Pyrates, and their Ship then lying at an Anchor, near one of the Islands, they had appointed to go ashore and fight, according to the Custom of the Pyrates: Mary Read was to the last Degree uneasy and anxious, for the Fate of her Lover; she would not have had him refuse the Challenge, because, she could not bear the Thoughts of his being branded with Cowardice; on the other Side, she dreaded the Event, and apprehended the Fellow might be too hard for him: When Love once enters into the Breast of one who has any Sparks of Generosity, it stirs the Heart up to the most noble Actions; in this Dilemma, she shew'd, that she fear'd more for his Life than she did for her own; for she took a Resolution of quarrelling with this Fellow herself, and having challenged him ashore, she appointed the Time two Hours sooner than that when he was to meet her Lover, where she fought him at Sword and Pistol, and killed him upon the Spot.

It is true, she had fought before, when she had been insulted by some of those Fellows, but now it was altogether in her Lover's Cause, she stood as it were betwixt him and Death, as if she could not live without him. If he had no regard for her before, this Action would have bound him to her for ever; but there was no Occasion for Ties or Obligation, his Inclination towards her was sufficient; in fine, they plighted their Troth to each other, which Mary Read said, she look'd upon to be as good a Marriage, in Conscience, as if it had been done by a Minister in Church; and to this was owing her great Belly, which she pleaded to save her Life.

She declared she had never committed Adultery or Fornication with any Man, she commended the Justice of the Court, before which she was try'd, for distinguishing the Nature of their Crimes; her Husband, as she call'd him, with several others, being acquitted; and being ask'd, who he was? She would not tell, but, said he was an honest Man, and had no Inclination to such Practices, and that they had both resolved to leave the Pyrates, the first Opportunity, and apply themselves to some honest Livelihood.

It is no doubt, but many had Compassion for her, yet the Court could not avoid finding her Guilty; for among other Things, one of the Evidences against her, deposed, that being taken by Rackam, and detain'd some Time on board, he fell accidentally into Discourse with Mary Read, whom he taking for a young Man, ask'd her, what Pleasure she could have in being concerned in such Enterprizes, where her Life was continually in Danger, by Fire or Sword; and not only so, but she must be sure of dying an ignominious Death, if she should be taken alive? She answer'd, that as to hanging, she thought it no great Hardship, for, were it not for that, every cowardly Fellow would turn Pyrate, and so infest the Seas, that Men of Courage must starve: That if it was put to the Choice of the Pyrates, they would not have the Punishment less than Death, the Fear of which kept some dastardly Rogues honest; that many of those who are now cheating the Widows and Orphans, and oppressing their poor Neighbours, who have no Money to obtain Justice, would then rob at Sea, and the Ocean would be crowded with Rogues, like the Land, and no Merchant would venture out; so that the Trade, in a little Time, would not be worth following.

Being found quick with Child, as has been observed, her Execution was respited, and it is possible she would have found Favour, but she was seiz'd with a violent Fever, soon after her Tryal, of which she died in Prison.

Questions for Discussion:
1. What does Mary Read's life reveal about the generally accepted role of women in the early 1700s?
2. How can Mary Read's activities be interpreted as rebellion against a system that allowed little freedom for women?

3. How did the various men Mary Read encountered throughout her life react to her cross-dressing?

Charles Johnson, *A General and True History of the Lives and Actions of the Most Famous Highwaymen, Murderers, Street-Robbers, &c.* (Birmingham: R. Walker, 1742), 167–69.

Various, "Pirate Articles" (ca. 1720s)

The idea of a pirate utopia or alternative society is most clearly documented in the crew articles they left behind. Articles were a kind of contract between captain and crew detailing the conditions under which they were to sail and emphasized the sailors' subordination to the master of the vessel. But pirate articles were distinctly different from the crew articles on a merchant ship in that they emphasized the crew's rights over the officers' powers. In some ways they were a complete inversion of the order established on commercial and naval ships.

Below are three different versions of pirate articles from the early eighteenth century. Bartholomew Roberts (1682–1722) was a fantastically successful Welsh pirate who captured hundreds of ships before his own death in combat with the British Navy. George Lowther (unknown–1723) was an officer on board a slave ship who led a successful mutiny and turned pirate; it is said he killed himself rather than face capture. John Phillips (unknown–1724) had a brief, bloody career as a pirate but faced a mutiny by his own crew, who threw him overboard to drown.

The Articles of Bartholomew Robert's Crew (circa 1720)

I. Every man has a vote in affairs of moment; has equal title to the fresh provisions or strong liquors at any time seized, and use them at pleasure unless a scarcity make it necessary for the good of all to vote a retrenchment.

II. Every man shall be called fairly in turn, by list, on board of prizes, because over and above their proper share, they were on these occasions allowed a shift of clothes. But if they defraud the Company to the value of a dollar, in plate, jewels or money, Marooning was the punishment. If the robbery was only between one another they contented themselves with slitting the ears and nose of him that was guilty, and set him on shore, not in an uninhabited place but somewhere where he was sure to encounter hardships.

III. No person to game at cards or dice for money.

IV. The lights and candles to be put out at eight o'clock at night. If any of the crew after that hour still remained inclined, they were to do it on the open deck.

V. To keep their piece, pistols and cutlass clean and fit for service.

VI. No boy or woman to be allowed amongst them. If any man were found seducing any of the latter sex, and carried her to sea disguised, he was to suffer Death.

VII. To desert the ship or their quarters in battle was punished with Death or Marooning.

VIII. No striking one another on board, but every man's quarrels to be ended on shore, at sword and pistol.

IX. No man to talk of breaking up their way of living till each has a share of £1,000. If, in order to do this, any man should lose a limb or become a cripple in their service, he was to have 800 dollars out of the publick stock, and for lesser hurts proportionately.

X. The Captain and the Quartermaster to receive two shares of a prize; the master, boatswain, and gunner, one share and a half, and other officers one and a quarter.

XI. The musicians to have rest on the sabbath day, but the other six days and nights none, without special favour.

The Articles of Captain George Lowther, & His Company (circa 1721)

I. The Captain is to have two full shares; the Master is to have one share and a half; the doctor, mate, gunner and boatswain, one share and a quarter.

II. He that shall be found guilty of taking up any unlawful weapon on board the privateer, or any prize, by us taken, so as to strike or abuse one another, in any regard, shall suffer what punishment the Captain and Majority of the Company shall think fit.

III. He that shall be found guilty of cowardice, in the time of engagement, shall suffer what Punishment the Captain and Majority shall think fit.

IV. If any Gold, Jewels, Silver, etc. be found on board of any prize or prizes, to the value of a piece-of-eight, and the finder do not deliver it to the quartermaster, in the space of 24 hours, shall suffer what punishment the Captain and Majority shall think fit.

V. He that is found guilty of gaming, or defrauding another to the value of a shilling, shall suffer what Punishment the Captain and majority of the Company shall think fit.

VI. He that shall have the misfortune to lose a limb, in time of engagement, shall have the sum of £150 sterling, and remain with the company as long as he shall think fit.

VII. Good quarters be given when called for.

VIII. He that sees a sail first, shall have the best pistol, or small arm, on board her.

The Articles on Board the *Revenge* Under Captain John Phillips (1723)

I. Every Man shall obey civil command; the Captain shall have one full share and a half in all prizes; the master, carpenter, boatswain and gunner shall have one share and quarter.

II. If any man shall offer to run away, or keep any secret from the Company, he shall be marooned, with one bottle of Powder, one bottle of water, one small arm, and shot.

III. If any man shall steal any thing in the company, or game to the value of a piece-of-eight, he shall be marooned or shot.

IV. If at any time we should meet another Marooner that man that shall sign his articles without the consent of our company, shall suffer such punishment as the captain and company shall think fit.

V. That man that shall strike another whilst these articles are in force, shall receive Moses's Law[1] on the bare Back.

VI. That man that shall snap his arms, or smoke tobacco in the hold, without a cap to his pipe, or carry a candle lighted without a lanthorn, shall suffer the same punishment as in the former article.

VII. That man that shall not keep his arms clean, fit for an engagement, or neglect his business, shall be cut off from his share, and suffer such other punishment as the captain and the company shall think fit.

VIII. If any man shall lose a joint in time of an engagement, he shall have 400 pieces-of-eight; if a limb, 800.

IX. If at any time you meet with a prudent woman, that man that offers to meddle with her, without her consent, shall suffer present death.

---

1   Moses's Law: thirty-nine blows with a whip.

Questions for Discussion:

1. According to the above documents, what was the primary concern of pirates when they wrote their articles?

2. What do these documents reveal about day-to-day life on board a pirate ship?

3. How do you think these articles differed from those on a merchant or naval vessel?

Charles Johnson, *A General History of the Robberies and Murders of the Most Notorious Pirates* (London: T. Warner, 1724), 182–84, 274–75, 307–8.

ENSLAVED AFRICANS AND SEAFARERS

The African slave trade was the largest involuntary movement of human beings in world history. Slavers ripped between ten and twelve million Africans from their homes and forced them onto ships that carried them across the ocean to lives of servitude, conducting backbreaking and menial work for the benefit of others. The background to the slave trade is a maritime one, in which blacks could be both cargo and crew.

The African slave trade and the relationship of seafaring to slavery has been the subject of significant scholarship in the last ten years. The relationship of Africans to the water should be of little surprise; they had vast networks of coastal and riverine commerce. Most African slaves found themselves delivered to slave ships not by a European style longboat, but by an African dugout paddled by other Africans. W. Jeffrey Bolster has examined the relationship of Africans and African Americans to the sea in his important work *Black Jacks*.[1] Bolster and others have found that blacks composed a large portion of seafarers in the age of sail.

In some ways the first passage below reinforces the traditional view of the slave trade. Typically the relationship of African Americans to the sea has been told as a slavery narrative, describing the horrors of the dreaded Middle Passage, the frequently lethal voyage from Africa to American slave markets. Few accounts remain of this experience from the enslaved Africans' point of view; the best known is Olaudah Equiano's autobiography. Equiano vividly describes the horrors of the Middle Passage. Once enslaved, he himself became a mariner, a fairly common occurrence in the eighteenth

---

1   W. Jeffrey Bolster, *Black Jacks: African American Seamen in the Age of Sail* (Cambridge, Mass.: Harvard University Press, 1997).

century, but, more unusually, he eventually escaped slavery and joined the fight against the slave trade.

Another enslaved mariner was Britton Hammon of Marshfield, Massachusetts. In his 1760 memoir he recalls his adventures as a seaman that reveal some of the interracial dynamics of the Atlantic World. Hammon's wages went to his master, but seafaring offered at least a temporary reprieve from a dreary New England winter. Unfortunately for Hammon, this particular voyage ended in disaster, and his adventure lasted almost thirteen years.

Both escaped slaves and free blacks often sought jobs as seamen, partly as an escape from the hardships of slavery and the oppressive racial hierarchy on land. Colonial newspapers frequently ran advertisements warning shipmasters not to hire escaped slaves or posting rewards for escaped slaves that give brief but vivid insights into the lives of African Americans. It may be surprising to some to note the mobility of black seafarers, the range of activities they were involved in, and their relations with white seafarers.

Olaudah Equiano, "Galling of the Chains" (ca. 1750s)

The following is an excerpt from chapter two of the memoirs of an enslaved African sailor named Olaudah Equiano (ca. 1745–1797). Equiano's memoir is an incredibly rare look at slavery from the viewpoint of an enslaved African. But there is some debate about the veracity of his account of his childhood; there is some evidence that Equiano was born in Carolina, rather than Africa.[1] Nonetheless, his book provides valuable insight to the process of enslavement and the dreaded Middle Passage across the Atlantic, and at the very least represents an important synthesis of the oral accounts that Equiano heard from other Africans.

For many historians, Equiano is the exemplar of an Atlantic World that arose as Europeans, Africans, and Americans interacted and exchanged ideas, commodities, and cultures around the shores of the Atlantic, a process expedited by maritime activities, including trade and warfare. This exchange was not always voluntary, as Equiano goes to great lengths to prove.

The first object which saluted my eyes when I arrived on the coast was the sea, and a slave ship, which was then riding at anchor, and

---

1   Vincent Carretta, *Equiano, the African: Biography of a Self-Made Man* (Athens: University of Georgia Press, 2005).

waiting for its cargo. These filled me with astonishment, which was soon converted into terror when I was carried on board. I was immediately handled and tossed up to see if I were sound by some of the crew; and I was now persuaded that I had gotten into a world of bad spirits, and that they were going to kill me. Their complexions too differing so much from ours, their long hair, and the language they spoke, (which was very different from any I had ever heard) united to confirm me in this belief. Indeed such were the horrors of my views and fears at the moment, that, if ten thousand worlds had been my own, I would have freely parted with them all to have exchanged my condition with that of the meanest slave in my own country. When I looked round the ship too and saw a large furnace or copper boiling, and a multitude of black people of every description chained together, every one of their countenances expressing dejection and sorrow, I no longer doubted of my fate; and, quite overpowered with horror and anguish, I fell motionless on the deck and fainted. When I recovered a little I found some black people about me, who I believed were some of those who brought me on board, and had been receiving their pay; they talked to me in order to cheer me, but all in vain. I asked them if we were not to be eaten by those white men with horrible looks, red faces, and loose hair. They told me I was not; and one of the crew brought me a small portion of spirituous liquor in a wine glass; but, being afraid of him, I would not take it out of his hand. One of the blacks therefore took it from him and gave it to me, and I took a little down my palate, which, instead of reviving me, as they thought it would, threw me into the greatest consternation at the strange feeling it produced, having never tasted any such liquor before. Soon after this the blacks who brought me on board went off, and left me abandoned to despair. I now saw myself deprived of all chance of returning to my native country, or even the least glimpse of hope of gaining the shore, which I now considered as friendly; and I even wished for my former slavery in preference to my present situation, which was filled with horrors of every kind, still heightened by my ignorance of what I was to undergo. I was not long suffered to indulge my grief; I was soon put down under the decks, and there I received such a salutation in my nostrils as I had never experienced in my life: so that, with the loathsomeness of the stench, and crying together, I became so sick and low that I was not able to eat, nor had I the least desire to taste any thing. I now wished for the last friend, Death, to relieve me; but soon, to my grief, two of the white men offered me eatables; and, on my refusing to eat, one of them held me fast by the hands, and laid me across I think the windlass, and tied my feet, while the other flogged me severely. I had never experienced any thing of this kind before; and although, not being used to the water, I naturally feared that element the first time I saw it, yet nevertheless, could I have got over the nettings, I would have jumped over the side, but I could not; and, besides, the crew used to watch us very closely who were not chained down to the decks, lest we should leap into the water: and I have seen some of these poor African prisoners most severely cut for attempting to do so, and hourly whipped for not eating. This indeed was often the case with myself. In a little time after, amongst the poor chained men, I found some of my own nation, which in a small degree gave ease to my mind. I inquired of these what was to be done with us; they gave me to understand we were to be carried to these white people's country to work for them. I then was a little revived, and thought, if it were no worse than working, my situation was not so desperate: but still I feared I should be put to death, the white people looked and acted, as I thought, in so savage a manner; for I had never seen among any people such instances of brutal cruelty; and this not only shewn towards us blacks, but also to some of the whites themselves. One white man in particular I saw, when we were permitted to be on deck, flogged so unmercifully with a large rope near the foremast, that he died in consequence of it; and they tossed him over the side as they would have done a brute. This made me fear these people the more; and I expected nothing less than to be treated in the same manner. I could not help expressing my fears and apprehensions to some of my countrymen: I asked them if these people had no country, but lived in this hollow place [the ship]: they told me they did not, but came from a distant one. 'Then,' said I, 'how comes it in all our country we never heard of them?' They told me because they lived so very far off. I then asked where were their women? had they any like themselves? I was told they had: 'and why,' said I, 'do we not see them?' they answered, because they were left behind. I asked how the vessel could go? they told me they could not tell; but that there were cloths put upon the masts by the help of the ropes I saw, and then the vessel went on; and the white men had some spell or magic they put in the water when they liked in order to stop the vessel. I was exceedingly amazed at this account, and really thought they were spirits. I therefore wished much to be from amongst them, for I expected they would sacrifice me: but my wishes were vain; for we were so quartered that it was impossible for any of us to make our escape. While we stayed on the coast I was mostly on deck; and one day, to my great astonishment, I saw one of these vessels coming in with the sails up. As soon as the whites saw it, they gave a great shout, at which we were amazed; and the more so as the vessel appeared larger by approaching nearer. At last she came to an anchor in my sight, and when the anchor was let go I and my countrymen who saw it were lost in astonishment to observe the vessel stop; and were not convinced it was done by magic. Soon after this the other ship got her boats out, and they came on board of us, and the people of both ships seemed very glad to see each other. Several of the strangers also shook hands with us black people, and made motions with their hands, signifying I suppose we were to go to their country; but we did not understand them. At last, when the ship we were in had got in all her cargo, they made ready with many fearful noises, and we were all put under deck, so that we could not see how they managed the vessel. But this disappointment was the least of my sorrow. The stench of the hold while we were on the coast was so intolerably loathsome, that it was dangerous to remain there for any time, and some of us had been permitted to stay on the deck for the fresh air; but now that the whole ship's cargo were confined together, it became absolutely pestilential. The closeness of the place, and the heat of the climate, added to the number in the ship, which was so crowded that each had scarcely room to turn himself, almost suffocated us. This produced copious perspirations, so that the air soon became unfit for respiration, from a variety of loathsome smells, and brought on a sickness among the slaves, of which many died, thus falling victims to the improvident avarice, as I may call it, of their purchasers. This wretched situation was again aggravated by the galling of the chains, now become insupportable; and the filth of the necessary tubs, into which the children often fell, and were almost suffocated. The shrieks of the women, and the groans of the dying, rendered the whole a scene of horror almost inconceivable. Happily perhaps for myself I was soon reduced so low here that it was thought necessary to keep me almost always on deck; and from my extreme youth I was not put in fetters. In this situation I expected every hour to share the fate of my companions, some of whom were almost daily brought upon deck at the point of death, which I began to hope would soon put an end to my miseries.

Often did I think many of the inhabitants of the deep much more happy than myself. I envied them the freedom they enjoyed, and as often wished I could change my condition for theirs. Every circumstance I met with served only to render my state more painful, and heighten my apprehensions, and my opinion of the cruelty of the whites. One day they had taken a number of fishes; and when they had killed and satisfied themselves with as many as they thought fit, to our astonishment who were on the deck, rather than give any of them to us to eat as we expected, they tossed the remaining fish into the sea again, although we begged and prayed for some as well as we could, but in vain; and some of my countrymen, being pressed by hunger, took an opportunity, when they thought no one saw them, of trying to get a little privately; but they were discovered, and the attempt procured them some very severe floggings. One day, when we had a smooth sea and moderate wind, two of my wearied countrymen who were chained together (I was near them at the time), preferring death to such a life of misery, somehow made through the nettings and jumped into the sea: immediately another quite dejected fellow, who, on account of his illness, was suffered to be out of irons, also followed their example; and I believe many more would very soon have done the same if they had not been prevented by the ship's crew, who were instantly alarmed. Those of us that were the most active were in a moment put down under the deck, and there was such a noise and confusion amongst the people of the ship as I never heard before, to stop her, and get the boat out to go after the slaves. However two of the wretches were drowned, but they got the other, and afterwards flogged him unmercifully for thus attempting to prefer death to slavery. In this manner we continued to undergo more hardships than I can now relate, hardships which are inseparable from this accursed trade. Many a time we were near suffocation from the want of fresh air, which we were often without for whole days together. This, and the stench of the necessary tubs, carried off many. During our passage I first saw flying fishes, which surprised me very much: they used frequently to fly across the ship, and many of them fell on the deck. I also now first saw the use of the quadrant; I had often with astonishment seen the mariners make observations with it, and I could not think what it meant. They at last took notice of my surprise; and one of them, willing to increase it, as well as to gratify my curiosity, made me one day look through it. The clouds appeared to me to be land, which disappeared as they passed along. This heightened my wonder; and I was now more persuaded than ever that I was in another world, and that every thing about me was magic. At last we came in sight of the island of Barbadoes, at which the whites on board gave a great shout, and made many signs of joy to us. We did not know what to think of this; but as the vessel drew nearer we plainly saw the harbour, and other ships of different kinds and sizes; and we soon anchored amongst them off Bridge Town. Many merchants and planters now came on board, though it was in the evening. They put us in separate parcels, and examined us attentively. They also made us jump, and pointed to the land, signifying we were to go there. We thought by this we should be eaten by these ugly men, as they appeared to us; and, when soon after we were all put down under the deck again, there was much dread and trembling among us, and nothing but bitter cries to be heard all the night from these apprehensions, insomuch that at last the white people got some old slaves from the land to pacify us. They told us we were not to be eaten, but to work, and were soon to go on land, where we should see many of our country people. This report eased us much; and sure enough, soon after we were landed, there came to us Africans of all languages. We were conducted immediately to the merchant's yard, where we were all pent up together like so many sheep in a fold, without regard to sex or age. As every object was new to me every thing I saw filled me with surprise. What struck me first was that the houses were built with bricks, in stories, and in every other respect different from those in Africa: but I was still more astonished on seeing people on horseback. I did not know what this could mean; and indeed I thought these people were full of nothing but magical arts. While I was in this astonishment one of my fellow prisoners spoke to a countryman of his about the horses, who said they were the same kind they had in their country. I understood them, though they were from a distant part of Africa, and I thought it odd I had not seen any horses there; but afterwards, when I came to converse with different Africans, I found they had many horses amongst them, and much larger than those I then saw. We were not many days in the merchant's custody before we were sold after their usual manner, which is this: On a signal given, (as the beat of a drum) the buyers rush at once into the yard where the slaves are confined, and make choice of that parcel they like best. The noise and clamour with which this is attended, and the eagerness visible in the countenances of the buyers, serve not a little to increase the apprehensions of the terrified Africans, who may well be supposed to consider them as the ministers of that destruction to which they think themselves devoted. In this manner, without scruple, are relations and friends separated, most of them never to see each other again. I remember in the vessel in which I was brought over, in the men's apartment, there were several brothers, who, in the sale, were sold in different lots; and it was very moving on this occasion to see and hear their cries at parting. O, ye nominal Christians! might not an African ask you, learned you this from your God, who says unto you, Do unto all men as you would men should do unto you? Is it not enough that we are torn from our country and friends to toil for your luxury and lust of gain? Must every tender feeling be likewise sacrificed to your avarice? Are the dearest friends and relations, now rendered more dear by their separation from their kindred, still to be parted from each other, and thus prevented from cheering the gloom of slavery with the small comfort of being together and mingling their sufferings and sorrows? Why are parents to lose their children, brothers their sisters, or husbands their wives? Surely this is a new refinement in cruelty, which, while it has no advantage to atone for it, thus aggravates distress, and adds fresh horrors even to the wretchedness of slavery.

Questions for Discussion:
1. What does Equiano's account reveal about the relationship between Europeans and Africans in the 1700s?
2. According to Equiano, how was order maintained on board the slave ship, both among the African slaves and the white crew?
3. How did the Africans on board this ship resist the fate of being enslaved for life?

Olaudah Equiano, *The Interesting Narrative of the Life of Olaudah Equiano, or Gustavus Vassa, The African* (Norwich, The Author, 1794), 46–57.

Britton Hammon, "Out of the Paw of the Lion" (1760)

Britton Hammon's memoir of his adventures as a sailor is a vivid reminder that not all sailors were free, and that slavery was an institution in all the American colonies. Although an enslaved African American, Hammon went to sea with his master's permission, suffered imprisonment for years, served in the Royal Navy, and finally reunited with his master in London by chance. His experiences may not have been so unusual; roughly a quarter of all male African Americans in Massachusetts went to sea. Nonetheless, this is a remarkable account of the many dangers that sailors encountered in the mid-1700s. Hammon's story was published in 1760, making him the first enslaved author to publish in America.

On Monday, 25th Day of *December*, 1747, with the leave of my Master, I went from *Marshfield*, with an Intention to go a Voyage to Sea, and the next Day, the 26th, got to *Plymouth*, where I immediately ship'd myself on board of a Sloop, Capt. *John Howland*, Master, bound to *Jamaica* and the *Bay*.[1] We sailed from *Plymouth* in a short Time, and after a pleasant Passage of about 30 Days, arrived at *Jamaica*; we was detain'd at *Jamaica* only 5 Days, from whence we sailed for the *Bay*, where we arrived safe in 10 Days. We loaded our Vessel with Logwood,[2] and sailed from the *Bay* the 25th Day of *May* following, and the 15th Day of *June*, we were cast away on *Cape-Florida*, about 5 Leagues from the Shore; being now destitute of every Help, we knew not what to do or what Course to take in this our sad Condition: The Captain was advised, intreated, and beg'd on, by every Person on board, to heave over but only 20 Ton of the *Wood*, and we should get clear, which if he had done, might have sav'd his Vessel and Cargo, and not only so, but his own Life, as well as the Lives of the Mate and Nine Hands, as I shall presently relate.

After being upon this Reef two Days, the Captain order'd the Boat to be hoisted out, and then ask'd who were willing to tarry on board? The whole Crew was for going on Shore at this Time, but as the Boat would not carry 12 Persons at once, and to prevent any Uneasiness, the Captain, a Passenger, and one Hand tarry'd on board, while the Mate, with Seven Hands besides myself, were order'd to go on Shore in the Boat, which as soon as we had reached, one half were to be Landed, and the other four to return to the Sloop, to fetch the Captain and the others on Shore. The Captain order'd us to take with us our Arms, Ammunition, Provisions and Necessaries for Cooking, as also a Sail to make a Tent of, to shelter us from the Weather; after having left the Sloop we stood towards the Shore, and being within Two Leagues

---

1 Bay: Bay of Compeche, in Central America.
2 Logwood: a kind of tree that grows in Central America. In Hammon's time it was highly valued as a commercial dye.

of the same, we espy'd a Number of Canoes, which we at first took to be Rocks, but soon found our Mistake, for we perceiv'd they moved towards us; we presently saw an English Colour hoisted in one of the Canoes, at the Sight of which we were not a little rejoiced, but on our advancing yet nearer, we found them, to our very great Surprize, to be *Indians* of which there were Sixty; being now so near them we could not possibly make our Escape; they soon came up with and boarded us, took away all our Arms Ammunition, and Provision. The whole Number of Canoes (being about Twenty), then made for the Sloop, except Two which they left to guard us, who order'd us to follow on with them; the Eighteen which made for the Sloop, went so much faster than we that they got on board above Three Hours before we came along side, and had kill'd Captain *Howland*, the Passenger and the other hand; we came to the Larboard side of the Sloop, and they order'd us round to the Starboard, and as we were passing round the Bow, we saw the whole Number of *Indians*, advancing forward and loading their Guns, upon which the Mate said, *"my Lads we are all dead Men,"* and before we had got round, they discharged their Small Arms upon us, and kill'd Three of our hands, viz. *Reuben Young of Cape-Cod*, Mate; *Joseph Little* and *Lemuel Doty* of *Plymouth*, upon which I immediately jump'd overboard, chusing rather to be drowned, than to be kill'd by those barbarous and inhuman Savages. In three or four Minutes after, I heard another Volley which dispatched the other five, viz. *John Nowland*, and *Nathaniel Rich*, both belonging to *Plymouth*, and *Elkanah Collymore*, and *James Webb*, Strangers, and *Moses Newmock*, Molatto. As soon as they had kill'd the whole of the People, one of the Canoes paddled after me, and soon came up with me, hawled me into the Canoe, and beat me most terribly with a Cut-lass, after that they ty'd me down, then this Canoe stood for the Sloop again and as soon as she came along side, the *Indians* on board the Sloop betook themselves to their Canoes, then set the Vessel on Fire, making a prodigious shouting and hallowing like so many Devils. As soon as the Vessel was burnt down to the Water's edge, the *Indians* stood for the Shore, together with our Boat, on board of which they put 5 hands. After we came to the Shore, they led me to their Huts, where I expected nothing but immediate Death, and as they spoke broken English, were often telling me, while coming from the Sloop to the Shore, that they intended to roast me alive. But the Providence of God order'd it otherways, for He appeared for my Help, *in this Mount*

of Difficulty, and they were better to me then my Fears, and soon un-
bound me, but set a Guard over me every Night. They kept me with
them about five Weeks, during which Time they us'd me pretty well,
and gave me boil'd Corn, which was what they often eat themselves.
The Way I made my Escape from these Villains was this; A Spanish Schooner arriving there from *St. Augustine*, the Master of which,
whose Name was *Romond*, asked the *Indians* to let me go on board
his Vessel, which they granted, and the Captain[1] knowing me very
well, weigh'd Anchor and carry'd me off to the *Havanna*, and after
being there four Days the *Indians* came after me, and insisted on having me again, as I was their Prisoner;—They made Application to the
Governor, and demanded me again from him; in answer to which the
Governor told them, that as they had put the whole Crew to Death,
they should not have me again, and so paid them Ten Dollars for me,
adding, that he would not have them kill any Person hereafter, but
take as many of them as they could, of those that should be cast away,
and bring them to him, for which he would pay them Ten Dollars a-
head. At the *Havanna* I lived with the Governor in the Castle about
a Twelve-month, where I was walking thro' the Street, I met with a
Press-Gang who immediately prest me, and put me into Goal, and
with a Number of others I was confin'd till next Morning, when we
were all brought out, and ask'd who would go on board the King's
Ships, four of which having been lately built, were bound to *Old-
Spain*, and on my refusing to serve on board, they put me in a close
Dungeon, where I was confin'd *Four Years and seven months*; during
which Time I often made application to the Governor, by Persons who
came to see the Prisoners, but they never acquainted him with it, nor
did he know all this Time what became of me, which was the means
of my being confin'd there so long. But kind Providence so order'd it,
that after I had been in this Place so long as the Time mention'd above
the Captain of a Merchantman, belonging to *Boston*, having sprung a
Leak was obliged to put into the *Havanna* to refit, and while he was at
Dinner at Mrs. *Betty Howard's*, she told the Captain of my deplorable
Condition, and said she would be glad, if he could by some means or
other relieve me; The Captain told Mrs. *Howard* he would use his best
Endeavours for my Relief and Enlargement.

---

1   Hammon noted, "The Way I came to know this Gentleman was, by his being taken last
     War by an English Privateer, and brought into Jamaica, while I was there."

Accordingly, after Dinner, came to the Prison, and ask'd the Keeper if he might see me; upon his Request I was brought out of the Dungeon, and after the Captain had Interrogated me, told me, he would intercede with the Governor for my Relief out of that miserable Place, which he did, and the next Day the Governor sent an Order to release me; I lived with the Governor about a Year after I was delivered from the Dungeon, in which Time I endeavour'd three Times to make my Escape, the last of which proved effectual; the first Time I got on board of Captain *Marsh*, an *English* Twenty Gun Ship, with a Number of others, and lay on board conceal'd that Night; and the next Day the Ship being under sail, I thought myself safe, and so made my Appearance upon Deck, but as soon as we were discovered the Captain ordered the Boat out, and sent us all on Shore. I intreated the Captain to let me, in particular, tarry on board, begging, and crying to him, to commiserate my unhappy Condition, and added, that I had been confin'd almost five Years in a close Dungeon, but the Captain would not hearken to any Intreaties, for fear of having the Governor's Displeasure, and so was obliged to go on Shore.

After being on Shore another Twelvemonth, I endeavour'd to make my Escape the second Time, by trying to get on board of a Sloop bound to *Jamaica*, and as I was going from the City to the Sloop, was unhappily taken by the Guard, and ordered back to the Castle, and there confined.—However, in a short Time I was set at Liberty, and order'd with a Number of others to carry the *Bishop*[1] from the Castle, thro' the Country, to confirm the old People, baptize Children, &c. for which he receives large Sums of Money. I was employ'd in this Service about Seven Months, during which Time I lived very well, and then returned to the Castle again, where I had my Liberty to walk about the City, and do Work for my self;—The *Beaver*, an *English* Man of War then lay in the Harbour, and having been informed by some of the Ship's Crew that she was to sail in a few Days, I had nothing now to do, but to seek an Opportunity how I should make my Escape.

Accordingly one Sunday Night the Lieutenant of the Ship with a Number of the Barge Crew were in a Tavern, and Mrs. *Howard* who had before been a Friend to me, interceded with the Lieutenant to carry me on board: the Lieutenant said he would with all his Heart,

1   Hammon here noted, "He is carried (by Way of Respect) in a large Two-arm Chair; the Chair is lin'd with crimson Velvet, and supported by eight Persons."

and immediately I went on board in the Barge. The next Day the *Spaniards* came along side the *Beaver*, and demanded me again, with a Number of others who had made their Escape from them, and got on board the Ship, but just before I did; but the Captain, who was a true *Englishman*, refus'd them, and said he could not answer it, to deliver up any *Englishmen* under *English* Colours. In a few Days we set Sail for *Jamaica*, where we arrived safe, after a short and pleasant Passage.

After being at *Jamaica* a short Time we sail'd for *London*, as convoy to a Fleet of Merchantmen, who all arrived safe in the *Downs*, I was turned over to another Ship, the *Arcenceil*, and there remained about a Month. From this Ship I went on board the *Sandwich* of 90 Guns; on board the *Sandwich*, I tarry'd 6 Weeks, and then was order'd on board the *Hercules*, Capt. *John Porter*, a 74 Gun Ship, we sail'd on a Cruize, and met with a *French* 84 Gun Ship, and had a very smart Engagement,[1] in which about 70 of our Hands were Kill'd and Wounded, the Captain lost his Leg in the Engagement, and I was Wounded in the Head by a small Shot. We should have taken this Ship, if they had not cut away the most of our Rigging; however, in about three Hours after, a 64 Gun Ship, came up with and took her. I was discharged from the *Hercules* the 12th Day of *May* 1759 (having been on board of that Ship 3 Months) on account of my being disabled in the Arm, and render'd incapable of Service, after being honourably paid the Wages due to me. I was put into the *Greenwich* Hospital[2] where I stay'd and soon recovered. I then ship'd myself a Cook on board Captain *Martyn*, an arm'd Ship in the King's Service. I was on board this Ship almost Two Months, and after being paid my Wages, was discharg'd in the Month of *October*. After my discharge from Captain *Martyn*, I was taken sick in *London* of a Fever, and was confin'd about 6 Weeks, where I expended all my Money, and left in very poor Circumstances; and unhappy for me I knew nothing of my *good Master's* being in *London* at this my very difficult Time. After I got well of my sickness, I ship'd myself on board of a large Ship bound to *Guinea*, and being in a publick House one Evening, I overheard a Number of Persons talking about Rigging a Vessel bound to *New-England*, I ask'd them to what Part of *New-England* this Vessel

---

1   Hammon notes, "A particular Account of this Engagement, has been Publish'd in the *Boston* News-Papers."

2   Greenwich Hospital: a hospital just outside London established to take care of sick, aged, or disabled sailors.

was bound? They told me, to *Boston*; and having ask'd them who was Commander? They told me, Capt. *Watt*; in a few Minutes after this the Mate of the Ship came in, and I ask'd him if Captain *Watt* did not want a Cook, who told me he did, and that the Captain would be in, in a few Minutes; and in about half an Hour the Captain came in, and then I ship'd myself at once, after begging off from the Ship bound to *Guinea*; I work'd on board Captain *Watt's* Ship almost Three Months, before she sail'd, and one Day being at Work in the Hold, I overheard some Persons on board mention the Name of *Winslow*, at the Name of which I was very inquisitive, and having ask'd what *Winslow* they were talking about? They told me it was *General Winslow*; and that he was one of the Passengers, I ask'd them what *General Winslow*? For I never knew *my good Master*, by that Title before; but after enquiring more particularly I found it must be *Master*, and in a few Days Time the Truth was joyfully verify'd by a happy Sight of his Person, which so overcome me, that I could not speak to him for some Time. *My good Master* was exceeding glad to see me, telling me that I was like one arose from the Dead, for he thought I had been Dead a great many Years, having heard nothing of me for almost Thirteen Years.

I think I have not deviated from Truth, in any particular of this my Narrative, and tho' I have omitted a great many Things, yet what is wrote may suffice to convince the Reader, that I have been most grievously afflicted, and yet thro' the Divine Goodness, as miraculously preserved, and delivered out of many Dangers; of which I desire to retain a *grateful Remembrance*, as long as I live in the World.

And now, That in the Providence of that GOD, who delivered his Servant David *out of the Paw of the Lion and out of the Paw of the Bear, I am freed from a* long *and* dreadful Captivity, among worse Savages than they; *And am return'd to my* own Native Land, to Shew how Great Things the Lord hath done for Me; *I would call upon all Men, and Say,* O Magnifie the Lord with Me, and let us Exalt his Name together! O that Men would Praise the Lord for His Goodness, and for his Wonderful Works to the Children of Men!

Questions for Discussion:
1. How did Hammon's race impact how Indians, Spaniards, and Englishmen treated him?
2. How did Hammon's life as a sailor give him opportunities and trouble that other enslaved Africans did not have?

3. How does Hammon's experience reflect the idea of an Atlantic World?

Britton Hammon, *A Narrative of the Uncommon Sufferings and Surprizing Deliverance of Britton Hammon, A Negro Man* (Boston: Green & Russell, 1760).

Various, "Run Away" (1745–1766)

African American seafarers, both enslaved and free, formed an important component of colonial America's maritime population. Furthermore, enslaved African Americans were valuable property that slavemasters were anxious to recover if they escaped. Newspaper advertisements for such escaped slaves were common fare in colonial newspapers, frequently offering sizable rewards. Such ads also reminded shipmasters that the punishment for carrying away a runaway slave was severe.

One element revealed in these ads is that black sailors, like other seafarers, were a highly mobile set of individuals. Their combined experiences linked black communities in Africa, the Caribbean, North America, and even European commercial centers like London. These ads also reveal details of black sailors' dress, conduct, activities, and even speech not found elsewhere, providing a rare insight into their daily lives.

The Pennsylvania Gazette, Philadelphia, July 4, 1745:

RUN away from the Sloop *Sparrow*, lately arrived from Barbadoes, Joseph Perry Commander, a Negro Man named John; he WAS BORN IN DOMINICA AND SPEAKS FRENCH, BUT VERY LITTLE ENGLISH, he is a very ill-featured Fellow, and has been much cut in his Back by often Whipping; his Clothing was only a Frock and Trowsers. Whoever brings him to John Yeats, Merchants in Philadelphia, shall have Twenty Shillings Reward, and reasonable Charges, paid by John Yeats.

The Pennsylvania Gazette, November 7, 1745:

Whereas Negro Jo (who formerly lived with Samuel Ogle, Esq.; then Governor of Maryland, as his cook) about 13 Months ago run away from the Subscriber, who was then at Annapolis, AND HAS SINCE BEEN OUT A VOYAGE IN ONE OF THE PRIVATEERS BELONGING TO PHILADELPHIA, and is returned there: These are to desire any Person to apprehend the said Negro, so that he may be had again, for which on their acquainting me therewith, they shall be rewarded with the Sum of Five Pounds, current Money: Or if the said

Negro will return to me, at my House in St. Mary's County, he shall be kindly received, and escape all Punishment for his Offence.
Philip Key.

Boston Weekly News-Letter, January 23, 1746:

RAN AWAY from his Master, Capt. John Steel, at the North End of Boston, the 17th Instant, a Young Negro Fellow, named Pompey SPEAKS PRETTY GOOD ENGLISH is about 19 or 20 Years of Age, is short in Stature and pretty long visaged, has been used to change his name; he had on a great Ratteen Coat, Waistcoat and Breeches, the coat pretty old, with white Metal Buttons, a Cotton and linnen Shirt, and ordinary Worsted Cap, and grey Yarn Stockings, he took with him an old Hat, and a Leather Jockey Cap, a pair of old black Stockings, and a new Ozenbrigs Frock: He has made several Attempts to get off in some Vessel, therefore all Masters of Vessels are cautioned not to entertain him.

Whoever shall apprehend the said Negro and carry him to said Master shall have Five Pounds old Tenor, and necessary Charges paid by John Steel.

The Pennsylvania Gazette, Philadelphia, July 3, 1746:

Run away from Samuel M'Call, jun. a Negro Man, named Tom, a very likely Fellow, about 22 or 23 Years of Age, about 5 Foot 10 Inches high, speaks good English, HAS BEEN A PRIVATEERING; has several good Cloaths on, with Check Shirts, some new; formerly belonged to Dr. Shaw of Burlington. Whoever secures the said Negro in any County Gaol[1] so that his Master may have him again, shall have a Pistole[2] Reward and reasonable Charges paid by Samuel M'Call.

N.B. He is a sensible, active Fellow, and runs well.

The Pennsylvania Gazette, Philadelphia, June 23, 1748:

RUN away from John Potts of Colebrookdale, Philadelphia county, Esq., about the 10th inst., a Spanish Negro Fellow, named John, of middle stature, about 30 years of age: Had on when he went away, only a shirt and trowsers, a cotton cap, a pair of old shoes; he is a cunning fellow and subject to make game at the ceremonial part of all reli-

---

1   Gaol: jail.
2   Pistole: gold coin.

gious worship except that of the papists; he is proud, and dislikes to be called a negroe, HAS FORMERLY BEEN A PRIVATEERING, and talks much (with a seeming pleasure) of the cruelties he then committed. Whoever takes up said Negroe, and takes him to his Master at Colebrookdale aforesaid, or secures him in any gaol shall have Thirty Shilling reward, and reasonable charges, paid by said John Potts or Thomas York.

The Boston Evening Post, October 3, 1748:

RAN away on the 19th of this Instant September, from his Master JOHN JOHNSON, of Boston, Jack-maker, a Negro Man Servant, named Joe, about 23 Years of Age, a likely Fellow, who had on when he went away a dark colored Fly Coat, with flat white Metal Buttons, a Swan Skin double breasted Jacket, Leather Deer Skin Breeches, a pair of high heel'd thick soled Shoes. He can play on the Flute, has a Scar on his upper Lip and SPEAKS GOOD ENGLISH. Whoever shall take him up and deliver him to his said Master, shall have Ten Pounds Reward, Old Tenor, and all reasonable Charges paid. All Masters of Vessels and others, are hereby cautioned against harbouring, concealing or carrying off said Negro, as they will avoid the Penalty of the Law.

Maryland Gazette, Annapolis, April 11, 1754:
Fifty Pistoles Reward
Annapolis, in Maryland, March 25, 1754.

RAN away on the 18th Instant with the Sloop *Hopewell*, belonging to the Subscriber, William Curtis, Master, the TWO FOLLOWING CONVICT SERVANTS, AND NEGRO MAN, viz: John Wright, a White Man, of a swarthy Complexion, very lusty, talks hoarse, and is much pitted with the Small Pox. John Smith, also a lusty White Man, with short black Hair. Toney, a yellowish Negro, and not quite so lusty, pretends to be a Portugese, speaks good English and pertly, is a good Hand by Water, also can do Cooper's Work, Butchering, &c. Had on or with him, a Dove colour'd Surtoot Coat.

They may have sundry Cloaths, Wigs, Linnen, Cash &c. belonging to the Captain, as it is believed they have murdered him; and the above Wright was seen with the Captain's Cloaths on, which were red; though he had Cloaths of sundry Colours with him: He also had a neat Silver hilted Sword, and Pistols mounted with Silver.

The Captain had the Register of the Sloop with him, but he was not endorsed thereon, as he was to return here to make up his Load, and clear at the proper Office. They were seen off Patuxent on the 22nd Instant, at which time the said Wright assumed Master, and took two Men with them, belonging to Schooner of Mr. James Dick's and Company one a White Man belonging to Capt. William Strachan, of London Town, who went on board with some Bread for them, at which Time they hoisted Sail, and cut their Boat adrift, and carried them off.

They had some Lumber on board, such as Staves, Heading, and Plank; also Rum, Molasses, Sugar, Linnen &c. &c.

The Sloop is about 45 Tons, Square sterned, with a Round House, with a Partition under dividing the Cabin and Steerage, the Waste black, yellow Gunwales and Drift Rails, and the Drift and Stern blue.

Whoever secures the said sloop and Goods so that the Owner may have her again, and the three White Servants and two Slaves, so that they may be brought to Justice, shall have FIFTY PISTOLES Reward, paid by
Patrick Creagh.

The Maryland Gazette, March 20, 1755:
Ten Pistoles Reward
Kent County Maryland, March 19, 1755.

WHEREAS THERE WERE SEVERAL Advertisements, (some of which were printed, and others of the same Signification written), dispersed through this Province, describing and offering a Reward of Two Pistoles, &c. for taking up a SERVANT MAN, NAMED JAMES FRANCIS, AND A MULATTO MAN SLAVE call'd Toby, both belonging to the subscriber, and ran away on the 11th Instant: And whereas it has been discovered since the Publishing of the said Advertisements, that they carried with them many more Things than is therein described, I do hereby again and farther give Notice that the White Man James Francis, is aged about 21 years, his Stature near five Feet and a half, slender bodied, with a smooth Face, almost beardless, born in England and bred a Farmer. The Mulatto is a lusty, well-set Country born Slave with a great Nose, wide Nostrils, full mouth'd, many Pimples in his Face; very slow in Speech, he is a tolerable Cooper and House Carpeter, and no doubt will endeavour to pass for a Free-Man;

Each hath a Felt Hat, Country Cloth Vest and Breeches, and Yarn Stockings: one of them has a light coloured loose Coat of Whitney or Duffel: The White Man a dark close bodied Coat, a striped short Vest of Everlasting, another of blue Fearnothing, with other Cloaths. The Slave has also many other valuable Garments; they took with them likewise a Gun, Powder and Shot, and are supposed either to cross, or go down Bay in a Pettiauger.[1]

Whoever brings the said Servant and Slave to the Subscriber on the Mouth of Chester River or to Thomas Ringgold at Chester-Town, shall have for a Reward Ten Pistoles and all reasonable Charges in taking and securing the said Servant and Slave, paid by
James Ringgold. Thomas Ringgold.

The New York Gazette, November 10, 1760:
Forty Dollars Reward

And all reasonable charges shall be paid to any Person that secures and brings to William Kelly, of the City of New York, merchant a Negro man named Norton Minors, who ran away from his masters Messrs. Bodkin and Ferrall of the Island of St. Croix, on the 1st day of July last; is by trade a Caulker and ship-carpenter; has lived at Newbury, in New-England; was the property of Mr. Mark Quane, who sold him to Mr. Craddock of Nevis, from whom the above gentlemen bought him about three years ago; is about 5 feet 8 inches high; age about 37 years; SPEAKS GOOD ENGLISH, CAN READ AND WRITE; AND IS A VERY SENSIBLE FELLOW: And his masters suspect he came off in the sloop Boscawen, Andrew Ford, Master, who sailed from the above Island the very day this fellow eloped, bound for Louisbourg.[2]

The New York Gazette, November 10, 1760:

RAN AWAY on the 9th Instant, October, in the Morning from the Subscriber, a Negro Man named JACK, a well set Fellow, about 5 feet 8 Inches high, full fac'd, much pitted with the Small-pox, snuffles when he speaks, READS ENGLISH, PRETENDS MUCH TO UNDERSTAND THE SCRIPTURES. Had on when he went away a Pair

---

1   Pettiauger: a small open boat.
2   Louisbourg: probably Louisbourg, a fortified French settlement on Cape Breton Island in modern-day Canada.

of Course Trowsers, stripped Jacket, and a Frock over it. Whoever takes up said Fellow and brings him to the subscriber shall have forty shillings and all reasonable Charges paid. All Masters of Vessels &c. are desired not to harbour him, or carry him off, as he or they may depend on being prosecuted as the Law directs.
Manuel Myers,
Linging in Stone Street.

The Boston Gazette and Country Journal, July 6, 1761:

RAN-away on the 28th Day of June 1761, from his Master, Ephraim Swift of Falmouth in the County of Barnstable, A Negro Man Servant named Peter, about 27 or 28 Years old, SPEAKS GOOD ENGLISH: had on when he went away a Beaveret Hat, a green worsted Capt, a close bodied Coat coloured with a green narrow Frieze Cape, a Great Coat, a black and white homespun Jacket, a flannel checked Shirt, grey yarn Stockings; also a flannel Jacket, and a Bundle of other Cloaths, and a Violin. He is very tall Fellow.

Whosoever shall apprehend the said Negro Fellow and commit him to any of his Majesty's Gaols, or secure him so as that his Master may have him again, shall have Five Dollars Reward, and all necessary Charges paid.
Ephraim Swift.

All Masters of Vessels and others are cautioned not to carry off or conceal the said Negro, as they would avoid the Penalty of the Law.

The New York Gazette or the Weekly Post-Boy, July 31, 1766:

RAN away from the Subscriber living in New-York, the Beginning of June Inst. a Negro Fellow named Charles, about five Feet ten Inches, very black, Pock-pitted, and remarkable for his white Teeth; SPEAKS BOTH FRENCH AND ENGLISH, JAMAICA BORN, marked under his left Breast P.C. Count; had on when he went away, a brown Jacket, and a blue short Waistcoat under it; a Pair of Trowsers, and a Sailor's round Hat. Whoever takes up said Negro, and secures him so that he may be had again shall have FORTY SHILLINGS Reward and all reasonable Charges paid by Andrew Myer in Dock-street.

N.B. All Masters of Vessels and others are hereby warned not to carry off said Servant, at their Peril, as they will answer as the law directs.

Questions for Discussion:

1. What do these advertisements reveal about interracial relations in the eighteenth century?

2. What patterns can be discerned from the above items that relate to the idea of an Atlantic World?

3. What does this document reveal about the seafaring experiences of black mariners in the eighteenth century?

"Eighteenth Century Slaves as Advertised by Their Masters," *The Journal of Negro History* 1, no. 2 (April 1916): 163–216.

UNRULY JACK TARS

Much of the tumult that presaged the American Revolution took place in coastal waters and the streets and wharves of seaports. Seafarers led American resistance to British colonial rule, a point best made by Jesse Lemisch's seminal 1968 article, "Jack Tar in the Streets."[1] In part this was because ports were where the most visible signs of royal authority existed, such as customhouses, admiralty courts, and the Royal Navy.

Lemisch argues that impressment, the British Navy's practice of forcing seafarers to serve on its warships, was deeply resented by seafarers and port communities. The presence of the Royal Navy's warships in colonial waters often had the effect of suppressing shipborne commerce as mariners feared they would be impressed. In both British and colonial ports, riots often broke out when "press gangs" came ashore and seized both sailors and landsmen. This should hardly be surprising given that these press gangs sometimes swept up hundreds of men at a time with little regard for their local status or if they were actually seamen or not.

Many of the British reforms that sparked so much American ire after 1763 were adjustments of maritime policy (especially a clamp-down on smuggling), and thus made sailors and others reliant on shipping increasingly restive. These problems grew worse with time, as Americans rejected several parliamentary efforts to tax American commerce. The 1770 Boston massacre, in which British soldiers shot several sailors and laborers, including a seaman of mixed ancestry named Crispus Attucks, exacerbated

---

1   Jesse Lemisch, "Jack Tar in the Streets: Merchant Seamen in the Politics of Revolutionary America," *William and Mary Quarterly* 3rd ser., 25, no. 3 (July 1968): 371–407.

anti-British feeling in the colonies. In 1772, Rhode Islanders, angry at the commander of HMS *Gaspee* for his strict enforcement of the Navigation Acts, burned that vessel one night after it ran aground. The British government moved to alleviate the situation by reducing taxes on colonial goods, with the lone exception of tea. The well-known result was the Boston Tea Party of December, 1773. Less well-known is that British tea faced similar opposition in other colonial ports like Philadelphia.

The following items illustrate how American maritime communities banded together to defy British authority. The first document is an official report on an anti-impressment riot in Boston. The second is the deposition of a British naval officer who had to deal with the wrath of angry Rhode Islanders who resented the Royal Navy's heavy-handed enforcement of the Navigation Acts. The third is the resolutions of patriots anxious to prevent entry of the detested tea into their port, a Philadelphian version of the Boston Tea Party.

William Shirley, "Knowles Riot" (1747)

The greatest of the impressment riots was the Knowles riot, which occurred in Boston in 1747. When the squadron under the command of Commodore Charles Knowles (1704–1777) sent press gangs ashore to press men for his fleet, both sailors and townspeople rose up in a violent protest. In a three-day-long inversion of the social hierarchy, the crowd seized a naval officer, beat local law enforcement officials, threatened the governor, smashed the windows of government buildings, and captured and burned a boat they believed belonged to the Royal Navy.

This report is written by William Shirley (1694–1771), the Royal Governor of Massachusetts, an Englishman sent out by the British government to administer this sometimes troublesome colony. Note in particular the response of Shirley and other British officials, who were willing to resort to massive violence to contain what they regarded as a mob out of control, and their ideas about Boston's democratic form of governance.

MY LORDS,

A riot, and Insult upon the King's Government lately happen'd here of so extraordinary a nature, that I think it my Duty to give your Lordships an Account of it.

It was occasion'd by an Impress made on the sixteenth of November at night out of all the Vessels in this Harbour, by Order of Commodore

Knowles, then on Board the *Canterbury*, for manning his Squadron; in which he confin'd himself to the Vessels on float,[1] and with design I am perswaded, to release upon a proper Application[2] the Inhabitants of the Town (three of which being Carpenter's Apprentices happen'd to be taken by the Press Gang in their general sweep) and as many of the Seamen belonging to outward bound Vessells, as could reasonably be desir'd; but the Tumult, which this proceeding produc'd, began early the next day before he was apply'd to for the discharge of any of the Impress'd Men, or had an Account given him of 'em.

The first notice, I had of the Mob, was given me between nine and ten o'clock in the forenoon by the Speaker of the House of Representatives, who had Pick'd up in the Streets Captain Derby of his Majesty's Ship *Alborough*, and the Purser of the *Canterbury*, and brought 'em under his Protection to me for Shelter in my House acquainting me at the same time, that the Mob consisted of about three hundred Seamen, all Strangers, (the greatest part Scotch) with Cutlasses and Clubs, and that they had seiz'd and detain'd in their Custody a Lieutenant of the *Lark*, whom they met with at his lodgings on Shoar; The next notice I had was about half an hour after by the Sheriff of the County, who with some of his Officers had been in pursuit of the Mob in order to recover the Man of War's Lieutenant, and to endeavour to disperse 'em; and who coming up with four of 'em separated from the others, had wrested a Cutlass from one and seiz'd two of 'em ; but being overtaken by the whole Mob, (who were appriz'd of this) as he was carrying those two to Goal, was assaulted, and Grievously wounded by 'em, and forc'd to deliver up his two Prisoners, and leave one of his Deputies in their hands, for whose life he assur'd me he was in fear.

Thereupon I immediately sent Orders to the Colonel of the Regiment to raise the Militia of the Town and suppress the Mob by force, and, if need was, to fire upon 'em with Ball; which were scarcely deliver'd to him, when they appear'd before my Gates, and part of 'em advanced directly through my Court yard up to my Door with the Lieutenant, two other Sea Officers and Mr. Knowles's Menial Servant in their Custody, that part of the Mob which stay'd at the outward Gate crying out to the party at my Door not to give up any of their Prison-

---

1   On float: Commodore Knowles promised to only impress seamen from ships in the harbor, not from the streets of Boston.

2   Release upon a proper Application: Knowles promised to release townspeople unintentionally scooped up by the press gangs.

ers to me. Upon this I immediately went out to 'em and demanded the cause of the Tumult, to which one of 'em arm'd with a Cutlass answer'd me in an Insolent manner it was caus'd by my unjustifiable Impress Warrant; whereupon I told 'em that the Impress was not made by my Warrant, nor with my knowledge; but that he was a very Impudent Rascal for his behaviour; and upon his still growing more Insolent, my Son in Law[1] who happen'd to follow me out, struck his Hat off his head, asking him if he knew, who he was talking to; this immediately silenced their Clamour, when I demanded of 'em, where the King's Officers were, that they had seiz'd; and they being shewn to me, I went up to the Lieutenant and bid him go into my House, and upon his telling me the Mob would not suffer him, I took him from among 'em, and putting him before me caus'd him to go in, as I did likewise the other three and follow'd 'em without Exchanging more words with the Mob, that I might avoid making any Promises or Terms with 'em; But my Son in Law, with the Speaker of the Assembly, the Colonel of the Regiment, and Captain of the *Massachusetts* Frigate,[2] who were now come into the House, stood some time at the Door parlying and endeavouring to Pacify 'em 'till upon the Tumult's increasing, and their threatening to recover the Sea Officers by force, if I did not deliver "em up again, or the Lieutenant did not come out to 'em and swear that he was not concern'd in the Impress, I sent an Under Sheriff, then lately come into my House, to desire the Gentlemen to let 'em know that I should consent to neither; and to retire into the House; and arm'd the Officers, who were now seven or eight in number, to stand upon their Defence, in case the Mob should be so outrageous, as to attempt to break into the House, and had the Door shut against 'em; upon which the Mob beset the House round, made some feint appearances of Attempting to force the Door open, abus'd the Under-sheriff in my Court yard (whom they beat and at last put in the Publick Stocks) and after behaving in a Tumultuous manner before the House about half an hour, left it.

By noon all the Officers of Mr. Knowles's Squadron of any Rank, who were on Shoar, except Captn. Erskine of the *Canterbury* (who had retir'd out of Town, where he was the day after, confin'd by a Mob) had retir'd to my House; and several Officers of my own, and the two

---

1   Son in Law: William Bollan.
2   *Massachusetts* Frigate: an armed ship operated by the colony, as opposed to a Royal Navy vessel.

Canada Regiments[1] came there to offer their Service for the protection of it; and about four in the afternoon I went to the Council Chamber the General Assembly being then sitting, to propose the immediate issuing of a Proclamation for dispersing the Mob, and discovering and apprehending the Ringleaders and others concern'd in it, and the same being just passed by the Board and the reward to be given being then under Consideration, the Mob now increas'd and join'd by some Inhabitants came to the Town House (just after candle light) arm'd as in the morning, assaulted the Council Chamber (myself and the Council being then sitting there and the House of Representatives adjourn'd) by throwing Stones and Brickbatts in at the Windows, and having broke all the Windows of the lower floor, where a few of the Militia Officers were assembled, forcibly enter'd into it, and oblig'd most of the Officers to retire up into the Council Chamber; where the Mob was expected soon to follow 'em up; but prevented by some few of the Officers below, who behav'd better.

In this Confusion two popular Members of the Council endeavour'd, but in vain, to appease the Mob by speaking to 'em from the Balcony of the Council Chamber; after which the Speaker of the House and others of the Assembly press'd me much to speak two or three words to 'em, only promising to use my endeavours with Mr. Knowles to get the Impress'd Inhabitants and some of the outward bound Seamen discharg'd; which, against my Inclinations, and to prevent their charging any bad Consequences, which might happen from this Tumult upon my refusal, I yielded to; and in this Parley one of the Mob, an Inhabitant of the Town call'd upon me to deliver up the Lieutenant of the *Lark*, which I refus'd to do; after which among other things he demanded of me, why a Boy, one Warren now under Sentence of death in Goal for being concern'd in a Press Gang, which kill'd two Sailors in this Town in the Act of Impressing, was not Executed; and I acquaint'd 'em his Execution was suspended by his Majesty's order 'till his pleasure shall be known upon it; whereupon the same Person, who was the Mob's Spokesman ask'd me "if I did not remember Porteous's Case[2] who was hang'd upon a sign post in Edinburgh." I told 'em very well, and that I hop'd they remember'd what the Consequence

---

1   Canada Regiments: units of colonial troops raised to fight the French in Canada.
2   Porteous's Case: during a 1736 riot in Edinburgh, John Porteous ordered his troops to
    fire into a crowd, killing several people. A few months later the people of Edinburgh
    lynched him.

of that proceeding was to the Inhabitants of the City; after which I thought it high time to make an end of parleying with the Mob, and retir'd into the Council Chamber: The Issue of this was that the Mob said they would call again at the Council Chamber the next day to know whether the Impressed men were Discharg'd; and went off to a Dock Yard upon proposal made among 'em to burn a Twenty gun ship now building there for his Majesty; whereupon I went to my own House accompanied with a party of Officers, Sir William Pepperrell,[1] and the Gentlemen of the Council; within a quarter of an Hour after which the Mob, who had been diverted from their purpose against the King's Ship by the sudden coming to shoar of a Barge, which they took to belong to one of Mr. Knowles's Squadron, seiz'd and carry'd it in Procession through the Town with an Intention to burn it in my Court Yard; upon which I order'd a party of Officers to go out and oppose their Entrance at my Outward Gate, which about ten of 'em immediately did, and upon the Appearance of the Mob's preparing to force that Gate open, Cock'd and presented their Muskets at 'em through an open Palisade fence, and had fir'd upon 'em, if Sir William Pepperrell had not instantly call'd out to the Officers to hold, 'till such, who might only be Spectators could be warn'd to separate from among the Mob; which they perceiving, and that the windows of the House were likewise lin'd with arm'd Officers, desisted and immediately alter'd their Scheme to that of burning the Barge in an out part of the Common, not discovering, 'till after it was burnt, that it really belong'd to a Master of a Scotch Vessell one of their Ringleaders. The Mob then separated and distributed themselves at the different Wharves and Ferry places, and at the Town Gates and other parts, to prevent any of the Sea Officers escaping out of the Town either by Water or Land in the Night; but at twelve o'clock I furnished Captain Derby and Captain Tailer and the Lieutt. of the *Lark*, with Horses out of my own Stable, and sent my Coachman with 'em for their guide, who conducted 'em along the beach clear of the Town Gates and Mob, about six miles out of Town, to a place where I order'd the Castle Barge[2] to be sent for 'em the next morning, and so they got safe on board Mr. Knowles.

The day following Mr. Knowles upon hearing of these outrages

---

1   Sir William Pepperell: a Massachusetts soldier in charge of that province's military efforts, recently knighted for capturing the French fortress of Louisbourg in Canada.
2   Castle Barge: the boat belonging to Castle William, the fort at the entrance to Boston harbor.

wrote me word, that he purpos'd to bring his whole Squadron before the Town[1] the next morning, but I dissuaded him from it, by
an immediate Answer to his Letter: In the Evening the Mob forcibly
search'd the Navy Hospital upon the Town Common in order to let
out what Seamen they could find there belonging to the King's Ships;
and seven or eight Private Houses for Officers, and took four or five
petty Officers; but soon releas'd 'em without any ill Usage, as they did
the same day Captain Erskine, whom they had suffer'd to remain in
a Gentleman's House upon his Parole, their chief intent appearing to
be, from the beginning, not to use the Officers ill any otherwise than
by detaining 'em, in hopes of Obliging Mr. Knowles to give up the
Impress'd men.

Your Lordships will doubtless by this time think the Militia of the
Town very tardy in not appearing yet under Arms, pursuant to my Orders for suppressing this outrageous Tumult; I thought 'em inexcus-
able and express'd my resentment at it by ordering three of the next
County Regiments, and part of the Regiment of Horse to be forthwith
rais'd, in Order to proceed to Boston, and in the mean time retiring
out of the Town, 'till I could assemble that force to quell the Insurrec-
tion; whereupon the Town has done everything in their power since,
to express their Abhorrence of these proceedings, and atone for their
Neglect; and though I think nothing can be said sufficient to excuse
'em, yet several things, may in extenuation of their faultiness; as the
suddenness of the Tumult, their not rightly understanding the Notice
given 'em by their Officers of my Orders, the mistaken notion that the
Impress was made on shoar; in which Persons had been haul'd out of
their beds and others wounded; which prov'd entirely false; that three
hundred men were Impress'd, whereas no more than forty eight were;
that many of the Inhabitants were taken among 'em; whereas only
three Carpenter's Apprentices were, and those by Accident; the recent
memory of two men's having been kill'd by a press Gang on Shoar; the
sufferings of some Merchants and Traders by Mr. Knowles's Impress,
who were Owners of outward bound Vessels ready to sail; their Uneasiness at the difference made between the Sugar Colony Islands and
his Majesty's Colonies upon the Northern Continent by the late Act of
Parliament exempting the former from Impresses of Seamen within

1   Before the town: Commodore Knowles is threatening to use his fleet's cannon to bom-
     bard Boston into submission.

their Limits, and the perswasion they have all over the Continent, that the Impressing of Seamen within any of his Majesty's Plantations, is illegal, by virtue of a Clause in a Statute of the [ ]¹ of Queen Anne, which they conceive to be perpetual, notwithstanding the Opinions of Sir Edward Northey, Sir Dudley Ryder and the late Solicitor General Strange, publish'd here to the contrary; and which nothing will remove, but a Judicial Determination, or an Act, or Clause in an Act of Parliament declaring the Clause in the former Act to be expir'd.

But what I think may be esteem'd the principal cause of the Mobbish turn in this Town, is it's Constitution; by which the Management of it is devolv'd upon the populace assembled in their Town Meetings; one of which may be called together at any time upon the Petition of ten of the meanest Inhabitants, who by their Constant attendance there generally are the majority and outvote the Gentlemen, Merchants, Substantial Traders and all the better part of the Inhabitants; to whom it is Irksome to attend at such meetings, except upon very extraordinary occasions; and by this means it happens, as it would do among any other Community in a Trading Seaport Town under the same Constitution, where there are about Twenty thousand Inhabitants, consisting among others of so many working Artificers, Seafaring Men, and low sort of people, that a factious and Mobbish Spirit is Cherish'd; whereas the same Inhabitants under a different Town-Constitution proper for the Government of so populous and Trading a place, would probably form as well dispos'd a Community for every part of his Majesty's Service, as any the King has under his Government.

Your Lordships will perceive by this Account that Mr. Knowles gave no just occasion for such a Tumult; he had lost near fifty men by Desertion since his Squadron lay in this Harbour, as he inform'd me, and that his Ships were short of their Complement; and I must add, that Captains of his Majesty's Ships have usually Impress'd out of Vessels on float in this Harbour, and am perswaded Mr. Knowles did not design to Impress any Inhabitants, twenty of whom he had, as he inform'd me, a little before Discharg'd; as I believe he wo'd have done most of the outward bound Sailors, if these outrages upon his Officers had not happen'd.

The whole Province is very angry at the Tardiness of the Militia of

---

1   Shirley meant to impose the reference to the statute, but never did.

the Town of Boston, and the House of Representatives was remarkably so.

Questions for Discussion:

1. What events and misunderstandings before the riot contributed to bad feelings against the Royal Navy in Boston?
2. Did this "mob" simply run amuck, or did it display organization and restraint in its actions?
3. What does this document reveal about social relations in colonial ports like Boston?

William Shirley to the Board of Trade, December 1, 1747, in *Correspondence of William Shirley, Governor of Massachusetts and Military Commander in America*, vol. 1, ed. Charles Henry Lincoln (New York: Macmillan, 1912), 412–19.

William Dickinson, "Burning the *Gaspee*" (1773)

By the early 1770s, many American colonists had become heartily sick of the Navigation Acts. Smuggling had long been a way of life for colonial merchants and sailors, but this period saw increasingly heavy-handed enforcement of the obnoxious commercial regulations by Crown-appointed customs officers and even the Royal Navy. His Majesty's schooner *Gaspee* had made itself particularly unwelcome in Rhode Island, inspecting every vessel it could as it patrolled Narragansett Bay. One night in June 1772, when the *Gaspee* happened to be grounded, a crowd of colonials rowed out to the vessel, seized it after a brief struggle in which the schooner's commander was dangerously wounded, then burned it to the waterline.

The British government responded with a thorough investigation of the *Gaspee* burning. But despite cash rewards, no credible witnesses came forward to identify those involved. The following document is a sworn deposition from that investigation. It was made by a junior officer belonging to the *Gaspee*. Admiral John Montagu of the Royal Navy then cross-examined him.

William Dickinson, midshipman of his Majesty's schooner *Gaspee*, sayeth: That the said schooner was at single anchor about three leagues[1] below Providence, in Rhode Island government, 10th of June, 1772, and about half past twelve o'clock in the night or morning, the watch

---

1   League: roughly three miles.

gave the alarm that a number of boats were coming down the river, and very near us, (being an exceeding dark night,) we hailed them, and ordered them to keep off. They instantly gave us three cheers, on which we fired at them with muskets, which they immediately returned with half a dozen muskets, (or thereabouts.) We then fired our pistols, on which they boarded us upon the starboard bow, and fired a number of small arms. Immediately Lieutenant Dudingston (her commander) cried out, "Good God, I am done for," and was wounded in his groin and arm. While we were disputing forward, relative to their boarding us, three other boats boarded us upon the quarter.[1] In the three boats which boarded us upon the quarter, there were thirty or forty men, at least, and in the whole, I suppose, about 150 in number, on which we thought proper (the Lieutenant being wounded) to surrender. When they had got possession of the schooner they used the people very ill, by pinioning of them, and throwing them into their boats, and refused the Lieutenant and officers any necessaries but what they had on, and not even suffered the commanding officer to have his papers, and robbed his servant of several silver spoons, and throwed his linen and apparel overboard. We were then sent ashore, in two different boats, the Lieutenant and part of the men in one boat, and myself with the rest of the people in the other boat, at the distance of about two miles asunder, as we found at daylight. I remained on the beach, and about half-past three o'clock saw the schooner on fire, and about half-past four I saw three boats put off from her, full of men, and rowed up towards Providence, and an hour after another boat came by her and landed her men at Pawtuxet.

Questions by Admiral Montagu.

Question.—How long had you been lying in Providence River?

Answer.—We came to an anchor there at about 4 o'clock in the afternoon of the 9th of June.

Q.—Had you sent any boat ashore?

A.—No, but employed sounding the Harbor.

Q.—Had you been at Providence before during the time you were upon that station?

A.—No.

Q.—Do you imagine that the people who boarded you, came from Providence?

---

1   Quarter: the aft part of the ship's side.

A.—Yes; I believe the most part, but cannot say all, as one boat landed her men at Pawtuxet.

Q.—What distance is Pawtuxet from Providence by land?

A.—Five miles.

Q.—What distance were the boats from the schooner when they were first seen?

A.—I was not upon deck at first myself, but when I saw them they were about 100 yards.

Q.—Why did you not fire your great guns at them?

A.—They boarded us upon the bows, and were so near to us that we had not time to get our guns out at the bow ports.

Q.—Did any of the people that boarded you appear like gentlemen?

A.—Yes; many of them appeared like men of credit and tradesmen, and but few like common men.

Q.—Did they make use of any opprobrious language?

A.—Yes; by threatening to put the Lieutenant to death, and calling us piratical rascals.

Q.—Where did you leave the *Beaver*?

A.—Off Golden Island, in the mouth of Secunet passage.

Q.—What distance from you?

A.—About twenty-five miles.

Q.—Could she be in sight when this happened?

A.—No; the main land is between.

Q.—Is there any thing more that you can recollect?

A.—Yes; one of the people took me by the collar, and said, "Damn you, where is your Pilot Doget." I answered he was discharged six weeks ago. He answered, "Damn your blood, you lie;" and said they would find him, and [illegible] him alive.

Q.—Did they suffer the Lieutenant to put on any clothes after he was wounded?

A.—No; he was in his shirt with his great coat over his shoulders, and a blanket round his body.

Q.—Was any other person wounded except the Lieutenant?

A.—Yes; one in the head.

And I further declare, that when Lieutenant Dudingston came on deck, I saw him go and stand by the starboard foreshrouds, in his shirt, with a pistol in one hand and a hanger[1] in the other. After he was

---

1   Hanger: officer's sword.

wounded he got aft and sat down by the cabin companion way, when the two ringleaders, with a number following them, came to him and said, "Now you piratical rascal, we have got you. Damn you, we will hang you all by the laws of Great Britain. Damn you, what made you fire when we answered you that the head sheriff was in the boat."

The Captain (N.B. The head sheriff and captain are fictitious names that the two ringleaders went by) said, "Stand aside and let me despatch the piratical dog." He then lifted a handspike over Mr. Dudingston's head, who asked "if they would give no quarters." They answered, "No." He then desired they would let me bind up his wounds, for he was shot, and showed them the wound in his left arm. They then said, "Damn your blood, you are shot by your own people." He was then taken down into the cabin by some of the mob. They then pinioned me and put me into the boat, where I remained for half an hour, when one of the mob called to their people in the boat to loose me for the Lieutenant wanted me. I went down in the cabin to him. He was laid on the after lockers, and one of the mob washing and binding up his wounds. The mob then got him on deck and put him in a boat and put off. Soon after, I was ordered into the boat again, and put off. In going on shore I saw a negro with the Lieutenant's hanger; being asked by another how he got it, he said he took it from the Captain.

Being down in the cabin with Lieutenant Dudingston, the ringleaders and some of the principal of the mob demanded his papers and orders for his proceeding in such piratical manner. I then showed them the commission from the Lords of the Admiralty, with all his orders and instructions that he had received from the Admiral, which they took and carried away. In going ashore one of the mob that rowed the boat said, that he and several more would not have been there, but that they were taken out of a house by force and compelled to go; that they beat a drum round the town of Providence in the evening to raise a mob.

W. DICKINSON.
Province of Massachusetts Bay,
Suffolk, sc. BOSTON, June 11, 1772.
The above named William Dickinson personally appearing, maketh solemn oath to the truth of the foregoing deposition, as wrote upon this and the six preceding pages, which is taken at the request of the Honorable John Montagu, Esq. Before me,
EDMUND QUINCY.

Questions for Discussion:

1. What does this document reveal about the power relationship between colonists and the Royal Navy?

2. What elements of colonial Rhode Island society attacked the *Gaspee*, and why might that be important for the investigators?

3. What was the point of the *Gaspee*'s attackers referring to Lieutenant Duddingston as a "pirate"?

William R. Staples, ed., *The Documentary History of the Destruction of the* Gaspee (Providence: Knowles, Vose, and Anthony, 1845), 12–14.

Anonymous, "Philadelphia Resolves" (1773)

While the Boston Tea Party of 1773 was the most famous, similar flare-ups occurred in other American port communities such as Philadelphia, on the Delaware River. Printed pamphlets warned Delaware pilots not to navigate the tea ship *Polly* up the river and threatened its captain with tar and feathering. As it happened, community leaders feared that violence would get out of hand and formed committees to head off actual violence, while still using its threat as a tool to achieve their ends. In this way Philadelphians ensured that the hated tea would not come ashore, that violence would be checked, and that revolutionary ideals would be preserved.

PHILADELPHIA.

Monday, December 17, 1773.

THE unanimity, spirit and zeal, which have heretofore animated all the colonies, from Boston to South-Carolina have been so eminently displayed in the opposition to the pernicious project of the East India Company, in sending Tea to America, while it remains subject to a Duty, and the Americans at the same time confined by the strongest prohibitory laws to import it only from Great Britain, that a particular account of the transactions of this city, cannot but be acceptable to all our readers, and every other friend of American liberty.

Upon the first advice of this measure, a general dissatisfaction was expressed, that, at a time when we were struggling with this oppressive Act, and an agreement subsisting not to import Tea while subject to the Duty, our fellow subjects in England should form a measure so directly tending to enforce the Act and again embroil us with our parent state. When it was also considered, that the proposed mode of disposing of the Tea tended to a monopoly, ever odious in a free country, a universal disapprobation shewed itself throughout the city. A publick Meeting of the inhabitants was held at the State House on the 18th October, at which great numbers attended and the sense of the city was expressed in the following resolves.

1. THAT the disposal of their own property is the inherent right of freemen; that there can be no property in that which another can, of right, take from us without our consent; that the claim of Parliament to tax America is, in other words a claim of right to levy contributions on us at pleasure.

2. That the duty imposed by Parliament upon tea landed in America, is a tax on the Americans, or levying contributions on them without their consent.

3. That the express purpose for which the tax is levyed on the Americans, namely for the support of government, administration of justice, and defence of his Majesty's dominions in America, has a direct tendency to render Assemblies useless, and to introduce arbitrary government and slavery.

4. That a virtuous and steady opposition to this ministerial plan of governing America, is absolutely necessary to preserve even the shadow of liberty, and is a duty which every freeman in America owes to his country, to himself and to his posterity.

5. That the resolution lately entered into by the East India Company to send out their Tea to America, subject to the payment of duties on its being landed here, is an open attempt to inforce this ministerial plan, and a violent attack upon the liberties of America.

6. That it is the duty of every American to oppose this attempt.

7. That whoever shall, directly or indirectly, countenance this attempt, or in any wise aid or abet in unloading, receiving, or vending the Tea sent, or to be sent out by the East India Company, while it remains subject to the payment of a duty here, is an enemy to his country.

8. That a Committee be immediately chosen to wait on those gentlemen, who, it is reported, are appointed by the East-India Company to receive and sell said Tea, and request them, from a regard to their own character, and the peace and good order of the city and province, immediately to resign their appointment.

In consequence of this appointment the Committee waited upon the Gentlemen in this city, who had been appointed Consignees of the expected cargo. They represented to them the detestation and abhorrence, in which this measure was held by their fellow Citizens, the danger and difficulties, which must attend the execution of so odious a trust, and expressed the united desire of the City, that they would renounce the commission, and engage not to intermeddle with the ship or cargo in any shape whatever. Some of the Commissioners resigned, in a manner that gave general satisfaction, others, in such equivocal terms as required farther explanation: However in a few days the resignation was complete. In this situation things remained for a few days. In the mean time, the general spirit and indignation rose to such a height, that it was thought proper to call another general Meeting of the principal Citizens, to consider and resolve upon such farther steps as might give weight, and ensure success to the unanimous opposition now formed. Accordingly a Meeting was had, for the above purpose, at which a great number of respectable Inhabitants attended; and it appeared to be the unanimous opinion, that the entry of the Ship at the Custom-House, or the landing any part of her cargo, would be attended with great danger and difficulty, and would directly tend to destroy that peace and good order, which ought to be preserved. An addition of twelve other Gentlemen was then made to the former Committee, and the general Meeting adjourned till the arrival of the Tea Ship. Information being given of that, the Price of Tea was suddenly advanced, though this was owing to a General Scarcity of that Article; yet all the Possessors of Tea, in order to give strength to the opposition, readily agreed to reduce the price, and sell what remained in their hands at a reasonable rate. Nothing now remained, but to keep up a proper correspondence and connection with the other Colonies, and to take all prudent and proper precautions on the arrival of the Tea Ship.

It is not easy to describe the anxiety and suspence of the City in this interval. Sundry reports of her arrival were received, which proved premature. But on Saturday evening last, an express came up from Chester, to inform the Town, that the Tea Ship, commanded by Capt. Ayres, with her detested Cargo, was arrived there, having followed another ship up the river so far.

The Committee met early the next morning, and being apprized of the arrival of Mr. Gilbert Barclay, the other Consignee, who came passenger in the ship they immediately went in a body to request his renunciation of the commission. Mr. Barclay politely attended the Committee, at the first request; and being made acquainted with the sentiments of the city, and the danger to which the public liberties of America were exposed by this measure, he, after expressing the particular hardship of his situation, also resigned the commission, in a manner which affected every one present.

The Committee then appointed three of their members to go to Chester, and two others to Gloucester Point, in order to have the earliest opportunity of meeting Capt. Ayres, and representing to him the sense of the Public, respecting his voyage and cargo. The Gentlemen, who had set out for Chester, receiving intelligence that the vessel had weighed anchor about 12 o'clock, and proceeded to town, returned. About two o'clock she appeared in sight of Gloucester Point, where a number of Inhabitants from the town had assembled with the Gentlemen from the Committee. As she passed along, she was hailed, and the Captain requested not to proceed farther, but to come on shore. This the Captain complied with, and was handed thro' a lane made by the People, to the Gentlemen appointed to confer with him. They represented to him the general sentiments, together with the danger and difficulties that would attend his refusal to comply with the wishes of the Inhabitants; and finally desired him to proceed with them to town, where he would be more fully informed of the temper and resolution of the People. He was accordingly accompanied to town, by a number of persons, where he was soon convinced of the truth and propriety of the representations, which had been made to him and agreed that upon the desire of the Inhabitants being publicly expressed, he would conduct himself accordingly. Some small rudeness being offered to the Captain afterwards in the street, by some boys, several Gentlemen interposed, and suppressed it before he received the least injury. Upon an hour's notice this morning, a public meeting was called, and the State-House not being sufficient to hold the numbers assembled, they adjourned into the Square. This meeting is allowed by all to be the most respectable, both in the numbers and rank of those who attended it, that has been known in this city. After a short introduction, the following resolutions were not only agreed to, but the public approbation testified in the warmest manner.

1. RESOLVED. That the Tea on board the ship *Polly*, Capt. Ayres, shall not be landed.

2. That Capt. Ayres shall neither enter nor report his vessel at the Custom-House.

3. That Capt. Ayres shall carry back the Tea immediately.

4. That Capt. Ayres shall immediately send a Pilot on board his vessel, with orders to take charge of her, and proceed with to Reedy-Island next high water.

5. That the Captain shall be allowed to stay in town till to-morrow, to provide necessaries for his voyage.

6. That he shall then be obliged to leave the town and proceed to his vessel, and make the best of his way out of our river and bay.

7. That a Committee of four Gentlemen be appointed to see these Resolves carried into execution.

The assembly were then informed of the spirit and resolution of New-York, Charles-Town, South-Carolina, and the conduct of the people of Boston, whereupon it was unanimously resolved,

That this assembly highly approve of the conduct and spirit of the people of New-York, Charles-Town, and Boston, and return their hearty thanks to the people of Boston for their resolution in destroying the Tea rather than suffering it to be landed. The whole business was conducted with a decorum and order worthy the importance of the cause. Capt. Ayres being present at this meeting, solemnly and publicly engaged, that he would literally comply with the sense of the city, as expressed in the above resolutions.

A proper supply of necessaries and fresh provisions being then procured, in about two hours the Tea-Ship weighed anchor from Gloucester Point, where she lay within sight of the town, and has proceeded, with her whole cargo, on her return to the East-India Company.

The Public think the conduct of those Gentlemen, whose goods are returned on board the Tea-Ship, ought not to pass unnoticed, as they have, upon this occasion, generously sacrificed their private interest to the public good.

Thus this important affair in which there has been so glorious an exertion of Public Virtue and Spirit, has been brought to a happy issue; by which the force of a law so obstinately persisted in to the prejudice of the national Commerce, for the sake of the principle on which it is founded, (a right of taxing the Americans without their consent,) has been effectually broken and the foundations of American Liberty more deeply laid than ever.

Questions for Discussion:

1. What was the basis of Philadelphian opposition to the East India Company's tea?

2. What does this document reveal about the revolutionary ideals of colonial Philadelphians?
3. What sorts of threats and bargains are made between the various parties in this encounter?

"Philadelphia, Monday, December 27, 1773." Broadside, Library of Congress, Rare Book and Special Collections Division.

2

REVOLUTION AND REPUBLIC

Seafarers and maritime concerns formed an important element of American society in the late eighteenth and nineteenth centuries. The coming revolution divided coastal communities; they experienced crowd actions and British reprisals that made ports like Boston, New York, and Philadelphia contentious places. The outbreak of the War of Independence in 1775 meant that the colonists were fighting the mightiest naval power on the planet. American naval efforts were not very successful, and one of the ironies of American independence was that a French king's fleet clinched the final victory against British domination in the Battle of the Capes off Yorktown, Virginia.

Independence brought a host of problems and opportunities to the American maritime community. Many of these questions predated the Revolution, such as maritime trade. Americans struggled to understand the role seaborne commerce would have in the economy, how to regulate and tax the nation's ports, and how to protect shipping from seizure by pirates and foreign nations. Indeed, through the War of 1812 many of the new nation's problems were related in one way or another to waterborne commerce, including establishing new trade routes, banning the importation of slaves, and protecting American sailors from impressment by foreign navies. As a result of these annoyances, the United States found it had to create a navy to protect American shipping from pirates and the predations of foreign powers such as France and Britain.

Inland waterways played a crucial role in the westward movement of American settlers. Whether it was the Great Lakes or the mighty western rivers, these freshwater bodies of water were rightly perceived as highways. Daring canal digging efforts like the Erie Canal connected the Great Lakes to important markets, and early river steamboats transformed how Americans traveled.

Race, too, remained an issue after independence. Americans remained unsure on racial issues. Native American communities were treated well when whites needed them, and very poorly when seen as an impediment to trade or agriculture. So, too, the position of the African American community was unclear. Some of the nation continued to embrace slavery, while other portions began to reject it. The burning question after the Revolution was what the free black community should do. A popular answer at the time was to sponsor the establishment of communities for American blacks in Africa.

After the War of 1812, America expanded westward, often by canal boat, river steamboat, or speedy clipper. This was the start of a golden age of American seafaring, with huge advances in shipbuilding and design, daring trading ventures to Asia, and the development of steam propulsion.

REVOLUTION AFLOAT

The American War of Independence was a nearly eight-year-long conflict, fought both on land and at sea. The British had an important advantage from the start: they possessed the world's mightiest navy, permitting them to bring the war to virtually any part of the long exposed coastline. The Americans, of course, had no navy at first. While the Continental Congress did authorize a navy in 1775, many Americans thought it was the height of folly to take on the British Navy. Congressman Samuel Chase of Maryland famously called it "the maddest idea in the World."

The events of the war supported Chase's idea. The various naval efforts of the war were largely failures. The British captured or destroyed virtually all the ships the Americans built. The Continental Navy only operated a successful fleet operation once. The great exception was the work of John Paul Jones, who launched a series of humbling raids on the British mainland. Jones's spirit is forever commemorated in his alleged words when called upon to surrender by a British frigate commander: "I have not yet begun to fight!"

One practical American response to a lack of naval power was to give privately owned vessels a government license, or "commission," to seize enemy merchant vessels. These private warships were called privateers, and there were almost 1500 privateering commissions issued between 1775 and 1783. Pursuing a naval strategy known as "guerre de course" (hunting warfare), privateers and ships of the state and Continental navies captured hundreds of British ships, depriving the enemy of supplies and bringing them to American ports where they were badly needed.

Luckily for historians, there is a wealth of information on the experiences of ordinary Americans who fought the Revolution at sea. In particular,

Michael Crawford's treatment of Christopher Prince's *Autobiography of a Yankee Mariner*[1] fully explores the career of a merchant mariner, naval seaman, and officer of a privateer in all its complexity.

Thomas Paine, "Common Sense" (1776)

No pamphleteer captured the spirit of the American Revolution as well as Thomas Paine (1737–1809), an English-born ne'er-do-well who developed increasingly radical political views as he entered middle age. He emigrated to America just before the Revolutionary War, took up the patriot cause, and published his famous pamphlet, *Common Sense*, in January 1776. The pamphlet was widely popular, and because of it many Americans decided that the best course for the Thirteen Colonies was total independence from Britain.

In this segment of *Common Sense*, Paine advocates the construction of an American Navy, explains the drawbacks of relying on the British Navy for protection, and proposes a way to keep an American fleet cheaply in times of peace. In typical Thomas Paine fashion, while some of his ideas are "common sense," others are clearly impractical.

No country on the globe is so happily situated, so internally capable of raising a fleet as America. Tar, timber, iron, and cordage are her natural produce. We need go abroad for nothing. Whereas the Dutch, who make large profits by hiring out their ships of war to the Spaniards and Portuguese, are obliged to import most of the materials they use. We ought to view the building a fleet as an article of commerce, it being the natural manufactory of this country. It is the best money we can lay out. A navy when finished is worth more than it cost. And is that nice point in national policy, in which commerce and protection are united. Let us build; if we want them not, we can sell; and by that means replace our paper currency with ready gold and silver. In point of manning a fleet, people in general run into great errors; it is not necessary that one fourth part should be sailors. . . . A few able and social sailors will soon instruct a sufficient number of active landmen in the common work of a ship. Wherefore, we never can be more capable to begin on maritime matters than now, while our timber is standing, our fisheries blocked up, and our sailors and

---

1   Michael J. Crawford, *Autobiography of a Yankee Mariner: Christopher Prince and the American Revolution* (Washington, D.C.: Brassey's, 2002).

shipwrights out of employ. Men of war, of seventy and eighty guns were built forty years ago in New-England, and why not the same now? Ship-building is America's greatest pride, and in which, she will in time excel the whole world. The great empires of the east are mostly inland, and consequently excluded from the possibility of rivaling her. Africa is in a state of barbarism; and no power in Europe, hath either such an extent of coast, or such an internal supply of materials. Where nature hath given the one, she has withheld the other; to America only hath she been liberal of both. The vast empire of Russia is almost shut out from the sea; wherefore, her boundless forests, her tar, iron, and cordage are only articles of commerce. In point of safety, ought we to be without a fleet? We are not the little people now, which we were sixty years ago; at that time we might have trusted our property in the streets, or fields rather; and slept securely without locks or bolts to our doors or windows. The case now is altered, and our methods of defence, ought to improve with our increase of property. A common pirate, twelve months ago, might have come up the Delaware, and laid the city of Philadelphia under instant contribution, for what sum he pleased; and the same might have happened to other places. Nay, any daring fellow, in a brig of fourteen or sixteen guns, might have robbed the whole Continent, and carried off half a million of money. These are circumstances which demand our attention, and point out the necessity of naval protection.

Some, perhaps, will say, that after we have made it up with Britain, she will protect us. Can we be so unwise as to mean, that she shall keep a navy in our harbours for that purpose? Common sense will tell us, that the power which hath endeavoured to subdue us, is of all others, the most improper to defend us. Conquest may be effected under the pretence of friendship; and ourselves, after a long and brave resistance, be at last cheated into slavery. And if her ships are not to be admitted into our harbours, I would ask, how is she to protect us? A navy three or four thousand miles off can be of little use, and on sudden emergencies, none at all. Wherefore, if we must hereafter protect ourselves, why not do it for ourselves? Why do it for another?

The English list of ships of war, is long and formidable, but not a tenth part of them are at any time fit for service, numbers of them not in being; yet their names are pompously continued in the list, if only a plank be left of the ship: and not a fifth part, of such as are fit for service, can be spared on any one station at one time. The East, and West

Indies, Mediterranean, Africa, and other parts over which Britain extends her claim, make large demands upon her navy. From a mixture of prejudice and inattention, we have contracted a false notion respecting the navy of England, and have talked as if we should have the whole of it to encounter at once, and for that reason, supposed, that we must have one as large; which not being instantly practicable, have been made use of by a set of disguised Tories to discourage our beginning thereon. Nothing can be farther from truth than this; for if America had only a twentieth part of the naval force of Britain, she would be by far an over match for her; because, as we neither have, nor claim any foreign dominion, our whole force would be employed on our own coast, where we should, in the long run, have two to one the advantage of those who had three or four thousand miles to sail over, before they could attack us, and the same distance to return in order to refit and recruit. And although Britain by her fleet, hath a check over our trade to Europe, we have as large a one over her trade to the West-Indies, which, by laying in the neighbourhood of the Continent, is entirely at its mercy.

Some method might be fallen on to keep up a naval force in time of peace, if we should not judge it necessary to support a constant navy. If premiums were to be given to merchants, to build and employ in their service, ships mounted with twenty, thirty, forty, or fifty guns, (the premiums to be in proportion to the loss of bulk to the merchants) fifty or sixty of those ships, with a few guard ships on constant duty, would keep up a sufficient navy, and that without burdening ourselves with the evil so loudly complained of in England, of suffering their fleet, in time of peace to lie rotting in the docks. To unite the sinews of commerce and defence is sound policy; for when our strength and our riches, play into each other's hand, we need fear no external enemy.

Questions for Discussion:

1. According to Paine, what advantages did the rebelling colonists have in maritime terms?

2. Why did Paine think it was unwise to rely on the British Navy for protection?

3. What disadvantages did Paine suggest the British fleet operated under?

George Rice Carpenter, ed., *American Prose: Selections with Critical Introductions* (New York: Macmillan, 1916), 68–70.

Robert Morris, "The Present State of Our Navy" (1776)

Robert Morris (1734–1806), a wealthy Philadelphia merchant, was a signer of the Declaration of Independence, the Articles of Confederation, and the Constitution, and was one of the most prominent American businessmen of his day, yet he remains little known. His role as the financial genius who kept the American Revolution financially afloat (if just) is certainly under-appreciated.

Already wealthy by the time of the Revolution, Morris was one of the few Americans to gain wealth during the war thanks to his investment in privateers. Morris, however, was also willing to make sacrifices, as when he sold his best ship, the *Black Prince*, to the Continental Navy, which renamed it the *Alfred*, the first ship in the Continental Navy. In this letter, Morris identifies some of the problems the Continental Congress had in establishing a viable navy.

Philadelphia, December 21, 1776.

You will doubtless be surprised that we have not made better progress with our Navy, because you are unacquainted with the many difficulties and causes of delay that have encountered us. The want of sea-coal for our anchor-smiths has been a great bar to our progress, the disappointment in our first attempts to cast cannon has been another, but above all, we have been hindered by the constant calling out of our Militia, in a manner that did not admit of the necessary tradesmen being exempted. You will wonder at this; it would be a long story to unfold the reasons, therefore suffice that it is so. Doctor *Franklin* can inform you of many particulars respecting the Flying-Camp; therefore, I shall give you the present state of our Navy, according to the best of my knowledge at this time.

The frigate in *New-Hampshire* is a very fine ship, completed in every particular, except the want of cannon, which was to have been cast in *Rhode-Island*, but the spirit of privateering has prevailed so eminently there, that they have sacrificed every other pursuit to it, both publick and private, as I am informed; and we have ordered the guns cast in *Connecticut* for that frigate to be sent to *Portsmouth*. As soon as they arrive, the *Raleigh* will be manned, and sail on a cruise.

At *Boston* they have also two fine frigates. The *Boston*, of twenty-four guns, I expect is at sea before this time, commanded by Captain *McNeil* a very clever officer. The other is nearly ready, commanded by Captain *Manly*.

In *Rhode-Island* were built the two worst frigates, as I have been informed by those that have seen the whole. These two are completely fitted, and were partly manned when we last heard from them; so that I hope they are now at sea.

In *Connecticut*, the frigate is said to be a fine ship; but she cannot get to sea this winter for want of cordage and other stores.

In *New-York*, two very fine frigates are blocked up by the enemy, and hauled into *Esopus Creek* for safety.

At this place, we have four very fine ships. One of them, the *Randolph*, Captain *Biddle*, of twenty-six twelve-pounders, will, I hope, go to sea in company with this letter; another, the *Delaware*, Captain *Alexander*, is getting ready, and I hope will get out this winter. The other two want guns, anchors, and men.

At *Baltimore*, is a fine frigate, now only waiting for an anchor and men.

Besides these, we have in service, the *Alfred, Columbus*, and *Reprisal*, ships from sixteen to twenty-four guns, the brigantines *Cabot, Camden, Andrew Doria*, and *Lexington*, of twelve to sixteen guns; the sloops *Providence, Hornet, Fly, Independence, Sachem*; and schooners *Wasp, Musquito*, and *Georgia Packet*, all in actual service; and they have had great success in taking valuable prizes, as indeed have numbers of privateers from all parts of *America*. We have besides, two very fine rowgalleys, built here, of ninety feet keel, but they are not yet rigged; and it has lately been determined by Congress to build some line-of-battle ships, and at all events to push forward and pay the utmost attention to an *American* Navy.

The greatest encouragement is given to seamen, which ought to be made known throughout *Europe*. Their pay in our Navy is eight dollars per month, with the best chance for prize money that men ever had, and liberty of discharges after every cruise, if they choose it. In the merchant service they now get from thirty to forty dollars per month; and this leads me to the state of our commerce.

In the Eastern States they are so intent on privateering that they mind little else. However, there is some exportation of produce from thence, and as to imports, they are the best supplied of any part of *America*, having been surprisingly successful in captures. *New-York* being in the hands of the enemy, we have nothing to say to it; and the produce of *New-Jersey* will be totally consumed by their army and ours. In this State, (*Pennsylvania*,) we had last season the worst crop of wheat ever known, both as to quantity and quality. This being our staple commodity, and stores prohibited, our merchants have been led to purchase much tobacco in *Maryland* and *Virginia*, and their ships are employed in the export of this article, with some flour, boards, beeswax, &c. We have a good many imports, but as fast as goods arrive, they are bought up for the Army, or for the use of neighbouring States, and therefore continue to bear high prices.

The value of ships has risen in the same enormous proportion with every thing else, and ships that were deemed worth £1,000 twelve months ago, now sell for £3,000, or upwards. Every article belonging to them is also excessively dear, and hard to be got, and the insolence and difficulty of seamen is beyond bearing. In *Maryland, Virginia, North-Carolina,* and *Georgia,* they have plenty of valuable produce on hand, but no ships to carry it away, and constant cruisers all along the coast make it very dangerous to send ships from one port to another; so that look which way you will, you find us surrounded with difficulties in the land service, in the sea service, and in our commerce.

Agriculture and mechanicks have their impediments, by the enlisting of soldiers, and frequent calls on the Militia. In short, nothing but the most arduous exertions, and virtuous conduct in the leaders, seconded by a spirited behaviour in the Army, and a patient endurance of hardships by the people in general, can long support the contest; therefore the Court of *France* should strike at once, as they will reap an immediate harvest. They may sell their manufactures for any price they please to ask; they will get in payment tobacco, rice, indigo, deerskins, furs, wheat, flour, iron, beeswax, lumber, fish, oil, whalebone, pot and pearl ashes, and various other articles, and, if they please, here is an ample field to employ their shipping, and raise seamen for their Navy.

Questions for Discussion:
1. What sorts of problems did the newly constructed Continental Navy vessels face?
2. What incentives did sailors have to serve on naval, merchant, or privateering vessels?
3. What commercial shipping problems were the southern colonies facing?

Peter Force, ed., *American Archives*, 5th ser., vol. 3 (Washington, 1853), 1335–36.

Continental Congress, "Instructions to Commanders of Privateers" (1776–1778)

Even before declaring independence, the Continental Congress set a course for conducting a naval war. Without a navy of its own, Congress settled on an expedient both familiar to American mariners and suited to colonial resources: privateering. Shipowners could easily fit out a merchant ship with a few cannon, acquire a commission from the government, and send it on a cruise to seize enemy ships. The privateer sent any vessels it captured back to port, where a court determined if it was a legitimate capture. If so, then the privateer's owners and the crew of the privateer split the proceeds, the bulk of which went to the owners. It could be immensely profitable for owners and crew alike, and the voyages were relatively short, making privateering more popular than regular naval service.

Privateering, however, could be prone to abuse; it could be a cover for piratical acts, smuggling, or trade with the enemy. Furthermore, privateersmen might attack neutral vessels, beat or rob prisoners, or plunder vessels before a court properly adjudicated the captured vessel. Congress acted to limit those abuses by printing the following set of instructions for the commanders of American privateers. With the war at sea increasingly being taken to European waters and the Caribbean, Congress expressed its concern that privateersmen be prudent in their conduct and not attack neutral shipping.

INSTRUCTIONS TO COMMANDERS OF PRIVATEERS

Continental Congress, April 3, 1776:

I. You may, by force of arms, attack, subdue and take all ships and other vessels belonging to the inhabitants of Great Britain, on the high seas, or between high water and low water mark, except ships and vessels bringing persons who intend to settle and reside in the United Colonies; or bringing arms, ammunition, or war-like stores, to the said colonies, for the use of such inhabitants thereof as are friends to the American cause, which you shall suffer to pass unmolested, the commanders thereof permitting a peaceable search and giving satisfactory information of the contents of the ladings and destinations of voyages.

II. You may, by force of arms, attack, subdue and take all ships and other vessels whatsoever, carrying soldiers, arms, gunpowder, ammunition, provisions, or any other contraband goods, to any of the British armies or ships of war employed against these colonies.

III. You shall bring such ships and vessels, as you shall take, with their guns, rigging, tackle, apparel, furniture, and ladings to some convenient port or ports of the United Colonies, that proceedings may thereupon be had in due form, before the courts which are or shall be appointed to hear and determine causes civil and maritime.

IV. You, or one of your chief officers, shall bring or send the master and pilot and one or more principal person or persons of the company of every ship or vessel by you taken, as soon after the capture as may be, to the judge or judges of such court as aforesaid, to be examined upon oath, and make answer to the interrogatories which may be propounded, touching the interest or property of the ship or vessel and her lading; and, at the same time, you shall deliver, or cause to be delivered to the judge or judges, all passes, sea-briefs, charter-parties, bills of lading, cockets,[1] letters and other documents and writings found on board, proving the said papers by the affidavit of yourself or of some other person present at the capture, to be produced as they were received, without fraud, addition, subduction[2] or embezzlement.

V. You shall keep and preserve every ship or vessel and cargo by you taken, until they shall, by a sentence of a court properly authorized, be adjudged lawful prizes; not selling, spoiling, wasting, or diminishing the same, or breaking the bulk thereof, nor suffering any such thing to be done.

VI. If you, or any of your officers or crew, shall, in cold blood, kill or maim, or by torture or otherwise, cruelly, inhumanly, and contrary to common usage and the practice of civilized nations in war, treat any person or persons surprized in the ship or vessel you shall take, the offender shall be severely punished.

VIII. You shall, by all convenient opportunities, send to Congress written accounts of the captures you shall make, with the number and names of the captives, copies of your journal from time to time, and intelligence of what may occur or be discovered concerning the designs of the enemy and the destination, motions and operations of their fleets and armies.

IX. One-third, at least, of your whole company shall be landsmen.

XI. You shall not ransom any prisoners or captives, but shall dispose of them in such manner as the Congress, or, if that be not sitting, in

---

1   Cockets: customhouse documents.
2   Subduction: taking away anything.

the colony whither they shall be brought, as the general assembly, convention, or council, or committee of safety, of such colony shall direct.

XII. You shall observe all such further instructions as Congress shall hereafter give in the premises, when you shall have notice thereof.

XIII. If you shall do anything contrary to these instructions, or to others hereafter to be given, or willingly suffer such thing to be done, you shall not only forfeit your commission and be liable to an action for breach of the condition of your bond, but be responsible to the party grieved for damages sustained by such malversation.[1]

A PROCLAMATION

Whereas Congress have received information and complaints, that "violences have been done by American armed vessels to neutral nations, in seizing ships belonging to their subjects and under their colours, and in making captures of those of the enemy whilst under the protection of neutral coasts, contrary to the usage and custom of nations": to the end that such unjustifiable and piratical acts, which reflect dishonour upon the national character of these states, may be in future effectually prevented, the said Congress hath thought proper to direct, enjoin and command, and they do hereby direct, enjoin and command, all captains, commanders and other officers and seamen belonging to any American armed vessels, to govern themselves strictly in all things agreeably to the tenor of their commissions, and the instructions and resolutions of Congress; particularly that they pay a sacred regard to the rights of neutral powers and the usage and custom of civilized nations, and on no pretence whatever presume to take or seize any ships or vessels belonging to the subjects of princes or powers in alliance with these United States, except they are employed in carrying contraband goods or soldiers to our enemies, and in such case that they conform to the stipulations contained in treaties subsisting between such princes or powers and these states; and that they do not capture, seize or plunder any ships or vessels of our enemies, being under the protection of neutral coasts, nations or princes, under the penalty of being condignly[2] punished therefore, and also of being bound to make satisfaction for all matters of damage and the

---

1   Malversation: misconduct.

2   Condignly: According to merit.

interest thereof by reparation, under the pain and obligation of their persons and goods. And further, the said Congress doth hereby resolve and declare, that persons willfully offending in any of the foregoing instances, if taken by any foreign powers in consequence thereof, will not be considered as having a right to claim protection from these states, but shall suffer such punishment as by the usage and custom of nations may be inflicted upon such offenders.

Given in Congress at York, in the state of Pennsylvania, this ninth day of May, Anno Domini 1778.

Questions for Discussion:
1. What sort of problems did privateers create for the Continental Congress?
2. What does this document reveal about how the Continental Congress thought privateering could advance its war aims?
3. What American ideals are revealed in these documents?

Gardner Weld Allen, *A Naval History of the American Revolution*, vol. 2 (Boston: Houghton, Mifflin and Company, 1913), 695–700.

Timothy Boardman, "Log-book of the *Oliver Cromwell*" (1778)

American naval efforts operated at several levels throughout the Revolutionary War. The Continental Congress had its own navy, but most states had navies, too, either for coastal defense or for carrying the war to the enemy. Timothy Boardman (1751–1838) served in the Connecticut militia before signing on board the ship *Oliver Cromwell* in 1778 as the ship's carpenter. While the *Oliver Cromwell* was a ship in Connecticut's state navy, it operated in much the same way as a privateer, preying on enemy merchant shipping. Like those on privateering vessels, this ship's crew received a share of whatever the ship captured rather than the monthly pay most naval personnel would expect. Boardman apparently did not care much for privateering; his captain had to cajole him aboard the ship for its return cruise from Charleston to Connecticut.

JOURNAL OF THE SECOND CRUISE.
April 7th the *Defence* had Five Men Broke out With the Small Pox.
9th they Lost a Man wth the Small Pox.

10th Exersis[d] Cannon & Musquetry.

11th Saw a Sail the *Defence* Spoke with her She was a Frenchman from Bourdeaux Bound to the West Indies.

13th Cros[d] the Tropick Shav[d] & Duck About 60 Men.[1]

14th at four Oclock Afternoon Saw a Sail Bearing ESE. We Gave Chase to her & Came Up With her at 8 Oclock She was a Large French Ship we Sent the Boat on Board of her She Informed us of two English Ships which She Left Sight of at the time we Saw her.

15th at Day Break We saw two Sail Bareing SEbS[2] Distance 2 Leagues We Gave Chase Under a Moderate Sail at 9 oClock P. M. Came Up with them they at First Shew French Colours[3] to Decoy us when we Came in About half a Mile of us she Ups with English Colours We had Continental Colours Flying We Engaged the Ship *Admiral Kepple* as Follows When We Came in About 20 Rods[4] of her We Gave her a Bow Gun She Soon Returned us a Stern Chaise[5] & then a Broad Side of Grape & Round Shot Cap[t] Orders Not to fire till we Can See the white of their Eyes We Got Close Under their Larbard[6] Quarter they Began Another Broad Side & then We Began & hel[d] Tuff & Tuff for About 9 Glasses[7] & Then she Struck to Us at the Same time the *Defence* Engaged the *Cyrus* who as the *Kepple* Struck Wore Round Under our Stem We Wore Ship & Gave her a Stern Chase at which She Immediately Struck. The Loss on our Side was One Kill[d] &; Six Wounded one Mortally Who Soon Died Our Ship was hull[d] 9 Times with Six Pound Shott Three of which Went through Our Birth[8] one of which wounded the Boatswains yeoman the Loss on their Side was two Kill[d] &; Six wounded their Larbourd quarter was well fill[d] with Shott one Nine Pounder went through her Main Mast. Imploy[d] in the After-noon Takeing out the Men & Maning the Prise[9] The *Kepple* Mounted 20 Guns 18 Six Pounders & two Wooden D[o] with about 45 Men, the *Cyrus* Mounted 16 Six Pounders with 35 Men Letters of

---

1 Shav[d] & Duck About 60 Men: apparently a "crossing the line" ceremony in which younger sailors were initiated by being ceremoniously shaved and ducked in the ocean. In this instance, the tropic crossed was probably the Tropic of Cancer.

2 SebS: abbreviation for south-east by south.

3 Colours: flag.

4 Rods: one rod equals sixteen and a half feet.

5 Stern Chaise: a cannon mounted in the stern to fire on pursuing vessels.

6 Larbard: the larboard, or port side of a vessel as one faced forward.

7 9 Glasses: on board sailing ships a glass was thirty minutes.

8 Birth: berth, or Boardman's sleeping quarters.

9 Prise: prize, the captured vessel.

Marque Bound from Bristol to Jamaica Laden with Dry Goods Paints & C.

18th Cap[t] Day Died.

19th Cap[t] Brown of The Ship *Adm[l] Kepple* &; Cap[t] Dike of the *Cyrus* with Three Ladies & 8 Men Sett off in a Long Boat for S[t] Kitts o[r] Cap[tns] Parker & Smedleys Permition.

20th Imploy[d] in taking things out of the Prise Viz. One Chist of Holland[1] a Quantity of Hatts & Shoes Cheeses Porter & Some Crockery Ware Small Arms Pistols Hangers[2] two Brass Barrel Blunderbusses a Quantity of Riggen & C.

21st At Three oClock Afternoon we wore Ship to the Southward The Prises Made Sail to the Northward we Lost Sight of them at Six.

May 2nd Sprung Our Foretopmast Struck it & Ship[d] Another in its Room.

8th Saw a Sail over Our Starboard bow We Gave Chase to her She was a French Guineaman[3] Bound to the Mole[4] With 612 Slaves on Board Our Cap[t] Put 6 Prisoners on Board of Her Left her Just at Dark.

11th At 5 o'Clock in the Morning Saw a Sail at the Windward two Leagues Distance Bearing Down Upon Us we Lay too for her till She Came in half Gun Shott of us the Man at Mast head Cry[d] out 4 Sail to the Leeward[5] Our Officers Concluded to Make Sail from her Supposing her to be a Frigate of 36 Guns after we Made Sail We Left as Fast as we wanted She Gave Over Chase at two oClock Afternoon She was the *Seaford* of 28 Guns.

22nd Sprung our Maintop sail Yard.

28th Made the Land at Port Royal.

29th the Ship Struck Bottom Thrice.[6]

30th Came over the Bar this Morning & Arriv[d] in this Harbour In Company with the Ship *Defence* Com[ed] by Sam[ll] Smedly. Charlestown, S[th.] C[na.] May ye 30th 1778.

JOURNAL OF THE THIRD CRUISE.

---

1 Chist of Holland: chest of Holland, perhaps a reference to a case of gin, or maybe a type of cloth.
2 Hangers: swords
3 Guineaman: slaveship.
4 The Mole: probably Môle Saint-Nicolas, a port in Haiti.
5 Leeward: downwind, an important consideration on a sailing vessel.
6 Ship Struck Bottom Thrice: Charleston, South Carolina, had a shallow sandbar across its seaward approaches that made entry for large ships difficult. In this instance, the *Oliver Cromwell* hit bottom three times before clearing the bar.

July 24 Weigh^d Anchor at 5 Fathom hole & Came Over the Bar In Comp^y with the *Notredame* a 16 Gun Brig & two Sloops. Mett a French Ship of 28 Guns on the Bar Bound in.

25th A Smooth Sea.

29th Saw A Sail Gave Chace.

30th Saw A Sail Gave Chace.

31st Saw two Sail Gave Chace. Light winds.

August 6th at half after Six Afternoon Saw a Sail & Gave Chace, at 11 Gave her a Bow Gun which Brought her too She was a Brig from New Orleans in Missippi Bound to Cape Francois a Spainard Went on Board Kept her All Night & Lett her Go at 10 °Clock the Next Day her Cargo was Furr & Lumber She had Some Englishmen on Board the Occasion of our Detaining her So Long.

7th At 5 O'Clock Afternoon Made the Land the Island of Abaco.[1]

8th at 10 O'Clock Harbour Island Bore East Dis^t 2 Leagues.

9th Hard Gales of wind.

10th Fresh Gales of wind & Heavy Squals.

11th Fresh Breeses & a Rough Sea.

12 at Six Afternoon Caught a Great Turtle which was Kook^d the Next Day for the Entertainment of the Gentlemen of the Fleet No Less than 13 Came on Board to Dine.

14 At 2 oClock P M Harbour Island Bore SbW 1 League Dis^t Sent the Yoll[2] on Shore The Brig Sent her Boat a Shore too.

15th The two Boats Returned with a two Mast Boat & 4 Men Belonging to New Providence Squally Night & Smart Thunder & Lightning.

16th Cros^d the Bahama Banks from 8 Fathom of water to 3¾ Came to Anchor at Night on the Bank.

17th Arrivd at the Abimenes Fill^d our Water Cask & Hogg^d Ship & Boot Top^d the Ship.[3]

18th At Day Break Weigh^d Anchor together with the Rice Thumper Fleet at Noon Parted with Them & Fired 18 Guns the Other fir'd their Guns Which was a 16 Gun Brigg the *Notredame* Command by Capt Hall A 10 Gun Sloop Com^d by Capt Robberts A 12 Gun Sloop Com^d by John Crappo or Petweet & Stood to the westward a cross^d the Gulf.

19th at Day the Cape of Floriday bore west we stood for it a Cross^d

---

1   Abaco: an island in the northern part of the Bahamas.

2   Yoll: yawl, an open rowing boat.

3   Hogg^d Ship & Boot Top^d the Ship: scraped the marine growth from its bottom.

the Gulf we Came out of the Gulf in five fathom of Water & Within 30 Rods of a Rieff in the Space of 15 Minutes in About a League of the Shore Which Surpris^d the Capt. & Other Officers we have the Ship in Stays & beat off the wind being moderate.

20th Saw a Sail & Gave her Chace & Came Up She was a Spaniard a Palacca[1] from Havanna Bound to Spain She Inform^d us of the Jamaica Fleet[2] that they Pass^d the Havanna ten Days Back Which made us Give over the Hopes of Seeing them.

22 Saw this Spaniard about a League to the Wind ward.

23 a Sunday, Saw a Ships Mast in Forenoon & Just at Night A Large Jamaica Puncheon Floating we hoisted out our Boat^s & went in Persuit of it but Could not Get it we Suppos^d it was full of Rum this Afternoon a Large Swell brok & Soon after A fine Breese Which Increas^d harder in the Morn^g.

24th Sun about two hours high we Saw white Water in About a Mile Under our Lee Bow we Saw the Breakers which was on the Bahama Banks which Surprisd our Officers & Men Greatly we Put our Ship About & had the Good Fortune to Clear them the wind Blew harder we Struck Top Gallant Yards & Lanch^d Top Gallant Masts Lay too Under one Leach of the Four Sail Got 6 Nine Pounders Down in the Lower hold & Cleard the Decks of unnecessary Lumber The Wind Continued verry hard The air was Verry Thick Just before Night the Sea Came in Over our Larboard Nettens on the Gangway. All the officers Advis^d to Cut away the Main Mast which we Did, Just at Dusk, All the hope we had was that it would not Blow harder, but it Continued harder till After Midnight About one oClock it Seemd to Blow in whirlwinds which oblig^d us to Cut away our Four Mast & Missen Mast. Soon after the Wind Chang^d to the Eastward which Greatly Encourag^d us Being Much Affraid of the Bahama Banks the fore Mast fell to the windward & Knock^d our Anchor off the Bow So that we Cut it away for fear it would Make a hole in the Bow of the Ship our Fore Mast Lay along Side for two hours After it fell, it Being Impossible to Get Clear of it We Bent our Cables for fear of the Banks that we Might try to Ride it out if we Got on.

25 Moderated Some But Verry Rough So that we Could Do no work.

---

1 Palacca: a two or three-masted vessel usually seen in the Mediterranean.
2 Jamaica Fleet: a large British convoy of merchant ships bound from Jamaica to England. Apparently the *Oliver Cromwell* had been looking to attack this valuable convoy.

26 Got a Jury Mast Upon the Main Mast.

27 Got up Jury Masts on the Fore & Mison Masts.

30 at 8 oClock in the Morning Saw a Brigg over our weather Bow 2 Leagues Dis[t] We Kept our Course She Stood the Same way Just at Night we gave her two Guns but She kept on at Night we Lost Sight of her.

31st at 5 in the Morning Saw the Brigg a Head Gave her Chace Came up with her about Noon we hoisted our Colours She hoisted English Colours, we Gave her one gun which made them come Tumbling Down.[1]

Sep[tr] 1st We Saw a Sail a Head Giving us Chace She hoisted Englis Colours & we & the Brigg hoisted English Colours She Came Down towards us we Put the Ship about & She Came Close too us we up Parts & Our Colours She put about & we Gave her about 12 Guns Bow Chaces & She Got Clear She was a Small Sloop of 6 or 8 Guns.

Sep[t] 2nd Got Soundings of Cape May 45 Fath[m].

Sep[t] 3rd at Night Lost Sight of The Prise.

Sep[t] 4th Saw a Sail A Privatier Schoner She kept Round us all Day & hoisted English Colours we hoisted English Colours but She thought Best Not to Speak with.

Sep[t] 5th Made the Land at 9 oClock in the Morning the South Side of Long Island against South Hampton & Came to Anchor Under Fishes Island at 12oClock at Night Saw five Sail at 2 Afternoon Standing to the Westward two of them Ships.

Sep[t] 6th 1778 New London. Arriv[d] in this Harbour.

Questions for Discussion:

1. What was the greatest danger the crew of the *Oliver Cromwell* faced?

2. What does this journal reveal about shipboard life on a warship in the age of sail?

3. What evidence does the Boardman journal reveal about the role of subterfuge in war at sea during the American Revolution?

Samuel W. Boardman, ed., *Log-book of Timothy Boardman: kept on board the privateer Oliver Cromwell, during a cruise from New London, Ct., to Charleston, S.C., and Return, in 1778* (Albany, N.Y.: Joel Munsell's Sons, 1885), 51–67.

---

1   ... made them come Tumbling Down: the British ship showed it surrendered by lowering its flag.

MARITIME POLITICAL ECONOMY

With independence came many problems, among them how to rebuild America's seaborne commerce. Political leaders such as James Madison and Alexander Hamilton struggled to understand the "political economy" (the interdependence of government, economy, and society) of the new nation. Heavily influenced by Adam Smith's book *Wealth of Nations*, both Madison and Hamilton sought to create a government that supported commercial enterprise but remained removed from it. The founders saw commercial shipping as an important part of the American economy because it would carry American agricultural goods to Europe.

The great exception to American enthusiasm for seaborne commerce was Thomas Jefferson, who had his own powerful views on what American society should become. A rural plantation owner, Jefferson naturally placed his trust in the soil and independent farmers as the future basis for American society. It should be no surprise that urban northerners like Alexander Hamilton possessed a different view, one that emphasized commerce and manufacturing. Jefferson and Hamilton came from fundamentally different worlds, and the agrarian/commercial divide soon manifested itself in American politics, with Jefferson's followers forming a "Democratic Republican" party and Hamilton's followers claiming the title "Federalists."

The differences between Hamilton and Jefferson were not merely political; often they reflected regional differences. While the Northeast looked to the sea as the source of its wealth both from the fisheries and overseas trade, western farmers sought American control of the Mississippi in order to send their produce to markets. Misunderstandings and local visions of the nation's prosperity led to severe tensions between coastal traders who tended to follow Hamilton's commercial vision and river farmers who favored Jefferson's agrarian ideals.

As it turned out, both sides were right. Americans did take to the water during the early republic, but farmers generated their largely agricultural cargoes. Coasting vessels and early river steamboats carried the surplus of American farms to burgeoning ports such as New York, New Orleans, and Baltimore. American agricultural staples, especially tobacco, flour, and cotton, streamed across the Atlantic to markets in western Europe, especially Britain. Delivering these goods were American sailors, a distinctive type of worker set apart from the rest of society by their world travels, salty jargon, and aggressive commercial spirit that led them to seek out new markets and compete with European and, above all, British shipping.

Thomas Jefferson, "Occupation of the Ocean" (1785)

Thomas Jefferson (1743–1826) was no lover of the sea. A gentleman farmer from inland Virginia, Jefferson idealized independent yeoman farmers rather than urban tradesmen merchants or seamen as the exemplar of American virtue. Nonetheless, maritime issues were too important to the young American republic for him to ignore. In this letter to John Jay, Jefferson, then serving as the American minister to France, lays out his ideas on seafaring commerce and the need for a navy.

> Paris, Aug. 23, 1785
>
> Dear Sir,—
>
> I shall sometimes ask your permission to your letters, not official but private. The present is of this kind and is occasioned by the question proposed in yours of June 14. "whether it would be useful to us to carry all our productions, or none?" Were we perfectly free to decide this question, I should reason as follows. We have now lands enough to employ an infinite number of people in their cultivation. Cultivators of the earth are the most valuable citizens. They are the most vigorous, the most independent, the most virtuous, & they are tied to their country & wedded to its liberty & interests by the most lasting bonds. As long therefore as they can find employment in this line, I would not convert them into mariners, artisans or anything else. But our citizens will find employment in this line till their numbers, & of course their productions, become too great for the demand both internal & foreign. This is not the case as yet, & probably will not be for a considerable time. As soon as it is, the surplus of hands must be turned to something else. I should then perhaps wish to turn them to the sea in preference to manufactures, because comparing the characters of the two classes I find the former the most valuable citizens. I consider the class of artificers as the panders of vice & the instruments by which the liberties of a country are generally overturned. However we are not free to decide this question on principles of theory only. Our people are decided in the opinion that it is necessary for us to take a share in the occupation of the ocean, & their established habits induce them to require that the sea be kept open to them, and that that line of policy be pursued which will render the use of that element as great as possible to them. I think it a duty in those entrusted with the administration of their affairs to conform themselves to the decided

choice of their constituents: and that therefore we should in every instance preserve an equality of right to them in the transportation of commodities, in the right of fishing, & in the other uses of the sea. But what will be the consequence? Frequent wars without a doubt. Their property will be violated on the sea, & in foreign ports, their persons will be insulted, imprisoned &c. for pretended debts, contracts, crimes, contraband, &c., &c. These insults must be resented, even if we had no feelings, yet to prevent their eternal repetition, or in other words, our commerce on the ocean & in other countries must be paid for by frequent war. The justest dispositions possible in ourselves will not secure us against it. It would be necessary that all other nations were just also. Justice indeed on our part will save us from those wars which would have been produced by a contrary disposition. But to prevent those produced by the wrongs of other nations? By putting ourselves in a condition to punish them. Weakness provokes insult & injury, while a condition to punish it often prevents it. This reasoning leads to the necessity of some naval force, that being the only weapon with which we can reach an enemy. I think it to our interest to punish the first insult; because an insult unpunished is the parent of many others. We are not at this moment in, a condition to do it, but we should put ourselves into it as soon as possible. If a war with England should take place, it seems to me that the first thing necessary would be a resolution to abandon the carrying trade because we cannot protect it. Foreign nations must in that case be invited to bring us what we want & to take our productions in their own bottoms. This alone could prevent the loss of those productions to us & the acquisition of them to our enemy. Our seamen might be employed in depredations on their trade. But how dreadfully we shall suffer on our coasts, if we have no force on the water, former experience has taught us. Indeed I look forward with horror to the very possible case of war with an European power, & think there is no protection against them but from the possession of some force on the sea. Our vicinity to their West India possessions & to the fisheries is a bridle which a small naval force on our part would hold in the mouths of the most powerful of these countries. I hope our land office will rid us of our debts, & that our first attention then will be to the beginning a naval force of some sort. This alone can countenance our people as carriers on the water, & I suppose them to be determined to continue such.

Questions for discussion:
1. What does this document reveal about Jefferson's vision for American society?
2. What does Jefferson see as some of the drawbacks to maritime commerce?
3. What role does Jefferson see for an American Navy?

Paul Leicester Ford, ed., *The Works of Thomas Jefferson*, vol. 4 (New York: G. P. Putnam's Sons, 1904), 449–51.

Alexander Hamilton, "Federalist No. 11" (1787)

Alexander Hamilton (1755?–1804) wrote this essay titled "The Utility of the Union in Respect to Commercial Relations and a Navy," in November 1787, under the pseudonym *Publius*. It was the eleventh of a series of essays in which Hamilton tried to persuade Americans to ratify the United States Constitution, which had been drafted in Philadelphia the previous summer, to replace the Articles of Confederation and form the basis for a new government. In this document, Hamilton advocates for a strong central government that could encourage and protect seaborne commerce. With the ratification of the Constitution, Hamilton became the nation's first Secretary of the Treasury, and while he held that post he established maritime policies that effectively supported American shipping.

To the People of the State of New York:
The importance of the Union, in a commercial light, is one of those points about which there is least room to entertain a difference of opinion, and which has, in fact, commanded the most general assent of men who have any acquaintance with the subject. This applies as well to our intercourse with foreign countries as with each other.
There are appearances to authorize a supposition that the adventurous spirit, which distinguishes the commercial character of America, has already excited uneasy sensations in several of the maritime powers of Europe. They seem to be apprehensive of our too great interference in that carrying trade, which is the support of their navigation and the foundation of their naval strength. Those of them which have colonies in America look forward to what this country is capable of becoming, with painful solicitude. They foresee the dangers that may threaten their American dominions from the neighborhood of States, which have all the dispositions, and would possess all the means, req-

uisite to the creation of a powerful marine. Impressions of this kind will naturally indicate the policy of fostering divisions among us, and of depriving us, as far as possible, of an ACTIVE COMMERCE in our own bottoms. This would answer the threefold purpose of preventing our interference in their navigation, of monopolizing the profits of our trade, and of clipping the wings by which we might soar to a dangerous greatness. Did not prudence forbid the detail, it would not be difficult to trace, by facts, the workings of this policy to the cabinets of ministers.

If we continue united, we may counteract a policy so unfriendly to our prosperity in a variety of ways. By prohibitory regulations, extending, at the same time, throughout the States, we may oblige foreign countries to bid against each other, for the privileges of our markets. This assertion will not appear chimerical to those who are able to appreciate the importance of the markets of three millions of people increasing in rapid progression, for the most part exclusively addicted to agriculture, and likely from local circumstances to remain so to any manufacturing nation; and the immense difference there would be to the trade and navigation of such a nation, between a direct communication in its own ships, and an indirect conveyance of its products and returns, to and from America, in the ships of another country. Suppose, for instance, we had a government in America, capable of excluding Great Britain (with whom we have at present no treaty of commerce) from all our ports; what would be the probable operation of this step upon her politics? Would it not enable us to negotiate, with the fairest prospect of success, for commercial privileges of the most valuable and extensive kind, in the dominions of that kingdom? When these questions have been asked, upon other occasions, they have received a plausible, but not a solid or satisfactory answer. It has been said that prohibitions on our part would produce no change in the system of Britain, because she could prosecute her trade with us through the medium of the Dutch, who would be her immediate customers and paymasters for those articles which were wanted for the supply of our markets. But would not her navigation be materially injured by the loss of the important advantage of being her own carrier in that trade? Would not the principal part of its profits be intercepted by the Dutch, as a compensation for their agency and risk? Would not the mere circumstance of freight occasion a considerable deduction? Would not so circuitous an intercourse facilitate the competitions of other nations, by enhancing the price of British commodities in our markets, and by transferring to other hands the management of this interesting branch of the British commerce?

A mature consideration of the objects suggested by these questions will justify a belief that the real disadvantages to Britain from such a state of things, conspiring with the pre-possessions of a great part of the nation in favor of the American trade, and with the importunities of the West India islands, would produce a relaxation in her present system, and would let us into the enjoyment of privileges in the markets of those islands elsewhere, from which our trade would derive the most substantial benefits. Such a point gained from the British government, and which could not be expected without an equivalent in exemptions and immunities in our markets, would be likely to have a correspondent effect on the conduct of other nations, who would not be inclined to see themselves altogether supplanted in our trade.

A further resource for influencing the conduct of European nations toward us, in this respect, would arise from the establishment of a federal navy. There can be no doubt that the continuance of the Union under an efficient government would put it in our power, at a period not very distant, to create a navy which, if it could not vie with those of the great maritime powers, would at least be of respectable weight if thrown into the scale of either of two contending parties. This would be more peculiarly the case in relation to operations in the West Indies. A few ships of the line, sent opportunely to the reinforcement of either side, would often be sufficient to decide the fate of a campaign, on the event of which interests of the greatest magnitude were suspended. Our position is, in this respect, a most commanding one. And if to this consideration we add that of the usefulness of supplies from this country, in the prosecution of military operations in the West Indies, it will readily be perceived that a situation so favorable would enable us to bargain with great advantage for commercial privileges. A price would be set not only upon our friendship, but upon our neutrality. By a steady adherence to the Union we may hope, erelong, to become the arbiter of Europe in America, and to be able to incline the balance of European competitions in this part of the world as our interest may dictate.

But in the reverse of this eligible situation, we shall discover that the rival ships of the parts would make them checks upon each other, and would frustrate all the tempting advantages which nature has

kindly placed within our reach. In a state so insignificant our commerce would be a prey to the wanton intermeddlings of all nations at
war with each other; who, having nothing to fear from us, would with
little scruple or remorse, supply their wants by depredations on our
property as often as it fell in their way. The rights of neutrality will
only be respected when they are defended by an adequate power. A
nation, despicable by its weakness, forfeits even the privilege of being
neutral.

Under a vigorous national government, the natural strength and
resources of the country, directed to a common interest, would baffle
all the combinations of European jealousy to restrain our growth. This
situation would even take away the motive to such combinations, by
inducing an impracticability of success. An active commerce, an extensive navigation, and a flourishing marine would then be the off-
spring of moral and physical necessity. We might defy the little arts of
the little politicians to control or vary the irresistible and unchange-
able course of nature.

But in a state of disunion, these combinations might exist and
might operate with success. It would be in the power of the maritime
nations, availing themselves of our universal impotence, to prescribe
the conditions of our political existence; and as they have a common
interest in being our carriers, and still more in preventing our becoming theirs, they would in all probability combine to embarrass our
navigation in such a manner as would in effect destroy it, and confine
us to a PASSIVE COMMERCE. We should then be compelled to content ourselves with the first price of our commodities, and to see the
profits of our trade snatched from us to enrich our enemies and per-
secutors. That unequaled spirit of enterprise, which signalizes the genius of the American merchants and navigators, and which is in itself
an inexhaustible mine of national wealth, would be stifled and lost,
and poverty and disgrace would overspread a country which, with
wisdom, might make herself the admiration and envy of the world.

There are rights of great moment to the trade of America which are
rights of the Union—I allude to the fisheries, to the navigation of the
Western lakes, and to that of the Mississippi. The dissolution of the
Confederacy would give room for delicate questions concerning the
future existence of these rights; which the interest of more powerful
partners would hardly fail to solve to our disadvantage. The disposition of Spain with regard to the Mississippi needs no comment. France

and Britain are concerned with us in the fisheries, and view them as of the utmost moment to their navigation. They, of course, would hardly remain long indifferent to that decided mastery, of which experience has shown us to be possessed in this valuable branch of traffic, and by which we are able to undersell those nations in their own markets. What more natural than that they should be disposed to exclude from the lists such dangerous competitors?

This branch of trade ought not to be considered as a partial benefit. All the navigating States may, in different degrees, advantageously participate in it, and under circumstances of a greater extension of mercantile capital, would not be unlikely to do it. As a nursery of seamen, it now is, or when time shall have more nearly assimilated the principles of navigation in the several States, will become, a universal resource. To the establishment of a navy, it must be indispensable.

To this great national object, a NAVY, union will contribute in various ways. Every institution will grow and flourish in proportion to the quantity and extent of the means concentrated towards its formation and support. A navy of the United States, as it would embrace the resources of all, is an object far less remote than a navy of any single State or partial confederacy, which would only embrace the resources of a single part. It happens, indeed, that different portions of confederated America possess each some peculiar advantage for this essential establishment. The more southern States furnish in greater abundance certain kinds of naval stores—tar, pitch, and turpentine. Their wood for the construction of ships is also of a more solid and lasting texture. The difference in the duration of the ships of which the navy might be composed, if chiefly constructed of Southern wood, would be of signal importance, either in the view of naval strength or of national economy. Some of the Southern and of the Middle States yield a greater plenty of iron, and of better quality. Seamen must chiefly be drawn from the Northern hive. The necessity of naval protection to external or maritime commerce does not require a particular elucidation, no more than the conduciveness of that species of commerce to the prosperity of a navy.

An unrestrained intercourse between the States themselves will advance the trade of each by an interchange of their respective productions, not only for the supply of reciprocal wants at home, but for exportation to foreign markets. The veins of commerce in every part will be replenished, and will acquire additional motion and vigor from a free circulation of the commodities of every part. Commercial enterprise will have much greater scope, from the diversity in the productions of different States. When the staple of one fails from a bad harvest or unproductive crop, it can call to its aid the staple of another. The variety, not less than the value, of products for exportation contributes to the activity of foreign commerce. It can be conducted upon much better terms with a large number of materials of a given value than with a small number of materials of the same value; arising from the competitions of trade and from the fluctuations of markets. Particular articles may be in great demand at certain periods, and unsalable at others; but if there be a variety of articles, it can scarcely happen that they should all be at one time in the latter predicament, and on this account the operations of the merchant would be less liable to any considerable obstruction or stagnation. The speculative trader will at once perceive the force of these observations, and will acknowledge that the aggregate balance of the commerce of the United States would bid fair to be much more favorable than that of the thirteen States without union or with partial unions.

It may perhaps be replied to this, that whether the States are united or disunited, there would still be an intimate intercourse between them which would answer the same ends; this intercourse would be fettered, interrupted, and narrowed by a multiplicity of causes, which in the course of these papers have been amply detailed. A unity of commercial, as well as political, interests, can only result from a unity of government.

There are other points of view in which this subject might be placed, of a striking and animating kind. But they would lead us too far into the regions of futurity, and would involve topics not proper for a newspaper discussion. I shall briefly observe, that our situation invites and our interests prompt us to aim at an ascendant in the system of American affairs. The world may politically, as well as geographically, be divided into four parts, each having a distinct set of interests. Unhappily for the other three, Europe, by her arms and by her negotiations, by force and by fraud, has, in different degrees, extended her dominion over them all. Africa, Asia, and America, have successively felt her domination. The superiority she has long maintained has tempted her to plume herself as the Mistress of the World, and to consider the rest of mankind as created for her benefit. Men admired as profound philosophers have, in direct terms, attributed to her inhabitants a physical superiority, and have gravely asserted that all animals, and with them the human species, degenerate in America—that even dogs cease to bark after having breathed awhile in our atmosphere. Facts have too long supported these arrogant pretensions of the Europeans. It belongs to us to vindicate the honor of the human race, and to teach that assuming brother, moderation. Union will enable us to do it. Disunion will add another victim to his triumphs. Let Americans disdain to be the instruments of European greatness! Let the thirteen States, bound together in a strict and indissoluble Union, concur in erecting one great American system, superior to the control of all transatlantic force or influence, and able to dictate the terms of the connection between the old and the new world!

Questions for Discussion:
1. What was Hamilton's economic vision for the newly created United States?
2. According to Hamilton, what advantages did a strong national government bring to maritime commerce?
3. What role did Hamilton foresee for an American Navy?

Henry Cabot Lodge, ed., *The Federalist: A Commentary on the Constitution of the United States* (New York: G. P. Putnam's Sons, 1888), 60–67.

Fisher Ames, "A Navigating People" (1793)

In January 1793, Congressman from Virginia James Madison made a speech in Congress calling for higher duties on imported goods and further restrictions against foreign ships entering American ports. Madison was a supporter of Jefferson, and both were increasingly concerned about the growth of maritime trade with the British. But New England's mercantile interests, which profited from this trade, opposed any interference with it. Congressman Fisher Ames (1758–1808) of Massachusetts, a state with considerable maritime interests, rose to refute Madison's ideas. To Ames it was folly to tinker with a policy that had proved so successful in reviving American seaborne commerce. Ames would prove to be a consistent critic of Jeffersonian trade policies and a noted leader of the Federalist party. Madison's differences with New England's commercial interests plagued him through the rest of his political career.

A question remains respecting the state of our *navigation*. If we pay no regard to the regulations of foreign nations, and ask, whether this valuable branch of our industry and capital is in a distressed and sickly state, we shall find it is in a strong and flourishing condition. If the quantity of shipping was declining, if it was unemployed, even at low freight, I should say it must be sustained and encouraged. No such thing is asserted. Seamen's wages are high, freights are high, and American bottoms in full employment. But the complaint is, our vessels are not permitted to go to the British West Indies. It is even affirmed, that no civilized country treats us so ill in that respect. Spain and Portugal prohibit the traffic to their possessions, not only in our vessels, but in their own, which, according to the style of the resolutions, is worse treatment than we meet with from the British. It is also asserted, and on as bad ground, that our vessels are excluded from most of the British markets.

This is not true in any sense. We are admitted into the greater number of her ports, in our own vessels; and by far the greater value of our exports is sold in British ports, into which our vessels are received, not only on a good footing, compared with other foreigners, but on terms of positive favor, on better terms than British vessels are admitted into our own ports. We are not subject to the alien duties; and the light money, &c., of 1s. 9d. sterling per ton is less than our foreign tonnage duty, not to mention the ten per cent, on the duties on goods in foreign bottoms.

But in the port of London our vessels are received free. It is for the unprejudiced mind to compare these facts with the assertions we have heard so confidently and so feelingly made by the mover of the resolutions, that we are excluded from most of their ports, and that no civilized nation treats our vessels so ill as the British. The tonnage of the vessels employed between Great Britain and her dependencies and the United States, is called two hundred and twenty thousand; and the whole of this is represented as our just right. The same gentleman speaks of our natural right to the carriage of our own articles, and that we may and ought to insist upon our equitable share. Yet soon after he uses the language of monopoly, and represents the whole carriage of imports and exports as the proper object of our efforts, and all that others carry as a clear loss to us. If an equitable share of the carriage means half, we have it already, and more, and our proportion is rapidly increasing. If any thing is meant by the natural right of carriage, one would imagine that it belongs to him, whoever he may be, who, having bought our produce, and made himself the owner, thinks proper to take it with him to his own country. It is neither our policy nor our design to check the sale of our produce. We invite every description of purchasers, because we expect to sell dearest, when the number and competition of the buyers is the greatest. For this reason the total exclusion of foreigners and their vessels from the purchase and carriage of our exports is an advantage in respect to navigation, which has disadvantage to balance it, in respect to the price of produce. It is with this reserve we ought to receive the remark, that the carriage of our exports should be our object rather than that of our imports. By going with our vessels into foreign ports we buy our imports in the best market. By giving a steady and moderate encouragement to our own shipping, without pretending violently to interrupt the course of business, experience will soon establish that order of things which is most beneficial to the exporter, the importer, and the ship-owner. The best interest of agriculture is the true interest of trade.

In a trade mutually beneficial, it is strangely absurd to consider the gain of others as our loss. Admitting it, however, for argument sake, yet it should be noticed that the loss of two hundred and twenty thousand tons of shipping is computed according to the apparent tonnage. Our vessels not being allowed to go to the British West Indies, their vessels, making frequent voyages, appear in the entries over and over again. In the trade to the European dominions of Great Britain, the distance being greater, our vessels are not so often entered. Both these circumstances give a false show to the amount of British tonnage, compared with the American. It is, however, very pleasing to the mind to see that our tonnage exceeds the British in the European trade. For various reasons, some of which will be mentioned hereafter, the tonnage in the West India trade is not the proper subject of calculation. In the European comparison, we have more tonnage in the British than in the French commerce; it is indeed more than four to one.

The great quantity of British tonnage employed in our trade is also, in a great measure, owing to the large capitals of their merchants employed in the buying and exporting our productions. If we would banish the ships, we must strike at the root, and banish the capital. And this, before we have capital of our own grown up to replace it, would be an operation of no little violence and injury to our southern brethren especially.

Independently of this circumstance, Great Britain is an active and intelligent rival in the navigation line. Her ships are dearer, and the provisioning [of] her seamen is, perhaps, rather dearer than ours; on the other hand, the rate of interest is lower in England, and so are seamen's wages. It would be improper, therefore, to consider the amount of British tonnage in our trade as a proof of a bad state of things, arising either from the restrictions of that government, or the negligence or timidity of this. We are to charge it to causes which are more connected with the natural competition of capital and industry, causes which, in fact, retarded the growth of our shipping more, when we were colonies, and our ships were free, than since the adoption of the present government.

It has been said with emphasis, that the constitution grew out of the complaints of the nation respecting commerce, especially that with the British dominions. What was then lamented by our patriots? Feebleness of the public counsels; the shadow of union, and scarcely the shadow of public credit; everywhere despondence, the pressure of evils, not only great, but portentous of civil distractions. These were the grievances; and what more was then desired than their remedies? Is it possible to survey this prosperous country and to assert that they have been delayed? Trade flourishes on our wharves, although it droops in speeches. Manufactures have risen, under the shade of protecting duties, from almost nothing to such a state that we are even told we can depend on the domestic supply, if the foreign should cease. The fisheries, which we found in decline, are in the most vigorous growth; the whale fishery, which our allies would have transferred to Dunkirk,[1] now extends over the whole ocean. To that hardy race of men the sea is but a park for hunting its monsters; such is their activity, the deepest abysses scarcely afford to their prey a hiding-place. Look around, and see how the frontier circle widens, how the interior improves, and let it be repeated, that the hopes of the people, when they formed this constitution, have been frustrated.

But if it should happen that our prejudices prove stronger than our senses; if it should be believed that our farmers and merchants see

---

1   Dunkirk: After the American Revolution, the French government attempted to recruit
     Nantucket whalemen to operate out of the port of Dunkirk, in France.

their products and ships and wharves going to decay together, and they are ignorant or silent on their own ruin; still the public documents would not disclose so alarming a state of our affairs. Our imports are obtained so plentifully and cheaply, that one of the avowed objects of the resolutions is, to make them scarcer and dearer. Our exports, so far from languishing, have increased two millions of dollars in a year. Our navigation is found to be augmented beyond the most sanguine expectation. We hear of the vast advantage the English derived from the navigation act; and we are asked, in a tone of accusation, shall we sit still and do nothing? Who is bold enough to say Congress has done nothing for the encouragement of American navigation? To counteract the navigation act, we have laid on British a higher tonnage than our own vessels pay in their ports; and what is much more effectual, we have imposed ten per cent, on the duties when the dutied articles are borne in foreign bottoms. We have also made the coasting trade a monopoly to our own vessels. Let those who have asserted that this is nothing, compare facts with the regulations which produced them.

. . .

Is not this increase of American shipping rapid enough? Many persons say it is too rapid, and attracts too much capital for the circumstances of the country. I cannot readily persuade myself to think so valuable a branch of employment thrives too fast. But a steady and sure encouragement is more to be relied on than violent methods of forcing its growth. It is not clear, that the quantity of our navigation, including our coasting and fishing vessels, is less in proportion to those of that nation; in that computation we shall probably find that we are already more a navigating people than the English.

As this is a growing country, we have the most stable ground of dependence on the corresponding growth of our navigation; and that the increasing demand for shipping will rather fall to the share of Americans than foreigners, is not to be denied. We did expect this from the nature of our own laws; we have been confirmed in it by experience; and we know that an American bottom is actually preferred to a foreign one. In cases where one partner is an American, and another a foreigner, the ship is made an American bottom. A fact of this kind overthrows a whole theory of reasoning on the necessity of further restrictions. It shows that the work of restriction is already done.

Questions for Discussion:

1. What did Ames's speech reveal about Madison's ideas on maritime trade?

2. How did Ames relate the success of American commercial policies to the success of the American Revolution?

3. What does this document reveal about the American relationship with the sea in the wake of the Revolution?

Fisher Ames, *Works of Fisher Ames: With a Selection from His Speeches and Correspondence*, vol. 2 (Boston: Little, Brown and Company, 1854), 18–22.

John Breckinridge, "Free Navigation of the Mississippi" (1793)

John Breckinridge (1760–1806), who was born in Virginia and moved to Kentucky, was one of many Americans to move west after the Revolution. Maritime issues loomed large in the consciousness of these new westerners because the Ohio and Mississippi rivers were natural highways on which they could transport their agricultural surpluses to larger markets. But Spain controlled the Mississippi's navigation, including the valuable port of New Orleans. From the close of the Revolution westerners demanded the right to market their produce in New Orleans and to use that port for shipping. The Spanish monarchy jealously guarded what it regarded as the privilege of navigating the Mississippi, although it did grant American use of the river in Pinckney's Treaty of 1795. The following petition penned by Breckinridge and printed in a Kentucky newspaper illustrates some of the dissatisfaction westerners had with the Federalist-dominated Washington administration.

TO THE INHABITANTS OF THE UNITED STATES WEST OF THE ALLEGANY AND APALACHIAN MOUNTAINS.

Fellow Citizens,

The Democratic Society of Kentucky, having had under consideration the measures necessary to obtain the exercise of your right to the free navigation of the Mississippi, have determined to address you upon that important topic. In so doing, they think, that they only use the undoubted right of Citizens, to consult for their common welfare. This measure is not dictated by party or faction, it is the consequence of unavoidable necessity. It has become so from the neglect shewn by the General Government, to obtain for those of the citizens of the United States, who are interested therein, the navigation of that River.

In the present age, when the rights of man have been fully investigated and declared by the voice of nations, and more particularly in America, where those rights were first developed and declared, it will not be necessary to prove, that the free navigation of the Mississippi is the natural right of the Inhabitants of the country watered by its streams. It cannot be believed, that the beneficent God of nature would have blessed this country with unparalleled fertility, and furnished it with a number of navigable streams, and that that fertility should be consumed at home, and those streams should not convey its superabundance to the climes far from it; for if we examine the wise diversity of the earth, as to climate and productions, lands, seas and rivers, we must discover the glorious plan of infinite beneficence to unite by the exchange of their surplus, various nations, and connect the ends of the earth, in the hands of commerce and mutual good offices. From the everlasting decrees of Providence, then, we derive this right; and must be criminal either to surrender or suffer it to be taken from us; without the most arduous struggle. But this right is ours, not only from nature but compact. We do not mean to urge this, as if a compact could give an additional sanction to a natural right; but to shew that our claim is derived from every source which can give it validity. The Navigation of the Mississippi was solemnly given and confirmed by Great Britain, to the citizens of the United States, by the provisional articles entered into at Paris,[1] between the two nations. More than eleven years have since elapsed, during which we have been denied the exercise of a right, founded upon such irrefragable grounds. What has been done by the former or present Government, during that period, on our behalf? In the former, we have been able to learn of no attempt to procure from the King of Spain, even an acknowledgment of our right. Repeated Memorials were presented to Congress upon the subject, but they were treated with a neglect bordering on contempt. They were laid upon the table, there to rest in endless oblivion. Once indeed, we know this subject was introduced into Congress, under the former Government; but it was by an unwarrantable and disgraceful proposition to barter away our right. The

---

1   Paris: The 1783 Treaty of Paris in which Great Britain formally recognized the sovereignty of the United States.

proposition was not adopted; the attempt being rendered abortive by the spirited and patriotic opposition of a part of the Union. The time at length came, when the voice of the people called for a change in the General Government; and the present Constitution of the United States was adopted. We then flattered ourselves that our rights would be protected; for we were taught to believe, that the former loose and weak confederation having been done away, the new government would possess the requisite energy. Memorials upon the subject were renewed: Six years have passed away, and our right is not yet obtained. Money is to be taken from us by an odious and oppressive excise; but the means of procuring it, by exercise of our just right, is denied. In the mean while, our brethren on the Eastern waters, possess every advantage which nature or compact can give them. Nay, we do not know that even one firm attempt to obtain it has been made. Alas! Is the energy of our Government not to be exerted against our enemies? Is it all to be reserved for her citizens?

Experience, Fellow-Citizens, has shewn that the General Government is unwilling that we should obtain the navigation of the River Mississippi. A local policy appears to have an undue weight in the Councils of the Union. It seems to be the object of that policy to prevent the population of this country, which would draw from the Eastern States their industrious Citizens. This conclusion inevitably follows from a consideration of the measures taken to prevent the purchase and settlement of the lands bordering on the Mississippi. Among those measures, the unconstitutional interference, which rescinded sales, by one of the States to private individuals makes a striking object. And perhaps, the fear of a successful rivalship in every article of their exports may have its weight. But, if they are not unwilling to do us justice, they are at least regardless of our rights and welfare. We have found prayers and supplications of no avail; and should we continue to load the table of Congress with memorials, from a part only, of the Western Country, it is too probable they would meet with a fate, similar to those which have formerly been presented. Let us, then, all unite our endeavors to the common cause. Let all join in a firm and manly Remonstrance to the President and Congress of the United States, stating our just and undoubted right to the Navigation of the Mississippi, remonstrating against the conduct of government with regard to that right, which must have been occasioned by local policy or neglect, and demanding of them speedy and effectual exertions for its attainment. We cannot doubt, that you will cordially and unanimously join in this measure. It can hardly be necessary to remind you, that considerable quantities of beef, pork, flour, hemp, tobacco, etc. the produce of this country, remain on hand for want of purchasers, or are sold at inadequate prices. Much greater quantities might be raised, if the Inhabitants were encouraged by a certain sale, which the free Navigation of the Mississippi would afford. An additional increase of those articles, and a greater variety of produce and manufactures would be supplied, by means of the encouragement, which the attainment of that great object would give to migration. But it is not only your own rights which you are to regard. Remember that your posterity have a claim to your exertions to obtain and secure that right. Let not your memory be stigmatized with a neglect of duty. Let not history record, that the Inhabitants of this beautiful country lost a most invaluable right and half the benefit bestowed upon it by a bountiful Providence, through your neglect and supineness. The present crisis is favorable. Spain is engaged in a war, which requires all her forces. If the present golden opportunity be suffered to pass without advantage, and she shall have concluded a peace with France,[1] we must then contend against her undivided strength.

But, what may be the event of the proposed application, is yet uncertain. We ought therefore, to be upon our guard, and watchful to seize the first favorable opportunity to gain our object. In order to do this, our union should be as perfect and lasting as possible. We propose, that societies should be formed in convenient districts, in every part of the Western country who shall preserve a correspondence upon this and every other subject of general concern. By means of these societies, we shall be enabled speedily to know what may be the result of our endeavors—to consult upon such further measures as may be necessary—to preserve union—and finally, by these means to secure success.

Remember, that it is a cause which ought to unite us—that that cause is indubitably just—that ourselves and posterity are interested—that the Crisis is favorable—and that it is only by union, that the object can be achieved. The obstacles are great, and so ought to be our efforts. Adverse fortune may attend us, but it shall never dispirit us. We

1   France: Breckinridge is pointing out that Spain was then at War with France, and it would be more difficult to gain concessions out of Spain if that war ended.

may for a while exhaust our wealth and strength in vain; but until the all-important object is procured, we pledge ourselves to you, and let us all pledge ourselves to each other, that our perseverance and our firmness will be inexhaustible.

By order of the Society
JOHN BRECKINRIDGE
Chairman.
December 13, 1793.

Questions for Discussion:
1. What does this document reveal about the importance of navigating the Mississippi and other western rivers?
2. What revolutionary or other ideals is Breckinridge espousing?
3. What does this document reveal about the relationship of maritime trade to partisan politics in the early republic?

———————
James Alton James, ed., *Readings in American History* (New York: Charles Scribner's Sons, 1914), 225–29.

MERCHANTS AND ENTREPRENEURS

After independence, merchants dominated commercial seafaring, but as the economy developed and changed, a new breed of entrepreneurs took the fore in the American economy. The difference is that while merchants essentially sought to "buy cheap and sell dear"—and sought out new markets to do so—entrepreneurs were much bolder, envisioning new ways of conducting business that reflected and sometimes led the changes and needs in society. Americans prospered in both roles during the early republic.

The manner in which merchants did business had remained much the same for hundreds of years, but that did not mean they did not eagerly seek out new markets. Relieved from British mercantilist restrictions after the Revolution, American merchants were quick to engage in trade with Asia. Yankee merchants brought back from Asia tea, porcelain, silks, and pepper, and held their own in a sometimes fierce and even dangerous business climate. Salem, Massachusetts, and its clever and determined merchants and mariners such as Elias H. Derby and George Nichols best illustrate the Yankee mercantile ideal.

Entrepreneurs were less conventional than merchants and were bolder in envisioning new ways to conduct business. They did not just want to expand trade, as did the merchants, but to fundamentally change it by creating new business practices and engaging with changing technologies. For the entrepreneur, new services such as scheduled packets and steamboats offered exciting new opportunities that could literally transform society. New York City, the heart of the new American business paradigm, was naturally the adopted home of entrepreneurs. One such entrepreneur was Robert Fulton, a transportation magnate who wanted to transform how Americans looked at travel through the use of reliable and profitable steamboats.

Elias H. Derby, "A Little Particular in These Orders" (1789)

Elias H. Derby (1739–1799) was America's first millionaire, a Salem, Massachusetts, merchant who prospered by investing in privateers during the American Revolution and who invested those profits in bold new ventures after independence. He took considerable risks in becoming one of the very first American merchants to trade with China, India, the Philippines, and Russia. He was successful in virtually all of his investments. The letter below, giving instructions to the captain of his ship *Astrea* and the supercargo (the agent in charge of selling the ship's cargo), reveals how merchants instructed the captains of their ships in conducting business overseas.

SALEM, February, 1789.
CAPT. JAMES MAGEE, JR., Mr. THOMAS H. PERKINS:
GENTS The ship *Astrea*, of which James Magee is master, and Mr. Thomas Perkins is supercargo, being ready for sea, I do advise and order you to come to sail, and make the best of your way for Batavia,[1] and on your arrival there you will dispose of such a part of the cargo as you think may be most for my interest.

I think you had best sell a few casks of the most ordinary ginseng, if you can get one dollar a pound for it. If you find the price of sugar to be low, you will then take into the ship as much of the best white kind as will floor her, and fifty thousand weight of coffee, if it is as low as we have heard—part of which you will be able to stow between the beams and the quintlings and fifteen thousand of saltpeter, if very low; some nutmegs, and fifty thousand weight of pepper; this you will stow in the fore peak, for fear of its injuring the teas. The sugar will save the expense of any stone ballast, and it will make a floor for the teas, &c., at Canton.

---

1   Batavia: modern-day Jakarta, in Indonesia.

At Batavia you must, if possible, get as much freight for Canton as will pay half or more of your charges that is, if it will not detain you too long, as by this addition of freight it will exceedingly help the voyage. You must endeavor to be the first ship with ginseng, for be assured you will do better alone than you will if there are three or four ships at Canton at the same time with you. If Messrs. Blanchard & Webb are at Batavia in the brigantine *Three Sisters*, and if they have not stock sufficient to load with coffee and sugar, and if it is low, and you think it for my advantage, then I would have you ship me some coffee or sugar, and a few nutmegs, &c., to complete his loading. If his brigantine can be sold for a large price, and sugar and coffee, &c., are too dear to make any large freight—in that case it possibly may be for my interest to have her sold, and for them to take passage with you to Canton: but this must not be done unless you, Dr. Blanchard, and Capt. Webb shall think it *greatly* for my interest. Or possibly they may sell their brigantine to advantage, and find some Dutch ship that would take their freight to St. Eustatia or Curaçao,[1] so as to make it very advantageous. But there are too often difficulties attending the sale of ships so far from home; it therefore must be well thought of before it is undertaken. One thing I have against it is, that I shall have too much property in the *Astrea*, and not know it in time to make my insurance; which ought to be taken into consideration. On your going round the Cape,[2] no doubt, you will see some India ships bound home; you will put letters on board two or three of them for me, acquainting me with the situation of the ship, and every thing you think I may wish to know. Capt. Magee and Mr. Perkins are to have 5 per cent. commission for the sales of the present cargo, and 2 ½ per cent. on the cargo home, and also 5 per cent. on the profit made on goods that may be purchased at Batavia and sold at Canton, or in any other similar case that may arise on the voyage. They are to have one half the passage money the other half belongs to the ship. The privilege of Capt. Magee is 5 per cent. of what the ship carries on cargo exclusive of adventures. The property of Mr. Perkins, it is understood, is to be on freight, which is to be paid for like the other freighters. It is orders that the ship's books shall be open to the inspection of the mates and doctor of the ship, so that they may know the whole business, as in

---

1 St. Eustatia or Curaçao: Dutch-controlled islands in the Caribbean.
2 Cape: Cape of Good Hope, the southern tip of Africa.

case of death or sickness it may be good service in the voyage. The Philadelphia beer is put up so strong, that it will not be approved of until it is made weaker: you had best try some of it first. The iron is English weight: you will remember there is 4 per cent. that you will gain if sold Dutch weight. As the ships will be about leaving Batavia at the time you are there; if so, you will best barter the small ginseng for something those ships may have on board, as no doubt it will do better in that way than at Canton. You will be carefull not to break any acts of trade while you are out on the voyage, to lay the ship and cargo liable to seizure, for my insurance will not make it good. All freight out and home, it is understood, belongs to the ship, as Capt. Magee is to fill his privilege with his own property. Be very careful of the expense attending the voyage, for I more fear that than any thing else; and remember that one dollar laid out while absent is two dollars out of the voyage. Pay particular attention to the quality of your goods, as your voyage very much depends on your attention to this. You will not forget what Mr. Shippey says to you on that head, of the green tea and nankeens. You are not to pay any moneys to the crew while absent from home, unless in a case of real necessity, and then they must allow an advance for the money. Annexed to these orders you have a list of such a cargo for my own account as I at present think may do best for me, but you will add or diminish any article as the price may be.

My own property, I suppose, will take the room of 500 chests, and your freight that you already engaged will take the room of about 500 chests, and then I compute you will have room for 500 chests more on freight, to make up the 1,500 which you think the ship will load on cargo. You must, at Canton or Batavia, endeavor to fill the ship with light freight; and, provided you can do it to advantage, as to take the less room: but this must not be done unless by calculation you find it greatly for my interest. And I again repeat that I would have the doctor and Mr. Bray made acquainted with the whole business of the voyage, for fear of accident, as, in case Mr. Perkins should fail, one or both of them might be of great service to the voyage. It is likewise my order that, in case of your sickness, you write a clause at the foot of these orders, putting the command of the ship into the person's hands that you think the most equal to it, not having any regard to the station *he* at present has in the ship. Among the silks, you will get me one or two pieces of the wide nankeen satin, and others you will get as directed.

Get me two pots of twenty pounds each of race ginger, that is well put up; and layout for my account fifteen or twenty pounds sterling in curiosities. There will be breakage room in the bilge of the ship, that nothing dry can go in; therefore, in the crop of the bilge you will put some boxes of China, such as are made suitable for such places, and filled with cups and saucers, some bowls, and any thing of the kind that may answer.

As to the sale of the ship *Astrea*, it will not do to think of it, on account of the freighters' goods; but if at Batavia or Canton you can agree to deliver her the next season for $20,000 or $25,000, you may do it, the danger of the seas, &c., excepted. Attend particularly to the writings for this contract. Provided that you wish to obtain more property home in the ship, it will be most agreeable to me to take such a part of the profit, or take it to come at their risk, and for me to have all above 40 per cent. for Hyson tea and light goods; but the goods must be of the best quality, and put in at the cash value; but do not take it on my risk without the property is insured before you leave Canton. If any goods are shipped from Canton in the ship, you will endeavor to get me the consignment, as it may serve some of my family at Boston. It is understood where I have one-third of the ginseng for the freight and commissions, as mentioned in the agreement, I am to allow Magee and Perkins the commission for the whole sales out. In case Mr. Blanchard is at Batavia, and purchasing coffee, sugar, and other articles, if he can, by taking those articles, put off some of your goods and give you this money, in any way not to injure his voyage, then I would have him do it. Provided you, by information, are fully convinced that you can make a freight from Batavia on coffee, sugar, cotton, rice, or any thing else, and you can sell my ginseng for a dollar a pound this weight, then I wish to have a third of my quantity sold, but not for less; but in a barter way you no doubt will do better.

Capt. Magee and Mr. Perkins Although I have been a little particular in these orders, I do not mean them as positive; and you have leave to break them in any part where you by calculation think it for my interest, excepting your breaking acts of trade, which I absolutely forbid. Not having to add, I commit you to the Almighty's protection, and remain your friend and employer,

ELIAS HASKET DERBY
Salem, 15th February, 1789.

We acknowledge the above to be a true copy of our orders this day received.

JAMES MAGEE.
THOMAS HAND. PERKINS

Questions for Discussion:
1. What patterns of world trade can be inferred from this document?
2. What did Derby's instructions about making the orders and the ship's books open to the mate and ship's doctor reveal about the danger of this voyage?
3. Based on this letter, what do these instructions tell us about Derby's business practices as a merchant?

———————

Freeman Hunt, *Lives of American Merchants*, vol. 2 (New York: Derby and Jackson, 1858), 61–65.

George Nichols, "Pepper Trade" (1802)

After the American Revolution, Salem produced a remarkable generation of merchant seafarers who reached out to new markets in Asia. One of those mariners was George Nichols (1778–1865), a Salem mariner who specialized in the Far East trade. In this memoir he assembled at age eighty, Nichols recounts that, only four weeks after his marriage, he left his Salem home on a two-year voyage to the East Indies as master of the ship *Active* seeking a cargo of black pepper. Nichols recalls the dangers of the pepper trade and the fierce competitive spirit among American ship captains.

I cruised for a day or two along the coast in search of a landing place, when I saw the masts of a ship in a small harbor. I entered, and found it was the port of Mukka, and the ship was the *America* of Salem, Capt. Briggs, master. I went ashore in my boat, and saw great numbers of Malays, all well armed. I soon negotiated with the Governor for a cargo of pepper. We fixed upon a price, but he said he could not deliver any to me until Capt. Briggs' vessel was loaded. Now the *America* was more than three times the size of the *Active*, and she had as yet received but half her cargo, so I declined waiting, unless the Governor would fix upon a time for me to begin to receive. It was finally agreed that I should begin to receive in a week, whether the *America* was loaded or not. Capt. Briggs objected strongly to this, and insisted upon having all the pepper that was brought until his cargo was completed. A week elapsed. I now used every argument in my power to induce Capt. B.- to come to some amicable terms, but all my efforts were fruitless. I told him if three hundred piculs[1] were brought in daily, he might have two of them, but if only two hundred, I should feel myself entitled to one hundred. "You shall not have a pound, if I can help it," was his reply. "If it has come to fighting," said I, "the hardest must fend off." Every effort was made by him to prevent me from getting pepper, notwithstanding which I got the first day one-fourth of all that was brought in, and the second day I got one-third. "Now," said I, "you see I can get pepper as well as you. It is a pity to quarrel about it. Let us work together harmoniously." But no, he would not yield to my wishes. A great deal of pepper was brought in from a village, which was about a half-mile distant from the harbor where our vessels lay. The natives brought it in bags upon their backs, and were obliged to cross a river about two feet deep. Capt. Briggs, thinking to get the advantage of me, employed his men, of whom he had about three times as many as I had, in transporting it through the water to his vessel. Seeing this, I observed to my men that I was very sorry to call upon them to do such drudgery as that, but I must do it, otherwise Capt. Briggs would obtain all the pepper. They replied with a great deal of feeling, "Capt. Nichols, we will go as far as Capt. Briggs' men, let them go as far as they may." So saying, they went cheerfully to work, and at the close of the day I found that we had one-half of all that had been received. I again renewed my offer to Capt. B-, but he declined it and replied to me as before. Observing on one occasion that a large quantity of pepper had been brought in boats during the night, I resolved to secure it, if possible. Accordingly I arose at daylight, jumped into my boat, and taking four of my men, with bags, rowed to the shore. We passed the *America* on our way, the crew of which were surprised to find us stirring so early, but when Capt. B- discovered our object, he, too, manned his boat and went ashore. He was too late, he found to his great mortification, to obtain any pepper; we had it all, a larger supply than we had received in any one day.

Before I had completed my cargo, I narrowly escaped being cut off by the natives. I was ashore one day receiving pepper, when Mr. Ward, joint supercargo with Capt. Briggs, saw one of his bags in the hands

---

1   Picul: or *pecul*, a weight that varied in different Asian countries from roughly 130 to 200 pounds.

of a native. He suddenly snatched it from him and ran off. The man enrages, drew his creese[1] and pursued him, but failing to get at him, he turned upon one of my men who was near, receiving peppers. The man sprang, the Malay after him, and immediately all the Malays drew their weapons. I was from one to two hundred yards distant at the time, and seeing the confusion I hastened to the spot to ascertain the cause. There I saw my man and the Malay within ten feet of him, with his drawn creese in his hand. To retreat was impossible, for the Malays were between me and my boats. So, alone and unarmed, I went into the midst of the natives, and they, perceiving that my designs were pacific, assisted me in arresting the offender. I clapped my hand upon his back, and asked him what he meant by such doings. Then sending for the Rajah, I complained of the man to him, and assured him if ever anything of the kind occurred again, I would immediately resort to my ship, fire upon the town and destroy it, adding, "You know I could do it." He assented, and after that I had no more trouble. It was now about noon, so I went aboard my vessel and dined. On my return one of the first persons I met was the Malay who attempted to kill my man. He was seated upon some bags of pepper, and being at leisure, I sat down by him. With his permission, I took his creese in my hand, and found, upon examination, that it was poisoned, and the least wound with it would have caused instant death. This Malay was a very civil, pleasant fellow, and one of the smartest men I ever knew. We afterwards became very good friends.

The morning after this adventure, Capt. Briggs left for a neighboring port, a few miles distant, though he had received only about two-thirds of his cargo. His reason for leaving, we may infer without much difficulty. From this time I received pepper about as fast as I could ship it. A few days after this, Capt. Thomas Webb, of the brig *George Washington*, came into port for a cargo of pepper. As my cargo was nearly completed, I requested him to wait till my vessel was loaded, and then he would have the market to himself. He agreed not to interfere with me, but fearing to be left there alone on account of the natives, he left the port in the course of a day or two. When Capt. W- first saw me ashore he eyed me with astonishment. "Why, you look like a devil," said he. I was dressed in striped, loose trousers, a thin jacket, without vest, an old slouched hat, and shoes without stock-

---

1   Creese: a *kris*, a distinctive Malayan dagger with a wavy blade.

ings, but the shoes I took off when wading through the water. Nothing pleased the natives more than to find me ready to conform to their customs. I often walked arm in arm with their leading men, went into their huts to light my cigars, and offering them some, would sit down and smoke with them. A little act of imprudence on my part came very near bringing me into serious difficulty with the Rajah. About the time I began to receive pepper, they raised the price of it one dollar on a picul. This was in consequence of their charging more in other ports. I met the Rajah and other leading men in a room, which they called their council chamber, and remonstrated with them upon raising the price, after the contract which they had made with me, but all to no purpose. In the excitement of the moment, I called the Rajah a bad man, which exasperated him very much. Conscious that I had erred, I immediately sought means to pacify him. I patted him on the shoulder and asked him to go with me into another room. I then offered to give him one hundred dollars if he would fulfill his contract with me, but he would not consent to do it for that sum. Finally I agreed to give him five hundred dollars, and told him that he could pocket the whole if he chose. This sum satisfied him. and secured his friendship. In less than a fortnight[1] after Capt. Briggs left Mukka I completed my cargo, and made arrangements to continue my voyage.

Questions for Discussion:
1. Why did Captains Nichols and Briggs compete so fiercely, even though they both came from Salem?
2. What was the relationship between trade and violence in this account of the pepper trade?
3. What efforts did Capt. Nichols make to understand the local Malay population?

Martha Nichols, *A Salem Shipmaster and Merchant: The Autobiography of George Nichols* (Boston: Four Seas Company, 1921), 65–73.

Robert Fulton, "The Steamboat Business" (1807)

Robert Fulton (1765–1814) is well-known as the man who made steamboats commercially viable. Born in Pennsylvania, as a young man Fulton traveled to Europe and studied engineering and experimented with steamboats. On

---

1   Fortnight: about two weeks.

his return to the United States, Fulton determined to create steamboat service between New York City and Albany and succeeded admirably with the *North River Steamboat* in 1807, the first commercial steamboat service in the world. Fulton was quickly copied by other businessmen and struggled to maintain his monopoly on steam navigation in New York waters.

Fulton was an entrepreneur who relied heavily on government support to get his innovative steamboat business going, making him what Burton W. Folsom, in his book *The Myth of the Robber Barons*, called a "political entrepreneur."[1] Folsom juxtaposed Fulton against another steamboat entrepreneur, Cornelius Vanderbilt, who fiercely opposed all government interference in business matters. The following letters written by Fulton reveal both his triumphs and concerns in inaugurating commercial steamboat service.

To the Editor of the *American Citizen*:

New York, August 20 [1807].

Sir:

I arrived this afternoon at 4 o'clock, [on] the steamboat from Albany. As the success of my experiment gives me great hope that such boats may be rendered of much importance to my country, to prevent erroneous opinions, and to give some satisfaction to the friends of useful improvements, you will have the goodness to publish the following statement of facts:

I left New York on Monday at 1 o'clock, and arrived at Clermont, the seat of Chancellor Livingston, at 1 o'clock on Tuesday, time 24 hours, distance 110 miles: On Wednesday I departed from the Chancellor's at 9 in the morning, and arrived at Albany at 5 in the afternoon, distance 40 miles, time 8 hours; the sum of this is 150 miles in 82 hours, equal near 5 miles an hour.

On Thursday at 9 o'clock in the morning I left Albany and arrived at the Chancellor's at 6 in the evening; I started from thence at 7, and arrived at New York on Friday at 4 in the afternoon; time 30 hours, space run through 150 miles, equal 5 miles an hour. Throughout the whole way my going and returning the wind was ahead; no advantage could be drawn from my sails the whole has therefore been performed by the power of the steam engine.

I am, Sir, Your most obedient,
ROBERT FULTON.

---

1   Burton W. Folsom, *The Myth of the Robber Barons* (Herndon, Va.: Young America's Foundation, 1991).

To Joel Barlow:

My steamboat voyage to Albany and back has turned out rather more favorably than I had calculated. The distance from New York to Albany is one hundred and fifty miles. I ran it up in thirty-two hours, and down in thirty. I had a light breeze against me the whole way, both going and coming; and the voyage has been performed wholly by the power of the steam-engine. I overtook many sloops and schooners beating to windward, and parted with them.

The power of propelling boats by steam is now fully proved. The morning I left New York there were not perhaps thirty persons in the city who believed that the boat would ever move one mile an hour or be of the least utility; and, while we were putting off from the wharf, which was crowded with spectators, I heard a number of sarcastic remarks. This is the way in which ignorant men compliment what they call philosophers and projectors.

Having employed much time, money, and zeal in accomplishing this work, it gives me, as it will you, great pleasure to see it answer my expectations. It will give a cheap and quick conveyance to the merchandize on the Mississippi, Missouri, and other great rivers, which are now laying open their treasures to the enterprise of our countrymen; and, altho the prospect of personal emolument has been some inducement to me, yet I feel infinitely more pleasure in reflecting on the immense advantage my country will derive.

To Robert Livingston:

New York,
Saturday, the 28 [29th] of August, 1807

Dear Sir:

On Saturday I wrote you that I arrived here on Friday at four o'clock, which made my voyage from Albany exactly thirty hours. We had a little wind on Friday morning, but no waves which produced any effect. I have been making every exertion to get off on Monday morning, but there has been much work to do—boarding all the sides, decking over the boiler and works, finishing each cabin with twelve berths to make them comfortable, and strengthening many parts of the iron work. So much to do, and the rain, which delays the caulkers, will, I fear, not let me off till Wednesday morning. Then, however, the boat will be as complete as she can be made—all strong and in good order and the men well organized, and I hope, nothing to do but to run her for six weeks or two months.

The first week, that is if she starts on Wednesday, she will make one trip to Albany and back. Every succeeding week she will run three trips—that is, two to Albany and one to New York, or two to New York and one to Albany, always having Sunday and four nights for rest to the crew. By carrying for the usual price there can be no doubt but the steamboat will have the preference because of the certainty and agreeable movements. I have seen the captain of the fine sloop from Hudson. He says the average of his passages have been forty-eight hours. For the steamboat it would have been thirty certain.

The persons who came down with me were so much pleased that they said were she established to run periodically they would never go in any thing else. I will have her registered and every thing done which I can recollect. Every thing looks well and I have no doubt will be very productive.

Yours truly,
ROBERT FULTON.

You may look for me Thursday morning about seven o'clock. I think it would be well to write to your brother Edward to get information on the velocity of the Mississippi, the size and form of the boats used, the number of hands and quantity of tons in each boat, the number of miles they make against the current in twelve hours, and the quantity of tons which go up the river in a year. On this point beg of him to be accurate.

To Captain Brink:

New York, Oct. 9, 1807.

Capt Brink:

Sir

Inclosed is the number of voyages which it is intended the Boat should run this season. You may have them published in the Albany papers.

As she is strongly man'd and every one except Jackson under your command, you must insist on each one doing his duty or turn him on shore and put another in his place. Everything must be kept in order, everything in its place, and all parts of the Boat scoured and clean. It is not sufficient to tell men to do a thing, but stand over them and make them do it. One pair of Quick and good eyes is worth six pair of hands in a commander. If the Boat is dirty and out of order the fault shall be yours. Let no man be Idle when there is the least thing to do, and make them move quick.

Run no risques of any kind when you meet or overtake vessels beating or crossing your way. Always run under their stern if there be the least doubt that you cannot clear their head by 50 yards or more. Give in the accounts of Receipts and expenses every week to the Chancellor.

Your most Obedient
ROBT. FULTON.

To Joel Barlow:

New York, June 28th, 1811.

Dear Barlow

My whole time is now occupied in building North River and Steam ferry boats, and in an interesting lawsuit to crush 22 Pirates who have clubbed their purses and copied my boats and have actually started my own Invention in opposition to me by running one trip to Albany: her machinery however gave way in the first voyage and she is now repairing, which will detain her I presume until we obtain an Injunction to stop her. A more infamous and outrageous attack upon mental property has not disgraced America. Thornton has been one of the great causes of it. In this interesting suit which places a great fortune at stake I want you to do two things for me immediately. First go or send Lee to Thornton's office and demand a certified copy of my transfer of one half of my United States patents to Robert R. Livingston and let the certificate state that such transfer is legally registered in the patent office, it may be certified by a Notary Public.

Questions for Discussion:
1. What evidence is there in these letters that Fulton had a vision for expanding steamboat service beyond the Hudson River?
2. What kind of business concerns did an innovator like Fulton have in initiating steamboat service?
3. What do these letters reveal about Fulton as an entrepreneur?

Alice Crary Sutcliffe, *Robert Fulton and the Clermont* (New York: Century Co., 1909), 222–23, 234–38, 253–54, 286–87.

PROTECTING AMERICAN SHIPPING AND SEAMEN

Independence brought its problems to American seafarers and merchants. The nation needed a strong central government to regulate trade, arrange commercial treaties, and protect American shipping. But there was no American naval force; the Continental Navy had disbanded at the end of the War of Independence. In order to protect and control coastal waters, Congress built and armed revenue cutters to stop smuggling. These tiny schooners comprised the nation's first sea service.

But the revenue cutters were coastal craft; they could not protect American shipping overseas. While the United States adopted Hugo Grotius's[1] idea that the sea was international territory and that all nations were free to use it for seafaring trade, many societies rejected that notion. This became clear to American merchants as early as 1784, when Moroccan vessels seized an American merchant ship and enslaved its crew. American diplomatic and naval efforts in the 1790s and years immediately following 1800 largely failed. As early as 1794, Congress began making the first tentative moves toward the creation of a navy that could protect American shipping overseas.

Sometimes foreign nations seized the sailors who manned vessels, rather than the ships and cargoes. The prime offender was Britain, which desperately needed sailors to man its navy during its wars against the French. The Royal Navy frequently impressed American sailors ashore in British ports or removed them from ships on the high seas. The American public deeply resented this practice, and the American government made repeated protests, but to little avail.

The most famous case of impressment occurred in 1807 when the British frigate *Leopard* stopped the American warship *Chesapeake* and demanded the return of some British sailors alleged to have deserted from the Royal Navy. When the American commander refused, *Leopard* fired on the American ship, compelling it to surrender, upon which British officers boarded *Chesapeake* and removed a number of sailors. The American public was outraged by this incident and demanded war. President Thomas Jefferson, however, knew the United States would fare badly in a conflict with Britain and so chose a different course: a complete embargo of American maritime commerce with Britain.

---

1   Hugo Grotius: (1583–1645), the author of *Mare Liberum* (*The Free Seas*), published in 1609. Grotius rejected the idea that a nation could claim sovereignty over portions of the ocean.

Ultimately, the failure to reach an understanding with Britain on these issues led to the War of 1812, which was fought at least in part to defend "Free Trade and Sailor's Rights."

Alexander Hamilton, "Instructions to Revenue Cutter Commanders" (1791)

The ratification of the Constitution in 1789 meant that the national government could at last effectively raise taxes. Most of the new national government's revenue came from tariffs and other taxes generated in the nation's seaports. To enforce these taxation measures, Congress authorized the Treasury department to man a fleet of small patrol craft dubbed *revenue cutters*. Between 1790 and 1798, these revenue cutters were the only armed vessels the federal government had afloat. Their primary mission remained the prevention of smuggling, but they also took on additional responsibilities such as rescuing vessels in distress. Today, the revenue cutter program is seen as the direct ancestor of the U.S. Coast Guard, making it the nation's oldest sea service. In this document, Secretary of the Treasury Alexander Hamilton sends out instructions to the commanders of the first revenue cutters to ensure that they understand their duties.

Treasury Department,

June 4th, 1791

Sir:

As you are speedily to enter upon the duties of your station it becomes proper briefly to point them out to you. Accordingly I send you a copy of the Act under which you have been appointed, and which are contained your powers and the objects to which you are to attend, and I shall add such observations as appears to me requisite to guide you in fulfilling the intent of that act.

It may be observed generally that it will be in a partial manner, the province of the Revenue Cutter to guard Revenue laws from all infractions, or breaches, either upon the coasts or within the bays, or upon the rivers and other waters of the United States, previous to the anchoring of vessels within the harbors for which they are respectively destined.

Hence, it will be necessary for you *from time to time to ply along the coasts in the neighborhood of your station, and to traverse the different parts of the waters which it comprehends*. To fix yourself constantly or even generally at one position, would in a great measure defeat the purpose of the establishment. It would confine your vigilance to a particular spot, and allow full scope to fraudulent practices, everywhere else. . . .

Careful attention is likewise due to the 13th and 14th sections of the act. It is of importance that vessels should not break bulk, or put out any part of their cargo even temporarily, previous to a regular entry and permission obtained, except in cases of real necessity, to be duly reported and proved. You will observe that besides the penalties on the masters and mates of the vessels from on board of which any goods shall have been illegally removed, the master or commander of the vessel or boat into which they may be received, and all persons aiding in the removal, are liable to a forfeiture of treble the value of the goods removed, and the vessel or boat into which they may be received is also subject to forfeiture. It is well known that one of the most extensive cases of illicit trade is that which is here intended to be guarded against—that of unlading goods before the arrival of a vessel into port, in coasters and other small vessels, which convey them clandestinely to land. Hence, the bare removal of goods from one vessel to another is made penal, though they may not have been landed. Nor will the pretext of their being intended to be replaced avail anything. The provisions of these sections admonish you to keep a careful eye upon the motions of coasting vessels, without, however, interrupting or embarrassing them unless where some strong ground of suspicion requires that they should be visited and examined. . . .

I have now noticed to you the principal parts of the law which immediately relate to the execution of your duty. It will, however, be incumbent upon you to make yourself acquainted with all the revenue laws, which concern foreign commerce, or the coasting trade—a knowledge of the whole spirit and tendency of which cannot but be a useful guide to you in your particular sphere. You will observe that the law contemplates the officers of cutters in certain cases remaining on board of vessels, until they arrive at their places of destination; and with a view to this it is that so many officers have been assigned to each cutter. It is not, however, expected that this will be done in every case, and it must be left to the discretion of the commanding officer when it shall be done—when there is a vessel, the lading of which is of very great value, or which has any considerable quantity of goods on deck, or in other situations from which they can readily be removed; or where the nature of the cargo is such as to admit more easily a clandestine landing, or from the highness of the duties to afford a more than ordinary temptation, or where a vessel is bound to a very interior district up long bays or rivers, or when any suspicious circumstances appear; in these and the like cases, it will be well to let an officer accompany the vessel to her place of destination. The want of a manifest will be a circumstance in favor of so doing. It will not, however, be advisable to make known the circumstances under which it is deemed most peculiarly proper to use these precautions; as it might sometimes unnecessarily give offense. It may be always left to be understood, that it is the practice whenever the state of the cutter renders it convenient. You are empowered, amongst other things, to affix seals on packages found in certain situations. For this purpose, proper seals will be prepared and transmitted. Till they are required, any other may be made use of. The principal design of this provision is to identify the packages found in such situations.

It will be expected that a regular journal be kept in each cutter, in the same manner, as far as circumstances are applicable, as is practiced in sea voyages, and that all occurrences, relative to the execution of the laws, and to the conduct of all vessels which come under their notice, be summarily noticed therein, and that a copy of this journal to the end of each month be regularly forwarded to the Treasury.

It has also occurred that the cutters may be rendered an instrument of useful information, concerning the coast, inlets, bays and rivers of the United States, and it will be particularly acceptable if the officers improve the opportunities they have (as far as shall be consistent with the duties they are to perform) in making such observations and experiments in respect to the objects, as may be useful in the interests of navigation, reporting the result, from time to time to the Treasury.

While I recommend in the strongest terms to the respective officers, activity, vigilance and firmness, I feel no less solicitude, that their deportment may be marked with prudence, moderation and good temper. Upon these last qualities, not less that the former, must depend the success, usefulness and consequently continuance of the establishment in which they are included. They cannot be insensible that there are some prepossessions against it, that the charge with which they are entrusted is a delicate one, and that it is easy by mismanagement, to produce serious and extensive clamor, disgust and alarm.

They will always keep in mind that their countrymen are freemen, and, as such, are impatient of everything that bears the least mark of a domineering spirit. They will, therefore, refrain, with the most guarded circumspection, from whatever has the semblance of haughtiness, rudeness, or insult. If obstacles occur, they will remember that they are under the particular protection of the laws and that they can meet with nothing disagreeable in the execution of their duty which these will not severely reprehend. This reflection, and a regard to the good of the service, will prevent, at all times a spirit of irritation or resentment. They will endeavor to overcome difficulties, if any are experienced, by a cool and temperate perseverance in their duty— by address and moderation, rather than by vehemence or violence. The former style of conduct will recommend them to the particular approbation of the President of the United States, while the reverse of it—even a single instance of outrage or intemperate or improper treatment of any person with whom they have anything to do, in the course of their duty, will meet with his pointed displeasure, and will be attended with correspondent consequences.

The foregoing observations are not dictated by any doubt of the prudence of any of those to whom they are addressed. These have been selected with so careful an attention to character, as to afford the strongest assurance, that their conduct will be that of good officers and good citizens. But, in an affair so delicate and important, it has been judged most advisable to listen to the suggestions of caution rather than of confidence, and to put all concerned on their guard against those sallies to which even good and prudent men are occasionally subject. It is not doubted that the instructions will be received as it ought to be, and will have its due effect. And that all may be apprized of what is expected you will communicate this part of your orders, particularly, to all your officers, and you will inculcate upon your men a correspondent disposition.

The 5th section of the Act, requires that all officers appointed pursuant to this Act, should take a certain oath therein specified. The Act of the 1st of June, 1789, requires that you should also take the oath to support the Constitution of the United States. These oaths, each of your officers must take before some Judge of the United States, if access can conveniently be had to one. If not, before some other magistrate, duly empowered to administer oaths, and a certificate from him, of the taking of it, must be transmitted to the Comptroller of the Treasury.

> I am sir, your obedient servant,
> ALEXANDER HAMILTON,
> Secretary of the Treasury

Questions for Discussion:

1. What does this document reveal about maritime trade circa 1791?

2. What does this document reveal about Hamilton's expectations about the duties of revenue cutters?

3. How are Hamilton's instructions on how revenue cutter captains should treat mariners related to the values Americans fought for in the American Revolution?

D. H. Smith, "The United States Revenue Cutter Service," *The United Service: A Monthly Review of Military and Naval Affairs* II, no. 5 (November, 1889), 465–66.

Samuel Calder, "Barbary Corsairs" (1793)

To the Islamic city-states of North Africa (often known as the Barbary states), the waters that lay before them were sovereign territory; any ship passing through those waters were required to pay a heavy tribute or face confiscation and the enslavement of the crew. Such actions angered American merchants, who called the actions *piracy*. But these North African seafarers were not seaborne criminals; they acted with the blessing and knowledge of their rulers and are better termed *corsairs*. The use of corsairs to tax or confiscate passing vessels was a time-honored tradition in the Mediterranean and vital to the economies of these city-states. In *The Barbary Wars: American Independence in the Atlantic World*,[1] historian Frank Lambert argues that the Barbary states merely waged a commercial war and that the American conflict with them was a struggle for economic freedom rather than a cultural or religious conflict.

To David Pearce, Junior, from Samuel Calder, Slave, Algiers, formerly Master of American Schooner *Jay*

ALGIERS Dec[r] 4th 1793

SIR

I wrote you on my first arrival here which perhaps may not come to hand, for fear of which I now write you informing you of my being Captured the 11th of Oct. by an Algerine Frigate of 26 Guns 50 Leagues S W. of Cape S[t] Vincent and brought to this place where I arrived the 30th of Oct. when we were all put on shore, where I found the unfortunate Crews of 10 more Americans all captured in October.

1 Frank Lambert, *The Barbary Wars: American Independence in the Atlantic World* (New York: Hill & Wang, 2005).

On our landing we were all put into Chains without the least distinction and put to hard labor from daylight until night with only the allowance of two small black loaves and Water & close confined at night we suffered much on board the Cruiser, for when they boarded us they even took the clothes from our backs & brought us on board almost naked in this situation they put us into the Cable Tier[1] without any thing, not even a blanket to Cover us where we remained until our arrival here without even a shirt to shift us. Death would be a great relief & more welcome than a continuance of our present situation, without a peace[2] you may be assured that the whole coast of Europe will be blockaded by their Cruisers, as they have been as far as Cape Ortegal, and it is not a doubt but they will go as far next Spring as the Channel of England, as they are building more Cruisers. They have now four Frigates from 26 to 46 Guns. Two Brigs of 24, four Zebecks[3] of 20 guns & four smaller ones which have all been at sea since their Truce with Portugal. The Cruisers that are now at sea we expect will bring in more Prizes tho' God forbid for the situation of the Convicts at the Castle would be happiness to our situation, for we think ourselves happy if we escape through the day being beat by our drivers, who carries a stick big enough to Knock a man down, and the innocent, often suffer with the guilty as they say we are all Christians. In my last letter to your father I gave him an account of what Cargo I had on board which was 650 Casks Raisins, 20 Casks Wine. 30 Jars of Raisins & 3$^{do.}$ of Grapes & 40 boxes d$^{o.}$ the gross Sales of my Cargo was 68-000^{rvns}[4] by which you will find the Cargo tho' damaged paid a Freight out and from the goodness of the fruit & wine, I make no doubt I should have done well had I got safe home as I got my Fruit 6^{rvns} cheaper than any that was then ship'd. But alas! All my hopes are blasted & whether ever I shall get away from this is entirely uncertain, indeed if I may judge by the unfortunate Cap$^{ts.}$ OBrien & Stevens who have been nine years here & most of their Crews are already Dead, & if our Country could not relieve so small a number what will they do where there is nearly 140 men in the 13 Vessels that's already taken &

---

1   Cable Tier: the section of a vessel where the anchor cables were stowed; a dark and uncomfortable compartment.
2   Calder here indicates that as long as the European powers are at war with one another, they will ignore the Barbary pirates.
3   Zebeck: sometimes spelled xebec, a type of Mediterranean sailing vessel.
4   rvn: some sort of coin, possibly a real de vellon.

we have no reason but to expect more however we have no Reason but to expect but that the Plague will in the course of a year take off many of us, as the last Plague took away 800 out of 2000 Slaves. I hope your father had the *Jay* Insured as I make no doubt you had the Cargo. I would if it was in my power forward you a regular Protest, but you know its impossible in this Country & I suppose one from a Slave would be of no importance. I am very sorry for your Misfortune but my Own is so much greater than yours that there is no Comparison.

Questions for Discussion:
1. What does this document reveal about the dangers American seamen faced?
2. What do Pearce's major concerns seem to be in this letter?
3. What can be learned from this document about the Barbary corsairs themselves?

Claude A. Swanson, ed., *Naval Documents Related to the United States Wars with the Barbary Powers*, vol. 1, *Naval Operations Including Diplomatic Background from 1785 through 1801* (Washington, D.C.: Government Printing Office, 1939), 57–58.

Congress, "Naval Armament Act" (1794)

The continued harassment of American shipping by North African corsairs moved Congress slowly in the direction of creating a permanent naval force. Diplomacy—including ransoming American sailors enslaved by the Barbary states along the northern shores of Africa—failed to produce the desired results, so Congress reluctantly turned to the expensive expedient of creating a navy. In 1794 President George Washington asked Congress to approve a bill that would create a naval force to protect American merchant vessels from the North African corsairs. There was considerable opposition to the idea; some congressmen were concerned about the expense of a navy, while others believed an American Navy would entangle the nation in foreign wars. Nonetheless, in March 1794, Congress passed An Act to Provide for a Naval Armament that authorized the creation of a fleet of six ships. In 1797 three frigates were launched, of which one, USS *Constitution*, still survives as the world's oldest commissioned warship afloat. In 1798 Congress authorized the creation of the Navy Department in order to protect American shipping—not from the Barbary states in the Mediterranean, but from French vessels in the Caribbean.

An Act to Provide for a Naval Armament, March 18, 1794

Whereas the depredations committed by the Algerine corsairs on the commerce of the United States, render it necessary that a naval force should be provided for its protection.

Sect. I. Be it therefore enacted by the Senate and House of Representatives of the United States of America in Congress assembled, That the President of the United States, be authorized to provide, equip and employ, four ships to carry forty guns each, and two ships to carry thirty-six guns each by purchase or otherwise.

Sect. II. And be it further enacted, That there shall be employed on board each of the said ships of forty guns, one captain, four lieutenants, one lieutenant of marines, one chaplain, one surgeon, and two surgeon's mates, and in each of the ships of thirty-six guns, one captain, three lieutenants, one lieutenant of marines, one surgeon, and one surgeon's mate, who shall be appointed, and commissioned, in like manner as other officers of the United States are.

Sect. III. And be it further enacted, That these shall be employed in each of the said ships, the following warrant officers, who shall be appointed by the President of the United States, to wit: one sailing master, one purser, one boatswain, one gunner, one sailmaker, one carpenter, and eight midshipmen; and the following petty officers, who shall be appointed by the captains of the ships, respectively, in which they are to be employed, viz. two master's mates, one captain's clerk, two boatswain's mates, one sailmaker's mate, two gunner's mates, one yeoman of the gun room, nine quarter gunners, (and for the four larger ships) two additional quarter gunners, two carpenter's mates, one armorer, one steward, one cooper, one master at arms, and one cook.

Sect. IV. And be it further enacted, That the crews of each of the said ships of forty-four guns, shall consist of 150 seamen, 100 midshipmen and ordinary seamen, one sergeant, one corporal, one drum, one fife and fifty marines; and that the crews of each of the said ships of thirty-six guns, shall consist of one hundred and thirty able seamen and midshipmen, ninety ordinary seamen, one sergeant, two corporals, one drum, one fife, and forty marines, over and above the officers herein before mentioned.

Sect. V. And be it further enacted, That the President of the United States, be and is hereby empowered to provide by purchase or otherwise, in lieu of said ships a naval force not exceeding in whole, that by this act directed, so, that no ship thus provided shall carry less than thirty-two guns; as he may so provide and proportion thereof, which in his discretion he may think proper.

Sect. VI. And be it further enacted, That the pay and subsistence of the respective commissioned and warrant officers be as follows: A captain, seventy-five dollars per month, and six rations per day; a lieutenant, forty dollars per month, and three rations per day; a lieutenant of marines, twenty-six dollars per month, and two rations per day; a chaplain, forty dollars per month, and two rations per day; a sailing-master, forty dollars per month, and two rations per day; a surgeon, fifty dollars per month, and two rations per day; a surgeon's mate, thirty dollars per month, and two rations per day; a purser, forty dollars per month, and two rations per day; a gunner, fourteen dollars per month, and two rations per day; a sailmaker, fourteen dollars per month, and two rations per day; a carpenter, fourteen dollars per month, and two rations per day.

Sect. VII. And be it further enacted, That the pay to be allowed to the petty officers, midshipmen, seamen, ordinary seamen, and marines, shall be fixed by the President of the United States. Provided, that the whole sum to be given for the whole pay aforesaid shall not exceed 27,000 dollars per month: and that each of the said persons shall be entitled to one ration per day.

Sect. VIII. That it be further enacted, That the ration shall consist of as follows: Sunday, one pound of bread, one pound and a half of beef, and half a pint of rice:—Monday, one pound of bread, one pound of pork, half a pint of peas or beans, and four ounces of cheese:—Tuesday, one pound of bread, one pound and a half of beef, and one pound of potatoes or turnips, and pudding:—Wednesday, one pound of bread, two ounces of butter, or in lieu thereof, six ounces of molasses, four ounces of cheese, and half a pint of rice:—Thursday, one pound of bread, one pound of pork, and half a pint of peas or beans:—Friday, one pound of bread, one pound of salt fish, two ounces of butter or one gill of oil, and one pound of potatoes:—Saturday, one pound of bread, one pound of pork, half a pint of peas or beans, and four ounces of cheese:—And there shall also be allowed one half pint of distilled spirits per day or in lieu thereof, one quart of beer per day, to each ration.

Sect. IX. Provided always, and be it further enacted, That if a peace shall take place between the United States and the regency of Algiers, that no further proceedings be had under this act.

Questions for Discussion:
1. What does this document reveal about the relationship between commercial shipping and the creation of the U.S. Navy?
2. What issues might a historian have in using this document to understand the past?
3. What does this document reveal about the lives of the officers and crews of the early U.S. Navy?

U.S. Congress. *Statutes at Large of the United States of America*, vol. 1 (Boston: Charles C. Little and James Brown, 1845), 350–51.

James Madison, "Impressment of American Seamen" (1803)

Few issues irked the American public more than the continued British impressment of American seamen into the Royal Navy. James Monroe captured the spirit of American anger when he wrote, "This dastardly practice must cease, our flag must protect the crew or the United States cannot consider themselves an independent nation." During its lengthy wars against revolutionary France and Napoleon Bonaparte, the British Navy desperately needed skilled seamen to man its huge fleet. Toward this end, British naval vessels frequently boarded vessels of any nationality and forced, or impressed, sailors even if they were American citizens; so-called press-gangs also impressed sailors in British ports. Paul A. Gilje, in *Liberty on the Waterfront*, estimated that the British Navy impressed some ten thousand Americans between 1793 and 1815.[1]

To help American sailors, the government issued documents called "protections" that testified that bearers were U.S. citizens. But not all sailors carried protections, foreign sailors often carried forged or fraudulent protections, and impressed sailors regularly found that Royal Navy officers simply ignored them or even tore them up. American Secretary of State James Madison (1751–1836) insisted that the American flag flown by merchant vessels afforded sailors the same protection they enjoyed on United States soil, but the British persisted in the practice until 1815. The following is a

---

1   Paul A. Gilje, *Liberty on the Waterfront: American Maritime Culture in the Age of Revolution* (Philadelphia: University of Pennsylvania Press, 2004).

report from Madison to President Thomas Jefferson, who then forwarded it to the Senate for its consideration.

Department of State, December 2, 1803.
Sir:

Agreeably to a resolution of the Senate, passed on the 22^d of last month, requesting the President of the united States to cause to be laid before them such information as may have been received relative to the violation of the flag of the United States, or to the impressment of any seaman in the service of the United States, by the agents of any foreign nation, I do myself the honor to transmit to you the enclosed abstract of impressments of persons belonging to American vessels, which, with the annexed extracts from the letters of some of our agents abroad, comprises all the information on the subject that has been received by this Department since the report to Congress, at its last session, relative to seamen. To the first mentioned document I have added a summary, showing the number of citizens of the United States impressed, and distinguishing those who had protections as citizens; those who are stated to be natives of the British dominions, and not stated to be naturalized as citizens; and those of all other countries, who are equally not stated to have been naturalized in the United States . . . .

Richard Rodman, on the 7th June, 1803, impressed at Hull, England, into the British service, from the American ship *Atlas*, Sweeny Wilson, master. It is not stated whether he had a protection, or of what country he is a citizen.

Dennis Sweeny, a native of Ireland, and without a protection, impressed on the 7th June, in the North sea, into the British frigate *Amelia*, Lord Proby, from the American ship *Washington*.

William Ireland, a native of Suffolk County, New York, impressed from the American ship *Alknomac*, John Gore, master, at Falmouth, Jamaica, by a pressgang belonging to the *Desirée*, Captain Ross, or the armed brig *Racoon*, though he showed a protection given by the collector at New York, dated 26th April last. This impressment was made on the 22^d June last.

John Dirks, Peter German, and James Peterson, natives of Denmark, impressed on the 29th June, from the barque *Pallas*, an American vessel, then lying at London. They had no protections.

Hiram Chaples, (a native of New York, but it is not stated that he had a protection,) was impressed on the 3^{d} day of July, from the American ship *Charleston*; Joseph Wyer, master, about twenty leagues from Sandy Hook, into the British frigate *Cambrian*.

Joseph Simonds, and Sylvester Pendleton, native Americans and residents of New York, and John Table, a black man, impressed about the 7th July, off the Texel, from the American schooner *Recovery*, Josiah Shackford, master, into the British sloop of war *Harpy*, Edmund Heywood, commander. Without protections.

Ephraim Vanduser, an American citizen and a native of New York, with a protection as such, impressed, from the schooner *Perseverance*, Daniel Coyle, master, on the 18th July, off Tiberoon, into the British sloop of war *Snake*.

Josiah Hunt, a native of Newburyport, Massachusetts, impressed the 17th July last, from the American brig *John*, Jonathan Titcomb, into the British ship *Emerald*, then in sight of Martinico. Without a protection.

John Whiting, a native of Gloucester, Massachusetts, impressed at the same time, from and into the same vessel. No protection in this case.

Nathaniel Keene, an American citizen, who had been in slavery in Algiers, and who had a protection, which he left, through forgetfulness, at New York, impressed on the 18th July, at Folkstone, into the British service, from the American ship *Maryland*, John Wickham, master.

Joseph Stevens, an American citizen, with a protection as such, impressed from the schooner *Perseverance*, Daniel Coyle, master, on the 18th July, off Tiberoon, into the British sloop of war *Snake*.

William Evans, an Englishman, without a protection, and Thomas Challis, an American citizen, impressed at Cork, on the 19th and 26th June, from the American ship *Joseph*, James Jameson, master.

Joseph Emerson, native of Lincoln County, Massachusetts, impressed from the American schooner *Harriet*, Nathaniel Knight, master, into the British schooner *St. Lucia*, Shipley, master, then lying in the road^1 of Basseterre, on the night of the 20th July. No protection.

Benjamin Eldridge and William Finney, native of Falmouth, Massachusetts, impressed on the 20th July from the American schooner *Hannah*, in the road of Basseterre, into the British schooner *St. Lucia*, Shipley, master. No protection.

---

1   Road: an open anchorage with little shelter from foul weather.

Three seamen, names unknown, belonging to the American vessel *Mark and Mary*, John Mooklar, master, were impressed, on the 29th July, into the *Emerald*, British vessel, Captain O'Brien, near the north end of Martinico, though the vessel from which they were taken was then in a leaky condition. Under these circumstances, Captain Mooklar was ordered to leave the coast of Martinico, as the island was blockaded, and he put into Dominica, but could stay there only a very short time, from the violence of the sea, which set into the harbor. He again put to sea, and before his return to Dominica sustained considerable loss in the washing overboard a great part of his deck cargo, which consisted of lumber. One of the men impressed had a custom-house protection.

William Whipp, native of New Haven, Connecticut, and John Simpson, of Virginia, impressed into the British sloop of war *Sylph*, July 30th, 1803, on the high seas, from the American ship *Phaeton*,— Boush, master. No protections.

George Arnold, native of Great Britain, and John Williamson, a Swede, both without protections, impressed the 31st July, on board the British frigate *Cambrian*, William Bradley, commander, from the American ship *Venus*, Lemuel Bruce, master, upon the high seas.

Two seamen, citizens of the United States, and possessed of protections as such, which they showed to the British officers, impressed into the British frigate *Boston*, Captain Douglas, just after she had passed the territorial line of the United States, about the last of July.

William Liddle, it is not stated whether he be a citizen of the United States, impressed from the *Juno*, the 3d August, on her passage from Norfolk to Amsterdam, into the British frigate *Thetis*.

John M'Evoy, (an Englishman, and without a protection,) impressed from the American brig *Paisly*, John Jackways, master, on the 9th August, into the British frigate *Boston*, Captain Douglas, off the Chesapeake.

James Farnish, mate, and Neil Lang, seaman, of the American brig *Drake*, on her voyage to Barbadoes, were impressed the 12th August last, upon the high seas, into a British frigate, name of which is not known. The crew which remained in the *Drake* were found to be too weak for working her; in consequence of which, the captain was obliged to put into Antigua, the nearest port that he could make, to the great loss of the adventure.

David Kitchall, a native citizen of the United States, at the mouth of Delaware bay, was impressed into the British ship *Leander*, captain

Cain, the 22^d August, 1803, from the American sloop *Hiland*, John Hand, master, on a voyage from Philadelphia to Alexandria. Kitchell, it is believed was without a custom-house protection.

Oliver Harris, native of Boston, on the 14th August, was impressed into the British ship *Blenheim*, from the American schooner *Harriet*, near the island of Martinique. No protection in this case.

Charles Tracy, an American citizen, impressed on the 25th August from the ship *Marion*, William D. Seton, off Delaware, into a British frigate, name unknown. No protection.

James Davis and Henry Wood, black men, impressed at Liverpool, on the 1st September, from the American ship *Chatham*. No protections.

Samuel Robinson, an American, with a protection, Christian Moldenham, and Christian Lowman, Danes, with Danish protections, impressed the 5th September, on the high seas, from the American ship Flora, Caleb Harrison, master, into the British frigate Cambrian.

Thomas Doyle, native of Philadelphia, and a seaman belonging to the American brig *Hector*, impressed at Lisbon, the 6th September, into the British sloop of war *Bittern*, than at that port. Doyle had a protection.

Samuel Watt, Andrew Pace, and John Davis, the former having a protection as an American citizen, and the two latter being natives and subjects of Great Britain, were impressed on the 11th September from the American ship *Charlotte*, Thomas Hasam, master, about ten miles east of Cape May, into the British sloop of war *Driver*.

James Matthews, chief mate of the schooner *Amazon*, John Murray, master, impressed on the 14th September, 1803, into the British armed brig *Geochi* Pine, in the West Indies. No protection.

William Watson, a native of Connecticut, and with a protection, impressed the 29th September from the American ship *Ontario*, Seaman Weeks, master, into the British frigate *Cambrian*, upon the high seas.

Thomas Cook and George Wilson, the former a native of New York, the latter of Scotland, both without protections, impressed October 1st from the ship *American Packet*, Solomon Swain, master, at sea, about eight leagues from the lighthouse at Sandy Hook, into the British frigate *Perseverance*.

Henry Cobb, a native of Falmouth, Massachusetts, impressed into the *Loire*, British ship. It is not stated when, or whether he had a protection.

Daniel Walker, native of Philadelphia, impressed from the American ship *Fox*, into the British frigate *Boston*. No protection, and the time of impressment not stated.

Jesse Dillings, native of Wethersfield, Connecticut, impressed into the *Dreadnought*, British ship. No protection; time not stated.

Richard Johnson, native of Middletown, Connecticut, impressed into the British service. No protection; time not stated.

Joseph Mace, native of Newburyport, Massachusetts, impressed into the British ship *Isis*. No protection; time not stated.

Samuel Hills, native of Providence, R.I. impressed into the English ship *Britannia*. He had a protection. Time not stated.

Henry Kipp, a native of Hamburgh, and a naturalized citizen of the United States; impressed into the British frigate *Endymion* from the American ship *Eagle*. No protection; time not stated.

William Chandler, a British subject, taken into the British service at Falmouth, Jamaica, from the American ship *Anna*, Caleb Johnson, master. No protection.

William Fegarie, belonging to the American brig *Sally*, claimed by the French at St. Pierre, Guadaloupe, as a citizen of France, and kept as such. Time not stated.

Nicholas Bullen, by birth a Frenchman, impressed into the service of France, from the American brig *Joseph*, at St. Pierre. Time not stated.

John Nicholson, a black man, with a certificate of freedom, impressed from the American brig *Canton*, at Surinam, into a Dutch frigate.

Questions for Discussion:
1. What does this document tell us about the crew composition of American ships?
2. What does this document tell us about where American ships conducted trade?
3. Based on this document, how effective were American efforts to protect its seamen?

James Madison, "Impressment of American Seamen," *American State Papers: Foreign Relations* 2:593–95 (New York: Gales and Seaton, 1832).

THE WAR OF 1812

In a speech to Congress in January 1812, Henry Clay commented that "If you wish to avoid foreign collision, you had better abandon the ocean." Indeed, American experiences on the oceans had been full of danger. Our first war with a foreign power was the Quasi-War with France, an undeclared naval war in the Caribbean to protect American shipping involved in the West Indies trade. Immediately after that conflict, the U.S. Navy deployed to the Mediterranean to fight an often frustrating war against North African pirates. Britain's high-handed treatment of American shipping and sailors ultimately resulted in the War of 1812, with Americans rallying to the call of "Free trade and sailors' rights."

When war finally did break out in 1812, the *London Times* dismissed the American Navy as "a few fir built frigates with strips of bunting, manned by sons of bitches and outlaws." This statement was symbolic of Britain's overconfidence in its naval mastery. American vessels such as USS *Constitution* proved they could defeat British warships in a number of one-on-one frigate duels. American privateers from ports such as Baltimore seized hundreds of enemy merchant ships, often hunting their quarry in Britain's home waters. American successes on the Great Lakes were even greater, especially the battle of Lake Erie in 1813, when an American fleet defeated and captured an entire British squadron. The American commander, Oliver Hazard Perry, famously reported "We have met the enemy and he is ours."

Yet the War of 1812 was not a great success. The overwhelming might of the British Navy blockaded American seaports, effectively halting seaborne commerce and bottling up American frigates. The war had never been popular in the commercial Northeast, and Federalist politicians benefited from anti-war sentiment. Most embarrassingly of all, a British raid captured Washington, D.C., with little effort and burned government buildings before retreating back to Chesapeake Bay. Nonetheless, the nation survived a conflict with the world's mightiest empire and survived intact, if just barely, and many Americans looked back with justifiable pride on the nation's naval victories in an otherwise largely bungled war effort.

James Madison, "War Message" (1812)

After years of friction over issues like impressment and free trade, President Madison attempts to persuade Congress to declare war on Great Britain in this carefully laid out argument of June 1812. One of the major issues for Americans was the ongoing issue of impressment, whereby the British Navy boarded American merchant vessels and forcibly carried away American sailors to serve in the Royal Navy. Impressment was the first topic President Madison mentioned when he asked Congress to declare war. But there are a number of issues mentioned in this speech, of which all save one—Indian attacks on American settlers that Madison suspected were incited by the British—had maritime roots.

WASHINGTON, June 1, 1812
To the Senate and House of Representatives of the United States:

I communicate to Congress certain documents, being a continuation of those heretofore laid before them on the subject of our affairs with Great Britain.

Without going back beyond the renewal in 1803 of the war[1] in which Great Britain is engaged, and omitting unrepaired wrongs of inferior magnitude, the conduct of her Government presents a series of acts hostile to the United States as an independent and neutral nation.

British cruisers have been in the continued practice of violating the American flag on the great highway of nations, and of seizing and carrying off persons sailing under it, not in the exercise of a belligerent right founded on the law of nations against an enemy, but of a municipal prerogative over British subjects. British jurisdiction is thus extended to neutral vessels in a situation where no laws can operate but the law of nations and the laws of the country to which the vessels belong, and a self-redress is assumed which, if British subjects were wrongfully detained and alone concerned, is that substitution of force for a resort to the responsible sovereign which falls within the definition of war. Should the seizure of British subjects in such cases be regarded as within the exercise of a belligerent right, the acknowledged laws of war, which forbid an article of captured property to be adjudged without a regular investigation before a competent tribunal, would imperiously demand the fairest trial where the sacred rights of persons were at issue. In place of such a trial these rights are subjected to the will of every petty commander.

The practice, hence, is so far from affecting British subjects alone that, under the pretext of searching for these, thousands of American citizens, under the safeguard of public law and of their national flag,

---

1   War: the Napoleonic War with France.

have been torn from their country and from everything dear to them; have been dragged on board ships of war of a foreign nation and exposed, under the severities of their discipline, to be exiled to the most distant and deadly climes, to risk their lives in the battles of their oppressors, and to be the melancholy instruments of taking away those of their own brethren.

Against this crying enormity, which Great Britain would be so prompt to avenge if committed against herself, the United States have in vain exhausted remonstrances and expostulations, and that no proof might be wanting of their conciliatory dispositions, and no pretext left for a continuance of the practice, the British Government was formally assured of the readiness of the United States to enter into arrangements such as could not be rejected if the recovery of British subjects were the real and the sole object. The communication passed without effect.

British cruisers have been in the practice also of violating the rights and the peace of our coasts. They hover over and harass our entering and departing commerce. To the most insulting pretensions they have added the most lawless proceedings in our very harbors, and have wantonly spilt American blood within the sanctuary of our territorial jurisdiction. The principles and rules enforced by that nation, when a neutral nation, against armed vessels of belligerents hovering near her coasts and disturbing her commerce are well known. When called on, nevertheless, by the United States to punish the greater offenses committed by her own vessels, her Government has bestowed on their commanders additional marks of honor and confidence.

Under pretended blockades,[1] without the presence of an adequate force and sometimes without the practicability of applying one, our commerce has been plundered in every sea, the great staples of our country have been cut off from their legitimate markets, and a destructive blow aimed at our agricultural and maritime interests. In aggravation of these predatory measures they have been considered as in force from the dates of their notification, a retrospective effect being thus added, as has been done in other important cases, to the unlawfulness of the course pursued, and to render the outrage the more signal these mock blockades have been reiterated and enforced

---

1   Pretended blockade: Madison is calling Britain's blockade of Europe illegal because they did not actually have enough ships to enforce such a blockade.

in the face of official communications from the British Government declaring as the true definition of a legal blockade that particular ports must be actually invested and previous warning given to vessels bound to them not to enter.

Not content with these occasional expedients for laying waste our neutral trade, the cabinet of Britain resorted at length to the sweeping system of blockades, under the name of orders in council, which has been molded and managed as might best suit its political views, its commercial jealousies, or the avidity of British cruisers.

To our remonstrances against the complicated and transcendent injustice of this innovation the first reply was that the orders were reluctantly adopted by Great Britain as a necessary retaliation on decrees of her enemy proclaiming a general blockade of the British Isles at a time when the naval force of that enemy dared not issue from his own ports. She was reminded without effect that her own prior blockades, unsupported by an adequate naval force actually applied and continued, were a bar to this plea; that executed edicts against millions of our property could not be retaliation on edicts confessedly impossible to be executed; that retaliation, to be just, should fall on the party setting the guilty example, not on an innocent party which was not even chargeable with an acquiescence in it.

When deprived of this flimsy veil for a prohibition of our trade with her enemy by the repeal of his prohibition of our trade with Great Britain, her cabinet, instead of a corresponding repeal or a practical discontinuance of its orders, formally avowed a determination to persist in them against the United States until the markets of her enemy should be laid open to British products, thus asserting an obligation on a neutral power to require one belligerent to encourage by its internal regulations the trade of another belligerent, contradicting her own practice toward all nations, in peace as well as in war, and betraying the insincerity of those professions which inculcated a belief that, having resorted to her orders with regret, she was anxious to find an occasion for putting an end to them. . . .

It has become, indeed, sufficiently certain that the commerce of the United States is to be sacrificed, not as interfering with the belligerent rights of Great Britain; not as supplying the wants of her enemies, which she herself supplies; but as interfering with the monopoly which she covets for her own commerce and navigation. She carries on a war against the lawful commerce of a friend that she may the better carry on a commerce with an enemy's commerce polluted by the forgeries and perjuries which are for the most part the only passports by which it can succeed.

Anxious to make every experiment short of the last resort of injured nations, the United States have withheld from Great Britain, under successive modifications, the benefits of a free intercourse with their market, the loss of which could not but outweigh the profits accruing from her restrictions of our commerce with other nations. And to entitle these experiments to the more favorable consideration they were so framed as to enable her to place her adversary under the exclusive operation of them. To these appeals her Government has been equally inflexible, as if willing to make sacrifices of every sort rather than yield to the claims of justice or renounce the errors of a false pride. Nay, so far were the attempts carried to overcome the attachment of the British cabinet to its unjust edicts that it received every encouragement within the competency of the executive branch of our Government to expect that a repeat of them would be followed by a war between the United States and France, unless the French edicts should also be repealed. Even this communication, although silencing forever the plea of a disposition in the United States to acquiesce in those edicts originally the sole plea for them, received no attention.
. . .

In reviewing the conduct of Great Britain toward the United States our attention is necessarily drawn to the warfare just renewed by the savages on one of our extensive frontiers a warfare which is known to spare neither age nor sex and to be distinguished by features peculiarly shocking to humanity. It is difficult to account for the activity and combinations which have for some time been developing themselves among tribes in constant intercourse with British traders and garrison without connecting their hostility with that influence and without recollecting the authenticated examples of such interpositions heretofore furnished by the officers and agents of that Government. Such is the spectacle of injuries and indignities which have been heaped on our country, and such the crisis which its unexampled forbearance and conciliatory efforts have not been able to avert. It might at least have been expected that an enlightened nation, if less urged by moral obligations or invited by friendly dispositions on the part of the United States, would have found in its true interest alone a sufficient motive to respect their rights and their tranquility on the high seas; that an enlarged policy would have favored that free and general circulation of commerce in which the British nation is at all times interested, and which in times of war is the best alleviation of its calamities to herself as well as to other belligerents; and more especially that the British cabinet would not, for the sake of a precarious and surreptitious intercourse with hostile markets, have persevered in a course of measures which necessarily put at hazard the invaluable market of a great and growing country, disposed to cultivate the mutual advantages of an active commerce.

Other counsels have prevailed. Our moderation and conciliation have had no other effect than to encourage perseverance and to enlarge pretensions. We behold our seafaring citizens still the daily victims of lawless violence, committed on the great common and highway of nations, even within sight of the country which owes them protection. We behold our vessels, freighted with the products of our soil and industry; or returning with the honest proceeds of them, wrested from their lawful destinations, confiscated by prize courts no longer the organs of public law but the instruments of arbitrary edicts, and their unfortunate crews dispersed and lost, or forced or inveigled in British ports into British fleets, whilst arguments are employed in support of these aggressions which have no foundation but in a principle equally supporting a claim to regulate our external commerce in all cases whatsoever.

We behold, in fine, on the side of Great Britain a state of war against the United States, and on the side of the United States a state of peace toward Great Britain.

Whether the United States shall continue passive under these progressive usurpations and these accumulating wrongs, or, opposing force to force in defense of their national rights, shall commit a just cause into the hands of the Almighty Disposer of Events, avoiding all connections which might entangle it in the contest or views of other powers, and preserving a constant readiness to concur in an honorable reestablishment of peace and friendship, is a solemn question which the Constitution wisely confides to the legislative department of the Government. In recommending it to their early deliberations I am happy in the assurance that the decision will be worthy the enlightened and patriotic councils of a virtuous, a free, and a powerful nation.

Having presented this view of the relations of the United States with Great Britain and of the solemn alternative growing out of them, I proceed to remark that the communications last made to Congress on the subject of our relations with France will have shewn that since the revocation of her decrees, as they violated the neutral rights of the United States, her Government has authorized illegal captures by its privateers and public ships, and that other outrages have been practiced on our vessels and our citizens. It will have been seen also that no indemnity had been provided or satisfactorily pledged for the extensive spoliations committed under the violent and retrospective orders of the French Government against the property of our citizens seized within the jurisdiction of France. I abstain at this time from recommending to the consideration of Congress definitive measures with respect to that nation, in the expectation that the result of un-closed discussions between our minister plenipotentiary at Paris and the French Government will speedily enable Congress to decide with greater advantage on the course due to the rights, the interests, and the honor of our country.

Questions for Discussion:
1. According to Madison, what are the maritime roots of the problems be-tween the United States and Britain?
2. What ideals does Madison expound in this message?
3. How does Madison frame his argument to make it more effective?

James D. Richardson, ed., *Compilation of the Messages and Papers of the Presidents, 1789–1897* (Washington, D.C.: Government Printing Office, 1896), 1: 499–505.

Usher Parsons, "Surgical Account of the Battle on Lake Erie" (1813)

The battle of Lake Erie was a great victory for the United States. Not only did Commander Oliver Hazard Perry capture the entire British fleet, con-sisting of two ships, two brigs, one schooner, and one sloop, but as detailed in Craig L. Symonds's *Decision at Sea*, the victory secured the upper Mid-west for the United States, allowing American forces to reoccupy Detroit and launch an offensive into Canada.[1] But the battle was not without cost. Casualties were heavy. Dr. Usher Parsons (1788–1868), a surgeon in the

1   Craig L. Symonds, *Decision at Sea: Five Naval Battles That Shaped American History* (New York: Oxford University Press, 2005).

U.S. Navy who served on USS *Lawrence*, wrote one of the most memorable accounts of the Battle of Lake Erie. It was a fiercely fought battle; in a letter to his parents, Parsons reported that no less than five cannonballs passed through the space in which he tended the wounded. In this account, written five years after the battle, Parsons recounts the difficulties of operating during and immediately after a naval battle in the age of sail.

Our force employed in this action consisted of nine vessels with about six hundred officers and men, and had been out of port four weeks, either cruising or lying at anchor in Put-in-Bay, a safe harbour among a cluster of islands near the head of the lake. The crews left port in good health, but shortly after were visited with an epidemic, which spread through the fleet, attacking about twenty or thirty in a day. It answered the description of a bilious remittent fever, was of short duration, except in a few instances, in which it degenerated into a typhus, and in only one instance proved fatal. So rapid were the recoveries, that, of above two hundred cases, only seventy-eight were reported unfit for duty on the day previous to the action. Thirty-one of these were on board the *Lawrence* and about the same number on board the *Niagara*, their whole crews being about one hundred and forty men each.

About 12 oclock, on a clear pleasant day, we met the enemy. The action soon became general and was severely felt; especially on board the *Lawrence*, the flag ship; two of the enemy's largest vessels engaging her, at a short distance, for nearly two hours; part of which time the men fell on board of her faster than they could be taken below. The vessel being shallow built afforded no cock-pit[1] or place of shelter for the wounded; they were therefore received on the ward room floor, which was about on a level with the surface of the water. Being only nine or ten feet square, this floor was soon covered, which made it necessary to pass the wounded out into another apartment, as fast as the bleeding could be stanched either by Ligatures or tourniquet. Indeed this was all that was attempted for their benefit during the engagement, except that in some instances division was made of a small portion of flesh, by which a dangling limb that annoyed the patient, was hanging from the body. Several, after receiving this treatment,

---

1   Cock-pit: during time of battle, the space on board a warship where the wounded were cared for. Ideally it was below the waterline, where enemy gunfire could not reach.

were again wounded, among whom was midshipman Lamb, who was moving from me with a tourniquet on the arm when he received a cannon ball in the chest; and a seaman brought down with both arms fractured, was afterwards struck by a cannon ball in the chest; and a seaman brought down with both arms fractured, was afterwards struck by a cannon ball in both lower extremities.

An hour's engagement had so far swept the deck, that new appeals for surgical aid were less frequent; a remission at this time, very desireable both to the wounded and myself; for the repeated request of the Commodore, to spare him another man had taken from me the last one I had to assist in moving the wounded, in fact many of the wounded themselves took the deck again at this critical moment. Our prospects nevertheless darkened, every new visitor from the deck bringing tidings still more dismal than the last, till finally it was announced that we had struck. The effect of this on the wounded was distressing in the extreme; medical aid was rejected and little else could be heard from them than "sink the ship" "let us all sink together" But this state of despair was short. The Commodore, who was still unhurt, had gone on board the *Niagara* and, with the small vessels bearing down upon the enemy, soon brought down the flags of their two heaviest ships, and thus changed the horrors of defeat into shouts of victory. But all the wounded were not permitted to mingle in the joy. The gallant Brooks, and some others were no more. They were too much exhausted by their wounds, to survive the confusions that immediately preceded this happy transition.

The action terminated shortly after three o'clock and, of about one hundred men reported fit for duty in the morning, twenty-one were found dead, and sixty-three wounded. The wounded arteries occupied my first attention, all which, except where amputation was required, were rendered secure before dark. Having no assistant (the surgeon on board with me being very sick) I deemed it safer to defer amputating till morning, and in the mean time suffered the tourniquets to remain on the limbs. Nothing more was done through the night than to administer opiates and preserve shattered limbs in a uniform position. At daylight a subject was on the table for amputation of the thigh, and at eleven o'clock all amputations were finished. The impatience of this class of the wounded, to meet the operation, rendered it necessary to take them in the same succession in which they fell. The compound and simple fractures were next attended to, then luxations,[1] lacerations, and contusions, all which occupied my time till twelve o'clock at night.

The day following I visited the wounded of the *Niagara*, who had lain till that time with their wounds undressed. I found the surgeon sick in bed with hands too feeble to execute the dictates of a feeling heart. Twenty-one wounded were mustered, most of whom were taken on board the *Lawrence* and dressed, and afterwards such as were lying in like manner on board the small vessels. In the course of the evening the sick were prescribed for, which was the first attention I had been able to render them since the action.

The whole number of wounded in the squadron was ninety-six. Of these, twenty-five were cases of compound fracture: viz: of the arm six; of the thigh, four; of the leg, eight; of the shoulder, three; of the ribs, three; and skull, one. Of simple fracture, there were four cases: viz. of the thigh, leg, arm and ribs. Grapeshot wounds, large and small were thirty-seven. There were two cases of concussion of the brain; three of the chest, and two of the pelvis. The contusions, large and small, were ten, and sprains, six.

Of the whole number, three died; viz: midshipman Claxton with compound fractures of the shoulder, in which a part of the clavicle, scapula, and humerus was carried away; a seaman with a mortification of the lower extremity, in which there had been a compound fracture, and another with a fracture of the skull, where a part of the cerebral substance was destroyed.

The compound fractures of the extremities were much retarded in their cure, by the frequent displacement of the bones, by the motion of the ship in rough weather, or by some other unlucky disturbance of the limb. In this way the bones in one case did not unite, until after forty days had elapsed, and in two or three other cases, not till after twenty-five days. The delay of amputations already mentioned had no effect on the success of the operations. Every case did well.

There were not more than two very singular wounds, or such as would be unlikely to occur in any sea engagement. In one of these cases a grapeshot four times as large as a musket ball, passed under the pyramidal muscle, without injuring the peritoneum. In the other, a cannister shot twice the size of a musket ball entered the eye, and on the fifth or sixth day was detected at the inside angle of the lower jaw

---

1   Luxations: dislocated limbs.

and cut out. In its passage it must have fractured the orbitar sphenoid bone, and passing under the temporal arch, inside the coronal process of the lower jaw, must have done great injury to the temporal muscle, and other soft parts, lying in its way.

The recovery of so great a proportion of the wounded may in a great measure be attributed to the following causes: First to the purity of the air. The patients were ranged along the upper deck, with no other shelter from the weather than a high awning to shade them. They continued in this situation for a fortnight, and when taken on shore, were placed in very spacious apartments, well ventilated. *Secondly*, to the supply of food best adapted to their cases, as fowls, fresh meat, milk, eggs and vegetables in abundance. The second day after the action, the farmers on the Ohio shore brought along side every article of the above description, that could be desired. *Thirdly*, to the happy state of mind which victory occasioned. The observations which I have been able to make on the wounded of three engagements have convinced me that this state of mind has greater effect than has generally been supposed; and that the surgeon on the conquering side will always be more successful, than the one, who has charge of the vanquished crew. *Lastly*, to the assistance rendered me by Commodore Perry and Mr. Davidson. The latter gentleman was a volunteer soldier among the Kentucky troops and engaged to serve on board the fleet during the action. After the action he rendered the wounded every aid in his power, continuing with them three months. And the Commodore seemed quite as solicitous for their welfare as he could possibly felt for the success of the battle.

Questions for Discussion:
1. What does this account tell us about naval combat in the age of sail?
2. According to this account, what were Parson's greatest concerns during the Battle of Lake Erie?
3. What does this account tell us about the state of naval medicine in 1813?

Usher Parsons, "Surgical Account of the Naval Battle on Lake Erie," *The New England Journal of Medicine and Surgery* 7, no. 4 (October, 1818): 313–16.

Zebulon R. Shipherd, "Sailors' Rights and Free Trade" (1814)

The War of 1812 was devastating for the American maritime community. Seaborne commerce came to a halt, and related trades and industries such as shipbuilding suffered as well. While seaports celebrated American naval victories, there was a great deal of concern about the merchant ships rotting in the nation's blockaded ports. Commercially oriented maritime communities protested the war in strong terms—as did Federalist politicians—but to no avail, and the war dragged on.

In the piece below, Federalist Congressman Zebulon R. Shipherd (1768–1841) of New York rose to speak on February 18, 1814, to address the House of Representatives on the question of taking a loan to fund the war. In this withering speech he strongly condemns the Madison administration's prosecution of the war and questions the idea that the nation entered the war to protect its seamen from impressment and to promote unfettered maritime trade.

Now, sir, let us inquire who are the men, that most loudly complain for the violation of "sailors' rights and free trade." Merchants? No. Those concerned in the navigation, the only employers of sailors? No. But men who rarely ever saw a ship or sailor. These men who have not, or ever will have any concern with foreign commerce or navigation, not only feel the most aggrieved by the impressment; but, strange to tell, they seem to know much about the number and circumstances of the impressed, than the very men who own the ships and employ the hands; and we are considered guilty of a barbarous incredulity, if we doubt the testimony of those gentlemen, when opposed to the evidence of men, who employ the sailors, and who live in the great commercial cities of the union.

Gentlemen from the interior possess amazing tenderness—they profess to feel a melting sympathy for their sufferings, and burn with indignation to avenge their wrongs, while the north and east, who employ nine-tenths of the sailors of the union, are so hard, they cannot feel for, and so blind they cannot perceive those mighty wrongs and agonies, so pathetically described on the other side, of the suffering sailors kidnapped by the unrelenting Britons. There is good reason why they neither feel nor see. The evils complained of, exist chiefly in the distempered imaginations of party zealots, are seen with jaundiced eyes; hence men with good sight and cool heads, are not beset with these phantoms.

Mr. Chairman, I have pointed out the men who are fighting for "free trade and sailors rights," and I have shewn you the men, whom gentlemen charge as being the enemies of both. Who are the former? Men who have no immediate interest in the subject of controversy;

who are the latter? Men who have acquired the support of themselves, their very subsistence, their wealth, by ships and by sailors. The former must have no experimental knowledge; the latter perfectly acquainted with every minutiæ.

The very sailors, sir, for whose grievances you continue the war, I venture to say, have been, and still are, opposed to your policy.

They, like other men, must regard their interests, so far as to value the services, from whence they obtain a subsistence. They can have no greater fancy for a system, of starvation than other men. It is true in profession; you are securing to them important rights; but in practice, you are annihilating the occupation for which they are only fitted; you have "taken away that on which they live;" you have robbed them of their bread. Before the war was declared, before any of those abominable restrictions which have maimed, crippled and annihilated our navigation, were fastened upon it, the sailors whose interests lies so near the hearts of the majority, notwithstanding the dangers of impressment, had not the least inclination to abandon the ocean; the high wages allowed them all the support, all the affluence, the heart of a sailor desires; food, clothes, grog, and tobacco. How is it now sir, in redressing their wrongs, you have destroyed their rights. They have been, and still are compelled to pine in want on your shores, live on charity, or seek that employment and subsistence, which their country has denied them, in the vessels of the enemy; yes sir, thousands of the very men, whose supposed injuries have produced such calamities to this nation, have sought employment from the nation, whose barbarity, as pretended, fills the sailor's heart with terror and dismay.

You will perceive, sir, the effect of your officious benevolence to the American Tars, you must perceive the melancholy fruits of your overweening fondness, to intermeddle with a concern, you neither understood or regarded. There is no fiction here, the facts are true.

Can you then, sir, wish any stronger evidence of the impolicy of your measures, than to see the foundation of your resentments pronounced; practically pronounced fictitious; the merchant struggling, notwithstanding restrictions, to gain the element where the government pronounced his interests in jeopardy, and preferring the risk to the safely you tender him.

The sailor, whose cause it is said we are fighting, seeking protection, employment and support, from his despoiler.[1]

---

1   Despoiler: the enemy, in this case the British.

Sir, who can be so blind as to believe your professions sincere? That you have laid your restrictions upon commerce from a friendship to that commerce; that you have declared war from a sincere desire to benefit the sailor, or the employment by which he lives. Experiments are not green; gentlemen must have learned the baneful effects of their policy long before war was, declared, and the opinions of men who best know, and are most interested in giving correct information.

It is a truth, sir, no one can contradict, that the party in power have ever been the foes of commerce, navigation, and all their appendages. From Mr. Jefferson down, the benefit of abandoning the ocean has been constantly urged. Long have they contended that our true policy consisted in leaving altogether the carrying even of our own production: to the carriers of Europe, and become terrapins.[1] Indeed, the object was entertained with so much fondness by the late President, that in the raptures of prophetic vision, hit strong passion burst forth while describing the glorious day *"when the planter and manufacturer should be seated side by side."* And, sir, this pleasing mania is by no means confined to that great inventor of modern *hydrophobia*;[2] the last message of the President[3] to this house at the opening of the session, after recounting the splendid victories and splendid failures of the last campaign, congratulates us upon one glorious advantage gained by the war—that the people have been driven from commerce to manufactories; that our losses and disasters are overbalanced by this acquisition. This, although not a literal quotation from the message, is its only obvious meaning.

An honorable colleague of mine (Mr. Taylor) some time since availed himself of this text, when speaking on the army bill, and delivered us a comment upon it to enforce the truth of the President's statement. I need not multiply proof that the party in power, from the beginning, have been the acknowledged foe of commerce and navigation. What blind infatuation then must bewilder the mind that can believe this war was declared to maintain *"Sailors' rights and free trade?"*

Questions for Discussion:
1. What does this document tell us about the political tensions that divided the nation during the War of 1812?

---

1   Terrapins: turtles, who react to danger by withdrawing into their shells.
2   Hydrophobia: literally "fear of water."
3   President: James Madison, President of the United States from 1809 to 1817.

2. According to Shipherd, what was the impact of the War of 1812 on the American maritime community?

3. What strengths or weaknesses does a congressional speech have for historians studying the War of 1812?

Zebulon R. Shipherd, "Sailors' Rights and Free Trade," in *The Massachusetts Manual, or, Political and Historical Register from June, 1814 to June, 1815*, ed. William Burdick (Boston: Charles Callender, 1814), 116–18.

WESTWARD BY BOAT

The wagon train may be the icon of westward movement, but water transportation had a major role to play in moving Americans to the frontier and sending their cash crops to national and world markets. It proved relatively easy for American farmers to send their crops and other produce to New Orleans down the Mississippi River on rafts and flatboats, but returning to Ohio or Kentucky back upstream was difficult. The new technology of the early nineteenth century would solve these problems and open the American Midwest to settlement and economic development.

Canals were one answer to the problems of western farmers. The Erie Canal, an engineering marvel of its day, connected Lake Erie and much of the upper Midwest to the Hudson River and ultimately to New York City. Completed in 1825, the canal dropped freight rates from Buffalo on Lake Erie to Albany on the Hudson River by 90 percent. Soon eastbound grain traveled to New York City, and westbound settlers traveled the opposite direction in specially constructed canal boats.

Steamboats offered another option, especially on the western rivers, because going upstream offered few problems to steamboats; in some senses, they actually performed better going upstream than downstream. Westerners were quick to perceive the advantages of steamboats. Four short years after commercial steamboat service started in New York, this advanced form of transportation was operating on the Mississippi. Within a decade after the War of 1812, dozens of steamboats plied the Mississippi, Ohio, Missouri, and Arkansas rivers, linking dozens of river ports together, moving goods and people at a speed and price unthinkable before the advent of steam power.

Western businessmen on the Great Lakes and western rivers quickly grasped that the rapid changes in transportation were opening the West. Community political and business leaders, termed *boosters*, competed fiercely to bring these modern amenities to their towns, hoping that their particular patch of wilderness could be transformed overnight into a bustling metropolis. Cities like Cincinnati did bloom almost overnight, but other settlements, like Black Rock, New York, failed in their efforts to become major ports and essentially disappeared, swallowed by their competitors.

De Witt Clinton, "Memorial to the Legislature of the State of New York" (1816)

The creation of the Erie Canal can largely be attributed to the determination of one New York politician, De Witt Clinton (1769–1828). He was a long-time mayor of New York City and served several terms as the governor of New York. One of Clinton's long-standing dreams had been the creation of a canal linking the Hudson River with Lake Erie. But canals were enormously expensive to build and required an engineering expertise that many thought could not be found in this country. Clinton realized that only the state possessed the financial wherewithal to undertake such a monumental effort. Evan Cornog, in *The Birth of Empire*,[1] reminds us that Clinton was also attempting to resurrect his political career at the same time.

In this piece, Clinton makes an appeal to New York's legislature for approval to build such a canal. The appeal was successful; Clinton himself broke ground on it, and on its completion in 1825 was one of the first to ride a barge from one end to the other. The canal itself was an enormous success, linking Midwestern farms and markets to New York City and beyond via an inexpensive and highly efficient waterway, one of the very first civil engineering marvels in the country.

> While we do not pretend that all the trade of our western world will centre in any given place, nor would it be desirable if it were practicable, because we sincerely wish the prosperity of all the states; yet we contend that our natural advantages are so transcendant, that it is in our power to obtain the greater part, and put successful competition at defiance. As all the other communications are impeded by mountains, the only formidable rivals of New-York for this great prize, are New-Orleans and Montreal, the former relying on the Mississippi, and the latter on the St. Lawrence.

---

1   Evan Cornog, *The Birth of Empire: DeWitt Clinton and the American Experience, 1769–1828* (New York: Oxford University Press, 1998).

In considering this subject, we will suppose the commencement of the canal somewhere near the outlet of Lake Erie.

The inducements for preferring one market to another, involve a variety of considerations: the principal are the cheapness and facility of transportation, and the goodness of the market. If a cultivator or manufacturer can convey his commodities with the same ease and expedition to New-York, and obtain a higher price for them than at Montreal or New-Orleans, and at the same time supply himself at a cheaper rate with such articles as he may want in return, he will undoubtedly prefer New-York. It ought also to be distinctly understood, that a difference in price may be equalized by a difference in the expense of conveyance, and that the vicinity of the market is at all times a consideration of great importance.

From Buffalo, at or near the supposed commencement of the canal, it is 450 miles to the city of New-York, and from that city to the ocean twenty miles. From Buffalo to Montreal 350 miles; from Montreal to the chops of the St. Lawrence, 450. From Buffalo to New-Orleans by the great lakes, and the Illinois River, 2,250 miles; from New-Orleans to the Gulf of Mexico 100. Hence, the distance from Buffalo to the ocean, by the way of New-York, is 470 miles; by Montreal, 800; and by New-Orleans, 2,350.

As the upper lakes have no important outlet but into Lake Erie, we are warranted in saying, that all their trade must be auxiliary to its trade, and that a favourable communication by water from Buffalo, will render New-York the great depot and warehouse of the western world.

In order, however, to obviate all objections that may be raised against the place of comparison, let us take three other positions: Chicago, near the southwest end of Lake Michigan, and of a creek of that name, which sometimes communicates with the Illinois, the nearest river from the lakes to the Mississippi; Detroit, on the river of that name, between Lake St. Clair and Erie; and Pittsburgh, at the confluence of the Alleghany and Monongahela Rivers, forming the head of the Ohio, and communicating with Le Bœuf by water, which is distant fifteen miles from Lake Erie.

The distance from Chicago to the Ocean by New-York, is about 1,200 miles. To the mouth of the Mississippi, by New-Orleans, near 1,600 miles, and to the mouth of the St. Lawrence, by Montreal, near 1,600 miles.

The distance from Detroit to the ocean by New-York, is near 700 miles. From Detroit to the ocean, by Montreal, is 1,050 miles. From Detroit to the ocean, pursuing the nearest route by Cleveland, down the Muskingum, 2,400 miles. The distance from Pittsburgh to the ocean, by Le Bœuf, Lake Erie, Buffalo, and New-York, is 700 miles. The same to the ocean by the Ohio and Mississippi, 2,150 miles.

These different comparative views show that New-York has, in every instance, a decided advantage over her great rivals. In other essential respects, the scale preponderates equally in her favour. Supposing a perfect equality of advantages as to the navigation of the lakes, yet from Buffalo, as the point of departure, there is no comparison of benefits. From that place, the voyager to Montreal has to encounter the inconvenience of a portage at the cataract of Niagara, to load and unload at least three times, to brave the tempests of Lake Ontario, and the rapids of the St. Lawrence.

In like manner the voyager to New-Orleans, has a portage between the Chicago and Illinois, an inconvenient navigation on the latter stream, besides the well-known obstacles and hazards of the Mississippi. And until the invention of steam-boats, and ascending navigation was considered almost impracticable. This inconvenience is, however, still forcibly experienced on that river, as well as on the St. Lawrence, between Montreal and Lake Ontario.

The navigation from Lake Erie to Albany, can be completed in ten days with perfect safety on the canal; and from Albany to New-York, there is the best sloop navigation in the world.

From Buffalo to Albany, a ton of commodities could be conveyed on the intended canal, for three dollars, and from Albany to New-York, according to the present prices of sloop transportation, for $2 80/100, and the return cargoes would be the same.

We have not sufficient data upon which to predicate very accurate estimates with regard to Montreal and New-Orleans; but we have no hesitation in saying, that the descending conveyance to the former, would be four times the expense, and to the latter, at least ten times, and that the cost of the ascending transportation would be greatly enhanced.

It has been stated by several of the most respectable citizens of Ohio, that the present expense of transportation by water from the city of New-York to Sandusky, including the carrying places, is $4 50/100 per hundred, and allowing it to cost two dollars per hundred, for transportation to Clinton, the geographical centre of the state, the whole expense would be $6 50/100, which is only fifty cents more than the transportation from Philadelphia to Pittsburgh, and at least $2 50/100 less than the transportation by land and water from these places, and that, in their opinion, New-York is the natural emporium of that trade, and that the whole commercial intercourse of the western country north of the Ohio, will be secured to her by the contemplated canal.

In addition to this, it may be stated, that the St. Lawrence is generally locked up by ice seven months in the year, during which time produce lies a dead weight on the hand of the owner; that the navigation from New-York to the ocean, is at all times easy, and seldom obstructed by ice, and that the passage from the Balize to New-Orleans is tedious; that perhaps one out of five of the western boatmen who descend the Mississippi, become victims to disease; and that many important articles of western production are injured or destroyed by the climate. New-York is, therefore, placed in a happy medium between the insalubrious heat of the Mississippi, and the severe cold of the St. Lawrence. She has also pre-eminent advantages, as to the goodness and extensiveness of her market. All the productions of the soil, and the fabrics of art, can command an adequate price, and foreign commodities can generally be procured at a lower rate. The trade of the Mississippi is already in the hands of her merchants, and although accidental and transient causes may have concurred to give Montreal an ascendency in some points, yet the superiority of New-York is founded in nature, and if improved by the wisdom of government, must always soar above competition.

Granting, however, that the rivals of New-York will command a considerable portion of the western trade, yet it must be obvious, from these united considerations, that she will engross more than sufficient to render her the greatest commercial city in the world. The whole line of canal will exhibit boats loaded with flour, pork, beef, pot and pearl ashes, flax-seed, wheat, barley, corn, hemp, wool, flax, lead, copper, salt, gypsum, coal, tar, fur, peltry, ginseng, beeswax, cheese, butter, lard, staves, lumber, and the other valuable productions of our country; and also, with merchandise from all parts of the world. Great manufacturing establishments will spring up; agriculture will establish its granaries, and commerce its warehouses in all directions. Villages, towns, and cities, will line the banks of the canal, and the shores of the Hudson from Erie to New-York. "The wilderness and the solitary place will become glad, and the desert will rejoice and blossom as the rose."[1]

While it is universally admitted that there ought to be a water communication between the great lakes and the tide-waters of the Hudson, a contrariety of opinion, greatly to be deplored, as tending to injure the whole undertaken, has risen with respect to the route that ought to be adopted. It is contended on the one side, that the canal should commence in the vicinity of the outlet of Lake Erie, and be carried in the most eligible direction across the country to the head-waters of the Mohawk River at Rome: from whence it should be continued along the valley of the Mohawk to the Hudson. It is, on the other side, insisted that it should be cut around the cataract of Niagara; that Lake Ontario should be navigated to the mouth of the Oswego River; that the navigation of that river, and Wood Creek, should be improved and pursued until the junction of the latter with the Mohawk at Rome. As to the expediency of a canal from Rome to the Hudson, there is no discrepancy of opinion; the route from Rome to the great lakes constitutes the subject of controversy.

If both plans were presented to the legislature, as worthy of patronage, and if the advocates of the route by Lake Ontario did not insist that their schemes should be exclusive, and of course, that its adoption should prove fatal to the other project, this question would not exhibit so serious an aspect. If two roads are made, that which is most accommodating will be preferred; but only if one is established, whether convenient or inconvenient to individuals, beneficial or detrimental to the public, it must necessarily be used. We are so fully persuaded of the superiority of the Erie Canal, that although we should greatly regret so useless an expenditure of public money as making a canal around the cataract of Niagara, yet we should not apprehend any danger from the competition of Montreal, if the former were established.

An invincible argument in favour of the Erie Canal, is, that it would diffuse the blessings of internal navigation over the most fertile and populous parts of the state, and supply the whole community with salt, gypsum, and in all probability coal. Whereas, the Ontario route would accommodate but an inconsiderable part of our territory, and instead

---

1   . . . rose: a biblical quote from Isaiah 35:1.

of being a great highway, leading directly to the object, it would be a circuitous by-road, inconvenient in all essential respects.

The most serious objection against the Ontario route, is, that it will inevitably enrich the territory of a foreign power, at the expense of the United States. If a canal is cut round the falls of Niagara, and no countervailing nor counteracting system is adopted in relation to Lake Erie, the commerce of the west is lost to us forever. When a vessel once descends into Ontario, she will pursue the course ordained by nature. The British government are fully aware of this, and are now taking the most active measures to facilitate the passage down the St. Lawrence.

It is not to be concealed, that a great portion of the productions of our western country are now transported to Montreal, even with all the inconveniences attending the navigation down the Seneca and Oswego Rivers; but if this route is improved in the way proposed, and the other not opened, the consequences will be most prejudicial. A barrel of flour is now transported from Cayuga Lake to Montreal for $1 50/100, and it cannot be conveyed to Albany for less than $2 50/100. This simple fact speaks a volume of admonitory instruction.

But in taking it for granted, that the Ontario route will bring the commerce of the west to New-York, yet the other ought to be preferred, on account of the superior facilities it affords.

In the first place, it is nearer. The distance from Buffalo to Rome, is less than 200 miles in the course of the intended canal; by Lake Ontario and Oswego, it is 232.

2. A loaded boat could pass from Buffalo to Rome by the Erie route, in less than seven days, and with entire safety. By the Ontario route, it will be perfectly uncertain, and not a little hazardous. After leaving the Niagara River, it would have to pass an inland sea to the extent of 127 miles, as boisterous and dangerous as the Atlantic. And besides a navigation of at least twenty miles over another lake, it would have to ascend two difficult streams for 55 miles; no calculation could then be made, either on the certainty or safety of this complicated and inconvenient navigation.

3. When a lake vessel would arrive at Buffalo, she would have to unload her cargo, and when this cargo arrived at Albany by the Erie Canal, it would be shifted on board of a river sloop, in order to be

transported to New-York. From the time of the first loading on the great lakes, to the last unloading at the storehouses in New-York, there would be three loadings and three unloadings on this route.

But when a lake vessel arrived with a view of passing the canal of Niagara, she would be obliged to shift her loading to that purpose, for it would be almost impracticable to use lake vessels on the Niagara River, on account of the difficulty of the ascending navigation. At Lewiston, or some other place on the Niagara, another change of cargo on board of a lake vessel for Ontario would be necessary: at Oswego another, and at Albany another; so that on this route, there would be five loadings and unloadings, before the commodities were stored in New-York.

This difference is an object of great consequence, and presents the most powerful objections against the Ontario route; for to the delay we must add the accumulated expense of these changes of the cargo, the storage, the waste, and damage, especially by theft, where the chances of depredation are increased by the merchandise passing through a multitude of hands, and the additional lake vessels, boats, and men that will be required, thereby increasing in this respect alone, the cost two-thirds above that attending the other course. And in general it may be observed, that the difference between a single and double freight, forms an immense saving. Goods are brought from Europe for twenty cents per cubic foot; whereas, the price from Philadelphia to Baltimore, is equal to ten cents. This shows how far articles once embarked, are conveyed with a very small addition of freight; and if such is the difference between a single and a double freight, how much greater must it be in the case under consideration?

Questions for Discussion:
1. What does this document reveal about the economic ambitions of New York and its connection to westward expansion?
2. What advantages did Clinton claim New York would have over New Orleans and Montreal if it built a canal to Lake Erie?
3. What does this document suggest about cooperation between government and business in the early republic?

David Hosack, *Memoir of De Witt Clinton* (New York: J. Seymour, 1829), 406–13.

Carl Bernhard Saxe-Weimar-Eisenach, "By Steamboat to Cincinnati" (1825)

America's western rivers proved almost ideal highways for the technological marvel of the day, the steamboat. The Mississippi and its feeders such as the Missouri and Ohio rivers provided tremendous access to the nation's interior. Furthermore, virgin forest lined the banks of these rivers, providing cheap and accessible fuel for the voracious appetite of the steamboats' fireboxes.

Carl Bernhard Saxe-Weimar-Eisenach (1792–1862) was a European nobleman and soldier who had fought in the wars against Napoleon. In the mid-1820s he arrived in North America and traveled extensively, including to what was then the American far West. Prince Bernhard proved a keen observer and seldom imposed aristocratic or snobbish views on his reader, instead providing a level-headed analysis of a country that fascinated him. In this selection, Bernhard reflects on steamboat travel on America's western rivers.

On the 30th of April I was very agreeably surprised by a visit from Colonel Wool, returning from an inspection on the Red river, the Arkansas, and New Orleans; he had ascended the stream in the steamboat *Washington*, and arrived in the night at Shippingport. Being on his return to Washington, he took his passage on board the steamboat *Atlanta*, for Pittsburgh. As this boat stopped at Cincinnati, whither it was my intention to go, I immediately concluded upon continuing my journey in the same boat, to enjoy as long as possible the society of so estimable a friend. We went on board between ten and eleven. The *Atlanta* was crowded with passengers, but we were fixed very comfortably and neatly. The greater of the passengers were from Natchez, who come with the intention of spending the summer in the healthier northern states. Among them was Major Chotard, who was going with his family to New York, whence he intended to embark for France; and Abbé Martial, a Frenchman, who had kept a boarding-school in New Orleans for a long time, and was at that time employed by the Bishop of Kentucky in Bairdstown, on whose account he was to travel in France and Italy.

Our trip up the river was very pleasant. The weather was fine; the shores of the Ohio became more and more interesting the higher we ascended the stream. In the afternoon, we perceived on the right shore the little town of Madison, situated on an eminence. It appeared to be in a flourishing condition, and contained many brick houses; a multitude of well-dressed persons were standing on the shore. Towards evening we passed the mouth of the Kentucky river on the left shore. The Kentucky river, according to the *Western Navigator*, is a beautiful river in Kentucky. It originates in the Cumberland mountains, is two hundred miles in length, one hundred and fifty of which are navigable. Its mouth is one hundred and sixty yards broad, and proves to be an excellent harbor for boats. The town occupies a very pretty situation; above its mouth, and farther down lies Prestonville. The flourishing town of Frankfort, the seat of government, is situated about sixty miles from the mouth of the river. The former is five hundred and twenty four and a half miles distant from Pittsburgh, fifty-seven and a half from Cincinnati, and fifty five and a half from Louisville. Shortly after leaving Louisville, we were followed by another steamboat called the *General Marion*, towards evening it reached, and wanted to pass us; a race took place, which discomposed us considerably, and became dangerous to a high degree. The boilers, being soon over-heated, might have burst and occasioned a great disaster; during this time we were so close together, that the railing, as well as the roofs of the wheels knocked against each other. The danger increased as night drew on, and particularly so as there were a great number of ladies on board, who were crying in a most piteous manner. One of them conducted herself most distractedly; she fell into hysteric fits, wanted to throw herself in the water on the opposite side of the boat, and could scarcely be prevented by three strong men. The heating of the boilers of the *General Marion* had been so violent, that they ran short of wood, and to their great confusion, and our extreme satisfaction, they were not only left behind, but were overtaken by the slow steam-boat *Ohio*: thus the *Atlanta* obtained a brilliant victory. Ten miles above the mouth, of the Kentucky river on the right shore, is the little town of Vevay, built and inhabited by Switzers. They planted vineyards, which it is said give them a good revenue. I regretted very much that we passed them by night, and thus were deprived of the view of Vevay. On the left shore is a small village called Ghent,[1] in honor of the treaty concluded in that city, in Flanders. I regretted not to have been able to visit that place, if only on account of the name. Without farther accident we went on the whole night, and next morn-

---

1   Ghent: the Treaty of Ghent ended the War of 1812.

ing found ourselves opposite to the mouth or the Great Miami, which joins the Ohio from the right shore. This stream forms the boundary between the states of Indiana and Ohio, and the *Western Navigator* makes the following observation concerning it. "The Great Miami is a considerable river, which takes its sources in Allen, Logan, Shelby, Merion, and Drake counties. It runs southerly through Miami and Montgomery counties, and receives in the last two considerable rivers, on the left the Mad river, and on the right the south-west fork. On entering Butler county the Miami takes a south-westerly direction, and flows into the Ohio at the south-west corner of this state, and the north-west one of Indiana. Its course is one hundred and twenty miles. Its sources situated between 40° and 41° lat. are in the vicinity of the Massassinaway, a branch of the Wabash, the Auglaize and St. Mary's, which are branches of the Maumée and the Sciota, its course is in general rapid, but without any considerable falls, and runs through a large and fertile valley which is partly submerged by high water. Near Dayton, about seventy-five miles from its mouth, the Miami receives on the east side the Mad river; from this place boats carrying three and four thousand barrels, may run into the Ohio during high water. The trial of ascending Mad river is seldom made, the stream being too rapid and there being a great many sand-banks and dams. The Miami has a diameter of one hundred and fifty yards during forty miles.

We found the shores or the Ohio well-cultivated, with orchards and Indian corn; we observed several very pretty country-seats. These shores are mostly elevated, and at the distance of about a mile we could perceive a chain of hills covered with woods, which made a fine prospect. Towards ten o'clock in the morning we reached Cincinnati, four hundred and forty-nine miles from Pittsburgh, one hundred and thirty-one from Louisville, and fourteen hundred and eighty from New Orleans. It is situated on the right shore of the Ohio, and built at the foot of a hill, which is surrounded by a half circle of higher hills covered with forests. This city presents a very fine aspect. The hills on the opposite side likewise form a half circle, and in this manner the hill on which Cincinnati is built, lies as it were in a basin. On the left shore, the Licking river flows into the Ohio. This, says the *Western Navigator*, is a considerable river in Kentucky, which, originating not far from the sources of the Cumberland and running about two hundred miles in a north-westerly direction; flows into the Ohio opposite Cincinnati. The towns of Newport and Covington, the former immediately above, and the latter below the mouth of the Licking river, are beautifully situated in Campbell county, Kentucky: Newport contains a military depöt of the United States. The shores near Cincinnati are rather steep, and to render the loading and unloading of boats more convenient, they are paved and provided with rings and chains of iron.

Before we could land, the health officers came on board to seek information respecting the health of the passengers, as great fears were entertained in Cincinnati of the small-pox, which was raging in Louisville. We took lodgings at Mack's, a good hotel, near the shore. Shortly after our arrival, I took a walk in town with Colonel Wool and Major Foster, of the sixth regiment, who came here to recruit. We visited some bookstores. The town contains about fifteen thousand inhabitants, and consists mostly of brick houses Some of the streets run parallel with the Ohio, and others form a right-angle with them, which makes them very regular; they are wide, well-paved, and have side-walks.

Questions for Discussion:
1. What does the document reveal about transportation on the western rivers?
2. What evidence is there in this passage that America's western rivers provided a vital highway connecting western cities?
3. What strengths or weaknesses does this document have for historians attempting to understand steamboat travel?

Bernhard, Duke of Saxe-Weimar-Eisenach, *Travels through North America, during the Years 1825 and 1826* (Philadelphia: Carey, Lea & Carey, 1828), 134–37.

Black Rock Gazette, "Launching the *Henry Clay*" (1825)

After the War of 1812, Americans looked to the Great Lakes as an enormous highway west. Part of the story was the digging of the Erie Canal. But a question remained as to the western terminus of that canal. Would it be Buffalo, or nearby Black Rock? The two communities competed mightily to attract the favor of the canal commissioners. This was perhaps the first of many such incidents in American history in which two nearby communities competed for canal access, a railroad, or a highway. Black Rock would ultimately lose this struggle to Buffalo, which eventually absorbed Black Rock within its city limits.

In the following newspaper article, Black Rock attempts to assert its dominance as New York's primary port on Lake Erie. Even the name of the ship launched is symbolic of the economic struggle Black Rock embarked upon: Henry Clay was a well-known politician and major proponent of canals.

On Thursday last, at eleven o'clock, in precise conformity with the previous notice, the Steam Boat, *Henry Clay*, was launched from the dock yard in this village into the new harbor. The day was beautiful, and the occasion honored by a great concourse of citizens and strangers, whom curiosity of business had drawn together. The wharves and ware-houses on each side, and the pier in front, of the yard, were filled with admiring spectators; and the new Steam Boat, *Pioneer*, was moored in the most convenient place to view the scene, and appropriated to the use of the ladies, who crowded her decks.

The *Henry Clay* is a beautiful boat, of the first class, and measures upwards of 300 tons. She was built by Mr. E. Meritt, a young artist of great promise, who served his apprenticeship with Messrs. Eckford & Brown, in New-York, and who built, last season, at that place, the new Steam Boat *Constitution*, now running between Troy and New-York. The size and model of the *Henry Clay* are precisely the same as those of the *Constitution*, with the exception of some trifling modifications, suggested by the builder, by way of improvement. The engine, which is on the low pressure principle, was made at Birbeck's Factory, in New-York, and was cast in the same moulds with that of the *Constitution*. As the navigation of the Lakes is somewhat hazardous, the owners have spared no pains or expense that would contribute to her security. In the quality of timber, strength of fastenings, and, we may add, neatness of workmanship, the *Henry Clay* is not surpassed by any vessel afloat. She is intended to ply, as a passage boat, between this place and Detroit, touching at the intermediate ports, and will probably make her first trip about the first of August.

After the launch, and a national salute fired from a six pounder on board the new boat, the owners and artificers, with a number of the gentlemen who had been launched in her, amongst whom were the Canal Commissioners, (General Van Rensselaer, Mr. Seymour, and Mr. Bouck) and several other distinguished strangers, repaired to Mr. Thayer's Hotel, and partook of a handsome dinner, provided by the

Directors. The following, among other toasts, were drank at the dinner, which was marked by hilarity and good cheer.

By Gen. Porter, (President of the board of Directors)—The *Henry Clay*. May her future course be marked by the gallant and lofty bearing that distinguishes the Statesman after whom she is named.

By Gen.Van Rensselaer—The Ohio Canals. Success to the enterprize and public spirit which projected them.

By Mr. Seymour—The Commerce of Lake Erie. May it richly reward the enterprising spirit of our countrymen.

By Mr. Beack—The memory of Robert Fulton.

By Mr. Mathews—The extremes of the Grand Canal Black Rock Harbour and the Albany Basin.

By Major Barton—The Territory of Michigan, Her increasing population gives life and spirit to the commerce of Lake Erie.

By Mr. Meritt, (the builder)—The Steam Boat *Henry Clay*. May she prove as advantageous to the Stockholders, as her namesake has to his country.

By J. L. Barton, (vice president)—The Steam Boat *Henry Clay*. Her elegant model and structure are the works of Meritt. In speed she stands not in fear of a Superior.

By J. G. Norton—The village of Black Rock. Its growing prosperity is evidence of its future greatness. (After the canal commissioners had retired.)

By Major Frazer—The President of the canal board—Gen. Stephen Van Rensselaer. In war, the citizen soldier; in peace, the patron of merit. His wealth is the Bank of the widow and orphan.

By Mr. Joy, of Buffalo—The canal commissioners of the state of New-York. May other states be equally successful in selecting officers to construct their works of internal improvement.

By Judge Slosson—The canal commissioners. Assailed by the rancor of political and local interest may they continue to deserve well of the state by pursuing a course which has no other object than her prosperity and glory, and no other rule but that of equal and exact justice to each of her citizens.

By a Guest—Nathan S. Roberts, Esq. Principal Engineer at the west. His skill in the construction of the Locks and canal on the Mountain Ridge, and his fearless stand in favor of the Black Rock Harbor, prove him, at once, the able Engineer, and honest Man.

By Mr. Andrews, (principal blacksmith)—The *Henry Clay*. May she last as long as the iron that binds her together.

By a Guest—Our Wives and Sweethearts. Pure as the waters of the Niagara—Beautiful as the model of our boat.

Questions for Discussion:
1. What does this document reveal about American attitudes toward waterborne commerce?
2. What do the after-dinner toasts say about the hopes and aspirations of Black Rock's business community?
3. How does this newspaper item attempt to establish the importance of Black Rock as a Lake port?

"Launch," *Black Rock Gazette* (Black Rock, N.Y.), June 14, 1825.

RACIAL DIVISIONS IN THE EARLY REPUBLIC

Paul Cuffe (1759–1817) is symbolic of the racial concerns that divided the early American republic. His mother was Native American and his father an enslaved African who bought his own freedom. Cuffe himself struggled throughout his life to gain acceptance by white-dominated society. Cuffe went to sea and gradually acquired enough capital to buy his own ship and ultimately a small fleet of vessels that were often captained and crewed exclusively by free blacks.

Cuffe whole-heartedly embraced his father's race. He refused to use the name of his father's owner, Slocum, and adopted his father's given name, Cuffe (sometimes spelled Cuffee) as his surname. He pushed for voting rights for blacks in Massachusetts and in 1811 made his first voyage to Africa to investigate the possibility of American blacks emigrating there to set up their own society.

Cuffe's Native American roots are less celebrated, but no less important. White Americans had a double standard for Native Americans. When whites deemed Indians useful, such as in the whaling industry or the West Coast otter-fur trade, they were eager to trade with or employ them. However, if the white community perceived Native Americans as a threat, or simply as an impediment to economic development, they quickly turned upon Indian communities, often with devastating results.

The problem for both blacks and Indians, or anyone of mixed race in this period, was that white Americans drew an increasingly sharp divide between themselves and persons of color. White slave masters forced enslaved blacks to labor, mostly growing crops like cotton, rice, or tobacco on lands expropriated from Indian tribes. The problem grew worse with time as racial attitudes hardened during the Jacksonian era.

Kasiascall, "Trading on the *Tonquin*" (1811)

According to historical geographer James R. Gibson's *Otter Skins, Boston Ships, and China Goods*,[1] the key American commodity that unlocked trade with China was the sea-otter pelts gathered by the peoples of the Pacific Northwest. In the late 1700s, a market for sea-otter furs developed in China owing to the tastes of the Manchu ruling class, who prized the furs for their warmth and luxurious appearance. American merchants discovered that they could buy these pelts from the native peoples of the Pacific Northwest relatively cheaply and then sell the pelts to the Chinese in return for tea, silk, and porcelain.

The Native Americans proved to be sophisticated and demanding partners, however. They often played British and American traders against one another to receive a higher price for their furs. Furthermore, if cheated or insulted, they could resort to violence and sometimes captured ships and killed their crews.

In the incident below, the trading ship *Tonquin*, owned by John Jacob Astor, suffered this fate. The vessel's master, an American naval officer on furlough named Jonathan Thorn, proved ill-suited for commercial dealings. Outraged by Thorn's actions, Native Americans seized his vessel with disastrous consequences for all concerned. This narrative is related by an Indian named Kasiascall under uncertain circumstances; while he claimed no part in the plot to capture the *Tonquin*, white fur traders deemed his behavior suspicious.

My name is Kasiascall, but the Chinooks and other Indians hereabout call me Lamazu. I belong to the Wick-a-nook tribe of Indians near Nootka Sound. I have often been on board ships. The whites call me Jack. I understand most of the languages that are spoken along the coast. I can speak some Chinook, too. I have been twice at this place before; once by land and once by sea. I saw the ship *Tonquin*; Captain Thorn was her commander. I went on board of her at Woody Point

---

1   James R. Gibson, *Otter Skins, Boston Ships, and China Goods: The Maritime Fur Trade of the Northwest Coast, 1785–1841* (Seattle: University of Washington Press, 1992).

harbour in June last. We remained there for two days. We then sailed for Vancouver's Island; and just as we had got to it, a gale of wind drove us to sea, and it was three days before we got back again. The fourth morning we cast anchor in Eyuck Whoola, Newcetu Bay. There we remained for some days; Indians going and coming, but not much trade. One day the Indians came on board in great numbers, but did not trade much, although they had plenty of skins. The prices offered did not please the Indians; so they carried back their furs again. The day following the chiefs came on board, and as usual asked the captain to show them such and such things, and state the lowest price, which he accordingly did. They did not, however, trade, but pressed the captain for presents, which he refused. The chiefs left the ship displeased at what they called stingy conduct in the captain, as they were accustomed to receive trifling presents from the traders on the coast.

In the evening of the same day, Mr. M'Kay and myself went on shore, and were well received by the chiefs, and saw a great many sea-otter skins with the Indians. We both returned to the ship the same evening. Next day the Indians came off to trade in great numbers. On their coming alongside, the captain ordered the boarding-netting to be put up round the ship, and would not allow more than ten on board at a time; but just as the trade had commenced, an Indian was detected cutting the boarding-netting with a knife in order to get on board. On being detected, he instantly jumped into one of the canoes which were alongside, and made his escape. The captain then, turning round, bade the chiefs to call him back. The chiefs smiled and said nothing, which irritated the captain, and he immediately laid hold of two of the chiefs, and threatened to hang them up unless they caused the delinquent to be brought back to be punished. The moment the chiefs were seized, all the Indians fled from the ship in consternation. The chiefs were kept on board all night with a guard over them. Food was offered them, but they would neither eat nor drink. Next day, however, the offender was brought to the ship and delivered up, when the captain ordered him to be stripped and tied up, but did not flog him. He was then dismissed. The chiefs were also liberated, and left the ship, refusing with disdain a present that was offered them, and vowing vengeance on the whites for the insult received.

Next day not an Indian came to the ship; but in the afternoon an old chief sent for Mr. M'Kay and myself to go to his lodge. We did so, and were very kindly treated. Mr. M'Kay was a great favourite among the Indians; and I have no doubt that the plot for destroying the ship was at this time fully arranged, and that it was intended, if possible, to save M'Kay's life in the general massacre. But not finding this practicable without the risk of discovery, he, as we shall soon learn, fell with the rest. When we were on shore we saw the chiefs, and they seemed all in good humour, and asked me if the captain was still angry; and on being assured that they would be well treated and kindly received by him if they went on board, they appeared highly pleased, and promised to go and trade the following day. Mr. M'Kay returned to the ship that evening, but I remained on shore till the next morning. When I got on board, Mr. M'Kay was walking backwards and forwards on deck in rather a gloomy mood, and considerably excited; himself and the captain having, as he told me, had some angry words between them respecting the two chiefs who had been kept prisoners on board, which was sorely against M'Kay's will.

As soon as I got on deck, he called me to him. "Well," said he, "are the Indians coming to trade to-day?" I said, "They are." "I wish they would not come," said he again; adding, "I am afraid there is an undercurrent at work. After the captain's late conduct to the chiefs, I do not like so sudden, so flattering a change. There is treachery in the case, or they differ from all other Indians I ever knew. I have told the captain so I have also suggested that all hands should be on the alert when the Indians are here; but he ridicules the suggestion as groundless. So let him have his own way." M'Kay then asked me my opinion. I told him it would be well to have the netting up. He then bid me go to the captain, and I went; but before I could speak to him, he called out, "Well, Kas, are the Indians coming to-day?" I said I thought so. He then asked "Are the chiefs in good humour yet?" I said I never saw them in better humour. "I humbled the fellows a little; they'll not be so saucy now; and we will get on much better," said the captain. At this moment M'Kay joined us, and repeated to the captain what he had just stated to me. The captain laughed; observing to M'Kay, "You pretend to know a great deal about the Indian character: you know nothing at all." And so the conversation dropt.

Mr. M'Kay's anxiety and perturbation of mind was increased by the manner in which the captain treated his advice; and having, to all appearance, a presentiment of what was brooding among the Indians, he refused going to breakfast that morning, put two pair of pistols in his pockets, and sat down on the larboard side of the quarter-deck in a pensive mood. In a short time afterwards, the Indians began to flock about the ship, both men and women, in great crowds, with their furs; and certainly I myself thought that there was not the least danger, particularly as the women accompanied the men to trade; but I was surprised that the captain did not put the netting up. It was the first time I ever saw a ship trade there without adopting that precaution. As soon as the Indians arrived, the captain, relying no doubt on the apparent reconciliation which had taken place between M'Kay and the chiefs on shore, and wishing perhaps to atone for the insult he had offered the latter, flew from one extreme to the other, receiving them with open arms, and admitting them on board without reserve, and without the usual precautions. The trade went on briskly, and at the captain's own prices. The Indians throwing the goods received into the canoes, which were alongside, with the women in them; but in doing so, they managed to conceal their knives about their persons, which circumstance was noticed by one of the men aloft, then by myself, and we warned the captain of it; but he treated the suggestions, as usual, with a smile of contempt, and no more was said about it; but in a moment or two afterwards, the captain began to suspect something himself, and was in the act of calling Mr. M'Kay to him, when the Indians in an instant raised the hideous yell of death, which echoed from stem to stern of the devoted ship, the women in the canoes immediately pushed off, and the massacre began. The conflict was bloody but short. The savages, with their naked knives and horrid yells, rushed on the unsuspecting and defenseless whites, who were dispersed all over the ship, and in five minutes' time the vessel was their own. M'Kay was the first man who fell, he shot one Indian, but was instantly killed and thrown overboard, and so sudden was the surprise that the captain had scarcely time to draw from his pocket a clasp-knife, with which he defended himself desperately, killed two, and wounded several more, till at last he fell dead in the crowd. The last man I saw alive was Stephen Weeks, the armorer. In the midst of the carnage, I leapt overboard, as did several other Indians, and we were taken up by the women in the canoes, who were yelling, whooping, and crying like so many fiends about the ship; but before I had got two gun-shots from the ship, and not ten minutes after I had left her, she blew up in the air with a fearful explosion, filling the whole place with broken fragments and mutilated bodies. The sight was terrific and overwhelming. Weeks must have been the man who blew up the ship, and by that awful act of revenge, one hundred and seventy-five Indians perished, and some of the canoes, although at a great distance off, had a narrow escape. The melancholy and fatal catastrophe spread desolation, lamentation, and terror throughout the whole tribe.

Scarcely anything belonging to the ship was saved by the Indians, and so terrifying was the effect, so awful the scene, when two other ships passed there soon afterwards, not an Indian would venture to go near them. I knew that the *Tonquin* belonged to the whites at Columbia, I was eighteen days on board of her, and had started long ago with the tidings of her tragical end; but falling sick, I was prevented from coming sooner. There might have been twenty-four days between the time the *Tonquin* left the Columbia and her destruction by the Indians.

Questions for Discussion:
1. What does this document reveal about racial relations in the Pacific Northwest in 1811?
2. According to Kasiascall, why did the *Tonquin* explode?
3. What are the strengths and weaknesses of this account for historians?

Alexander Ross, "Adventures of the First Settlers on the Oregon or Columbia River," in *Early Western Travels, 1748–1846*. Series of Annotated Reprints of Some of the Best and Rarest Contemporary Volumes of Travel, ed. Reuben Gold Thwaites, vol. 7 (Cleveland, Ohio: A. H. Clark Co., 1904), 165–70.

Peter Williams Jr., "His Voyages Are All Over" (1817)

Late in life, Paul Cuffe had a growing interest in returning free blacks to Africa, where they could set up their own society. In 1811 he travelled to Africa in one of his own ships. In 1815 he returned to Africa, taking nine African families at his personal expense. These voyages can be seen as precursors to the efforts of the American Colonization Society (ACS) formed in 1817 to send free African Americans to Africa as an alternative to emancipation in the United States.

In the piece below, a free black minister commemorates the efforts of Paul Cuffe to promote African emigration. Peter Williams Jr. (1786–1840) was a free black born in New York City who rose to prominence in the free black community as a religious leader. After the War of 1812, Williams began to advocate emigration to Africa and began a regular correspondence with Paul Cuffe, who relied on Williams and the free black community in New York City to spread the word about African emigration.

Under this impression, he turned his thoughts to the British settlement at Sierra Leone; and, in 1811, finding his property sufficient to warrant the undertaking, and believing it to be his duty to appropriate part of what God had given him to the benefit of his and our unhappy race, he embarked on board of his own brig, manned entirely by persons of color, and sailed to the land of his forefathers, in the hope of benefiting its natives and descendants.

Arrived at the colony, he made himself acquainted with its condition, and held a number of conversations with the governor and principal inhabitants; in which he suggested a number of important improvements.—Among other things, he recommended the formation of a society for the purposes of promoting the interests of its members and of the colonists in general; which measure was immediately adopted, and the society named "The Friendly Society of Sierra Leone." From thence he sailed to England, where, meeting with every mark of attention and respect, he was favored with an opportunity of opening his views to the board of managers of the African Institution; who, cordially acquiescing in all his plans, gave him authority to carry over from the United States a few colored persons of good character, to instruct the colonists in agriculture and the mechanical arts. After this he returned to Sierra Leone, carrying with him some goods as a consignment to the Friendly Society, to encourage them in the way of trade; which having safely delivered, and given them some salutary instructions, he set sail and returned again to his native land.

Thus terminated his first mission to Africa—a mission fraught with the most happy consequences; undertaken from the purest motives of benevolence, and solely at his own expense and risk.

Returned to the bosom of his family and friends, where every comfort awaited his command, he could not think of enjoying repose while he reflected that he might, in any degree, administer to the relief of the multitudes of his brethren, who were groaning under the yoke of bondage, or groping in the dark and horrible night of heathenish superstition and ignorance.—Scarcely had the first transports of rejoicing at his return, time to subside, before he commenced his preparations for a second voyage; not discouraged by the labors and dangers he had past, and unmindful of the ease which the decline of life requires, and to which his long-continued and earnest exertions gave him a peculiar claim. In the hope of finding persons of the description given by the African Institution, he visited most of the large cities in the Union, held frequent conferences with the most reputable men of color, and also with those among the whites who had distinguished themselves as the friends of the Africans; and recommended to the colored people to form associations for the furtherance of the benevolent work in which he was engaged. The results were, the formation of two societies, one in Philadelphia, and the other in New York, and the discovery of a number of proper persons, who were willing to go with him and settle in Africa.—But, unfortunately; before he found himself in readiness for his voyage, the war commenced between this country and Great Britain. This put a bar in the way of his operations, which he was so anxious to remove, that he traveled from his home at Westport, to the city of Washington, to solicit the government to favour his views, and to let him depart and carry with him those persons and their effects whom he had engaged to go and settle in Sierra Leone. He was, however, unsuccessful in the attempt. His general plan was highly and universally approbated, but the policy of the government would not admit of such an intercourse with an enemy's colony.

He had now no alternative but to stay at home and wait the event of the war. But the delay, thus occasioned, instead of being suffered to damp his ardor, was improved by him to the maturing of his plans, and extending his correspondence, which already embraced some of the first characters in Great Britain and America. After the termination of the war, he with all convenient speed prepared for his departure, and in Dec. 1815, he took on board his brig 38 persons of the dispersed race of Africa; and after a voyage of 55 days, landed them safely on the soil of their progenitors.

It is proper to remark that capt. C. in his zeal for the welfare of his brethren, had exceeded the instructions of the institution at London. They had advised him not to carry over, in the first instance, more than 6 or 8 persons; consequently, he had no claim on them for the passage and other expenses attending the removal of any over that number. But this he had previously considered, and generously resolved to bear the burden of the expense himself, rather than any of those whom he had engaged should be deprived of an opportunity of going where they might be so usefully employed. He moreover foresaw, that when these persons were landed at Sierra Leone, it would be necessary to make such provision for the destitute as would support them until they were enabled to provide for themselves.

For this also he had to apply to his own resources, so that in this voyage he expended out of his own private funds between three and four thousand dollars, for the benefit of the colony.

Whether this sum will ever be made up to his heirs, is not for me to determine, but whether it is so or not, this act of his deserves to be placed on record, and handed down to posterity as a proof of the warmth of his benevolence, and of the purity and disinterestedness of his attachment to the African race.

On the arrival of Capt. Cuffee at Sierra Leone, he presented his passengers to the governor, who gave each family a lot of ground in the town, besides from 30 to 50 acres of land (according to their number) on a spot about two miles distant from it. Afterwards, in a letter which he wrote to England, (in answer to one which he had received, requiring him to say what should be done for the advantage of the new comers,) he prudently advised, that a house should be built for the accommodation of their families on each of their farms.

His stay at the colony, at this time, was about two months, and when he took his departure, particularly from those whom he brought over with him, it was like a father taking leave of his children, receiving the tokens of their overflowing affection, and with pious admonitions, commending them to the protection of God.

Oh! Never, never to be forgotten scene. When the doleful tidings shall be there announced, that he is numbered with the dead, what tears will flow at the recollection of its every circumstance.

The exclusion of American vessels from the trade of the British colonies, by the late treaty, rendered Capt. C. (in order that he might prosecute his designs) very solicitous to obtain a license for his vessel to trade to Sierra Leone. He had, indeed, been urged to connect himself with the institution of London, and to sail as supercargo in British bottoms and to British ports; but with this he was unwilling to comply, though he knew the business would be very lucrative. Considering himself (to use his own phraseology) as a member of the whole African family he was unwilling to leave that part of it which was in America, in its present state.—"My wish," said he, "is for the good of this people universally." His last voyage had been undertaken at the risk of having his vessel and cargo seized and condemned; and, though he escaped, he could not think it advisable to run the same hazard again. He, therefore, wrote to his friends in England, to try to obtain a license for his vessel, and to make some other arrangements which he deemed necessary for another voyage. Whether these arrangements were ever made, I cannot say, but if they were, it was not until after he was seized with that complaint which terminated his labours and his life. He was taken ill sometime in February, and expired on the 7th day of September, in the 39th year of his age.

During his illness, the subject of meliorating the condition of his brethren, continued deeply impressed on his mind, and occupied his decaying powers in an extensive correspondence with their friends; and, though he was unable to serve them as he had done, he was gratified at finding his views adopted by a number of the most benevolent and influential men in the American Union.

Such was the public character. Such was the warmth of his benevolence, the activity of his zeal, and the extent of his labours, in behalf of the African race. Indeed his whole life may be said to have been spent in their service. To their benefit he devoted the acquisitions of his youth, the time of his later years, and even the thoughts of his dying pillow.

As a private man, he was just and upright in all his dealings, an affectionate husband, a kind father, a good neighbor, and a faithful friend. Pious without ostentation, and warmly attached to the principle of Quakerism; he manifested, in all his deportment, that he was a true disciple of Jesus; and cherished a charitable disposition to professors of every denomination, who walked according to the leading principles of the gospel.—Regardless of the honors and the pleasures of the world, in humble imitation of his divine master, he went from place to place doing good, looking not for his reward among men, but in the favor of his heavenly father.—Thus walking in the ways of piety and usefulness, in the smiles of an approving conscience, and the favor of God; he enjoyed through life, an unusual serenity and satisfaction of mind, and when the fatal messenger arrived to cut the bonds of mortality, it found him in peace, ready and willing to depart. In that solemnly interesting period, when nature with him was struggling in the pangs of dissolution, such a calmness and serenity overspread his soul, and manifested itself in his countenance and actions, that the heart of the greatest reprobate, at beholding him, would have responded the wish, "let me die the death of the righteous, and let my last end be like his."

A short time previous to his exit, feeling sensible that it was near, he called his family together to bid them adieu. It was an affecting scene. A scene of inexpressible solemnity—of tears and bitter anguish, on the one hand, and Christian firmness and resignation on the other. His wife and children, and several other relatives, being all assembled around him, the good old man reached forth his enfeebled hand, and after shaking hand with each, and given them some pious advice, he commended them to the tender mercies of Jehovah, and bade them all a final farewell. After this his mind seemed almost entirely occupied with the eternal world. "Not many days hence," said he to one of his neighbors who came to visit him, "not many days hence, and ye shall see the glory of God; I know that my works are all gone to judgment before me;" but he subjoined, "it is well, it is all well." I could add many particulars, but it is unnecessary. He is gone. He lived the life, and died the death, of a Christian. He is gone whence he shall never return, and where he shall contend no more with raging billows, and with howling storms. His voyages are all over, he has made his last—and it was to the haven of eternal repose.

Questions for Discussion:
1. According to Williams, what were Cuffe's reasons for bringing free blacks to Africa?
2. What does this document reveal about the lives of free African Americans in the early republic?
3. According to Williams, what obstacles did Cuffe encounter in settling free blacks in Africa?

Peter Williams Jr., "A Discourse Delivered on the Death of Capt. Paul Cuffee," in American Colonization Society, *Third Annual Report of the American Society for Colonizing the Free People of Colour of the United States* (Washington: Davis and Force, 1820), 115–20.

Charleston Courier, "South Carolina vs. Daley" (1824)

Both Indians and blacks faced discrimination, as did any non-white seafarers in the early republic. But determining race could be very difficult. What constituted being black? Native American? White? This question came to the fore in the early 1820s in the port of Charleston, South Carolina, which had a long-standing fear of slave rebellions fomented by free blacks. In 1823 the South Carolina legislature passed a law that required any "free negroes or persons of colour, as cooks, stewards, or mariners" who entered that port to be imprisoned in the local jail as long as his ship was in port, and to be returned when his ship sailed. Massachusetts, and other maritime states with large numbers of African American seafarers, objected strongly to these laws and in 1844 sent a representative to Charleston to deal with the issue. Hostile Charlestonians quickly chased the representative and his daughter out of Charleston; friends spirited them on board a departing ship to escape threatened mob violence.

In this legal case reported by the *Charleston Courier*, a South Carolina court attempts to determine if this law applies to Amos Daley, a Native American sailor from Rhode Island.

State of South Carolina vs. Daley

Mr. EDITOR: as this case appears to have excited some degree of interest among our fellow citizens, and as only a very partial account of it has yet been published, the following report, drawn up by one present at and concerned in the trial, may not be unacceptable to your readers:

Amos Daley, a native of Rhode Island, claiming to be a free Indian of the Narragansett tribe, was arraigned before a court formed under the act of 1823, for having returned into the State, contrary to the provisions of said act, after having received official warning of the consequences of such return.

The court consisted of John H. Mitchell, Q.U., and Joseph Cole, William McDow, and John Huger, Esqrs., freeholders. The trial came on on Tuesday, the 22d of June. Mr. Holmes, Solicitor of the South Carolina Association, for the prosecution; Messrs. Courtenay and McCrady for the prisoner.

On opening the court, the presiding, officer read its proceedings at the last meeting, and the testimony of Andrew Bay, Q.U. a witness on behalf of the prosecution, which was as follows:

That he committed the prisoner, Amos Daley, to jail, having arrived here in the schooner *Fox*, Rose, master, on the 22d day of April last; that on the 3d of May last he was released, and, on his description and marks, age, &c., being duly recorded, witness warned the prisoner never to return here again, and warned, also, Captain Rose of the consequences which would ensue should he be brought into this State; that the prisoner did return to Charleston, (notwithstanding the warning aforesaid,) in the same vessel, commanded by the same captain, and witness again had the prisoner arrested and committed on the 16th of the present mouth of June, agreeably to the directions of the act of December, 1823.

The court then entered into the examination of witnesses on the part of the prisoner. Three witnesses were called, viz: Perry Rose, master of the schooner *Fox*; James Gilbert, mate; and Mr. R. B. Lawton.

Captain Rose was first sworn, and testified: That he well knew the prisoner's mother to be a Narragansett Indian, with straight black hair; also knew his father, husband to the woman, his mother; that he, also, was a Narragansett Indian, with straight black hair; that his father was a freeholder, owning a farm, and that the prisoner was entitled to all the rights and privileges of citizenship in Rhode Island; that the prisoner was of Warwick; that these Indians trace their descent through the women.

The mate, James Gilbert, was next sworn. He had seen the woman, called the mother of the prisoner, and she was an Indian squaw; he had also seen the man called his father; he, too, was an Indian. Both father and mother have straight hair. Witness had no doubt that the prisoner was a free Indian. He had known the prisoner since the time of the last war; that it was customary to call Indians colored men.

Mr. Lawton, being then sworn, said: That he was brought up in Rhode Island, and lived there until he was 15 years old. He knew the Indians of the Narragansett tribe very well, and the features of the prisoner were those of the tribe he claimed to belong to. On his cross examination, he stated that the Narragansetts, like all other Indians traced their descent always through the women; that the hair of the prisoner was not like the generality of Indians, but that he had seen genuine squaws of that tribe, who were old, with very curly hair; he thought, however, the hair of the prisoner rather against him; that negroes are not very plenty among the Narragansetts; that it was not uncommon to call Indians men of color.

Messrs. Turnbull and Hugar, were now called, on the part of the prosecution.

Mr. Turnbull, being sworn, said: That Captain Rose (thinking erroneously that he had something to do with the prosecution) had complained to him of the hard fate of the prisoner; that the captain told him he knew the prisoner's mother, and she was an Indian, but that he did not know his father; that he (witness) had seen Indians of various tribes; the complexion was not the test of genuine blood, but the long straight hair was the characteristic universally relied on. The prisoner was not darker than many Indians he had seen. He never was among the Narragansett Indians.

Next was sworn Mr. A. Hugar, who testified: That he was present with Mr. Turnbull when he conversed with the captain. The captain then said be knew the prisoner's mother, very well; she was brought up in his family, and was an Indian; but, on being asked whether he knew the father, he had answered nearly in these words: "That he knew nothing at all about the father." He, too, (witness,) had traveled much among the Indians; and he considered the hair, not the complexion, the test of genuine blood.

Here the examination of witnesses closed. It was conceded that he (Fox) had come from a foreign port, and, that the captain was not liable, under the act, for bringing the prisoner into the State. The sheriff's book was produced. The prisoner's hair was woolly. The following is the copy of a certificate in possession of the prisoner, which was adduced on the trial:

> *To whom concerned:*
> STATE OF RHODE ISLAND, *ss:*
> I hereby certify that Amos Daley, a man of color, was born in the town of Warwick, in this State, on the 15th day of September, A.D. 1800, and is the son of William Daley, by Susannah, his wife, as appears of record.
> JOHN REYNOLDS *Town Clerk.*
> NORTH KINGSTON, *December* 27, 1823.

Messrs. Courtenay and McCrady, for the prisoner, contended that the evidence adduced was conclusive as to the prisoner's national character, and brought him within the exception of the act and at least sufficient to throw the *onus probandi* on the prosecution, and bound the court. The former gentleman then endeavored to show that, even if the prisoner were within the letter, he was clearly without the equity of the act. As it was no offense in the captain to bring him in, he was bound in bonds so to do, and the prisoner could not prevent it. And further argued, that the act itself was unconstitutional and void, under the 2d section of the 4th article of the Constitution of the United States: "that the citizens of each State shall be entitled to all privileges and immunities of citizens in the several States," the prisoner being a citizen of Rhode Island. The latter denied the constitutionality of the law, also, but relied on the 8th section of the 1st article of the Constitution of the United States: "Congress shall have power to regulate commerce with foreign nations, and among the several States, and with the Indian tribes;" the act being an interference with navigation, which, in the case of Gibbons *vs.* Ogden, had been decided to be an essential part of commerce, and beyond the control of the States. Further: that the act of 1823 clashed with the commercial regulations of the United States.

Mr. Holmes, in reply, denied that sufficient evidence had been adduced on the part of the prisoner to throw the "*onus*" on the prosecution; and that the prisoner was obliged to prove himself within the exception of the act; contended that the captain's evidence was worthless, as he had contradicted himself; and that the prisoner and captain both came within the equity of the act, both having been warned, but the captain happened to escape the letter; that Mr. Courtenay's construction of the Constitution had been refuted in the Missouri question by our ablest statesmen; that the part of the Constitution and the case relied on by Mr. McCrady were wholly inapplicable to the case before the court; seemed to doubt the principles in Gibbons *vs.* Ogden, and thought we should await the judgment of the Supreme Court in our own case before we yielded.

The court, after consideration, adjudged the prisoner guilty; but, in consequence of its appearing that he had not returned voluntarily, only sentenced him to receive twelve lashes on his bare back the same afternoon, at 5 o'clock, in the work-house.

Questions for Discussion:
1. What does this document reveal about racial relations in 1824?
2. What sort of evidence did both sides use to determine Amos Daley's race?
3. On what grounds did South Carolina authorities flog Amos Daley?

U.S. House Committee on Commerce, *Free Colored Seamen: Majority and Minority Reports*, 27th Cong., 3rd sess., H. Report 27–80, (January 20, 1843), 18–21.

3

ANTEBELLUM SEAFARING

The perceived romance and adventure of the sailor's life, despite its many hardships, drew many Americans to the nation's ports. On the very first page of *Moby Dick*, Herman Melville reported that landsmen lined the New York City waterfront "posted like silent sentinels all around the town . . . thousands upon thousands of mortal men fixed in ocean reveries. Some leaning against the spiles; some seated upon the pier-heads; some looking over the bulwarks of ships from China; some high aloft in the rigging. . . . They must get just as nigh the water as they possibly can without falling in. And there they stand—miles of them—leagues. Inlanders all, they come from lanes and alleys, streets and avenues north, east, south, and west. Yet here they all unite."

The seafarers in this period—whether a young Frederick Law Olmsted in his short and unhappy experiences in the China trade, a steamboat pilot like Samuel Clemens, or a young Frederick Douglass escaping from slavery dressed as a sailor—were representative of American society, ideals, and concepts like reform, business, technological change, freedom, race, and gender. Furthermore, seafarers like Olmsted, Clemens, and Douglass went on to shape how Americans perceived themselves. Other authors such as James Fenimore Cooper, Richard Henry Dana, Walt Whitman, Henry David Thoreau, and of course Herman Melville joined them in creating a literature that reflected the many connections antebellum America had with the sea.

Sailors also contributed to the American fascination with speed, a by-product of a transportation revolution that completely reshaped the lives of all Americans. The young nation was in a hurry, and shipowners and masters were happy to oblige. As the French writer Alexis de Tocqueville noted, American seafarers "sets sail while the storm is still rumbling; by night as well as by day he spreads full sails to the wind; he repairs storm damage as he goes; and when at last he draws near the end of his voyage, he flies toward the coast as if he could already see the port. . . . The American is often shipwrecked, but no other sailor crosses the sea as fast as he." The passion for speed transferred itself to steamboats, too. Riverboats raced one another on the nation's western rivers, endangering passengers and crew who nonetheless cheered on their speeding vessels. In particular, American steam packets competed fiercely with British steamers for the fastest crossing of the North Atlantic.

The antebellum period was thus the golden age of American seafaring. There were more seamen pursuing more varied trades than ever before, from the western rivers to the South Pacific, and they brought a new prosperity to American seaport communities. Steamboats ruled the western rivers, immigrants crossed the Atlantic on sailing vessels, whaleships ventured to the far reaches of the Pacific, and fishermen sailed to the stormy Grand Banks.

Yet there were problems, too. Women in maritime communities often suffered cruelly during the absence of sailor husbands, brothers, and fathers. Seamen themselves had to endure often horrific conditions and brutal discipline. Steamboats frequently burned, collided, or simply blew up as mariners struggled to understand the complexity of steam navigation. Reformers attempted to grapple with these problems, with mixed results.

African American mariners were an important part of maritime America. Frederick Law Olmsted noted a Virginia steamboat crewed entirely by blacks. Lewis Temple invented a new harpoon for New Bedford's whaling industry, which employed many African Americans. Yet racism grew worse in these years, and black seafarers found themselves increasingly marginalized. Enslaved blacks faced horrific conditions and many sought to escape in boats or ships—not all successfully.

The Civil War itself visited many troubles on Americans. For naval officers, new technologies threatened the old, and combat itself was both an opportunity and a peril at the same time. Commercial mariners, whether blockade runners or Yankee whalemen in the Pacific, faced capture and possibly the destruction of their vessels. The war devastated commercial shipping, and with the exception of the Western rivers and Great Lakes, saw a decline in deep-sea shipping that proved remarkably difficult to reverse.

THE GOLDEN AGE

As early as 1825, Daniel Webster boasted that the United States had "a commerce which leaves no sea unexplored." The nation prospered mightily in the antebellum period, which many consider the golden age of American seafaring. As Andrew Gibson and Arthur Donovan note in *The Abandoned*

Ocean,[1] the size, beauty, and speed of American sailing ships, especially the full-rigged wooden clippers, were testimonies to the skill and abilities of the nation's merchants, seamen, and shipwrights. For a brief but glorious moment, American shipping seemed to dominate world shipping.

But as Gibson and Donovan note, clippers also represented the end for American shipping. Clippers were the products of a traditional shipbuilding craft rather than of scientific naval architecture. Steamships could offer more dependable service, and iron ships were more durable. Market forces were moving beyond a world of wood and sail to an era of steam and iron, but the American business community found itself ill-equipped to make that transition, and Britain reasserted its commercial maritime predominance by embracing new technologies.

This section examines the relationship between American seafaring, national identity, and commerce. Utilizing the observations of French author Alexis de Tocqueville as well as that of American entrepreneurs such as Edward Knight Collins, it looks at the centrality of seaborne commerce to American self-identity in the antebellum period, as well as the commercial factors that impacted shipping.

Jeremiah N. Reynolds, "A Commercial and Enterprising People" (1828)

Americans' competitive spirit played out on the Pacific Ocean, too. In this piece, Jeremiah N. Reynolds (1799–1858), a newspaper editor and lecturer, vigorously propounds to Congress the benefits of exploring the Pacific Ocean and the Antarctic. He had some experience in the Pacific, having volunteered to sail with USS *Potomac* on an expedition to punish a Sumatran community that had seized the Salem trading vessel *Friendship* and killed most of its crew. On his return to the U.S., Reynolds wrote a book about his experience and urged Congress to send naval vessels to the Pacific to chart and explore it. Eventually Congress authorized a six-vessel naval squadron known as the United States Exploring Expedition under the command of Lieutenant Charles Wilkes.

Maritime historian Nathaniel Philbrick followed the exploits and misadventures of the amateur scientists of the Wilkes expedition in *Sea of Glory: America's Voyage of Discovery—The U.S. Exploring Expedition, 1838–1842*.[2]

1   Andrew Gibson and Arthur Donovan, *The Abandoned Ocean: A History of United States Maritime Policy* (Columbia: University of South Carolina Press, 2000).
2   Nathaniel Philbrick, *Sea of Glory: America's Voyage of Discovery—The U.S. Exploring Expedition, 1838–1842* (New York: Viking Penguin, 2003).

During its four-year voyage between 1838 and 1842, the expedition made significant progress in charting portions of Antarctica and the Pacific, including the Oregon coast and many islands in the South Pacific. Furthermore, the expedition's botanists and other scientists gathered valuable data and samples that became the heart of the Smithsonian's collections at its founding in 1846.

No one who has reflected on the vast resources of the earth, "which is our inheritance," can doubt that a large portion of it contains many things which may be turned to good account by the enterprise and good management of our people; and those are the true profits of commerce. The great mass of the intelligence of the country is for it, and is calling on the national legislature for aid in the undertaking.

The States, whose legislative bodies have sanctioned it, are represented on the floor of Congress by one hundred and twenty-nine members, to say nothing of the memorials from large cities and other places, and the aggregate of citizens of these States, near six millions.

We have been an industrious, a commercial and enterprising people, and have taken advantage of the knowledge of others, as well as of their trade; for, although our entrance and our clearance, without looking at our immense coasting trade, amounted to eight thousand seven hundred and sixty-six vessels, yet not one of those were sailed a mile by a chart made by us, except we may suppose the chart of George's bank may have been used by a few of the navigators of these vessels. We are dependent on other nations for our nautical instruments as well as charts and if we except *Bowditch's Navigation*,[1] an improvement on Hamilton Moore's book of the same kind, we have not a nautical table or book in our navy, or amongst our merchantmen, the product of our own science and skill; and we are now among the three first commercial nations of the world, and have more shipping and commerce than all the nations of Europe had together when Columbus discovered this continent, but a little more than three centuries since; and our navy, young as it is, has more effective force in it than the combined navies of the world could have amounted to at that period. Out of the discovery of this continent, and a passage to the

---

1   *Bowditch's Navigation*: Nathaniel Bowditch's *The New American Practical Navigator*, first published in 1802 and still in use today.

Indies, grew up the naval powers of Europe. On the acquisition of the New World, Spain enlarged her marine; France and England theirs, to hold sway with Spain; and that of the Netherlands sprang from the extent of their trade, connected with the wise policy of enlarging and protecting it.

Our commercial and national importance cannot be supported without a navy, or our navy without commerce,—and a nursery for our seamen. The citizens of Maine, of New York, of Georgia, of Ohio, and of the great valley of the Mississippi, are as deeply interested in the existence of our gallant navy, and of the extension of our commerce, as they are interested in the perpetuity of our institutions and the liberty of our country. Indeed, liberty and commerce have been *twin sisters* in all past ages, and countries and times; they have stood side by side, moved hand in hand. Wherever the soil has been congenial to the one, there has flourished the other also; in a word, they have lived, they have flourished, or they have died together.

Commerce has constantly increased with the knowledge or man; yet it has been undergoing perpetual revolutions. These changes and revolutions have often mocked the vigilance of the wary, and the calculations of the sagacious; but there is now a fundamental principle on which commerce is based, which will lead the intelligent merchant and the wise government to foresee and prepare for most of these changes; and that principle consists in an intimate knowledge of all seas, climates, islands, continents, of every river and mountain, and every plain of the globe, and all their productions, and of the nature, habits and character of all races of men; and this information should be corrected and revised with every season.

The commercial nations of the world have done much, and much remains to be accomplished. We stand a solitary instance among those who are considered commercial, as never having put forth a particle of strength, or expended a dollar of our money, to add to the accumulated stock of commercial and geographical knowledge, except in partially exploring our own territory.

When our naval commanders and hardy tars have achieved a victory on the deep, they have to seek our harbors, and conduct their prizes into port, by tables and charts furnished perhaps by the very people whom they have vanquished.

Is it honorable for the United States to use forever the knowledge furnished us by others, to teach us how to shun a rock, escape a shoal, or find a harbor, and add nothing to the great mass of information that previous ages and other nations have brought to our hands?

Tyre, Greece, Carthage, Venice, Florence,[1] whose commerce has ceased, and whose opulence is gone forever, have still left the historic glory of having shown succeeding ages the way to wealth, and honor, and power, by means of knowledge. The ancient commercial and naval monuments are theirs, and every niche of the modern temple of Neptune is filled by others—not ourselves. The exports, and more emphatically the imports of the United States, her receipts and expenditures, are written on every pillar erected by commerce on every sea and in every clime; but the amount of her subscription stock to erect these pillars, and for the advancement of knowledge, is nowhere to be found.

To open new sources of traffic and of commercial wealth, has gratified the pride as well as the avarice of man, in every age; and the adventurous deeds by which this has been achieved, have been commemorated by every historian, poet, and even fabulist in all past times; for the Argonautic expedition for the golden fleece, as given us by the poets and mythologists, is only in the form of a generous and munificent commemoration of the voyage of one who ventured much to open a new path to commerce, for the aggrandizement of his own country.

We have been plundered by the English and French, by Spaniards and Neapolitans, Danes, Norwegians, and the Barbary powers,[2] while our commerce was extending everywhere, and protected nowhere. Some of these insults and depredations have been settled for, and others are quietly, but surely, approximating to a day of *restitution* or *retribution.* The spirit of the nation is aroused on these subjects, and can never sleep again; honor, justice, feeling, conscious of physical strength, all forbid it. Have we not, then, reached a degree of mental strength that will enable us to find our way about the globe without leading-strings? And are we forever to take the highway others have laid out for us and fixed with mile-stones and guide-boards? Permit me to conclude, in humble imitation of the great discoverer of this

---

1   Tyre, Greece, Carthage, Venice, Florence: historic city-states that prospered from maritime trade in the Mediterranean.
2   Barbary powers: North African city-states that had a record of attacking American shipping.

continent to his patrons: *We fear no storms, no icebergs, no monsters of the deep, in any sea; we will conduct ourselves with prudence, and discretion, and judgment; and, if we succeed, the glory and profit will be yours; if we perish in our attempt, we alone shall suffer, for the very inquiry after us will redound to your honor.*

Questions for Discussion:

1. What does this document reveal about how Americans viewed themselves?

2. What are the different reasons Reynolds uses to argue that the United States must contribute to the charting of the world's oceans?

3. How does Reynolds view the relationship between commercial shipping and the Navy?

Jeremiah N. Reynolds, "Naval Exploring Expedition," *American State Papers: Naval Affairs* 3:193–94 (Washington: Gales and Seaton, 1860).

Alexis de Tocqueville, "Born to Rule the Seas" (1831)

Alexis de Tocqueville (1805–1859) was a French nobleman who traveled to the United States in the 1830s just as the market revolution, westward expansion, and Jacksonian democracy radically transformed American society. Tocqueville was fascinated by the American pursuit of wealth, and how that pursuit interacted with egalitarian ideals. Tocqueville also noted the maritime greatness of the United States, the success of its merchants, the boldness of its mariners, and claimed this American pursuit of wealth was nothing short of "heroic." In this excerpt, de Tocqueville considers American maritime efforts, both on the high seas and on the western rivers, and why both were so successful.

It is difficult to say for what reason the Americans can trade at a lower rate than other nations; and one is at first led to attribute this circumstance to the physical or natural advantages which are within their reach; but this supposition is erroneous. The American vessels cost almost as much to build as our own; they are not better built, and they generally last for a shorter time. The pay of the American sailor is more considerable than the pay on board European ships; which is proved by the great number of Europeans who are to be met with in the merchant vessels of the United States. But I am of opinion that the true cause of their superiority must not be sought for in physical advantages, but that it is wholly attributable to their moral and intellectual qualities. . . .

The Americans have introduced a similar system into their commercial speculations; and they do for cheapness what the French did for conquest. The European sailor navigates with prudence; he only sets sail when the weather is favorable; if an unforseen accident befalls him, he puts into port; at night he furls a portion of his canvas; and when the whitening billows intimate the vicinity of land, he checks his way, and takes an observation of the sun. But the American neglects these precautions and braves these dangers. He weighs anchor in the midst of tempestuous gales; by night and by day he spreads his sheets to the wind; he repairs as he goes along such damage as his vessel may have sustained from the storm; and when he at last approaches the term of his voyage, he darts onward to the shore as if he already descried a port. The Americans are often shipwrecked, but no trader crosses the seas so rapidly. And as they perform the same distance in a shorter time, they can perform it at a cheaper rate.

The European touches several times at different ports in the course of a long voyage; he loses a good deal of precious time in making the harbor, or in waiting for a favorable wind to leave it; and he pays daily dues to be allowed to remain there. The American starts from Boston to go to purchase tea in China; he arrives at Canton, stays there a few days, and then returns. In less than two years he has sailed as far as the entire circumference of the globe, and he has seen land but once. It is true that during a voyage of eight or ten months he has drunk brackish water and lived upon salt meat; that he has been in a continual contest with the sea, with disease, and with a tedious existence; but upon his return he can sell a pound of his tea for a half-penny less than the English merchant, and his purpose is accomplished.

I cannot better explain my meaning than by saying that the Americans affect a sort of heroism in their manner of trading. But the European merchant will always find it very difficult to imitate his American competitor, who, in adopting the system which I have just described, follows not only a calculation of his gain, but an impulse of his nature. . . .

As long as the sailors of the United States retain these inspiriting advantages, and the practical superiority which they derive from them, they will not only continue to supply the wants of the producers and consumers of their own country, but they will tend more and more to become, like the English, the factors of all other peoples.[1] This prediction has already begun to be realized; we perceive that the American traders are introducing themselves as intermediate agents in the commerce of several European nations;[2] and America will offer a still wider field to their enterprise. . . .

An attentive examination of what is going on in the United States will easily convince us that two opposite tendencies exist in that country, like two distinct currents flowing in contrary directions in the same channel. The Union has now existed for forty-five years, and in the course of that time a vast number of provincial prejudices, which were at first hostile to its power, have died away. The patriotic feeling which attached each of the Americans to his own native State is become less exclusive; and the different parts of the Union have become more intimately connected the better they have become acquainted with each other. The post,[3] that great instrument of intellectual intercourse, now reaches into the backwoods; and steamboats have established daily means of communication between the different points of the coast. An inland navigation of unexampled rapidity conveys commodities up and down the rivers of the country.[4] And to these facilities of nature and art may be added those restless cravings, that busy-mindedness, and love of self, which are constantly urging the American into active life, and bringing him into contact with his fellow-citizens. He crosses the country in every direction; he visits all the various populations of the land; and there is not a province in France in which the natives are so well known to each other as the 13,000,000 of men who cover the territory of the United States.

Reason shows and experience proves that no commercial prosperity can be durable if it cannot be united, in case of need, to naval

---

1   Tocqueville here notes "It must not be supposed that English vessels are exclusively employed in transporting foreign produce into England, or British produce to foreign countries; at the present day the merchant shipping of England may be regarded in the light of a vast system of public conveyances, ready to serve all the producers of the world, and to open communications between all peoples. The maritime genius of the Americans prompts them to enter into competition with the English."
2   Tocqueville notes that "Part of the commerce of the Mediterranean is already carried on by American vessels."
3   Post: mail system.
4   Tocqueville notes "In the course of ten years, from 1821 to 1831, 271 steamboats have been launched upon the rivers which water the valley of the Mississippi alone. In 1829 259 steamboats existed in the United States."

force. This truth is as well understood in the United States as it can be anywhere else: the Americans are already able to make their flag respected; in a few years they will be able to make it feared. I am convinced that the dismemberment of the Union would not have the effect of diminishing the naval power of the Americans, but that it would powerfully contribute to increase it. At the present time the commercial States are connected with others which have not the same interests, and which frequently yield an unwilling consent to the increase of a maritime power by which they are only indirectly benefited. If, on the contrary, the commercial States of the Union formed one independent nation, commerce would become the foremost of their national interests; they would consequently be willing to make very great sacrifices to protect their shipping, and nothing would prevent them from pursuing their designs upon this point.

Nations, as well as men, almost always betray the most prominent features of their future destiny in their earliest years. When I contemplate the ardor with which the Anglo-Americans prosecute commercial enterprise, the advantages which befriend them, and the success of their undertakings, I cannot refrain from believing that they will one day become the first maritime power of the globe. They are born to rule the seas, as the Romans were to conquer the world.

Questions for Discussion:
1. According to de Tocqueville, how does the American sailor represent certain American national attributes?
2. With what commercial attributes does de Tocqueville credit American mariners?
3. According to de Tocqueville, in what way have steamboats bound Americans together?

_____

Alexis de Tocqueville, *Democracy in America* (New York: A. S. Barnes & Co., 1851), 459–65.

Edward Knight Collins, "Memorial to Congress" (1851)

By the 1840s, American merchant shipping posed a serious threat to British commercial dominance of the North Atlantic. That competition was keenest in the steamer packet trades, especially between the British Cunard Line and the American Collins Line, operated by Edward Knight Collins

(1802–1878). The following jingle to the tune of *Yankee Doodle Dandy* captured some of the spirit of that competition:

A steamer of the Collins Line,
A Yankee Doodle Notion,
Has also quickest cut the brine
Across the Atlantic Ocean.
And British agents, no way slow,
Her merits to discover,
Have been and bought her just to tow
The Cunard packets over!

The competition, fueled by government subsidies, continued into the 1850s with larger and more powerful steamers built annually. Stephen Fox has caught the spirit of this competition, and its relationship to the rise of international capitalism, in *Transatlantic: Samuel Cunard, Isambard Brunel, and the Great Atlantic Steamships*.[1] Ultimately it was the Collins Line, which was dogged by bad luck (including the sinking of two of its best steamers with large loss of life), that stumbled first. American economic problems, followed by a devastating Civil War, ensured that American steamers could not resume the competition, and Britain would continue to dominate the North Atlantic.

The undersigned, contractors for carrying the United States Mail between New York and Liverpool, respectfully ask the attention of Congress to the statements and the petition of this their memorial.

It is now about four years since your memorialists entered into a contract with the Secretary of the Navy for building five steamships, to be employed as a mail line between this country and England. At that time England enjoyed undisputed supremacy in the steam navigation of the Atlantic, and monopolized the carriage of the passengers and letters of the world. In the interval that has since elapsed, your memorialists have built four steamers of the largest size, with accommodations for the comfort of passengers far exceeding every thing of the kind before known; of a speed that compares favorably with that of the steamers of the competing English lines, and which they

---

1   Stephen Fox, *Transatlantic: Samuel Cunard, Isambard Brunel, and the Great Atlantic Steamships* (New York: HarperCollins, 2003).

attained only after ten years' experience; notwithstanding the inexperience and consequent inferiority of their engineers and firemen, the
steamers of the American line have made the shortest passages to the
westward, and, with but two exceptions, (and those of three hours
only) the shortest passage to the eastward, that have ever yet been
accomplished. It is admitted on both sides of the water, that the ships
and their steam machinery, are equal to the best of British build and
manufacture. This success has been attained at a very great expense,
and under very disadvantageous circumstances.

The manufacture of machinery, much larger than had ever before
been built in this country, was disproportionately expensive (much
larger than was anticipated) and the materials employed in it were
better and higher-priced than were ever before used for the same
purposes. The cost was still enhanced (in comparison with that of
the British lines) by the high prices of labor; and the result is, that
when the line is completed, so great will have been the original outlay
that the insurance alone will amount to $228,000, being considerably
more than one-half the sum agreed to be paid by Government for the
transportation of the mails. Add to this, that the American line suffer disadvantages from the inexperience of its engineers and firemen,
besides paying them 50 per cent more than is paid by the English
steamers; and it will hardly be necessary to add, that your memorialists cannot maintain a successful competition with them except upon
the grant of such aid from our own Government, as on the basis of
tonnage will correspond to that which the English admiralty extends
to the Cunard line. Even on the same terms, the system of maintaining
steam-packets convertible into war steamers, is recommended by its
economy; for the cost to Government of laying up in ordinary[1] such a
steamer as the *Baltic*, or the *Pacific*,[2] with interest on the outlay, dete-
rioration, &c., would be $150,000 per annum; as may be ascertained
by reference to the accounts of the steamer *Mississippi*.[3]

Your memorialists therefore respectfully solicit from Congress an
extension of the time in which to refund the money loaned to them by
the Government, so that it may be repaid 10 per cent. annually; that
amount to be deducted from the last quarterly payment in each year.

They also pray that authority may be given to the Secretary of the

---

1   Ordinary: decommissioning a vessel and putting it aside for use at a later date.
2   *Baltic*, or the *Pacific*: two of Collins's steamers.
3   *Mississippi*: USS *Mississippi*, an American steam warship launched in 1841.

Navy[1] to increase their annual compensation, having regard to the tonnage and dimensions of the steamers employed, and to the average per ton allowed to the other American lines, by their existing contracts.

Your memorialists further pray that the steamers, in time of peace, may be placed under the executive control of your memorialists, and be officered by them, as they apprehend that they can in no other way secure that entire responsibility which is indispensable to the perfect efficiency and safety of the service.

Your memorialists respectfully represent, that they have entered upon this enterprise with no exclusive views of commercial profit, but on national grounds, and to prevent the undisputed supremacy of the seas from falling into the hands of a rival power. The contract of your memorialists calls for ships of 2,000 tons burthen. Your memorialists were soon persuaded that with steamers of this size they could never compete successfully with the improvements and increase of the British line; and they determined to augment their bulk to about 3,000 tons. The enterprise was commenced by an incorporated company, who were the assignees of the original contractors. Of the stock but $1,100,000 was subscribed, and the difference between that and $2,500,000, the entire amount which has been expended, has been made up, with the exception of the Government advance of $385,000, mainly by the directors of the company. Any portion of this stock may be obtained at par by any one who is disposed to purchase it.

Your memorialists have little expectation of deriving pecuniary advantages from this contract, even with the solicited alterations. They are merely anxious that it should be put upon grounds which will enable them to meet the extraordinary efforts of the British steamers and the British Government and people, with an efficient and successful competition. The question has assumed a national interest. If it is understood that the American line will be sustained by the American Government, to the extent necessary to place it on an equal footing with the British steamers, your memorialists have no doubt that, on this route, to which all the energies of Great Britain, commercial and governmental, have been directed, they will be able to achieve a complete triumph. If this aid is withheld, there is no doubt that British

---

1   Navy: to receive a subsidy, the Collins Line ships were designed to be turned into auxiliary naval vessels in time of war.

capital and experience, backed by the assistance of the Government, will outstrip all American competition.

Your memorialists have said that they have not entered upon this enterprise with the mere expectation of pecuniary advantages. They now declare that, if their petition should be granted by the Government, they will, at any time within six months after the passage of the act which they solicit, surrender their contract, with all its incidents and advantages, to the Secretary of the Navy, or to any individuals that may be indicated by him, on the repayment to them of the actual disbursements that have accrued in its execution. They desire merely that the monopoly which has hitherto been enjoyed may be wrestled from our commercial rivals, and that the supremacy upon the ocean, which will result to the most efficient steam-marine of the world, may be at least shared with Great Britain by the United States. They believe that on this ground they will not appeal to the American Government in vain, but that all the necessary legislative aid for the accomplishment of this most desirable object will be readily granted by the representatives of the American people.

Questions for Discussion:
1. What does this document reveal about the commercial competition between the United States and Britain?
2. According to Collins, what disadvantages did American steamships have in competing with the British?
3. What compelling evidence did Collins give for continued subsidies from the U.S. government?

Edward Knight Collins, *The Supremacy of the Seas, or Facts, Views, Statements, and Opinions relating to the American & British Steamers* (Washington: Gideon and Co., 1851), 3–5.

Robert B. Forbes, "The Present Spirit of Navigation" (1855)

Robert B. Forbes (1804–1889) was a sea captain, merchant, shipbuilder, and prolific author of maritime books and pamphlets. Forbes's claim to fame among seafarers was the invention of the "Forbes rig" for sailing vessels, which allowed fewer sailors to safely handle sailing vessels in storms. Forbes engaged in numerous philanthropic activities, such as sending USS *Jamestown* to relieve Irish famine sufferers in 1847, efforts to make seafaring safer, and the establishment of the Sailor's Snug Harbor in Boston in

1855. In his day Forbes was one of the best-informed Americans concerning maritime matters, a forward-thinking seafarer who advocated screw pro-pellers, lifeboats, and other innovations and fearlessly advocated for them in numerous pamphlets and articles. Yet Forbes did not embrace all change, and in the following extract from his *A New Rig for Ships*, he expresses some ambivalence about changes in seafaring.

Great progress has been made, within the last twenty-five or thirty years, in the equipment and fit-out of the merchant ships of the United States, and particularly during the last five years. In consequence, ships are now more easily managed by smaller crews than formerly.

The adoption of chain cables, looked upon at first with distrust, is universal; iron trusses, iron futtock shrouds, iron bands to yards, friction roller-sheaves, patent steering-gear, ventilators, and many smaller articles, have come into general use. The labor of fitting and working ships is much reduced. The rigger, with his mass of "puddings," "mousings," "cat-harpings," "bentick shrouds," "top-burtons," "rolling tackles," buoys and buoy-ropes,[1] has been obliged to give way, in a great measure, to the blacksmith. Jack[2] is almost ready to go to sea for the love of it; and insurance offices are only kept open for lounging places, where the newspapers and the gossip of the day may be indulged in, the President and Directors occasionally putting their hands in their pockets to pay for some old ship that should have been condemned before starting! Chronometers, barometers, and thermometers, have crowded out lunars, azimuths, and amplitudes. Heaving the lead has become a matter of tradition; the commander who makes the best passage is the best fellow, no matter what risk he runs. The everlast-ing spirit of go-a-head-ism rules paramount. Seamen, however, have not improved, except in the important matter of temperance, in the same ratio that ships and their rigging have improved. I speak more especially of the Jacks. The old pig-tail *Agamemnons*, the Sons of Trafalgar,[3] and the younger Sons of Victory, who sailed and fought

---

1   The rigger . . . : these are references to rigging once made out of rope that had been replaced by iron parts.
2   Jack: an ordinary sailor, as opposed to a mate or master.
3   *Agamemnons* . . . Trafalgar: Forbes here refers to the old-style British sailors who served during the Napoleonic War at battles such as Trafalgar, the greatest naval victory of the age.

with Bainbridge, Hull,[1] and others of our own side of the Atlantic the old privateersmen, full of oaths, tobacco, and rum, all are gone! And in many respects, it is fortunate that we know them no more. But they had their uses; and, generally speaking, always, when sober and at sea, they were sailors of the first water, ready and expert to obey any orders against an enemy or against the elements. They were the men not to be ashamed of a reef taken in during the darkest squall; they could straighten out their twelve or fifteen fathoms of line, and melodiously sing the "marks" and "deeps;"[2] they had a religious pride in saying, "Ay, ay, sir!" to every order, and generally in obeying any seamanlike demand. In short, half a dozen of them in a gale of wind were worth ten of the men now rating as seamen.

One great cause of this falling off in the quality of marlinspike sailors is the discovery of gold in California. Another prominent cause is to be found in the greatly-increased competition among shipowners, whereby economy is necessarily the first object. It is becoming unfashionable to have ships come and go in what once was considered fine order. The freight-list is the great object. It is very seldom that the eye is gratified with a ship coming into port looking neat and trim about her spars and rigging. The booming-gun, at departure and on arrival, is no longer heard. Everybody goes and comes back, no matter what part of the world he has been to, without causing any remark. The leveling power of steam has told the story of his ship's loading, her time of sailing, &c.; the profit, or more likely the loss, on the cargo, is already calculated; the arrival of the ship is a mere fact to hear all about in the newsroom. No one asks or cares whether she looks well or ill; her sails may be clewed up, and left hanging for a week in such style as would make an old tar weep, or she may be as trim as any of the old *Unions, Georges, Zephyrs,* or *Panthers*; nobody cares. From my country residence, I daily see ships coming and going—gallant ships, well commanded, well officered, and only pretty well manned; and many of them carry the spirit of economy so far that they do not show their national flag. Ships meet on the ocean now-a-days, and pass each other by, without showing bunting, or asking a question, unless

---

1 Bainbridge, Hull: William Bainbridge and Isaac Hull, American naval officers who served with distinction in the War of 1812.

2 "marks" and "deeps": maritime jargon used when using a sounding lead, a heavy lead weight attached to a marked line that determined the depth of water.

it be about the price of cotton, or the value of freight. "What is your longitude?" "Are you in want of anything?" "Pleasant passage to you," and "Report me, on arrival; all well," are expressions no longer known to the language. If a man ask the first question, he is considered a fool; he is lost, and don't know where he is! If the second, he would be considered even less wise, and entirely opposed to the owner's interest; and, as for reporting him, steam will do that long before he gets home. All these little nothings combine to depreciate the quality of the sailor; the inducements to commerce at home, render the sailor's vocation less popular daily; discipline is no longer maintained as formerly, and we are getting slip-shod.

Questions for Discussion:
1. What does this document reveal about American maritime enterprise in the 1850s?
2. What was the "present spirit of navigation" about which Forbes wrote and how did it relate to American society as a whole?
3. What major changes did Forbes see in the maritime industry, and which did he like or dislike?

Robert B. Forbes, "The Present Spirit of Navigation," *Monthly Nautical Magazine, and Quarterly Review*, II (April–September 1855): 256–58.

PERILS OF SEAFARING

The American public had a morbid interest in death in the antebellum period, encouraging authors like Edgar Allan Poe to pen his only full-length novel, *The Narrative of Arthur Gordon Pym of Nantucket*, a tale that included accounts of shipwreck, mutiny, and cannibalism. But American readers did not have to turn to fiction to read about maritime disasters; compendiums of shipwreck tales, such as Charles Ellms's 1841 *Shipwrecks and Disasters at Sea*, and works that specialized in a special type of marine disaster, such as James T. Lloyd's 1856 *Lloyd's Steamboat Directory, and Disasters on the Western Waters*, were plentiful.

Indeed, the common element sailors shared was the danger inherent to seafaring, no matter whether on a freshwater river or a clipper rounding Cape Horn, a sailor's life was fraught with peril. The following accounts explore the dangers of seafaring in a number of maritime trades. The first piece is fairly typical of the sensationalism of many marine disaster accounts, in this case, describing an explosion on a river steamboat. Steamboats had an alarming tendency to burn or explode before better engineering and government regulations made them safer. The next piece, a transcript of testimony related to the fire on the steamboat *Lexington*, reminds us that technology brings new dangers and that regulations, of themselves, are not sufficient to ensure safety. The third piece looks at the more traditional shipwreck of a sailing vessel loaded with Irish immigrants from the perspective of those on shore surveying the remains of the vessel and the corpses scattered on the beach. The final item is a fragment of the journal of Samuel Millet, a young sailor who went on a whaling voyage from which he never returned; a whale killed him.

Anonymous, "Explosion on the *Helen McGregor*" (1830)

Not all maritime disasters happen at sea. Some of America's greatest maritime disasters involved ships on the Great Lakes and western rivers. American steamboats were notoriously unsafe because their pilots chose to run them at dangerous speeds and the engine designs themselves were unsafe. Between 1825 and 1850, some 1,400 people died in steamboat explosions. In that period about 185 steamboats blew up on western waters, while only 45 exploded in other waters. Steamboats were opening up the nation to westward expansion, but at a terrible cost in human lives. Nonetheless, steamboats quickly became a popular form of travel. Because of their speed and convenience, they were the preferred mode for those traveling in what was then the American west.

Unlike sailing vessel disasters, boiler explosions on steamboats often occurred very suddenly and in this case within feet of the wharf. Some sixty people died in the *Helen McGregor* tragedy, sparking a congressional investigation into steamboat safety. By the end of the 1830s, Congress had belatedly passed a steamboat inspection law to prevent further tragedies such as this one.

FATAL EXPLOSION OF THE BOILER
ON BOARD
THE STEAM BOAT
HELEN McGREGOR,
At Memphis, on the Mississippi.

The following is a description, by a passenger, of one of the most fatal steamboat disasters that has ever occurred on the western waters.

On the morning of the 24th of February, 1830, the *Helen McGregor* stopped at Memphis, on the Mississippi river, to deliver freight and land a number of passengers, who resided in that section of Tennessee. The time occupied in so doing could not have exceeded three quarters of an hour. When the boat landed, I went ashore to see a gentleman with whom I had some business. I found him on the beach, and after a short conversation, I returned to the boat. I recollect looking at my watch as I passed the gang-way. It was half past eight o'clock. A great number of persons were standing on what is called the boiler deck, being that part of the upper deck situated immediately over the boilers. It was crowded to excess, and presented one dense mass of human bodies. In a few minutes we sat down to breakfast in the cabin. The table, although extending the whole length of the cabin, was completely filled, there being upwards of sixty cabin passengers, among whom were several ladies and children. The number of passengers on board, deck and cabin united, was between four and five hundred. I had almost finished my breakfast, when the pilot rung his bell for the engineer to put the machinery in motion. The boat having just shoved off, I was in the act of raising my cup to my lips, the ting-ling of the pilot bell yet on my ear, when I heard an explosion, resembling the discharge of a small piece of artillery. The report was perhaps louder than usual in such cases; for an exclamation was half uttered by me, that the gun was well loaded, when the rushing sound of steam, and the rattling of glass in some of the cabin windows, checked my speech, and told me too well what had occurred. I almost involuntarily bent my head and body down to the floor—a vague idea seemed to shoot across my mind that more than one boiler might burst, and that by assuming this posture, the destroying matter would pass over without touching me.

The general cry of, "a boiler has burst," resounded from one end of the table to the other; and, as if by a simultaneous movement, all started on their feet. Then commenced a general race to the ladies' cabin, which lay more towards the stern of the boat. All regard to order or deference to sex seemed to be lost in the struggle for which should be first and farthest removed from the dreaded boilers. The danger had already passed away. I remained standing by the chair on which I had been previously sitting. Only one or two persons staid in the cabin with me. As yet no more than half a minute had elapsed since the explosion; but, in that brief space, how had the scene changed! In that "drop of time" what confusion, distress, and dismay! An instant before, and all were in the quiet repose of security—another, and they were overwhelmed with alarm or consternation. It is but justice to say, that in this scene of terror, the ladies exhibited a degree of firmness worthy of all praise. No screaming, no fainting—their fears, when uttered, were not for themselves, but for their husbands and children.

I advanced from my position to one of the cabin doors, for the purpose of inquiring who were injured, when, just as I reached it, a man entered at the opposite one, both his hands covering his face, and exclaiming, "Oh God! Oh God! I am ruined!" He immediately began to tear off his clothes. When stripped, he presented a most shocking spectacle: his face was entirely black—his body without a particle of skin. He had been flayed alive. He gave me his name, and place of abode—then sunk in a state of exhaustion and agony on the floor. I assisted in placing him on a mattress taken from one of the berths, and covered him with blankets. He complained of heat and cold as at once oppressing him. He bore his torments with manly fortitude, yet a convulsive shriek would occasionally burst from him. His wife, his children, were his constant theme—it was hard to die without seeing them—"it was hard to go without bidding them one farewell." Oil and cotton were applied to his wounds; but he soon became insensible to earthly misery. Before I had done attending to him, the whole floor of the cabin was covered with unfortunate sufferers. Some bore up under the horrors of their situation with a degree of resolution amounting to heroism. Others were wholly overcome by the sense of pain, the suddenness of the disaster, and the near approach of death, which even to them was evident—whose pangs they already felt. Some implored us, as an act of humanity, to complete the work of destruction, and free them from present suffering. One entreated the presence of a clergyman, to pray by him, declaring he was not fit to die. I inquired—none could be had. On every side were heard groans, and mingled exclamations of grief and despair.

To add to the confusion, persons were every moment running about to learn the fate of their friends and relatives—fathers, sons, brothers—for in this scene of unmixed calamity, it was impossible to say who were saved, or who had perished. The countenances of many were so much disfigured as to be past recognition. My attention, after some time, was particularly drawn towards a poor fellow, who lay unnoticed on the floor, without uttering a single word of complaint.

He was at a little distance removed from the rest. He was not much scalded; but one of his thighs was broken, and a principal artery had been severed, from which the blood was gushing rapidly. He betrayed no displeasure at the apparent neglect with which he was treated—he was perfectly calm. I spoke to him: he said "he was very weak, but felt himself going—it would soon be over." A gentleman ran for one of the physicians. He came, and declared that if expedition were used, he might be preserved by amputating the limb; but that, to effect this, It would be necessary to remove him from the boat. Unfortunately the boat was not sufficiently near to run a plank ashore. We were obliged to wait until it could be close hauled. I stood by him, calling for help. We placed him on a mattress, and bore him to the guards. There we were detained some time from the cause we have mentioned. Never did any thing appear to me so slow as the movements of those engaged in hauling the boat.

I knew, and he knew, that delay was death—that life was fast ebbing. I could not take my gaze from his face—there all was coolness and resignation. No word or gesture indicative of impatience escaped him. He perceived by my loud, and perhaps angry tone of voice, how much I was excited by what I thought the barbarous slowness of those around: he begged me not to take so much trouble—that they were doing their best. At length we got him on shore. It was too late—he was too much exhausted, and died immediately after the amputation.

So soon as I was relieved from attending on those in the cabin, I went to examine that part of the boat where the boiler had burst. It was a complete wreck—a picture of destruction. It bore ample testimony to the tremendous force of that power which the ingenuity of man had brought to his aid. The steam had given every thing a whitish hue; the boilers were displaced; the deck had fallen down; the machinery was broken and disordered. Bricks, dirt, and rubbish, were scattered about. Close by the bowsprit was a large rent, through which I was told the boiler, after exploding, had passed out, carrying one or two men in its mouth. Several dead bodies were lying around. Their fate had been an enviable one compared with that of others: they could scarcely have been conscious of a pang ere they had ceased to be. On the starboard wheel-house lay a human body, in which life was not yet extinct, though apparently there was no sensibility remaining. The body must have been thrown from the boiler-deck, a distance of thirty feet. The whole of the forehead had been blown away: the brains were still beating. Tufts of hair, shreds of clothing, and splotches of blood might be seen in every direction. A piece of skin was picked up by a gentleman, on board, which appeared to have been pealed off by the force of the steam. It extended from the middle of the arm down to the tips of the fingers, the nails adhering to it. So dreadful had been the force, that not a particle of the flesh adhered to it. The most skilful operator could scarcely have effected such a result. Several died from inhaling the steam or gas, whose skin was almost uninjured.

The number of lives lost, will, in all probability, never be distinctly known. Many were seen flung into the river, most of whom sunk to rise no more. Could the survivors have been kept together until the list of passengers was called, the precise loss would have been ascertained. That however, though it had been attempted, would, under the circumstances, have been next to impossible.

Judging from the crowd which I saw on the boiler-deck immediately before the explosion, and the statement which I received as to the number of those who succeeded in swimming out after they were cast into the river, I am inclined to believe that between fifty and sixty must have perished.

The cabin passengers escaped, owing to the peculiar construction of the boat. Just behind the boilers were several large iron posts, supporting, I think, the boiler deck: across each post was a large circular plate of iron of between one and two inches in thickness. One of these posts was placed exactly opposite the head of the boiler which burst, being the second one on the starboard side. Against this plate the head struck, and penetrated to the depth of an inch; then broke, and flew off at an angle, entering a cotton bale to the depth of a foot. The boiler head was in point blank range with the breakfast table in the cabin; and had it not been obstructed by the iron post, must have made a clear sweep of those who were seated at the table.

To render any satisfactory account of the cause which produced the explosion, can hardly be expected from one who possesses no scientific or practical knowledge on the subject, and who previously thereto was paying no attention to the management of the boat. The captain appeared to be very active and diligent in attending to his duty. He was on the boiler deck when the explosion occurred, was materially injured by that event, and must have been ignorant of the mismanagement, if any there were.

From the engineer alone could the true explanation be afforded; and, if indeed it was really attributable to negligence, it can scarcely be supposed he will lay the blame on himself. If I might venture a suggestion in relation thereto, I would assign the following causes:—That the water in the starboard boilers had become low, in consequence of that side of the boat resting upon the ground during our stay at Memphis; that, though the fires were kept up some time before we shoved off, that the head which burst had been cracked for a considerable time; that the boiler was extremely heated, and the water, thrown in when the boat was again in motion, was at once converted into steam; and the flues not being sufficiently large to carry it off as soon as it was generated, nor the boiler head of a strength capable of resisting its action, the explosion was a natural result.

Questions for discussion:
1. What does this document reveal about traveling on steamboats?
2. What does this account reveal about American attitudes toward death and danger in 1830?
3. What is the goal of the author in publishing this account?

Archibald Duncan, *The Mariner's Chronicle: Containing Narratives of the Most Remarkable Disasters at Sea* (New Haven, Conn.: R. M. Treadway, 1834), 453–57.

John Clark, "*Lexington* Testimony" (1840)

On January 14, 1840, the steamer *Lexington* sank in Long Island Sound after a fire broke out on board. Cornelius Vanderbilt, a former steamboat captain himself, built the *Lexington* in 1835 to be the "fastest in the world." But the *Lexington* had a fatal flaw: when its operators converted it from a wood-burning vessel to a coal burner in 1839 it made the wooden vessel much more vulnerable to fire. Heat or a spark from the super-heated smokestack caused a fire on the freight deck which quickly communicated itself to the cargo of some 150 bales of cotton. The fire, subsequent drownings, and deaths from exposure killed 139 of the 143 passengers and crew aboard; of the four survivors, only one was a passenger.

The testimony that follows is a portion of the investigation launched in the aftermath of the *Lexington* sinking. The witness, John Clark, was the steamboat inspector responsible for certifying the *Lexington*'s safety. Not only did Clark display a remarkable arrogance during the inquest, but he had the misfortune to face Richard M. Hoe, a very knowledgeable juror who asked Clark some difficult questions.

John Clark examined.—I was a machinist, but I am now an inspector of steamboats, under the act of Congress; I reside at 33 Essex street; I was acquainted with the steamboat *Lexington*, and inspected her the 1ˢᵗ of October last; she was all correct, and we gave a certificate. The whole top of the boiler was removed down to the flue last fall. The bottom was also repaired; I do not believe the steering department of the boat belongs to our duty; we do not examine the steering gear; we have nothing to do with that, only the engine and boiler; I did examine the steering apparatus it was two rods under the promenade deck, with hide ropes round the wheel. These ropes were within ten feet fore and aft of the sternpost and the tiller wheel [Here the coroner read the law to the witness, but the latter persisted that he had nothing to do with the steering apparatus].

By the Witness—I only consider myself bound to inspect the hull, boiler, and machinery; I go first on deck, then below, and look about, when I inspect a vessel nothing more than look at the wood and iron.

Coroner.—Have you ever condemned a boat?

Witness.—We never condemned any boat. We have restricted them to a certain amount of steam.

Juror.—Well, when you inspect a boat you look at the wood, and do nothing else?

Witness.—Yes, we take our fees.

Coroner.—What boats have you ever restricted to a certain amount of steam?

Witness.—Why, some of the ferry-boats on the North river. A year ago last fall, we restricted the *Rhode Island*, because the boiler was rather weak. We have also restricted the *William Young*, and the *Superior*.

Juror.—Was the restriction complied with?

Witness.—I suppose so.

Coroner.—Did you ever restrict the *Nimrod*?

Witness.—Yes; because she wanted a new boiler.

Juror.—Was any restriction ever put on the *Lexington*?

Witness.—No, sir.

Juror.—How do you examine the hull of a vessel?

Witness.—Why, I examine it.

Juror.—How?

Witness.—With my eyes.

Juror.—Do you mean to say that you see every vessel that is hauled out of the water?

Witness.—Yes.

Juror.—Well, we want to know your mode of proceeding.

Witness.—Well, I go and inquire the boat's age. How much do you suppose I am to do for five dollars?

Juror.—No matter, sir, about the fee; we want to know your mode of proceeding.

Witness.—Why, I examine the hull, and I look at the engine; I have worked at and made almost every kind of engine for the last thirty years.

Juror.—Mr. Coroner, am I in order in asking this question: how he found the hull of the steamer *William Young*?

Coroner.—Yes, sir.

Witness.—Well I think he is not, sir.

Juror.—Oh, I have several other boats to question him on, sir.

Witness.—Well, sir, this juror may be a steamboat owner, and may wish to get up a prejudice against a particular boat.

Coroner.—About the *William Young*, sir?

Witness.—Why we gave her a certificate that she was of such an age, and was suitable to run the river with a certain amount of steam. The boiler was an old one. We gave her a certificate last October.

Juror.—Have you examined the *Providence*, of Newburg?

Witness.—Not this year.

Juror.—Why, then, do you allow her to run?

Witness.—Why, it is the duty of the master to apply, or run the risk of being informed against. [Here, the coroner stated he had some doubts about the propriety of examining the witness as to particular steamboats, except as they referred to the case of the *Lexington*.]

Juror.—In due deference to your better judgment, sir, I think he is bound to say how he proceeds in the examining of steamboats. It is the opinion of the jury, that the inspectors have passed steamboats as safe, and given them certificates when they were not worthy of it. If we are traveling out of the road, why, we submit to your correction.

Coroner.—I do not think this man is on his trial; and all that we have to do, is to inquire about the *Lexington*.

Juror.—Why, sir, suppose it could be proved that he has examined and passed boats unworthy of it, would it not be a fair presumption that he may have done the same in the case of the *Lexington*?

[The answer of the coroner escaped the reporter.]

Question.—Are you interested in the *Lexington*?

Answer.—I have not a cent invested in any steamboat whatever. I think the *Lexington* was not so well calculated to carry freight as passengers, although she was strong enough to carry anything. We gave the *William Young* a different certificate to that given to the *Lexington*.

Juror.—Do you think you have a right to give such a certificate?

Coroner.—I don't think he is bound to answer.

Witness.—Why, if you pump me in that way, you will get out the secrets of every body's boat.

Juror.—How many bales of cotton could the *Lexington* carry?

Witness.—I did not think she could carry one with safety; as it regards safety from fire I mean.

Questions for Discussion:

1. What does this testimony reveal about American attitudes toward safety in 1840?

2. What does Clark's testimony reveal about the standards for steamboat inspection in 1840?

3. What limits does the transcript of court testimony place on the reader?

Testimony of John Clark, 26th Cong., 1st sess., 1840, S. Rep. 241, 22–24, in *Public Documents Printed by Order of the Senate of the United States* (Washington: Blair and Rives, 1840).

Henry David Thoreau, "Wreck of the *St. John*" (1849)

Herman Melville captured the essence of the Irish immigrant passage in his novel *Redburn*, comparing their quarters to dog kennels, describing the families "packed like slaves on a slave ship" and the shortage of food on such ships. The horrors of the immigrant ships were proverbial, but with the advent of the "Potato Famine" in Ireland, the choice for many was to starve to death or undertake this dangerous voyage. The ship that wrecked in this instance, the *St. John*, was probably typical in that it was a so-called famine ship loaded with emigrants from Galway, Ireland. Roughly one hundred people died in the disaster; only some twenty persons survived, including the captain.

The wreck of the *St. John* is reported by Henry David Thoreau (1817–1862), a famous American writer and philosopher, best known today for his essay *Walden*. In this piece, Thoreau explores humanity's relationship to the sea by walking along the beaches of Cape Cod and talking with the fishermen and sailors he meets along the way. He recounts the grisly experience of coming across the shipwreck of a vessel that had been carrying Irish immigrants to Boston.

We left Concord, Massachusetts, on Tuesday, October 9th, 1849. On reaching Boston, we found that the Provincetown steamer, which should have got in the day before, had not yet arrived, on account of a violent storm; and, as we noticed in the streets a handbill headed, "Death! One hundred and forty-five lives lost at Cohasset," we decided to go by way of Cohasset. We found many Irish in the cars, going to identify bodies and to sympathize with the survivors, and also to attend the funeral which was to take place in the afternoon; and when we arrived at Cohasset, it appeared that nearly all the passengers were bound for the beach, which was about a mile distant, and many other persons were flocking in from the neighboring country. There were several hundreds of them streaming off over Cohasset common in that direction, some on foot and some in wagons, and among them were some sportsmen in their hunting-jackets, with their guns, and game-bags, and dogs. As we passed the graveyard we saw a large hole, like a cellar, freshly dug there, and, just before reaching the shore, by a pleasantly winding and rocky road, we met several hay-riggings and farm-wagons coming away toward the meeting-house, each loaded with three large, rough deal boxes. We did not need to ask what was in them. The owners of the wagons were made the undertakers. Many horses in carriages were fastened to the fences near the shore, and, for a mile or more, up and down, the beach was covered with people looking out for bodies, and examining the fragments of the wreck. There was a small island called Brook Island, with a hut on it, lying just off the shore. This is said to be the rockiest shore in Massachusetts, from Nantasket to Scituate, hard sienitic rocks, which the waves have laid bare, but have not been able to crumble. It has been the scene of many a shipwreck.

The brig *St. John*, from Galway, Ireland, laden with emigrants, was wrecked on Sunday morning; it was now Tuesday morning, and the sea was still breaking violently on the rocks. There were eighteen or twenty of the same large boxes that I have mentioned, lying on a green hill-side, a few rods from the water, and surrounded by a crowd. The bodies which had been recovered, twenty-seven or eight in all, had been collected there. Some were rapidly nailing down the lids, others were carting the boxes away, and others were lifting the lids, which were yet loose, and peeping under the cloths, for each body, with such rags as still adhered to it, was covered loosely with a white sheet. I witnessed no signs of grief, but there was a sober despatch of business which was affecting. One man was seeking to identify a particular body, and one undertaker or carpenter was calling to another to know in what box a certain child was put. I saw many marble feet and matted heads as the cloths were raised, and one livid, swollen, and mangled body of a drowned girl, who probably had intended to go out to service in some American family, to which some rags still adhered, with a string, half concealed by the flesh, about its swollen neck; the coiled-up wreck of a human hulk, gashed by the rocks or fishes, so that the bone and muscle were exposed, but quite bloodless, merely red and white, with wide-open and staring eyes, yet lustreless, dead-lights; or like the cabin windows of a stranded vessel, filled with sand. Sometimes there were two or more children, or a parent and child, in the same box, and on the lid would perhaps be written with red chalk, "Bridget such-a-one, and sister's child." The surrounding sward was covered with bits of sails and clothing. I have since heard, from one who lives by this beach, that a woman who had come over before, but had left her infant behind for her sister to bring, came and looked into these boxes, and saw in one, probably the same whose superscription I have quoted, her child in her sister's arms, as if the sister had meant to be found thus; and within three days after, the mother died from the effect of that sight.

We turned from this and walked along the rocky shore. In the first cove were strewn what seemed the fragments of a vessel, in small pieces mixed with sand and sea-weed, and great quantities of feathers; but it looked so old and rusty, that I at first took it to be some old wreck which had lain there many years. I even thought of Captain Kidd, and that the feathers were those which sea-fowl had cast there; and perhaps there might be some tradition about it in the neighborhood. I asked a sailor if that was the *St. John*. He said it was. I asked him where she struck. He pointed to a rock in front of us, a mile from the shore, called the Grampus Rock, and added,

"You can see a part of her now sticking up; it looks like a small boat."

I saw it. It was thought to be held by the chain-cables and the anchors. I asked if the bodies which I saw were all that were drowned.

"Not a quarter of them," said he.

"Where are the rest?"

"Most of them right underneath that piece you see."

It appeared to us that there was enough rubbish to make the wreck of a large vessel in this cove alone, and that it would take many days to cart it off. It was several feet deep, and here and there was a bonnet or a jacket on it. In the very midst of the crowd about this wreck, there were men with carts busily collecting the sea-weed which the storm had cast up, and conveying it beyond the reach of the tide, though they were often obliged to separate fragments of clothing from it, and they might at any moment have found a human body under it. Drown who might, they did not forget that this weed was a valuable manure. This shipwreck had not produced a visible vibration in the fabric of society.

About a mile south we could see, rising above the rocks, the masts of the British brig which the *St. John* had endeavored to follow, which had slipped her cables, and, by good luck, run into the mouth of Cohasset Harbor. A little further along the shore we saw a man's clothes on a rock; further, a woman's scarf, a gown, a straw bonnet, the brig's caboose, and one of her masts high and dry, broken into several pieces. In another rocky cove, several rods from the water, and behind rocks twenty feet high, lay a part of one side of the vessel, still hanging together. It was, perhaps, forty feet long, by fourteen wide. I was even more surprised at the power of the waves, exhibited on this shattered fragment, than I had been at the sight of the smaller fragments before. The largest timbers and iron braces were broken superfluously, and I saw that no material could withstand the power of the waves; that iron must go to pieces in such a case, and an iron vessel would be cracked up like an egg-shell on the rocks. Some of these timbers, however, were so rotten that I could almost thrust my umbrella through them. They told us that some were saved on this piece, and also showed where the sea had heaved it into this cove, which was now dry. When I saw where it had come in, and in what condition, I wondered that any had been saved on it. A little further on a crowd of men was collected around the mate of the *St. John*, who was telling his story. He was a slim-looking youth, who spoke of the captain as the master, and seemed a little excited. He was saying that when they jumped into the boat, she filled, and, the vessel lurching, the weight of the water in the boat caused the painter to break, and so they were separated. Whereat one man came away, saying:

"Well, I don't see but he tells a straight story enough. You see, the weight of the water in the boat broke the painter. A boat full of water is very heavy," and so on, in a loud and impertinently earnest tone, as if he had a bet depending on it, but had no humane interest in the matter. Another, a large man, stood near by upon a rock, gazing into the sea, and chewing large quids of tobacco, as if that habit were forever confirmed with him.

"Come," says another to his companion, "let's be off. We've seen the whole of it. It's no use to stay to the funeral."

Further, we saw one standing upon a rock, who, we were told, was one that was saved. He was a sober-looking man, dressed in a jacket and gray pantaloons, with his hands in the pockets. I asked him a few questions, which he answered; but he seemed unwilling to talk about it, and soon walked away. By his side stood one of the life-boat men, in an oil-cloth jacket, who told us how they went to the relief of the British brig, thinking that the boat of the *St. John*, which they passed on the way, held all her crew, for the waves prevented their seeing those who were on the vessel, though they might have saved some had they known there were any there. A little further was the flag of the *St. John* spread on a rock to dry, and held down by stones at the corners. This frail, but essential and significant portion of the vessel, which had so long been the sport of the winds, was sure to reach the shore. There were one or two houses visible from these rocks, in which were some of the survivors recovering from the shock which their bodies and minds had sustained. One was not expected to live.

We kept on down the shore as far as a promontory called Whitehead, that we might see more of the Cohasset Rocks. In a little cove, within half a mile, there were an old man and his son collecting, with their team, the sea-weed which that fatal storm had cast up, as serenely employed as if there had never been a wreck in the world, though they were within sight of the Grampus Rock, on which the *St. John* had struck. The old man had heard that there was a wreck, and knew most of the particulars, but he said that he had not been up there since it happened. It was the wrecked weed that concerned him most, rock-weed, kelp, and sea-weed, as he named them, which he carted to his barn-yard; and those bodies were to him but other weeds which the tide cast up, but which were of no use to him. We afterwards came to the life-boat in its harbor, waiting for another emergency, and in the afternoon we saw the funeral procession at a distance, at the head of which walked the captain with the other survivors.

On the whole, it was not so impressive a scene as I might have expected. If I had found one body cast upon the beach in some lonely place, it would have affected me more. I sympathized rather with the winds and waves, as if to toss and mangle these poor human bodies was the order of the day. If this was the law of Nature, why waste any time in awe or pity? If the last day were come, we should not think so much about the separation of friends or the blighted prospects of individuals. I saw that corpses might be multiplied, as on the field of battle, till they no longer affected us in any degree, as exceptions to the common lot of humanity. Take all the graveyards together, they are always the majority. It is the individual and private that demands our sympathy. A man can attend but one funeral in the course of his life, can behold but one corpse. Yet I saw that the inhabitants of the shore would be not a little affected by this event. They would watch there many days and nights for the sea to give up its dead, and their imaginations and sympathies would supply the place of mourners far away, who as yet knew not of the wreck. Many days after this, something white was seen floating on the water by one who was sauntering on the beach. It was approached in a boat, and found to be the body of a woman, which had risen in an upright position, whose white cap was blown back with the wind. I saw that the beauty of the shore itself was wrecked for many a lonely walker there, until he could perceive, at last, how its beauty was enhanced by wrecks like this, and it acquired thus a rarer and sublimer beauty still.

Why care for these dead bodies? They really have no friends but the worms or fishes. Their owners were coming to the New World, as Columbus and the Pilgrims did, they were within a mile of its shores; but, before they could reach it, they emigrated to a newer world than ever Columbus dreamed of, yet one of whose existence we believe that there is far more universal and convincing evidence—though it has not yet been discovered by science—than Columbus had of this; not merely mariners' tales and some paltry drift-wood and sea-weed, but a continual drift and instinct to all our shores. I saw their empty hulks that came to land; but they themselves, meanwhile, were cast upon some shore yet further west, toward which we are all tending, and which we shall reach at last, it may be through storm and darkness, as they did. No doubt, we have reason to thank God that they have not been "shipwrecked into life again." The mariner who makes the safest port in Heaven, perchance, seems to his friends on earth to be shipwrecked, for they deem Boston Harbor the better place; though perhaps invisible to them, a skilful pilot comes to meet him, and the fairest and balmiest gales blow off that coast, his good ship makes the land in halcyon days, and he kisses the shore in rapture there, while his old hulk tosses in the surf here. It is hard to part with one's body, but, no doubt, it is easy enough to do without it when once it is gone. All their plans and hopes burst like a bubble! Infants by the score dashed on the rocks by the enraged Atlantic Ocean! No, no! If the *St. John* did not make her port here, she has been telegraphed there. The strongest wind cannot stagger a Spirit; it is a Spirit's breath. A just man's purpose cannot be split on any Grampus or material rock, but itself will split rocks till it succeeds.

Questions for Discussion:
1. What does this piece tell us about Thoreau's perception of the power of the ocean?
2. What does this piece tell the reader about the Irish immigrants coming to America?
3. What strengths or weaknesses does a literary account such as this have for historians?

Henry David Thoreau, *Cape Cod* (Boston: Houghton Mifflin, 1893), 4–14.

Samuel Millet, "Whaling Journal" (1849)

America's whaling industry peaked in the late 1840s to early 1850s. While the fleets based themselves in ports like New Bedford or Nantucket in Massachusetts, after independence they increasingly sought out the whale population of the Pacific Ocean. These voyages frequently lasted for years, alternating between weeks of tedium and the frenzied activity of the hunt, and then processing the whale carcasses for their oil, teeth, baleen, or even bone. As in other "fisheries," whalemen received as their pay a portion of the ship's catch after deductions for expenses rather than a monthly predetermined sum. Younger, inexperienced whalemen received much smaller shares (termed *lays*) than officers. And no one received any money if they killed no whales.

Samuel Millet is symbolic of the thousands of American youths who took to the sea in pursuit of whales. For many American boys, seafaring was a rite of passage that represented a transition to manhood. Facing danger and overcoming one's fears "manfully" was an important benchmark on the road to manhood and therefore worth recording in detail in a journal. Their experiences have been captured by the late Briton Busch in his monograph *Whaling Will Never Do for Me.*[1]

June 16. This day about two o'clock P. M. a cry came from the masthead "There she blows, there she b-l-o-w-s, there she blo-ws," for the first time. The captain hailed the masthead "Where aways" and the answer came back "Four points off the weather bow." In a moment all hands were up in the rigging looking in the direction pointed out by the men at the masthead and in a little while he could be seen plain from the deck. All was now excitement for each boat's crew was eager to be the first to strike the whale. When within about a mile of the whale we could see him lie rolling on the surface and spouting. We soon saw many more whales, some showing flukes which is a sure sign that they are going down, but they usually do not stay down more than ten or fifteen minutes where there is a school of whales together. When there is a lone whale he will sometimes stay down an hour. When we advanced to within three-quarters of a mile from the whales all three boats were ordered to lower and they all dashed away with rapid strides towards the place of slaughter. I was in the waist boat. We pulled to windward ahead of the whales but they milled around and went to the leeward coming nearer to the starboard boat which was headed by the "old man," as the sailors call him, and as the whale passed the Captain's boat he fastened to him and shortly was able to lance him. I got alongside so that I had a fair view. After they got fast they let the whale run a while and then hauled in enough line to get near enough to lance him which is the most dangerous part of the engagement for then he begins to go in his fury and if he does hit any part of the boat he will stave it and most likely to kill someone. In this

---

1   Briton Cooper Busch, *Whaling Will Never Do for Me: The American Whaleman in the Nineteenth Century* (Lexington: University Press of Kentucky, 1994).

case no one was hurt and soon he began to spout thick blood and we soon found ourselves in a sea of blood for some distance around us. After a whale is dead there remains a good deal to be done for the oil is tryed out[1] and stored down. It was late in the evening before we got the whale alongside and made fast which is done with a fluke chain; a large chain with a bite in it put around the flukes and coming in through the hawser hole and belayed around the bits. Then the main topsail is hauled back until the whale is cut in. This is done with long handled spades with one man overboard to make fast to the pieces which are hauled on board by a large fall which is taken around the windlass and then hove in. The head is turned up and dipped out with a bucket, some making from forty to fifty barrels as the head makes about one third of the oil taken from a whale. This whale was a small one and did not make but forty-five barrels. While cutting him in the sharks were so thick one could see forty or fifty at once and the man that was on the whale was obliged to have a rope fastened around under his arms to haul him up at any minute to keep the sharks from devouring him for they would come upon the whale clear out of the water and carry off pieces that I should judge weighed from eight to ten pounds or more. As we did not get the whale along side until dark we had to keep a sharp lookout all night. At daylight Sunday morning, "all hands ahoy," with three loud raps on scuttle, awoke me and in a few minutes all hands were heaving in the whale with a loud "yoho, heave, ho, he." By two o'clock P.M. we had the try works hot and trying out the blubber. It took three days to try it out and store it down, in the bottom of the hole, with only four hours sleep out of the twenty-four and at one time I was at the helm six hours without being relieved. By this time I have been through all the many processes that I will have to go so many times. Our grub begins to be very bad for our bread and beef were of the meanest quality and our water stinks so that it can be smelt half the ships length and so thick it can hardly be sucked through the teeth, partly because it is so old, and partly because it being stored in old oil casks. This is nothing uncommon, however, for whalemen.

June 20. Spoke the brig *America* of Mattapoisett, Capt. Lambert, and raised whales the next day. Took one, with the *America's* crew,

---

1   Tryed out: tried out, the process in which whale blubber was processed for the oil it contained.

and as the two ships kept together we were obliged to divide our oil which was in all sixty-five barrels sperm. Bad weather all the time we were trying out with some very heavy squalls.

June 24. Saw whales about six o'clock and lowered all three boats at once and were very fortunate to take another whale but it was hard work as the sun was very hot and there was not a ripple on the blue expanse except what was made by the whales and sharks and occasionally a dolphin gliding by on the smooth surface of the broad Atlantic. There was a gentle undulating that seemed like the hard breathing of some huge monster, but we had white water enough when we got amongst the whales and sharks. I was beset by a blue shark of monstrous size which came at me over the gunwale of the boat and I very narrowly escaped him and then he swerved around the boat and nearly bit the blade off the steering oar and then coming at my oar with such force as to almost wrench it from my hands and taking out quite a large piece of the blade. The second mate, who had charge of our boat, was obliged to take his spade and kill him. This time we were three days in trying out and storing down our whale which made us thirty five barrels sperm. The *America's* crew took in sight of us a whale that made them about the same amount of oil. After dividing our oil we parted company.

June 27. Spoke bark *Dr. Franklin* of Westport. Took a porpoise it being the first we have taken. It is very good dish when one has nothing but salt junk and hard bread to eat and when fried or made into sausage is quite equal to any that is made at home.

July 2. Since the 26th of June we lowered the boats three times, once for black fish and twice for whales but were not fortunate enough to take any.

July 4. All hands were called at sunrise. After turning the reefs out of the topsails and scrubbing off decks we were called to breakfast. Every morning before breakfast decks are scrubbed not excepting Sunday. After breakfast this morning we were set to working on some old sails and kept at work all day without speaking to each other as we are not allowed to talk while at work in the waist and so I was left alone to meditate on the past and paint in my own imagination the bright future when I should return to my own dear native land.

July 6. Spoke the bark *Persia* and brig *Rodman* both of New Bedford. The *Persia*, six months out, with 145 barrels of sperm and *Rodman*, fourteen months out with 165 barrels sperm and bound home.

The crew were rather discouraged for some of them would go home in debt without anything to pay for their outfits with and this is one great evil in going a-whaling for it is too much like lottery business.

July 8. Spoke bark *President* of Westport and also next day saw five sail in sight all at one time. During the short time I have been engaged in this kind of business I have visited quite a number of vessels, some from Nantucket, New Bedford, Westport, Mattapoisett, and some from the Cape. I have seen many a homesick fellow that would have given anything in the world, if he had it, if he could only get his feet again on Yankee soil. But they must submit to their hard fate and live like dogs for perhaps two or three more years.

July 21. Spoke a German ship from Bremen bound to Mobile with 235 passengers. She was a noble ship and her sides were as smooth as a glass bottle. The Dutch captain, for such he proved to be for our captain could hardly make out from him where he was from or where bound to, said he had seen a good many whales the week before but our mate said "dam him he can't tell a whale from a porpoise."

July 26. As we lay becalmed all day under a burning sun, towards night most of the crew went overboard to bathe and cool themselves and seeing so many of my shipmates diving off from the fore rigging I followed suit but there were some that would not go for they said they would not be food for the sharks. Those who did go paid no regard to the sharks although they were around the ship most of the time and but a little time before one very large shark was seen along-side the ship. The steward being the best swimmer swam under the ship going down on one side and coming up on the other. A sailor's constant exposure to danger makes him a stranger to fear and he will hazard danger that would make a landsman quail.

July 28. After sundown, as I was standing on the windlass, I saw a school of black fish and when the Captain saw them he ordered all of the boats to be lowered and in a few minutes all three of the boats were in chase but they did not come up with them. The captain's boat was beset with a shark and whilst he was snapping at the bow of the boat the captain killed him with the harpoon. This is often the case that whale boats are assailed by sharks and should they get stove at such a time a part of the crew would be sure to be devoured by them.

August 3. Spoke the bark *Chase* of New Bedford, fitted out to whale it for four months and a half and then go to California. I was happy to find two men from North Bridgewater, that I acquainted with, and I spent three or four hours on board with them. She was later reported in Fayal[1] with 250 barrels of sperm. The same day spoke a bark from Provincetown three months out with 150 barrels sperm.

August 6. The steward had a fit and I think he suffered the most of any person I ever saw for it took four men to hold him and the blood at times would gush from his nostrils. At four o'clock came on squally and remained so through the night. The next day raised a large whale but it blew so hard with squalls of rain that they could not keep sight of him from the boats for the mist was so thick that he could not be seen from the mast-head only at times. After pulling about four hours and the boat within half a mile of the whale, the "old man" got into a passion and ordered me to run up the signal for the boat to return. He then cleared away his own boat but when he found two of his boat crew were unable to go he was in a rage and said he wished to God we were all sick. When the boat came on board night came on and we saw no more of the whale. It is now five weeks since we saw a whale spout. As before, the weather continued to be squally and blowing hard until the eleventh, during which time we lay-to under double-reefed topsails and we could not go on deck without getting wet so we kept wet most of the time. We were forced to beat about all the time in this heavy weather. It may well be said a sailor's life is exciting and one of continued privation and exposure. It is seldom that he long has a bright sky, fair wind, and smooth sea. The next day raised a school of whales and all the boats were lowered. About two o'clock I went in the Captain's boat and dropping right a-stem of the ship, as the whales were to windward of us, we lay there a few minutes and the whales came down to leeward of us, and then we set our boat sail and although it blew quite fresh, we sailed after them. In a few minutes the Captain luffed his boat to and we found ourselves along side a very large whale. The boat steerer fastened to him and he brought his flukes up right over the boat so that it covered us with water. Then starting off with the velocity of a steam engine, it seemed that the boat went right through some of the seas and we could not get our breath only at times. This did not last long and the whale rose to the surface and lay rolling from side to side. The Captain sung out, "Hawl line, hawl like Hell, sonny," as he used to do as but one of us was

---

1   Fayal: or Faial, is one of the Portuguese-owned Azore Islands in the Atlantic Ocean, a well-known port of call for many American whaling vessels.

out of his teens in the old man's boatcrew. When we had hauled up
to him again he lay in a sea of blood which was fast flowing from his
wounds. Before the Captain could get a chance to lance him he was
off again and the harpoon was drawn out of him. We did not see him
again and neither of the other boats got fast to a whale. This made our
Captain curse his bad luck enough to send the boat where he said he
hoped the whale had gone which was straight to Hell. We then made
the best of our way on board again and got our boats on board a good
half hour after sundown. We then got our supper but it was not a very
tempting meal for it consisted of a quart of the meanest tea and some
hard bread so hard that it would take twenty-four hours to soak it
soft and our beef was so coarse-grained it was more like eating straw
than meat. This is all the food we now see or have for months except
a small duff twice a week and this would answer for some school boy
to use for a foot ball if they could get nothing better. However, this is
common fare for whalemen.

August 21. On going to the masthead early in the morning I raised
two schools of sperm whales and this time I stayed onboard and kept
ship while all three boats went after the whales and they sailed on the
wind pulling with the oars at the same time until the last speck of the
boat fails were seen to sink neath the horizon from the masthead. It
was late in the afternoon before all were again on board being very
much fatigued. They starting so early in the morning they were unable
to get anything to eat before their start. All hands had another hard
day's work without anything to show for it.

August 25. Spoke brig *Gem* of Beverly, Captain Haynes, four and a
half months out with 150 barrels of sperm.

August 27. I met with a very sad accident. It was blowing hard and
the ship rolling heavily and I went to take a kid of beans which was
handed me at the scuttle, when my foot slipped and I spilt some on me
and scalded me very bad but I kept the kid right-side up until I could
set it down. I was confined below for some time.

September 2. This morning started blowing very hard from the
S.W. and it continued to blow harder and harder and before night we
were obliged to lay-to under close-reefed main-topsail and fore and
main spencer and fore-top-mast stay-sail. About four o'clock, as I had
the morning watch, I saw our stay-sail split and before we could get it
in it blew nearly all away like a bag of feathers shook out at the sport
of the wind. At daylight all hands were called and the foregallant-sail

yard was sent down and the boats hoisted up to the davits and everything secured as snug as we could for the seas were every moment
breaking over our little bark, fore and aft. All hands went below, except one boat's crew, and amused themselves, both fore and aft, by
playing checkers or cards and not regarding the violence of the storm
any more than if they had been on *terra firma*. We were far from being
dry below, as well as on deck, for we had to lay in our bunks and let the
water run down on us most all of the time during the gale which lasted
three days and nights and we did not have a dry stitch to our backs.

Questions for Discussion:
1. According to Millet, what dangers did whalemen face?
2. How does this journal excerpt chronicle Millet's transition from boy to
man?
3. Who might Millet have looked to as a role model for manliness on this
voyage?

Samuel Millet, *A Whaling Voyage in the Bark* Willis (Boston, Privately printed,
1924), 4–13.

LAUNCHING SOCIAL AND LABOR REFORM

Reform movements flourished in the early republic. Temperance, banning
corporal punishment, and moral improvement were the order of the day in
American society after 1820; the maritime world was not immune to these
causes. Many of the reform movements were religiously based by-products
of the "Second Great Awakening," a remarkable burst of religious fervor
that lasted from the 1790s to the 1830s.

Many reformers chose to work on the aspects of sailors' lives that were
most visible: the disorderly "sailor towns" in the waterfront sections of
American ports where drunkenness, prostitution, and crime were rife.
Reform-minded groups distributed Bibles and pamphlets, preached on the
waterfront, often in special seamen's churches (termed *bethels*), and operated "temperance boardinghouses" for sailors as an alternative to the rowdy
taverns and boardinghouses they often stayed in while ashore. To some
this was high-minded reform, but to others it smacked of social control
imposed by local elites.

One of the most enduring reform movements was the temperance movement, which wanted to reduce alcohol consumption, especially of hard

liquor. Seamen, well-known for their hard-drinking ways, were soon targeted by reformers. One impact of temperance was the gradual disappearance of a daily liquor ration for both merchant and naval seamen. Some seamen, such as Joseph Bates, joined the cause and became leaders in the movement.

Not all reform was religiously based, however. Some of the reform movements were deeply influenced by American egalitarian ideals of legal equality for all free white men. This egalitarian ideal discouraged demeaning corporal punishments such as flogging, both ashore and afloat. The movement to ban corporal punishment, while often supported by religious reformers, was often legalistic. The writings of Richard Henry Dana Jr., a Boston attorney who wrote a compelling account of his two-year experience as a common sailor, convinced many Americans that flogging must end.

The antebellum period also saw the rise of a nascent working-class consciousness that rejected many of the bourgeois ideals reformers attempted to impose. These Americans saw the reformers as oppressors who wanted to control them. Many working-class white Americans viewed reformers as well-heeled hypocrites who gladly oppressed them by keeping wages low, even as they espoused the rhetoric of freedom for southern slaves. For some, as demonstrated in the 1851 "Fisherman's Song," the answer was to create unions and go on strike to get their due from a pretentious middle class.

Joseph Bates, "Temperance Ship" (1828)

Joseph Bates (1792–1872) was a Massachusetts-born mariner and leading figure in the creation of the Seventh-day Adventist Church. Bates began sailing at age fifteen as a cabin boy and experienced many adventures, including impressment into the Royal Navy and imprisonment in the notorious Dartmoor prison in England. During his seafaring career, Bates observed time and again the effect heavy drinking had on sailors. In this piece, taken from his autobiography, Bates reflects on his efforts as a sea captain to impose moral order by eliminating his crew's liquor ration.

We sailed from New Bedford on the morning of Aug. 9, 1827. I found it much more trying to part with my family and friends this time than ever before.

Our pilot now left us with a strong breeze wafting us out once more into the boisterous ocean for a long voyage. As usual, our anchors were now stowed away, and everything was secured in case we should be overtaken by a storm. As the night set in, on taking our departure from Gay Head Light, distant about fifteen miles, all hands were called aft on the quarter-deck. All but one were strangers to me, as they had come from Boston the day before. I read our names and agreement to perform this voyage, from the shipping papers, and requested their attention while I stated the rules and regulations which I wished to be observed during our voyage.

I spoke to them of the importance of cultivating kind feelings toward each other while we were alone on the ocean, during our contemplated voyage. I stated that I had frequently seen bitter feelings and continued hatred arise on shipboard by not calling the men by their proper names. Said I, "Here is the name of William Jones; now let it be remembered while we are performing this voyage that we all call his name William. Here is John Robinson; call him John. Here is James Stubbs; call him James. We shall not allow any Bills, or Jacks, or Jims, to be called here." In like manner I read all their names, with those of the first and second mates, and requested them always to address one another in a respectful manner, and to call themselves by their proper names; and if the officers addressed them otherwise, I wished it reported to me.

Another rule was, that I should allow no swearing during the voyage. Said William Dunn, "I have always had that privilege, sir." "Well," said I, "you cannot have it here," and quoted the third commandment, and was endeavoring to show how wicked it was to swear, when he said, "I can't help it, sir!" I replied, "Then I will help you to help it." He began to reason about it, and said, "When I am called up in the night to reef topsails in bad weather, and things don't go right, I swear before I think of it." Said I to him, "If you do so here, I will tell you what I will do with you; I will call you down and send you below, and let your shipmates do your duty for you." Dunn saw that such a course would disgrace him, and he said, "I will try, sir."

Another rule was, that we should allow no washing nor mending clothes on Sundays. I said to the crew, "I have a good assortment of books and papers which you may have access to every Sunday. I shall also endeavor to instruct you, that we may keep that day holy unto the Lord. You shall have every Saturday afternoon to wash and mend your clothes, both at sea and in harbor, and I shall expect you to appear every Sunday morning with clean clothes. When we arrive in port you may have the same Saturday afternoon in your turn to go on shore and see the place, and get what you wish, if you return on board at night sober; for we shall observe the Sabbath on board in port, and not grant any liberty on shore Sunday."

At this, Dunn remarked again, "That's the sailor's privilege, and I have always had the liberty of going on shore Sundays, and" "I know that very well," said I, interrupting him, "but I cannot give you that liberty," and endeavored to show the crew how wrong it was to violate God's holy day, and how much better they would enjoy themselves in reading and improving their minds than in joining all the wickedness that sailors were in the habit of in foreign ports on that day.

"Another thing I want to tell you is, that we have no liquor, or intoxicating drinks, on board." "I am glad of that!" said John R. Perhaps this was the first voyage he had ever sailed without it. Said I, "We have one junk-bottle of brandy, and one also of gin, in the medicine chest; this I shall administer to you like the other medicine when I think you need it. This is all the liquor we have on board, and all that I intend shall be on board this vessel during our voyage; and I here strictly forbid any of you bringing anything of the kind on board when you have liberty to go on shore in foreign ports. And I would that I could persuade you never to drink it when on shore. When you are called to do duty during your watch below, we shall expect you to come up readily and cheerfully, and you shall retire again as soon as the work is performed, and also have your forenoon watch below. If you adhere to these rules, and behave yourselves like men, you shall be kindly treated, and our voyage will prove a pleasant one." I then knelt down and commended ourselves to the great God, whose tender mercies are over all the works of his hands, to protect and guide us on our way over the ocean to our destined port. . . .

During our homeward-bound passage, our crew seemed more thoughtful and attentive to the religious instructions we were endeavoring to impart to them. It was evident that the Spirit of the Lord was at work in our midst. One James S. gave good evidence of a thorough conversion to God, and was very happy during our voyage home. Religion seemed to be his whole theme. One night in his watch on deck, while relating to me his experience, he said, "Don't you remember the first night out on our voyage from home, when you had all hands called aft on the quarter-deck, and gave them rules for the voyage?" "Yes," I replied. "Well, sir, I was then at the helm, and when you finished, and knelt down on the quarter-deck and prayed with us, if at that time you had taken up a handspike and knocked me down at the helm, I should not have felt worse; for I had never seen such a thing before." Thomas B. also professed conversion at that time.

Our passage home was pleasant, with the exception of a heavy gale which troubled us some, but the good Lord delivered us from its over-whelming influence, and we soon after arrived safely in the harbor of New York City. The first news from home was that my honored father had died some six weeks before my arrival. This was a trying provi-dence for which I was not prepared. He had lived nearly seventy-nine years, and I had always found him in his place at the head of the family after my long voyages, and it seemed to me that I had not one seri-ous thought but that I should see him there again if I lived to return home.

While in the city I had the pleasure of attending an evening bethel prayer-meeting on board a ship lying at the wharf. I enjoyed it very much. Such meetings were then in their infancy, but since that time it is common enough to see the bethel flag on Sunday morning on board the ships for meeting, on both the east and north sides of the river, for the benefit of sailors and young men that are often wandering about the city without home or friends. Many, doubtless, have been saved from ruin by the efforts of those engaged in these benevolent institu-tions, while other homeless ones, who have not had such influences to restrain them, have been driven to deeds of desperation, or yielded to feelings of despair. The trying experience of my early days made me familiar with such scenes.

On one of my previous voyages, I had prevailed on a young man to accompany me to his home in Massachusetts. And while I was in the city this time, as I was passing through the park, among many others whom I saw was a young man seated in the shade, looking very melancholy, quite similar to the one just mentioned, and not far from the same place. I seated myself beside him, and asked him why he appeared so melancholy. At first he hesitated, but soon began to inform me that he was in a destitute state, having nothing to do, and nowhere to go. He said his brother had employed him in his apoth-ecary store in the city, but he had recently failed and broken up, and left the city, and that now he was without home and friends. I asked him where his parents lived. He replied, "In Massachusetts. My father is a Congregationalist preacher, near Boston." I invited him to go on board my vessel, be one of my crew, and I would land him within sixty miles of his home. He readily accepted my offer, and on our arrival in New Bedford, Mass., his father came for him, and expressed much gratitude to me for his safe return and the privilege of again meeting with his son.

On our arrival in New York, my crew, with one exception, chose to remain on board and discharge the cargo, and not have their discharge as was customary on arriving from a foreign port. They preferred, also, to continue in their stations until we arrived in New Bedford, where the *Empress* was to proceed, to fit out for another voyage. After discharging our cargo, we sailed and arrived in New Bedford about the 20th of June, 1828—twenty-one years from the time I sailed from thence on my first European voyage, in the capacity of cabin boy.

Some of my men inquired when I was going on another voyage, and expressed a wish to wait for me, and also their satisfaction with the last as being their best voyage. It was some satisfaction to me to know that seamen were susceptible of moral reform on the ocean (as proved in this instance) as well as on the land; and I believe that such reforms can generally be accomplished where the officers are ready and willing to enter into it. It has been argued by too many that sailors continue to addict themselves to so many bad habits that it is about useless to attempt their reform. I think it will be safe to say that the habitual use of intoxicating drink is the most debasing and formidable of all their habits. But if governments, ship-owners, and captains, had not always provided it for them on board their war and trading ships, as a beverage, tens of thousands of intelligent and most enterprising young men would have been saved, and would have been as great a blessing to their friends, their country, and the church, as farmers, doctors, lawyers, and other tradesmen and professional men have been.

Having had some knowledge of these things, I had resolved in the fear of God to attempt a reform, though temperance societies were then in their infancy, and temperance ships unknown. And when I made the announcement at the commencement of our last voyage that there was no intoxicating drink on board, only what pertained to the medicine chest, and one man shouted that he was "glad of it," this lone voice on the ocean in behalf of this work of reform from a stranger, manifesting his joy because there was no liquor on board to tempt him, was cheering to me, and a strong evidence of the power of human influence. I believe that he was also deeply affected, and I cannot now recollect that he used it in any way while under my command, nor any of the others, except Wm. Dunn, whom I had to reprove once or twice during the voyage for drinking while he was on duty on shore.

Then what had been considered so necessary an article to stimulate the sailor in the performance of his duty proved not only unnecessary, but the withholding of it was shown to be a great blessing in our case.

Questions for Discussion:
1. As a sea captain, what advantages did Bates's religious views have in operating his vessel?
2. How were Bates's ideals related to the reform movements in American society?
3. How did Bates's crew respond to his efforts?

James White, *The Early Life and Later Experience and Labors of Elder Joseph Bates* (Battle Creek, Mich.: Steam Press of the Seventh Day Adventist Publishing Association, 1868), 207–29.

Richard Henry Dana Jr., "Flogging on the *Pilgrim*" (1840)

Richard Henry Dana Jr. (1815–1882) is best remembered for his account of shipping out as an ordinary sailor on the brig *Pilgrim* on a voyage to California. Entitled *Two Years Before the Mast*, Dana intended for this book to reveal life at sea as it really was; the effort proved successful, and the book quickly became a best seller. In this selection, perhaps the most famous in the book, Dana describes the harsh discipline captains frequently dealt out to their crews, often for the most trivial of offenses. *Two Years Before the Mast* thus became instrumental in the American public's demand that flogging (long banned on shore) be abolished on ships, both in the Navy and on merchant vessels.

Dana himself, however, was ambivalent about flogging. While his memories of the floggings on board the *Pilgrim* clearly display his horror at the scene, he also maintained that flogging should remain an option for shipmasters as a "last resort." In fact, abolishing flogging was a complex process, as revealed by historians such as Myra C. Glenn.[1] Congress finally abolished

---

1 Myra C. Glenn, "The Naval Reform Campaign Against Flogging: A Case Study in Changing Attitudes Toward Corporal Punishment, 1830–1850," *American Quarterly* 35:4 (Autumn, 1983): 408–25.

flogging on most ships in 1850, although there were efforts to revive it by some naval officers.

For several days the captain seemed very much out of humor. Nothing went right, or fast enough for him. He quarreled with the cook, and threatened to flog him for throwing wood on deck; and had a dispute with the mate about reeving a Spanish burton;[1] the mate saying that he was right, and had been taught how to do it by a man who was a sailor! This, the captain took in dudgeon, and they were at sword's points at once. But his displeasure was chiefly turned against a large, heavy-moulded fellow from the Middle States, who was called Sam. This man hesitated in his speech, and was rather slow in his motions, but was a pretty good sailor, and always seemed to do his best; but the captain took a dislike to him, thought he was surly, and lazy; and "if you once give a dog a bad name"—as the sailor-phrase is—"he may as well jump overboard." The captain found fault with everything this man did, and hazed him for dropping a marlinespike from the main-yard, where he was at work. This, of course, was an accident, but it was set down against him. The captain was on board all day Friday, and everything went on hard and disagreeably. "The more you drive a man, the less he will do," was as true with us as with any other people. We worked late Friday night, and were turned-to early Saturday morning. About ten o'clock the captain ordered our new officer, Russell, who by this time had become thoroughly disliked by all the crew, to get the gig ready to take him ashore. John, the Swede, was sitting in the boat alongside, and Russell and myself were standing by the main hatchway, waiting for the captain, who was down in the hold, where the crew were at work, when we heard his voice raised in violent dispute with somebody, whether it was with the mate, or one of the crew, I could not tell; and then came blows and scuffling. I ran to the side and beckoned to John, who came up, and we leaned down the hatchway; and though we could see no one, yet we knew that the captain had the advantage, for his voice was loud and clear

"You see your condition! You see your condition! Will you ever give me any more of your jaw?" No answer; and then came wrestling and heaving, as though the man was trying to turn him. "You may as well

---

1   Spanish burton: a highly complex arrangement of blocks and tackle.

keep still, for I have got you," said the captain. Then came the question, "Will you ever give me any more of your jaw?"

"I never gave you any, sir," said Sam; for it was his voice that we heard, though low and half choked.

"That's not what I ask you. Will you ever be impudent to me again?"

"I never have been, sir," said Sam.

"Answer my question, or I'll make a spread eagle of you! I'll flog you, by Gd."

"I'm no negro slave," said Sam.

"Then I'll make you one," said the captain; and he came to the hatch-way, and sprang on deck, threw off his coat, and rolling up his sleeves, called out to the mate—"Seize that man up, Mr. A-! Seize him up! Make a spread eagle of him! I'll teach you all who is master aboard!"

The crew and officers followed the captain up the hatchway, and after repeated orders the mate laid hold of Sam, who made no resistance, and carried him to the gangway.

"What are you going to flog that man for, sir?" said John, the Swede, to the captain.

Upon hearing this, the captain turned upon him, but knowing him to be quick and resolute, he ordered the steward to bring the irons, and calling upon Russell to help him, went up to John.

"Let me alone," said John. "I'm willing to be put in irons. You need not use any force;" and putting out his hands, the captain slipped the irons on, and sent him aft to the quarterdeck. Sam by this time was seized up, as it is called, that is, placed against the shrouds, with his wrists made fast to the shrouds, his jacket off, and his back exposed. The captain stood on the break of the deck, a few feet from him, and a little raised, so as to have a good swing at him, and held in his hand the bight of a thick, strong rope. The officers stood round, and the crew grouped together in the waist. All these preparations made me feel sick and almost faint, angry and excited as I was. A man—a human being, made in God's likeness—fastened up and flogged like a beast! A man, too, whom I had lived with and eaten with for months, and knew almost as well as a brother. The first and almost uncontrollable impulse was resistance. But what was to be done? The time for it had gone by. The two best men were fast, and there were only two beside myself, and a small boy of ten or twelve years of age. And then there were (beside the captain) three officers, steward, agent and clerk. But beside the numbers, what is there for sailors to do? If they resist, it is mutiny; and if they succeed, and take the vessel, it is piracy. If they ever yield again, their punishment must come; and if they do not yield, they are pirates for life. If a sailor resist his commander, he resists the law, and piracy or submission are his only alternatives. Bad as it was, it must be borne. It is what a sailor ships for. Swinging the rope over his head, and bending his body so as to give it full force, the captain brought it down upon the poor fellow's back. Once, twice;—six times. "Will you ever give me any more of your jaw?" The man writhed with pain, but said not a word. Three times more. This was too much, and he muttered something which I could not hear; this brought as many more as the man could stand; when the captain ordered him to be cut down, and to go forward.

"Now for you," said the captain, making up to John and taking his irons off. As soon as he was loose, he ran forward to the forecastle. "Bring that man aft," shouted the captain. The second mate, who had been a shipmate of John's, stood still in the waist, and the mate walked slowly forward; but our third officer, anxious to show his zeal, sprang forward over the windlass, and laid hold of John; but he soon threw him from him. At this moment I would have given worlds for the power to help the poor fellow; but it was all in vain. The captain stood on the quarter-deck, bare-headed, his eyes flashing with rage, and his face as red as blood, swinging the rope, and calling out to his officers, "Drag him aft! Lay hold of him! I'll sweeten him!" etc., etc. The mate now went forward and told John quietly to go aft; and he, seeing resistance in vain, threw the blackguard third mate from him; said he would go aft of himself; that they should not drag him; and went up to the gangway and held out his hands; but as soon as the captain began to make him fast, the indignity was too much, and he began to resist; but the mate and Russell holding him, he was soon seized up. When he was made fast, he turned to the captain, who stood turning up his sleeves and getting ready for the blow, and asked him what he was to be flogged for. "Have I ever refused my duty, sir? Have you ever known me to hang back, or to be insolent, or not to know my work?"

"No," said the captain, "it is not that I flog you for; I flog you for your interference—for asking questions."

"Can't a man ask a question here without being flogged?"

"No," shouted the captain; "nobody shall open his mouth aboard this vessel, but myself;" and began laying the blows upon his back, swinging half round between each blow, to give it full effect. As he went on, his passion increased, and he danced about the deck, calling out as he swung the rope; "If you want to know what I flog you for, I'll tell you. It's because I like to do it!—because I like to do it!—It suits me! That's what I do it for!"

The man writhed under the pain, until he could endure it no longer, when he called out, with an exclamation more common among foreigners than with us "Oh, Jesus Christ! Oh, Jesus Christ!"

"Don't call on Jesus Christ," shouted the captain; "he can't help you. Call on Captain T-, he's the man! He can help you! Jesus Christ can't help you now!"

At these words, which I never shall forget, my blood ran cold. I could look on no longer. Disgusted, sick, and horror-struck, I turned away and leaned over the rail, and looked down into the water. A few rapid thoughts of my own situation, and of the prospect of future revenge, crossed my mind; but the falling of the blows and the cries of the man called me back at once. At length they ceased, and turning round, I found that the mate, at a signal from the captain had cut him down. Almost doubled up with pain, the man walked slowly forward, and went down into the forecastle. Every one else stood still at his post, while the captain, swelling with rage and with the importance of his achievement, walked the quarter-deck, and at each turn, as he came forward, calling out to us, "You see your condition! You see where I've got you all, and you know what to expect!" "You've been mistaken in me—you didn't know what I was! Now you know what I am!"—"I'll make you toe the mark, every soul of you, or I'll flog you all, fore and aft, from the boy, up!" "You've got a driver over you! Yes, a slave-driver a negro-driver! I'll see who'll tell me he isn't a negro slave!" With this and the like matter, equally calculated to quiet us, and to allay any apprehensions of future trouble, he entertained us for about ten minutes, when he went below. Soon after, John came aft, with his bare back covered with stripes and wales in every direction, and dreadfully swollen, and asked the steward to ask the captain to let him have some salve, or balsam, to put upon it. "No," said the captain, who heard him from below; "tell him to put his shirt on; that's the best thing for him; and pull me ashore in the boat. Nobody is going to lay-up on board this vessel." He then called to Mr. Russell to take those men and two others in the boat, and pull him ashore. I went for one. The two men could hardly bend their backs, and the captain called to them to "give way," "give way" but finding they did their best, he let them alone. The agent was in the stern sheets, but during the whole pull—a league or more—not a word was spoken. We landed; the captain, agent, and officer went up to the house, and left us with the boat. I, and the man with me, staid near the boat, while John and Sam walked slowly away, and sat down on the rocks. They talked some time together, but at length separated, each sitting alone. I had some fears of John. He was a foreigner, and violently tempered, and under suffering; and he had his knife with him, and the captain was to come down alone to the boat. But nothing happened; and we went quietly on board. The captain was probably armed, and if either of them had lifted a hand against him, they would have had nothing before them but flight, and starvation in the woods of California, or capture by the soldiers and Indian blood-hounds, whom the offer of twenty dollars would have set upon them.

After the day's work was done, we went down into the forecastle, and ate our plain supper; but not a word was spoken. It was Saturday night; but there was no song—no "sweethearts and wives." A gloom was over everything. The two men lay in their berths, groaning with pain, and we all turned in, but for myself, not to sleep. A sound coming now and then from the berths of the two men showed that they were awake, as awake they must have been, for they could hardly lie in one posture a moment; the dim, swinging lamp of the forecastle shed its light over the dark hole in which we lived; and many and various reflections and purposes coursed through my mind. I thought of our situation, living under a tyranny; of the character of the country we were in; of the length of the voyage, and of the uncertainty attending our return to America; and then, if we should return, of the prospect of obtaining justice and satisfaction for these poor men; and vowed that if God should ever give me the means, I would do something to redress the grievances and relieve the sufferings of that poor class of beings, of whom I then was one.

Questions for Discussion:
1. What does this document reveal about working conditions on American vessels in the antebellum period?
2. How can this flogging be connected to antebellum racial segregation and the attitudes white Americans had about their place in society?

3. What did Dana find that sailors could do about a captain who wanted to flog them?

Richard Henry Dana Jr., *Two Years Before the Mast* (New York: P. F. Collier & Son, 1909), 104–9.

Anonymous, "The Fisherman's Song" (1851)

Fishing was an important maritime activity for many coastal communities, but the most commercially valuable was the cod fishery of New England. While this industry had originally been based on Cape Ann north of Boston, by 1850 Maine led the nation in fishing tonnage. Much of this fishing took place on the Grand Banks, a shallow area of the Atlantic south of Newfoundland known for its unpredictable weather. Once there, the fishermen hand-lined for cod from the decks of their anchored schooners.

It was undoubtedly a dangerous way to make a living. And for many fishermen it promised little in the way of profits as shoreside merchants frequently took advantage of the fishermen by inflating prices of goods and attempting to pay the lowest price possible for the fish they bought. Printed in Portland, Maine, in 1851, this song sheet celebrates the fisherman's life even as it criticizes their treatment ashore. Further information on Maine's antebellum fisheries can be gained from Wayne O'Leary's book *Maine Sea Fisheries*.[1]

Come all you hardy fishermen who plough the raging main,
And listen while I sing to you the hardships of the same
About the first of April boys, it is the time to start,
And leave all's near and dear behind with a sad aching heart.
Our colors then we do display to show we mean to sail,
And does the wind prove prosperous and blow a pleasing gale
We steer away good East South East, Cape Sable[2] for to clear,
But still our hearts we leave behind with those most near and dear.
But soon the wind increases fast to a tremendous gale,
And now my boys 'tis call all hands the word is take in sail,
With quick dispatch the work is done, the sails all reefed snug,

1   Wayne M. O'Leary, *Maine Sea Fisheries: The Rise and Fall of a Native Industry, 1830–1890* (Boston: Northeastern University Press, 1996).
2   Cape Sable: the southern tip of Nova Scotia.

While some green hands are sick as death and heaving up their cud.
Now running under close reefed sails with most uncommon speed,
Our noble vessel leaps and bounds like a high mettled steed;
Now tow'ring high on mountain waves, now sunk in their abyss,
While raging tempests around us roar, which seem to threaten
    death.
The snow comes on in angry gusts accompanied with hail,
Our noble vessel labors hard
again we shorten sail
Madly she leaps from wave to wave and cuts the wildest pranks,
Our captain says at this great rate we soon shall reach the Banks.[1]
When on the Bank and anchor down, our toil begins afresh,
Sometimes we cannot catch enough of fish to make a mess;
Hard all the day we have to toil and keep watch in the night,
And often try a week or two and cannot feel a bite.
The weather on the Banks is rough to an intense degree,
While we poor souls are tossed about, our homes are on the sea,
Shut out from all society and from its dear confines,
Like poor dejected convicts, who are exiled for their crimes.
And yet some ignorant land lubbers are often heard to say,
Fishermen get their money in a very easy way;
The dolt, whoever he may be, sinner, saint or priest,
Should always have what he deserves, a kick from a dumb beast.
But no digression I intend, for yet we're on the Banks,
And do we e'er get home again to God we owe the thanks,
The Bank we mortally abhor and here we hate to dwell,
Its character is near allied to that conceived of hell.
Chords of affliction are our lines, and currents liquid wrath,
The haddock are the devils imps and skates his refuse trash;
The ice and snow our flesh will freeze, and cause us acute pain,
For whether burnt or froze you know the anguish is the same.
But since we have successful been and caught a fare of fish,
Now we will leave this direful Bank with joy and happiness;
Our prayers are now for a fair breeze to waft us on our way
Why moves the lazy craft so slow, while loved ones mourn our stay.
O 'tis a thought sublime, that man can find a way and force,

---

1   Banks: the Grand Banks, a series of underwater plateaus southeast of Newfoundland
    that were some of the best fishing grounds in the Atlantic.

Where all is trackless and compel the winds to aid his course;
Those agents of Almighty power to lend their untimed wings,
And in their course to bear him on to the most distant climes.
And now again our native hills appear unto our view,
Such transports now we do enjoy, as landsmen never knew;
Absence and toil endears our homes and makes us love them more,
For none know how to prize their homes who always stay on shore.
Though in our absence, landsmen may have had a pleasant time,
But now we have returned again they can't begin to shine.
The fishermen, when on the land, the first class do compose,
A likelier set cannot be met when in their Sunday clothes.
The ladies too do them respect and on them lavish smiles,
Among the best they choose their wives all round for many miles,
Possessed of all good qualities, both free from stain and blot,
While landsmen have a second choice among the refuse lot.
And when we get a fare of fish we're somewhat satisfied,
And do they sell for a good price, we're still more gratified;
For those who catch the fish, of course should to their interest look,
But frequently the largest fish are caught without a hook.
Some of our shoremen are great rogues, and some are honest men,
The ratio is we estimate, one honest one in ten;
And some profess themselves to be good abolitionists,
While they do hold white slaves themselves how wonderful it is.
Our merchants are a set of knaves, on cheating they are bent,
For when we have their goods on tick they put on twelve per cent.
They cheat us in a double sense, for only look at this,
They set the price upon their goods likewise upon our fish.
O that the fishermen would rise, and in their strength put down
These suckers who oppress them so, with which our land abounds;
Union is strength, in every sense, and this we all believe,
And it united, to a man, great things we might achieve.
But should you say that we are poor, and can't our rights defend,
In answer I would say, the rich upon the poor depend;
Strike from the world the lab'ring class, lay them beneath the
    ground,
And in short space there'd be no trace of human beings found.
The men of pleasure lazy souls, likewise our Congress men,
Would sooner starve than till the soil, on this you may depend;
One quarter of the world at large, maintain the other three,

And this is no rough estimate, in it wise men agree.
But what I'm going to suggest, and which I think is right,
That would the fishermen combine, and for higher wages strike,
Their grievances they would redress, and would these suckers foil,
Who hold them now in slavery, and thrive upon their toil.
My song has run to a great length, and some it may offend,
The truth does always offend most, on this you may depend;
None but the guilty will be vexed, and on it wish a curse,
So now you have it, good or bad, for better or for worse.

Questions for Discussion:
1. What does this song reveal about ordinary fishermen's lives?
2. What evidence does this song provide about how fishermen viewed themselves as distinct from the rest of society?
3. What grievances did fishermen have against political leaders, reformers, merchants, and landsmen in general?

"The Fisherman's Song," (Portland, Maine: Harmon & Williams, 1851), Library of Congress, Rare Book and Special Collections Division.

Master Shipwrights Association, "Arbitrary and Unjust Demands" (1863)

The second half of the nineteenth century saw a dramatic change in shipbuilding. Ship construction moved from wood to iron to steel; fewer and fewer ships relied on sail, instead using coal-powered steam engines; and the relationship of shipyard owners to their workers changed as well. These were complex transitions, often accompanied by considerable controversy as society responded to technological change. Historian William H. Thiesen, in *Industrializing American Shipbuilding*,[1] examines the process whereby American shipbuilding evolved from a craft based on traditions, instincts, and handmade models to an engineering-based industry with highly trained naval architects who used abstract mathematics to create ship designs.

The transition in shipbuilding was not merely technical; it had social ramifications, too. In this item, a letter from shipyard operators protest-

1   William H. Thiesen, *Industrializing American Shipbuilding: The Transformation of Ship Design and Construction, 1820–1920* (Gainesville: University Press of Florida, 2006).

ing a labor strike, the alienation of owners from producers is evident. The background to this strike is the federal government's enormous demand for ships built in New York City during the Civil War. The issue was money: the shipyard workers saw the Master Shipwrights Association as a "combination of capitalists who were getting rich off the profits derived from their labor," while the shipyard operators claimed their worker's claims were "arbitrary and unjust." For a time, some six thousand strikers united, slowing work on the dozens of ironclads under construction around New York harbor, but eventually the strikers faltered, and by Christmas day the strike was over.

New York, 17ᵗʰ Novʳ 1863
Hon. S. P. Chase
Secretary of the Treasury
Sir

In accordance with your request recently made to a committee representing the Master Shipwrights of New York and vicinity, they herewith respectfully submit the following for your consideration.

The *Association* known as the *Master Shipwrights Association* of this city is composed exclusively of Employers in the construction and repairs of sailing and steam vessels, and embraces every firm with one exception now conducting such a business in this city & vicinity. The objects sought to be attained by the *Association* is protection against the arbitrary and unjust demands made by their employees for increased rates of labor, and to oppose all combinations & organizations that would arbitrarily deprive us of the right of fixing the compensation of labor, as heretofore.

The past records of our business amply demonstrate the fact that all reasonable and just demands for increased wages have been promptly & cheerfully acceded to, and moreover have always been in excess of those paid in any other branch of mechanics.

As to the Association known as the *Along Shore Shipwrights Association*—It is composed and its affairs controlled principally by the foreign element of workingmen, a very large proportion being the most inferior mechanics. Their object is the precise reverse of the *"Master Shipwrights Association"* viz—to obtain the largest possible amount of wages for the smallest amount of labor, and to accomplish this, they not only refuse to work themselves at less than *their* fixed rate of wages, but prohibit those who are well disposed from laboring, and in order more effectually to accomplish their ends, a portion of the *employees in the Navy Yard* are members of the said Association, and from the proceeds of their wages (they remaining employed) contribute somewhat to the aid of the strikers while they are unemployed, knowing that the Government will by regulation increase the rate of their labor, should the outside strike prove successful.

The *ultimate effect of such strikes* if carried out successfully will be a necessity on the part of employers and contractors to require a very large margin for profits on every contract for work that is made, as the invariable experience and singular with similar combinations has been that one successful strike is speedily followed by another, and that the men do less work for the increased rate of wages.

As to *the present & probable duration of the strike* we would state that four weeks have elapsed since its commencement, and that present appearances indicate a speedy breaking up of the "Association." We believe that result will be reached within the present month.

We regret our inability to give you *positive* information relative to the price of labor paid by Mr. Ezra Buckman of this city to the carpenters employed by him in making repairs on Coast Survey Steamer *Vixen*, as his books are not accessible to members of our Association. We can only say that all those employed by him upon the said vessel have testified to their receiving the advance demanded, and moreover that Buckman makes no denial of the charge.

The compensation now paid to Carpenters employed in the repair of vessels designated as "old work" is three dollars per day. Nine hours constitutes a days work.

The *wages paid to carpenters* employed in the construction of vessels is $2.75 per day. *The time worked is as follows.* From the 20th March to the 20th Septr. Work commences at 7 A.M., and terminates at 6 P.M., with an intermission of one hour for dinner making 10 hours of working time. From the latter date (20th Septr.) labor commences at 7 A.M. & terminates at sun down, this system being continued until the 20th of March when the 10 hours is again resumed. The time thus made by carpenters on new work averages 9 hours & 36 minutes for every working day of the year.

As to the *approximate differences* in cost of building an one hundred thousand dollar vessel at the present rate, and that now demanded by our workmen, we could say that the amount would be not less than seven thousand dollars, which would include the labor in all departments, Engineers only excepted.

Very Respectfully
Committee of the Master Shipwrights Association of N. York

Questions for Discussion:
1. What does this document reveal about relations between shipyard workers and shipyard operators in the mid-nineteenth century?
2. What does this document reveal about the working conditions in American shipyards in the 1860s?
3. What are the differences between the "Along Shore Shipwrights Association" and the "Master Shipwrights Association?"

Committee of the Master Shipwrights Association to Secretary of the Treasury Samuel P. Chase, November 17, 1862. National Archives and Records Administration RG 26: "Records of the United States Coast Guard," Entry 155: Miscellaneous Correspondence of the Revenue Cutter Service, 1793–1910.

SAILORS AND WOMEN

The Victorian era, with its emphasis on home, hearth, and family, saw a new sentimentalization of the parting of seafarer from sweetheart. One newspaper proclaimed "We can hardly conceive a situation more wretched than that of the wife of an active sailor. . . . the anxiety to which her husband subjects her to, will prey upon and finally destroy the finest constitution. Every wind that blows is a source of fear; every rain that falls causes sorrow; every cloud that rises is big with the fate of her nearest friend." Pamphlets, poems, and prints all emphasized the bittersweet separation of sailors from their families.

The opposite side of the maudlin sentimentality for loved ones at home was the anger many mariners felt at being victimized ashore. An unseemly combination of unscrupulous boardinghouse proprietors, prostitutes, crooked saloonkeepers, and devious chandlers worked to deprive sailors of their pay as soon as possible. Many sailors, eager to enjoy themselves after a long voyage, fell prey to these schemers and discovered that months of hard work bought only moments of fleeting pleasure once in port.

Taken together, these documents give a broad understanding of the complicated relationships between mariners and women in the antebellum years. Readers wanting to know more may want to refer to the collec-

tion of articles edited by Margaret S. Creighton and Lisa Norling entitled
*Iron Men, Wooden Women: Gender and Seafaring in the Atlantic World,
1700–1920.*[1]

Anonymous, "The Wives of Nantucket" (1843)

Sailors often left their sweethearts behind, sometimes for years at a time.
Whaling communities such as Nantucket were especially prone to this, and
undoubtedly it must have been very difficult emotionally for both the men
and women of Nantucket. While a few captains' wives were able to join their
husbands at sea, for most it was a long and lonely wait. Lisa Norling, writing about the lives of these women in her monograph *Captain Ahab Had
a Wife: New England Women and the Whalefishery*, explores the "separate
spheres" men and women inhabited in Victorian society.[2] Norling finds that
society's emphasis on the sentimental aspects of women's relations with
sailors devalued the work they performed in their husbands' absence. In
this anonymous piece reproduced in the *Sailor's Magazine*, we get a maudlin view of the emotional gamut whalers' wives experienced.

If there is any place under heaven where the heart-rending pangs
incident on the separation of near and dear friends are acutely felt,
it is in Nantucket. The young wife, who has been married scarce two
months, feels that she is called upon to part with all that to her seems
worth living for, when she learns that in a few days her husband leaves
for a four years' voyage. What sad reflections crowd upon her mind
as she makes the necessary preparation for his departure. She fears to
think that death may overtake him ere the voyage is ended, and that he
may *never return*. She tries to be cheerful, at least to appear so, in the
presence of her husband, but the unbidden tears will gush forth and
chase each other down her cheek, until at last she is compelled to retire to the privacy of her chamber, and there give vent to her feelings.
And thus she goes on from day to day, until at last the dreaded hour
approaches when they must part. Who but the wife herself can, describe her feelings at such a painful moment! Thank Heaven, we have

1   Margaret S. Creighton and Lisa Norling, *Iron Men, Wooden Women: Gender and Seafaring in the Atlantic World, 1700–1920* (Baltimore: Johns Hopkins University Press,
1996).

2   Lisa Norling, *Captain Ahab Had a Wife: New England Women & the Whalefishery,
1720–1870* (Chapel Hill: University of North Carolina Press, 2000).

neither experienced nor witnessed such a separation, and we hope we never shall. *Four years!* think of it ye who have your husbands, and friends, and all that go to make home happy year after year; think what would be your feelings were you placed in like situations with our Nantucket women. We will not attempt to describe the anguish of parting: language would fail us were we to attempt it. None but those who have passed through such a trial can tell us how much they suffer. How gloomy does every thing appear as night draws nigh to the lonely wife. How does the merry laugh of a passer-by grate upon her ear; for to her it seems downright sacrilege to be gay at such a moment. But if the approach of night is gloomy, what must her feelings be when she retires to her chamber for the night? Sad and long are the hours of that night, and morning finds her very little more resigned than she was the night previous. Time moderates her grief, but never obliterates her feelings of sadness. Month after month passes away, and the time has arrived when her husband ought to be heard from. Each whaling report is perused with anxiety and fear, in hopes that intelligence may be gleaned of the absent one. But she is doomed to further disappointment; there is no news for her. For several months more she is kept in suspense, fearful that the next intelligence will be that the ship in which he embarked is lost. By-and-by a vague rumor is circulated that, her husband was heard of, but where, when; or by whom, she cannot learn. Her anxiety is increased, and she prays most fervently for a letter. Perhaps at the expiration of twelve or fifteen months, the long wished for letter reaches her—some six or eight months after it was written—which is the first certain intelligence she has had. She feels thankful, but, a feeling of sadness will come over as she thinks of the long and anxious months she has yet to pass ere her husband's return.

The time has at length arrived when the long absent one may be daily expected. The flag-staff on which the American flag is hoisted when a ship has arrived is watched daily, for weeks, and oftentimes months, before him who she looks for arrives. Frequently, however, after a month or two of anxious looking for, some ship arriving brings the unwelcome information that her husband will not be home for six or eight months. Here is a fresh disappointment, and she feels it more intensely, since she had reasons to expect him every day. "Hope deferred maketh the heart sad," and the lonely wife feels this to be true in her case. She feels that it is hard that she should be so disappointed, yet tries to *appear* resigned, for it is impossible that she should be *really* resigned to her hard fate. The additional months have glided away, and again is the wife watching the flag-staff, hoping every moment to see the signal for a ship in sight displayed. A few weeks passed in this way and her troubles appear about to cease, for a messenger has brought the news that her husband is nearing the bar,[1] and in a few hours she will see him. The heart bounds with delight, and she gives utterance to her feelings in deep and fervent thanks to the Ruler of heaven and earth. But alas! That we should be compelled to chronicle another disappointment; it is *not* her husband's ship, as she learns at the expiration of an hour or two from some friend who had been down to the wharf to greet the expected husband. The report was premature. What a change comes over her at the intelligence. She feels her spirits sink within her, and dark and sorrowful are her thoughts. The next day she is again informed that her husband is approaching the bar. Between hope and fear she passes a few hours, until at last she actually sees him from whom she has been separated *four years*, approach the house. She briefly ejaculates her thanks for his safe return as she hears his well known step when he opens the outer door. We leave the meeting scene to be supplied by our readers.

Such is a feeble picture of what those women undergo whose husbands do business on the mighty deep. Certainly their trials are neither few nor far between. It is often the case that a husband departs on another voyage in six or eight weeks after his return.

Questions for Discussion:
1. What do these images reveal about Victorian ideals concerning relationships between men and women?
2. How does this piece relate to the Victorian concept of "separate spheres" for men and women in port communities?
3. How did Nantucket women attempt to deal with the emotional hardship of prolonged separation from their seafaring husbands?

Anonymous, "The Wives of Nantucket," *Sailor's Magazine* (December 1843): 115–16.

---

1   Bar: a sandbar at the approaches to Nantucket's harbor.

Nathaniel Currier, "Sailor's Adieu and Return" (1847)

Nathaniel Currier (1813–1888) came to fame in 1840 when he produced a popular print of the steamboat *Lexington* burning in Long Island Sound. Currier's prints became widely popular, made possible by the use of cheap immigrant labor to hand-tint them and advances in technology that made printing inexpensive. He further obliged the public by creating a huge range of images of American life, many of them nautical in nature. Many were also maudlin, reflecting popular tastes and Victorian sentimentality.

In this series, Currier explores the anxiety produced by sailors' separation from their loved ones. Currier was meticulous in his detail; note especially the second print, where the sailor is holding letters from his sweetheart in his right hand and looking at a miniature portrait of her in his left. Typical of many Currier prints, the details reveal change over time and exploit a sentimental scene.

THE SAILOR'S ADIEU.

"The Sailor's Adieu," ca. 1847. Lithograph by Nathaniel Currier, courtesy of the Library of Congress # LC-USZC2-2979.

"The Sailor Far-Far at Sea," ca. 1845. Lithograph by Nathaniel Currier, courtesy of the Library of Congress # LC-USZC2-2978.

"The Sailor's Return," ca. 1845. Lithograph by Nathaniel Currier, courtesy of the Library of Congress # LC-USZC2-2980.

Questions for Discussion:

1. What do these images reveal about Victorian ideals concerning relationships between men and women?
2. How do these images reflect or distort the actual and the stereotypical?
3. What clues does the artist give of departure, return, or the duration of the voyage?

Library of Congress, Prints & Photographs Division, LC-USZC2-2979, LC-USZC2-2978, and LC-USZC2-2980.

Joseph G. Clark, "Land Sharks" (1848)

Sailors faced dangers ashore as well as at sea. In every large port there was a "sailortown" that was well-equipped to provide services such as boarding houses, taverns, and chandleries. But there were also dishonest men and women prepared to take advantage of sailors, who often received substantial sums of money for their months of labor at sea and were known to spend it frivolously. Sailors became known as easy prey for a whole host of waterfront criminals. New York in particular became known for its tough waterfront, and in this 1848 account Joseph G. Clark, freshly returned from the Navy's Wilkes Expedition to the Pacific, details the sort of troubles his shipmates found themselves in once ashore.

The below account is particularly troubling in that it shows the seamier side of sailors' time ashore. Clark paints a picture of victimized seafarers, innocents who squander their hard-earned pay on women not worthy of their attention. Clark's arguments may have some merit, but it is not clear that sailors were only mere victims; they could also be victimizers. An article that reflects some of these complexities is Linda Maloney's "Doxies at Dockside: Prostitution and American Maritime Society, 1800–1900."[1]

As it is probable that this volume will be read by many a brother sailor, it may not be inappropriate to recur to incidents connected with landlords, and some, I am sorry to say, are not only *lordly*, but perfidious. To those who have had fewer facilities of judging of the character of the "land sharks" than myself; who have observed less of their intrigues and stratagems, it may be serviceable as a means of avoiding the tyrants' power. All may be aware of the fact that as the

---

1   Linda Maloney, "Doxies at Dockside: Prostitution and American Maritime Society, 1800–1900," in *Ships, Seafaring and Society: Essays in Maritime History*, ed. Timothy J. Runyan (Detroit: Wayne State University Press, 1987), 217–25.

hardy sailor returns from a long voyage, with his hard-earned wages, this class of men—if the term is appropriate—is ever ready to defraud such as may come within their iron grasp, but by what means this is effected, some may yet be ignorant. They are, apparently, unmoved by the tears and moans of kindred, as they see loved ones drawn into the vortex of dissipation and licentiousness, indifferent to the common claims of humanity. Money they wish and money they will have, though they wade through seas of blood to accomplish their ends; though the widowed mother toils in sorrow and wastes her ebbing energies as the direct consequence, or orphan children supplicate a meager pittance from a frigid, heartless world. Is this severe language? I would that it were untrue, that it were the fitful imaginations of a disordered brain, but many, ah! too many can sadly vouch for its truthfulness.

Those employed in our naval service, are far more in danger from this source than other seamen; they are longer from the hallowed influences of home, and the refining, reclaiming tendencies of fireside associations. They are also more exposed to the hardships, dangers and unfavorable influences of a marine life, and consequently have an almost irresistible desire to "enjoy themselves" (what *enjoyments*!) by throwing off all restraint and plunging into a senseless hilarity and inebriation. Again, they ordinarily have larger amounts of money when they come on shore, and, as a natural consequence, soon come within the contaminating grasp of these modern *harpies*, and they seldom escape from their talons until their funds are gone, and they are plunged low in the depths of degradation and ruin, by this arch enemy, for such he must be, however artful his pretended friendship may be. This apparent friendship seems very carefully graduated by the amount of remaining funds, and its last impulse dies away, as the last cent falls into his misery-tilled coffers.

The "vilest of the vile," of both sexes, are brought into requisition, when a man-of-war[1] is reported, and a great many *new* boarding houses are opened for the occasion. The whole fraternity of conspirators now form their plans, and the whole wharf in the vicinity of the ship is crowded with landlords and runners, and as often as a sailor raises his head above the netting, he is hailed with "mess-mate," "ship-mate," with other familiar appellations which are most coaxingly ap-

---

1 Man-of-war: warship.

plied to him, while their countenances and hearts are living exem-
plifications of the sentiment expressed by Shakespeare, "A man may
smile and smile, and be a villain; " but as the sailor is a stranger to this
clan of *new* boarding masters, and as he is too frank and honest himself to suspect their insincerity, they often succeed in decoying large
numbers of them into their dens of infamy. The result is, that the fruit
of years of toil is dissipated in about as many days, and their pleasant
homes(?) are soon transformed into very forbidding ones, and the
victims, for whom they expressed so much regard, are required to
find *new* quarters. The purse being empty, the bags and chests are next
rifled, and not a vestige of decent clothing remains which can become
available. Exorbitant and imaginary bills, with downright robbery for
the climax, soon terminate the sailor's tarry on shore. Diseased, degraded and dispirited, he is soon obliged to ship or perhaps this is
done for him by his ever-watchful *guardian*, and his advance secured,
and when he is reinstated on the deck of the receiving ship,[1] he is
cared as little for by the landlords as the brutes that are slaughtered
for his convenience.

These things were once transacted openly, but now more cunning
and management are requisite; they have recourse to every plot which
they can devise, to facilitate the accomplishment of their unworthy
designs. Draymen[2] are bribed to obtain their clothes: hammocks, &c.,
under pretence of conveying them to houses of good reputation, but
instead of this, they are carried where the premeditated plunder is
effected.

New York abounds in just such places, and sailors, on coming into
port, must be exceedingly careful how they select a boarding place,
especially if they design to visit their friends, and devote their earnings to more consistent objects. They must be continually on the alert,
lest they are robbed while sober, but if they can be induced to quaff
the fatal cup, they may bid adieu to pleasing associations with friends,
and the sweets of domestic life.

These secret plans are skillfully digested, and faithfully executed.
Runners and accomplices are employed and bountifully compensated,
making it a regular business to underrate all respectable "homes," and

---

1   Receiving ship: a ship the Navy put recruits on until they were assigned to another
    vessel.
2   Draymen: cart drivers.

temperance boarding houses;[1] intoxicating drink is an important agent in the work of destruction. These emissaries will distinguish themselves by their coarse imprecations, profane curses and vulgar epithets; nothing appears too harsh that can be said respecting such homes for the sailor, as, they are well aware, tend directly to abridge their nefarious business. Their mental powers, it would seem, are taxed to concoct falsehoods which shall be sufficiently libelous to prejudice seamen against such places, where they know that they will be beyond their reach. Should these fabrications fail, their next resort, perchance, is to get their baggage into the hands of some bribed coach-man, under the pretext of conveying it to a temperance house, and a liberal fee will ensure the safe arrival at some degraded and degrading den of infamy, and before the sailor is aware of the character of the place, his things are under the control of an intriguing landlord, and it is with the utmost difficulty that he can recover his property, without a legal interference, during which delay, should not his pockets or his chest be rifled, he may regard himself as fortunate. An individual who will be guilty of such cowardly and contemptible intrigue, will not be very scrupulous when he has his victim within his grasp; what he fails to get by permission, he will take by force.

Another stratagem is to employ some shrewd individual to com-mence the work of destruction while at sea, who under the garb of a shipmate can practice his deception and be credited, however much he might traduce respectable establishments, and discolor the merits of other resorts, of which he is a base hireling and utters falsehoods for the same reason that he engages in his ordinary employments.

It is ordinarily true, that the payment on board of a man-of-war does not occur until some days after their arrival at port; of this cir-cumstance, the landlord is fully aware, and soon avails himself of this advantage. His agent is furnished with funds, and very generously—as it might seem—supplies their present wants by loaning money or oth-erwise, but is particularly careful to be present at the time of payment, and receives the check from the purser, of course losing nothing by his investment.

The last, though not the least of these arts which are devised to defraud the mariner, of which I shall make mention, is performed by woman, *woman* did I say? I will not thus dishonor that name, ever dear

---

1   Temperance boarding houses: boarding houses that prohibited drinking alcohol.

to the virtuous. Degraded and unprincipled females, by feigned smiles and hypocritical and specious graces, insinuate themselves into favor with the unsuspecting sailor, extorting from him valuable presents, or otherwise making large draughts upon his funds, often relinquishing their victim only when the last dollar is transferred to their hands, with not even an apology for an equivalent. These individuals know well the frankness, kind-heartedness and generosity of the sailor, and effect his ruin when other efforts less fascinating, might fail. Numerous instances of this kind have come under my own observation, but a few will suffice to illustrate the effects of such devices to extort presents by abusing the sailor's generosity, and the consequent treatment. Two seamen with whom I was acquainted, had returned from a cruise up the Mediterranean, one receiving $280, and the other $310. The landlord had a wife and daughters who were adepts in this kind of robbery. I was shown a valuable silk dress, beside a considerable amount of jewelry which had been presented by these seamen. These were given on Monday; on Thursday they were driven from the house, and on Friday, while I was standing with them, these females passed us, arm in arm with seamen who had more recently returned, who might have shared a similar fate at the next arrival. As they passed us on the sidewalk, the same beautiful and rich dress was drawn aside, that it might not come in *contact with that of the donor*, while the remark was distinctly heard, *"I wish these filthy scamps would keep clear of the sidewalks, and not spoil people's nice clothes."* This occurred in *eight days* after their arrival, and what became of the $590, I will leave the reader to infer.

This is but one of *many* similar incidents, and those who have long been familiar with this subject, will, I think, sustain me in the assertion that "not one half has been told." They know well that the daughters and wife of the landlord, richly attired, promenade the public resorts, displaying the fruits of toil on the "mountain wave," the lavish gifts of the afterwards despised sailor.

Questions for Discussion:

1. What does this document tell us about popular attitudes toward seafarers in antebellum America?

2. What does Clark's account reveal about relations between mariners and women in antebellum ports?

3. What does this document tell us about the needs, desires, and attitudes of antebellum sailors?

Joseph G. Clark, *Light and Shadows of Sailor Life* (Boston: Benjamin B. Mussey & Co., 1848), 255–61.

PACIFIC EXPANSION

The late 1840s and 1850s saw an enormous rise in interest in the nation's West Coast and the Pacific Ocean in general. The background to Pacific expansion was the idea of *Manifest Destiny*, a term coined by journalist John L. O'Sullivan in 1845. The term labeled a rather vague idea held by many Americans that God had preordained that the United States should spread from the Atlantic to the Pacific—and possibly beyond.

Interest in exploiting the Pacific's natural resources, notably whale oil and gold, went hand in hand with the notion of Manifest Destiny. The 1840s were the peak years for the American whale fishery, with an average of over six hundred Yankee vessels scouring the seas for whales per year. These whalemen entered new seas in pursuit of their quarry, gaining a unique knowledge of the largely uncharted Pacific, especially the northern latitudes off Alaska. Whaleships were often some of the first representatives of the United States to encounter foreign cultures. Some such societies suffered cruelly from contact, especially from disease, while others, like the Japanese, imprisoned American whalemen who wrecked on their shores.

The discovery of gold in California just weeks after Mexico formally ceded it to the United States also sparked public interest in the West Coast. Speed was an essential component to success, and the fastest way to California in 1849 was on board a new type of America sailing vessel known as a clipper. These "greyhounds of the sea" could shave more than a month off the sea voyage to California. The destination in California was almost always San Francisco, whose 1848 population of 1,000 blossomed to 25,000 in 1849. By 1860 the United States was a Pacific as well as an Atlantic nation. The maritime elements of westward expansion have only relatively recently reentered the historical consciousness in works like Charles R. Schultz's social history, *Forty-Niners 'Round the Horn*.[1]

The Navy played a part in this expansion both by facilitating navigation and by opening new markets. By charting the expanses of the Pacific and

---

1   Charles R. Schultz, *Forty-Niners 'Round the Horn* (Columbia: University of South Carolina Press, 1999).

publishing data on ocean currents and prevailing winds, naval officers made navigation safer. The Navy also punished pirates, hunted down mutineers, and negotiated commercial treaties—sometimes over a cannon barrel, as when it forced the reclusive nation of Japan to open its ports to western shipping.

Nancy Bolles, "Whaling Wife" (1851)

Nancy Bolles, the wife of Captain John Bolles, was one of a number of "whaling wives" who, rather than spending long periods of their married lives alone in New England, chose to accompany their sea captain husbands on dangerous voyages to the Pacific that often lasted several years. In Bolles's case, she also chose to bring her two children, John and Isabel, on board the whaling ship *Alert* of New London, Connecticut, for a whaling voyage in the Pacific Ocean. The lives of New England's whaling wives has been explored in detail by maritime historian Joan Druett in books like *She Was a Sister Sailor*.[1]

In this letter to her sisters, Bolles describes her life on the *Alert* and the places she visited. No grammarian, Bolles's account is valuable in that it reflects the views of a rather ordinary woman encountering new cultures.

Mowee.[2] March 25th 1851

Dear Sisters,

This is the first chance I have had of writing to you since we left the Western Islands.[3] So you see that I improve the first oppertunity to let you know how we have been getting along the four first weeks after leaving home I was verry seasick, so that I did not sit up all day in the time; and for four or five months I was seasick a good part of the time. John and Isabel got along verry well. John was seasick a verry little Isabel was not sick any, John had to take all of the care of them when first out, do their washing, and take care of me too. We had a verry heavy thunder storm in the gulf Stream the lightning struck our mast, but the rain pour'd down in such torrents that it prevented seting the ship on fire. We had a verry quick passage to the Western Islands; I went ashore to Flores and Fayal, the Portagues men, women, and children

---

1 Joan Druett, *She Was a Sister Sailor: The Whaling Journals of Mary Brewster, 1845–1851* (Mystic, Conn.: Mystic Seaport Museum, 1992).

2 Mowee: Maui, one of the Hawaiian Islands.

3 Western Islands: the Azores, a common stop for whaling ships seeking additional crew.

flock'd to meet us from all quarter, we went to the American Consul's[1] and thare I stayed a good part of the day, they lived in the greatest luxery and ease of any place I was ever to, it was indeed the beautifulest spot I ever beheld, thare was three or four acres coverd with flowring trees shrubury and plants, from all parts of the world; thare was the orange tree and evergreen arbours interwoven with roses and flowers of every coler and hue; indeed I cannot paint the beauty of the spot to you, I have read of such places but I never thought they existed before, I wish you could see it, but I did not enjoy the pleasure of seeing it as I should if I had been well. There I saw professor Webster daughter she married the American Consul son Mr. Dabney and lives in the family with them she had one child and was going to have another soon. Next day John went ashore to Terceira I did not go for I did not feel well enough, here he got the rest of his recruits which consisted Potatoes Beets onions Cabage Pumkins and Cucumbers and a few oranges and Lemons. After leaving the Islands we ware in warm weather for about two months, the next land we made was Tristand Acunha[2] and Inaccessible Islands and from thare to Goughfs Island[3] which is not inhabited nether can you land on account of the surf, here the boats loward and went in shore a fishing and caught as many fish as we could eat fresh some red and yellow ones which was verry prety; they brought abord some Pinguins which was quite a curiosoty for me to see. The boats loward and took four blackfish since we have been out not such ones as you catch on Perkins rocks, but fish that was 20 feet long and four made 10 barrels of oil, thare flesh looks more like beef than it does like fish that we get to home. Thare is plenty of sea birds of every description from snowey white to a jet black and in size they verry as much as they do in colour, the largest is as large again as a goose. Thare is plenty of fish Paupasses[4] Sharks Swordfish Albicoars Flying fish Skipjacks and jumpers and a great many others that I will not take the trouble to mention. The next land we made was the Island of Amsterdam[5] here again the boats went in shore a fishing, John loward his boat and took John Isabel and me and went in shore we tried to land,

---

1   American Consul's: the American government had minor officials, termed consuls, stationed in ports around the world to facilitate trade and oversee the interests of American citizens abroad.
2   Tristand Acunha: Tristan da Cunha, a very remote British island in the South Atlantic.
3   Gough Island: a part of the Tristan da Cunha group of islands.
4   Paupasses: porpoises.
5   Island of Amsterdam: an isolated volcanic island in the southern Indian Ocean.

but could find any place where I could get up the side of the mountain; some of the men got up but thare was not much growing on the Island we got a good lot of fish, and a few Craw fish which is like Lobsters only they have no big claws; the boats took as many fish as we wanted fresh and we salted 12 barrels, they was the fatest and best fish I ever saw; we calculated to of made the Island of St Pauls[1] whare we could went ashore, but the wind did not prove favorable and so we proceeded on our voige. Nether of these Islands was not inhabited. The first whale we took was a large Sperm whale that John got he thought it would of made 60 barrels of oil, but the weather came on verry bad so that he could not cut it in, we lay too with it along side one week, and finally had to cut off and loose it at last. Since the mate has took a Sperm whale that made 31 barrels and the Second mate a right whale that made 55 barrels of oil. We have now got in warm weather again, having been in cold windy and rainy weather for four months; we have been round New Holland[2] and New Zealand, we have not found whale as we exspecked; and the weather has been verry bad. Had we of stayed at home till Septtember we should been just as well off. We have not fleeted below but one night, then the wind blew tremendous hard and the sea run mountains high we did not know but our house on deck would go to pieces, but it is standing yet. The galley went over one night and stove to pieces breaking the stove and everything that was in it, it broke 2 iron boilers 1 large copper boiler the teakettle and 3 large saucepans all to pieces, and I do not know what we should of done, had it not been for two irons boilers that was below and the utensils that belonged to my stove. We have not spoke but one whale ship since we have been out that was the *William Hamilton* of New Bedford, the captain and mate came aboard of our ship, the mate took quite a liking to little John he said that he would willingly pay three dollars a month if he could have him aboard of his ship to play with.

Monday Jan. 13th to day we made we made the Island of Pit-Carins,[3] this is a small Island settled by English men that mutineer'd aboard of an English ship, took her from the captain and went to the Sosiety Island[4] and got some taheitian women then went to Pit-Carins and run the ship ashore and took everything out of her and settled on the

---

1   Island of St. Pauls: another volcanic island in the southern Indian Ocean.

2   New Holland: Australia.

3   Pit-Carins: Pitcairn Island, famously populated by the descendants of the mutineers from HMS *Bounty*.

4   Sosiety Island: Society Islands, now a part of French Polynesia.

Island. The climate is very warm, the children the most of them go entirely naked, the women go bare headed and barefooted and ware petticoats and wrappers, the men dress verry much like our country-men. The inhabitants are half white and speak our language, which is verry plesant to those that visit the Island, they consist of 162 in number, they are verry pious and never eat without asking a bless-ing and retuning thanks, they have family prayers every morning in thare families and meetings every Sabbath; I stayed ashore two days and one night, everything was new and interesting to me, thare was some verry pretty flowering trees and shrubery, and all kind of fruit, Oranges Lemons Limes Cocoa-nuts Pine-apples Breadfruit Bananas Plantain Mumy apples Water melons Sweet potatoes and Yams the mumy apple grows on trees and is about as large as common sized muskmelon and tast verry much like one, thare was not much fruit that was ripe but we got a little of all sorts; thare was one Captains wife ashore that had been thare 7 months, she had a child 3 weeks old and was expecting her husband every day thare was another Captain that left his wife there some time she die'd two months ago with the consumption, she had it when she left home, they was both from Nan-tucket. We had three men runaway here, but all the men on the Island turn'd out and look'd till they found them, they will not have anyone stop here to stay, because the Island is so small that they think as the inhabitants increase that they will have to leave some of them and find and go some whare else to live.

I think that I have told you enough about Pit Carins so I will give you a little discription of our crew, we have a verry good lot of of-fercers and boat steerers, three of the boat steerers are portagues the other one belongs to New London ferry. Mr. Chipman he steer John,[1] he is a first rate man and well fitted to occupy a higher office if he only would let liquor alone. Our steward is a verry good cook but will lie so that I cannot tell any thing by what he says. The cook is so dirty that I exspect that he and his galley will go adrift yet in slush.[2] The crew some of them are a poor miserable set, we have one man that has been sick all of the voige but he has fight with most every man in the focastle. And another that has pretended to be blind, crazy and sick, he is the quereest specimen of human nature that I ever saw, by his looks and appearance you would think that he was foolish. But he

---

1   he steer John: i.e., served as the boatsteerer on her husband John's whaleboat.
2   Slush: the grease left over from cooking salt pork.

can converse on any subject, equal to any man on board of the ship, the men are all of the time a peeking upon him, and if they would let him alone he would begin a quarrel with them. And if they only point anything at him he will hollow sware and cry you would think he was almost kill'd, he got his rasor one night and pretended that he was going to cut his throat. And at another time he was missing, we thought he had jumped overboard, all hands was called up out of thare births, and looked the ship all over, and finally found him at last down in the hole stowed away under some staves of cask, he pretended that he was afraid that some of the men was going to flog him; At another time he got to jawing with some of the men aft and John told him to go forward and stay there, so he went to the side of the ship and jumped over board, all was excitement for a little while, for we did not know but he would drown'd at first, but I do not think that he had such a though himself, he knew that the ship was not going verry fast and that he could swim till the boat picked him up, he swimed toward the boat like a good fellow till the boat got most to him then he turned and went the other way and told them to let him drown'd, I do not think thare is one aboard the ship but would be glad to get rid of him, We are now on our way to the Sanwish Islands[1] we have cruised about three weeks on the line for Sperm whale, John has took two that made 36 barrels and the third mate one that that made 6 barrels of oil. John has got to be a great stout boy I do not think you would hardly know him he has grown so he has not had but one sick spell and that was soon after we left home, he is in his elements aboard of the ship he is harpooning and lanceing whales and pulling ropes all of the time. He wants to know every little while whare Granmars house and grandpars boats is but I think he has almost forgot all about home. Tell his grandfather that he will be large enough to help him farm it when he get home. Isabel has been a verry good child and a verry well one, although I have had to feed her ever since I left home, I have been sick so much that I have not had scarcely any milk for her, when I was seasick I vomited till I vomited blood and rais'd it which left my stomach in a verry week state and a pain in my breast that and my old complaint has keep me sick and complaining all of the voige. But I have got along verry well, and like whaling so far much better than I exspected I should, I have been as contented here with my family as I should of been at home. The time has pass'd so rapidly that I

---

1   Sanwish Islands: Sandwich Islands, now known as the Hawaiian Islands.

can hardly realise that so many months has passed since I left you, give yourselves no uneasiness about me for I have got along so far as well as I should at home.

March 2th we anchord in the harbor of Hilo on the island of Owyhee.[1] So I will give you a little discription of my first visit on shore. Thare is but three white families on this part of the island. One is a minister one a Doctor and the other a school teacher they all belong to the mission, the minister sent down his waggon drawn by two cannackers[2] to the shore for the children and me to ride up to the house. Some of the way I rode in the waggon and some of the way I rode pigback, for we came to a stream of water that was as deep as the cannackers waist so one of them took John on his shoulder and the other me and carried us across I exspecked every minute when he would fall down with me but I arrived safe on the other side, I saw a great deal that was new to me and the place was verry pleasant only it rained every day while we was thare and that was 16 days we had a verry bad time a getting out of the harbor, we waited a number of day for a fair wind and finally got under way, but did not have wind enough to get out of the harbor. And so the pilot had to anchor in a rather bad place. That night the wind blew verry hard, we put over both anchors, at midnight in a verry hard squall our chain broke and we lost one anchor, the other drag'd and we came verry near going ashore but they payed out all of the chain to the big anchor and got up a small one from below which brough her up, but we exspected all night the ship would go ashore, John took the children and me and carried us aboard of a merchant ship that lay in the harbor and we stayed thare till morning, all of the next day we could not get under way and that night the wind blew and we was in as much danger as ever, the first and second mate locked up thare chest so as to save thare clothes if the ship went to pieces in the surf they thought thare chest would wash ashore. But toward morning we got up the anchors and with much hard labour in towing the ship before night we made out to get to sea again. And the next day we anchored in the harbor of Mowee here I shall stay with the children while John is gone on the northwest, there is but four white families on this part of the Island, but a great many white men. I am to stay with Alford Bush he is a bachelor and his sister keeps house for him, she is Capt. Long's wife from New Lon-

---

1   Owyhee: Hawaii.
2   Cannackers: Kanaka, or native Hawaiian.

don she came to Calaforna with her husband and she left Calaforna and came here and keeps house for her brother she is a young women and has no Children. She expects her husband here to stay in three or four months. I do not like the idear of staying here much I had rather go to the northwest, but I have ben sick so much that I think as well as John that it will be for the best for me not to go so I shall try and content myself as well as I can here. It is most probable that we shall have to stay another season, and I hope then I shall be able to go with him. He has considerable trouble with his men here two has run away one he has discharge because he was not good for any thing another he has had to pay 36 dollars for and leave him in the hospittle to get rid of him five that could not get a chance to runaway has come and wanted thare discharge but John would not discharge them and so they went below and refus'd duty, and he has had to handcuff them and put them below they all in debt to the ship about 100 dollars and so they want to get away and go to calafornia. I guess by this time, you are growing weary of my simple letter and so I will draw it to a close. John has laughed at me a good deal about it he thinks I had better send you his journal that it will do just as well, but I tell him that I am afraid you will have to pay to much postage on it.[1] I intend this letter for all of you I cannot get a chance to write any more and I do not think it nesesary, for I have written all I can think of to write, and I know that you all will have a chance to read it. I have not heard from home since I left, I hope you will all take the trouble to write for I would like to hear from you verry much I like to hear from father and mother, and I should like to step in and see them if I could and the rest of you but I do not know when I shall, and if I meet you no more on earth I hope I shall meet you all in heaven, for we must all soon leave this world and try the unseen realities of eternity. So I must bid you farewell may the blessing of God rest with you.

> I remain your affectionate sister
> Nancy.

Questions for Discussion:
1. What does this document reveal about Bolles's attitude toward foreign people and places?
2. What does this document reveal about the lives of women who chose to sail with their sea captain husbands?

---

1   Postage on it: in 1851 the recipient of a letter had to pay for it, rather than the sender.

3. What does this document reveal about the whaling industry and seafaring life in 1851?

Nancy Bolles, Letter, 1851. VFM 1655, Manuscripts Collection, G. W. Blunt White Library, Mystic Seaport Museum, Inc.

Matthew Fontaine Maury, "The Winds and Currents of the Seas— Fast Sailing" (1853)

The antebellum years saw the rise of American interest in science, especially when it was directly applicable to practical matters like navigation. Foremost among the nation's scientists who attempted to understand the world's oceans was Navy lieutenant Matthew Fontaine Maury (1806–1873), the "pathfinder of the seas." Using diverse sources, such as logbooks from commercial vessels, Maury aggregated an enormous amount of information about wind patterns, currents, weather, and incidentally, whale migrations, especially in the vast Pacific. Maury published this data in his 1851 book, *Explanation and Sailing Directions*, which "put within reach of the young and inexperienced mariner, a summary of the experience of thousands of voyages." This information had very practical implications for navigators, who could shave whole weeks off long voyages by using Maury's information.

Maury's timing in publishing his data was very good, for Americans were in a tremendous rush to sail to California. Gold miners and others were willing to pay premium prices to sail on the fastest ships of the day, the lofty and beautiful clippers. In the below passage, Maury analyzes the fastest passages by two of the most famous of these clippers, the *Sovereign of the Seas* and the *Flying Cloud*. The names of the vessels are indicative of the pride and competitiveness of their owners.

NATIONAL OBSERVATORY, WASHINGTON, May 10,1853.
SIR:—

The clipper-ship *Sovereign of the Seas*[1] (McKay)[2] has made such an extraordinary run that I beg to make it the subject matter of an official

---

1   *Sovereign of the Seas*: an extremely fast clipper ship built in 1852 by famous shipbuilder Donald McKay (1810–1880) in East Boston, Massachusetts.

2   McKay: Lauchlan McKay (1811–1895), master of the *Sovereign of the Seas* and the younger brother of its builder.

report. It is due to builders, owners, and masters, as well as to navigation, that such an achievement should be made known.

This ship is one of the glorious fleet of a thousand sail that is voluntarily engaged in making observations for wind and current charts. She it is, it will be recollected, who, taking them for her guide, made the extraordinary run of 103 days from New York to San Francisco, both crossing the equator in the Pacific and arriving in port on the day predicted.

Little or nothing, except what conjecture suggested, was known as to the winds in this part of the ocean. The results of my investigations elsewhere with regard to winds and the circulation of the atmosphere had enabled me to announce, as a theoretical deduction, that the winds in the "variables" of the South Pacific would probably be found to prevail from the westward with a tradewind-like regularity. Returning from the Sandwich Islands to New York in the remarkably short run of 82 day, she passed through a part of the Great South Sea which has been seldom traversed by traders—at least I have the records of none such.

Between the parallels of 45 degrees and 55 degrees S., from the meridian of the Cape of Good Hope eastward around to that of Cape Horn, there is no land or other disturbing agent to interrupt the wind in its regular circuits. Here the winds would be found blowing from the west with greater force than from the east in the trade-wind region, and giving rise to that long rolling swell peculiar to those regions of the Pacific, they would enable ships steering east to make the most remarkable runs that have ever been accomplished under canvas.

The *Sovereign of the Seas* has afforded the most beautiful illustration as to the correctness of these theoretical deductions.

Leaving Oahu for New York, via Cape Horn, 18th of February last, she stood to the southward through the belts both of the northeast and southeast trades, making a course good on the average through them a little to the west of south. She finally got clear of them March 6th, after crossing the parallel of 45° south upon the meridian of 164° west.

The 8th and 9th she was in the "horse latitude" weather of the southern hemi-sphere. So far her run had been good, but there was nothing remarkable in it.

Having crossed the parallel of 48° south, she found herself on the 10th fairly within the trade-like west winds of the Southern ocean, and here commenced a succession of the most extraordinary day's runs that have ever been linked together across the ocean.

From March 8th to March 31st. from the parallel of 48° south in the Pacific to 35° south in the Atlantic, during an interval of twenty-two days, that ship made 29° of latitude and 126° of longitude; her shortest day's run during the interval—determined by calculation, not by the log—being one hundred and fifty knots.[1] The wind all this time is not recorded once with easting in it. It was steady and fresh from the westward.

In these twenty-two days that ship made 5,391 nautical miles. But that you may the more conveniently contrast her performance with that of railroad cars and river steamers, I will quote her in statute miles.

Here, then, is a ship under canvas, and with the winds alone as a propelling power, and with a crew, too, so short, the captain informs me, that she was but half manned, accomplishing in twenty-two days the enormous run of 6,245 miles, (one-fourth the distance round the earth,) and making the daily average of two hundred and eighty-three statute miles and nine-tenths (283.9). During eleven of these days consecutively her daily average was 354 statute miles, and during four days, also consecutively, she averaged as high as 398¾ statute miles.

From noon of one to the noon[2] of the next day, the greatest distance made was 869 knots, or 419 miles; and the greatest rate reported by the captain is 18 knots, or 21 statute miles, the hour. This is pretty fair railroad speed.

The greatest distance ever before performed from noon to noon, on the ocean, was 374 knots, (433¼ statute miles,) by the clipper-ship *Flying Cloud*, in her celebrated passage of 89 days and 21 hours to San Francisco, in 1851, and which yet stands unequalled. I say, from noon to noon, because from noon to noon was not, with either of these ships, the exact measure of twenty-four hours.

The *Flying Cloud* was going to the northward and westward, and on the day of her great run she made 4 deg. 40 min. of longitude, which in time is 19 min. 4 sec.; that is, her noon to noon for that day was 24 hours 19 min. 4 sec.

---

1   Knots: Maury here is using the term *knot* in place of *nautical miles*, a usage that has fallen out of favor.
2   Noon: in ship's logbooks, a twenty-four-hour day commenced at noon.

On the other hand, the *Sovereign of the Seas* was steering to the eastward, and on the day of her great run she made 8 deg. 44 min. of longitude, which in time is 34 min. 66 sec.; that is, her noon to noon for that day was only 23 hours 25 min. 4 sec. longitude.

Thus the *Flying Cloud*'s run in 24 hours 19 min. 4 sec. was 433¼ statute miles, and the other 419 in 23 hours 25 min. 4 sec.

Reducing these runs each to the performance pro rata, according to the log, for 24 hours, we have for the former ship 427.5 against 427.6 by the latter; that is, the best 24 consecutive hours' run by the *Sovereign of the Seas* exceeds the best consecutive 24 hours of the *Flying Cloud* only by *one-tenth* part of a mile.

These two ships are certainly *par nobile*, but the great day's performance of each does not prove the *Sovereign of the Seas* to be a faster ship than the *Flying Cloud*. The *Sovereign of the Seas* had in her favor that long rolling swell from the westward that is peculiar to high southern latitudes, and which helped mightily to heave her along. All seamen who have doubled Cape Horn know what it is, and I need not describe it.

It is true the *Flying Cloud*, on her great day, had during the "latter part strong gales and high seas running," still those high seas were not like that long rolling Cape Horn swell that comes from the westward with such a heaving force, and which had been chasing the *Sovereign of the Seas* steadily for ten days.

On the other hand, it may be urged in favor of the latter that she was short-handed, with foretopmast disabled, and jury topgallant-mast. Her abstract log, it should also be mentioned, says nothing as to the force of the wind, the heave of the sea, or the sails set; while that of the *Flying Cloud* is quite full upon these points.

Though I am unwilling therefore to decide against the *Flying Cloud* as to the greatest day's run ever made, it is clear that her competitor has borne off the palm as to the length of time for which she has kept up her great speed. Her log stops March 3d, latitude 33 deg. 16 min. north, 432 nautical miles in a straight line from Sandy Hook.

Taking it, therefore, for the seventy-nine days for which she gives it, and stating the distance by straight line from her place at noon of one day to the noon of the next, it appears that her daily average was 222.7 statute miles, making the whole distance sailed during the interval to be 17,597 statute miles; which gives for canvas the remarkable achievement of accomplishing a distance more than two-thirds of that which it requires to encircle the earth, at the average rate of nine miles and upwards the hour for 1,896 consecutive hours.

As I write this, the abstract of another ship, the *Comet*, E. C. Gardiner, from San Francisco to New York, is received. She, too, has made an extraordinary run. She made the passage in 83½ days, sailing during the interval 17,496 statute miles, and averaging 210 miles a day. She, however, except merely by doubling Cape Horn, did not run through the region of the trade-like winds and heaving swells of the South Pacific, which favored the *Sovereign of the Seas* to such an extent, and therefore no fair comparison can be made as to the relative sailing qualities of these two ships.

There is another circumstance, however, connected with this voyage of the *Sovereign of the Seas* which is worthy of attention, for it is significant, and a fact illustrative of the revolutions in the way of business which are being quietly wrought by the time-saving devices of the age.

This splendid ship, after unloading her cargo in California, was sent to glean after our whalemen, and she came home with oil gathered from them at the Sandwich Islands.

This adventurous class of our fellow citizens resort there in such numbers, that the fees annually paid by the government for the relief of the sick and disabled seamen there amount to upwards of $50,000.

Now, if the Pacific Railway were built, the thousands of American seamen and the fleets of American whaleships that annually resort to those islands for refreshment and repairs, would resort to California. There they would be in their own country, the oil would probably be sent home on railway instead of by clipper ships, and all the advantage of refitting so many ships, of treating and recruiting so many men, would insure to the benefit, of our own citizens.

Respectfully,
M. F. MAURY, Lieutenant U.S.N.

Hon. JAS. C. DOBBIN, Secretary of the Navy, Wash.

Questions for Discussion:
1. What does this document reveal about the connection between scientific navigation and seaborne commerce?
2. What does this document reveal about American abilities and desires to expand westward into the Pacific?

3. What does this document suggest about the interconnections between American naval and commercial goals?

Matthew Fontaine Maury, "The Winds and Currents of the Seas—Fast Sailing," *The Merchants' Magazine and Commercial Review* 29 (June–December, 1853): 114–16.

United States "Treaty of Kanagawa" (1854)

The United States Navy's role in the antebellum period was largely one of protecting and promoting trade, and the various ships and squadrons assigned to the Pacific played a major role in supporting American seaborne commerce. That included suppressing piracy in the East Indies, pursuing mutineers from the whaleship *Globe,* creating ocean charts as did Matthew F. Maury, or opening trade with nations like Japan, as Commodore Matthew Calbraith Perry (1794–1858) did between 1852 and 1854.

Japan before 1852 was a closed society, with minimal trade relations with the outside world. The American government had made several efforts to open trade relations with Japan, but all failed. In the early 1850s, the American government, concerned for the fate of shipwrecked American whalemen imprisoned in Japan and desiring a coaling station in the Far East, sent a squadron under the command of Commodore Perry to open Japan. Perry finally succeeded in opening negotiations in 1852, in part because the steamships under his command overawed the Japanese. In 1854 the Japanese government signed a commercial treaty with the United States and soon entered a phase of rapid westernization.

The United States of America and the empire of Japan, desiring to establish firm, lasting and sincere friendship between the two nations, have resolved to fix, in a manner clear and positive by means of a treaty or general convention of peace and amity, the rules which shall in future be mutually observed in the intercourse of their respective countries; for which most desirable object the President of the United States has conferred full powers on his commissioner, Matthew Calbraith Perry, special ambassador of the United States to Japan and the August sovereign of Japan has given similar full powers to his commissioners, Hayashi-Daigaku-no-kami, Ido, Prince of Tsus-Sima; Izawa, Prince of Mmimasaki; and Udono, member of the Board of Revenue.

And the said commissioners after having exchanged their said full powers and duly considered the premises, have agreed to the following articles:

Article I—There shall be a perfect, permanent and universal peace, and a sincere and cordial amity, between the United States of America on the one part and between their people, respectfully, (respectively,) without exception of persons or places.

Article II—The port of Simoda, in the principality of Idzu and the port of Hakodadi, in the pricipality of Matsmai are granted by the Japanese as ports for the reception for American ships, where they can be supplied with wood, water, provisions and coal, and other articles their necessities may require, as far as the Japanese have them. The time for opening the first named port is immediately on signing this treaty; the last named port is to be opened immediately after the same day in the ensuing Japanese year.

Note—A tariff of prices shall be given by the Japanese officers of the things which they can furnish, payment for which shall be made in gold, and silver coin.

Article III—Whenever ships of the United States are thrown or wrecked on the coast of Japan, the Japanese vessels will assist them, and carry their crews to Simoda or Hakodadi and hand them over to their countrymen appointed to receive them. Whatever articles the shipwrecked men may have preserved shall likewise be restored and the expenses incurred in the rescue and support of Americans and Japanese who may thus be thrown up on the shores of either nation are not to be refunded.

Article IV—Those shipwrecked persons and other citizens of the United States shall be free as in the other countries and not subjected to confinement but shall be amenable to just laws.

Article V—Shipwrecked men and other citizens of the United States, temporarily living at Simoda and Hakodadi, shall not be subject to such restrictions and confinement as the Dutch and Chinese are at Nagasaki but shall be free at Simoda to go where they please within the limits of seven Japanese miles from a small island in the harbor of Simoda, marked on the accompanying chart hereto appended; and shall in like manner be free to go where they please at Hakodadi, within limits to be defined after the visit of the United States squadron to that place.

Article VI—If there be any other sort of goods wanted or any business which shall require to be arranged, there shall be careful deliberation between the particles in order to settle such matters.

Article VII—It is agreed that ships of the United States resorting to the ports open to them, shall be permitted to exchange gold and silver coin and articles of goods for other articles of goods under such regulations as shall be temporarily established by the Japanese government for that purpose. It is stipulated, however that the ships of the United States shall be permitted to carry away whatever articles they are unwilling to exchange.

Article VIII—Wood, water provisions, coal and goods required shall only be procured through the agency of Japanese officers appointed for that purpose, and in no other manner.

Article IX—It is agreed, that if, at any future day, the government of Japan shall grant to any other nation or nations privileges and advantages which are not herein granted to the United states and the citizens thereof, that these same privileges and advantages shall be granted likewise to the United States and to the citizens thereof without any consultation or delay.

Article X—Ships of the United States shall be permitted to resort to no other ports in Japan but Simoda and Hakodadi, unless in distress or forced by stress of weather.

Article XI—There shall be appointed by the government of the United States consuls or agents to reside in Simoda at any time after the expiration of eighteen months from the date of the signing of this treaty; provided that either of the two governments deem such arrangement necessary.

Article XII—The present convention, having been concluded and duly signed, shall be obligatory, and faithfully observed by the United States of America, and Japan and by the citizens and subjects of each respective power; and it is to be ratified and approved by the President of the United States, by and with the advice and consent of the Senate thereof, and by the August Sovereign of Japan, and the ratification shall be exchanged within eighteen months from the date of the signature therefore, or sooner if practicable.

In faith, whereof, we, the respective plenipotentiaries of the United States of America and the empire of Japan aforesaid have signed and sealed these presents.

Done at Kanagawa, this thirty-first day of March, in the year of our Lord Jesus Christ one thousand eight hundred and fifty-four and of Kayei the seventh year, third month and third day.

Questions for Discussion:
1. What does this document reveal about the Navy's role in supporting American seaborne trade?
2. What does this treaty reveal about Japanese concerns?
3. How does this document reflect American maritime concerns in the Far East?

Hunter Miller, ed., *Treaties and Other International Acts of the United States of America*, vol. 6 (Washington, D.C.: Government Printing Office, 1942), 440–42.

New York Daily Tribune, "A Heroine of the Sea" (1857)

While the vast majority of seafarers were men, a few women went to sea as well, a fact that historians have recently been exploring in detail. One of the most famous of these women was Eleanor Prentiss Creesy, who was fascinated by navigation and was an early follower of Matthew Fontaine Maury's sailing charts. Creesy acted as navigator on the famous clipper ship *Flying Cloud*, which her husband commanded. Together they broke a world record, sailing from New York and arriving in San Francisco in a mere eighty-nine days, a record that stood until 1989.

Mary Patten (1837–1861), who sailed on the clipper her husband commanded, *Neptune's Car*, was another such navigating wife. Clipper ships such as the *Neptune's Car* were the fastest and most beautiful ships afloat before the Civil War, technological marvels best known for their swift passages from New York to San Francisco on the dangerous Cape Horn route. The following is a newspaper account of how Patten took command of her husband's ship after he became ill. She was only nineteen at the time and pregnant, and had to deal with the hostility of the first mate and the incompetence of the second mate, not to mention the usual dangers of seafaring. It is a truly remarkable story of perseverance in the face of adversity, and it is easy to see why the U.S. Merchant Marine Academy commemorated Mary Patten by naming the school's infirmary after her.

Among the noble band of women who, by their heroic bearing, under great trial and suffering, have won for themselves imperishable fame, Mary A. Patten may claim a prominent position. Mrs. Patten is a native of Boston, and but 20 years of age. Her husband, Capt. Joshua A. Patten, sailed from this port in July last, for San Francisco, as commander of the clipper ship *Neptune's Car*, of Foster and Nickerson's line, and it was during this voyage that his wife rendered herself so distinguished. Capt. Patten is well known in this port, and at the eastward, as a young and rising seaman; and the vessels under his command have made some of the swiftest passages on record. He took command of the *Neptune's Car* about two years ago, and made his first voyage in her to San Francisco in 90 days. On that occasion Mrs. Patten accompanied him to San Francisco, China, London, and back to New York. His next voyage was that last year to San Francisco, in which his wife again accompanied him. The *Neptune's Car* left port at the same time with the clippers *Romance of the Seas*, *Intrepid*, and two others, the names of which we do not remember. As usual with commanders in the Pacific trade, Capt. Patten wished to get his ship into port ahead of his rivals. He soon found, however, that his first mate slept during half his watch on the quarter deck, while he kept the ship under reefed courses, and after repeated remonstrance had proved unavailing he found it necessary to remove him. After that he undertook to discharge the mate's duties as well as his own, and in consequence of fatigue was taken sick, while passing through the Straits of Lemaire, around the Horn, and in a short time brain fever developed itself.

From that time, up to the period of her arrival at San Francisco, Mrs. Patten was both nurse and navigator. When her husband was taken sick the ship was given in charge of the second mate. He, however, was but an indifferent navigator, and although he knew how to take an observation, he could not work up the reckoning. Mrs. Patten, who, on her previous voyage, had studied navigation as a pastime, now took observations, worked up the reckoning by chronometer time, laid the ship's courses, and performed most of the other duties of the captain of the ship. During this time her husband was delirious with the fever, and she shaved his head, and devised every means in her power to soothe and restore him. To this end, she studied medicine to know how to treat his case intelligently, and in course of time succeeded in carrying him alive through the crisis of his complaint.

About one week after the Captain fell sick the mate wrote a letter to Mrs. Patten, reminding her of the dangers of the coast and the great responsibility she had assumed, and offering to take charge of the ship. She replied that, in the judgment of her husband, he was unfit to be mate, and therefore could not be considered qualified to fill the post of commander. Stung by this rebuff, the fellow tried to stir up the crew to mutiny against her; but she called the other mates and sailors aft, and appealed to them to support her in her hour of trial. To a man they resolved to stand by her and the ship, come what might. It was pleasant to witness their cheerful obedience to her orders, as each man vied with his fellows in the performance of his duties.

By the time the ship came nearly up to the latitude of Valparaiso, Capt. Patten had somewhat recovered from the fever, although far too weak for any mental or physical exertion, and the mate, after promise of doing better in future, had partially resumed duty. But Mrs. Patten discovering that he was steering the ship out of her course, and making for Valparaiso, appraised her husband of the fact. The mate was summoned below and asked to explain his conduct, which he did by saying that he could not keep the ship nearer her course. Capt. Patten then had his cot moved to a part of the cabin from which he could view the "tell-tale" of the compass, and soon found that the mate was still steering for Valparaiso. He then sent for the four mates and the sailors, promoting the second officer to his place. Then he gave orders that under no circumstances was his ship to be taken into any other port than San Francisco. Soon after he had a relapse, and for 25 days before the vessel reached port he was totally blind. At length San Francisco was reached in safety, after a short voyage of 120 days, the vessel beating three out of four of her competitors.

The safety of the ship and the preservation of her husband's life were wholly due to the constant care and watchfulness of Mrs. Patten. On her arrival she informed the consignee of the vessel that for fifty nights previous she had not undressed herself.

Some time in December last we published the only account of this remarkable instance of female fortitude which had been given, in an extract from a commercial letter to the owners in this city. Yesterday we received a note from our ship-news collector, stating that Mrs. Patten and her husband were in this city, having arrived in the steamer *George Law*. We found them at the Battery Hotel, and obtained an interview with Mrs. Patten. She was assiduously attending her husband as heretofore, but his situation is such as to preclude all hope of recovery. Before leaving San Francisco, deafness was added to his other afflictions, and he now lies upon his couch insensible to everything but the kind offices of his beloved companion, and so weak that he may expire at any moment. Occasionally he speaks to his wife, sometimes lucidly, but oftener in a wild and incoherent manner. Mrs. Patten's brother, Mr. Brown, we believe, who is foreman of a shipyard in Boston, is in attendance upon his sister and brother-in-law. From him we learned that Capt. Patten had been taken care of by his brother Masons in San Francisco, and Dr. Harris, one of the fraternity, had watched over him on his way home. On leaving San Francisco, he seemed to rally considerably, but on reaching a warm latitude he relapsed, and has sunk to the hopeless state in which we found him. The Masons of this city, having been advised from San Francisco of his intended departure for home, were waiting for the *George Law* on her arrival, and brought him on a litter to the Battery Hotel, where they have since watched over him.

With that modesty which generally distinguishes true merit, Mrs. Patten begged to be excused from speaking about herself. She said that she had done no more than her duty, and as the recollection of her trials and suffering evidently gave her pain, we could not do otherwise than respect her feelings. Few persons would imagine that the woman who behaved so bravely, and endured so much for her husband's sake, is a slender New England girl, scarcely twenty years old. She is a lady of medium height, with black hair, large, dark, lustrous eyes, and very pleasing features. Her health is very much impaired from the hardships which she has undergone, and she is very near the period of maternity. Yet she does not spare herself in the least, but is most faithful and constant in her attentions to her husband. We have been informed that she is in strained circumstances, and although she might and doubtless would shrink from assistance from others, yet it seems to me that this is a case in which our merchants may do themselves honor, by a liberal recognition of her heroic conduct. The Board of Underwriters, we understand, have voted or will vote her $1,000. Considering that the ship and cargo were worth nearly $350,000, and that to her skill and decision they are mainly indebted for its safety, under most severe circumstances for the weather was unusually severe we think, looking at the matter from a purely pecuniary point of view, the least they should have done would have been to give her a check for $5,000. Not only did she safely take the ship from Cape Horn to San Francisco, but both vessel and cargo were in better trim than any of her competitors when she reached port. Of course the owners of the ship will do handsomely by Mrs. Patten, but were the merchants of New York to make up a liberal purse it would prove highly acceptable to the widow (as she almost certainly soon will be) and her small family.

Capt. Patten is a native of Rockland, Maine, and has risen from the forecastle solely by his own exertions. Mrs. Patten and her brother will convey him to their home in Boston today by the steamer, if the weather will permit. That she has the entire sympathies of this community in her trying affliction she may be fully assured, and also that by her good deeds she has added another laurel to the honor of her sex.

Questions for Discussion:
1. Does this newspaper article celebrate Mrs. Patten as a mariner or as the model of a good wife?
2. What does this document reveal about sailing to California on a clipper ship?
3. What rewards did Patten seek for her performance, and what did she actually receive for her conduct?

"A Heroine of the Sea," *New York Daily Tribune*, February 18, 1857.

SLAVES AND SAILORS

Slavery was an important issue for maritime America. Many American seamen were not white in the antebellum period: large numbers of African Americans, Native Americans, and others sailed on American ships. But the question of race and slavery became more complex in the 1820s when South Carolina's legislature passed the Negro Seamen Act in order to prevent black sailors from encouraging slave revolts in ports like Charleston. These laws, enacted throughout the Deep South, required shipmasters to hand over black seamen for imprisonment for the duration of a vessel's stay in port. While the federal court system found this approach illegal, South Carolina simply ignored the courts and did as it pleased. Black seamen responded by trying to avoid southern ports or leaving seafaring altogether.

But not everyone in America condoned slavery. Led by William Lloyd Garrison (himself the son of a sailor), a handful of religious reformers termed *abolitionists* embarked on a crusade to end slavery. Abolitionists

came together in 1839 to fund the legal defense of Africans illegally enslaved in the *Amistad* case. Abolitionists even assisted slaves in escaping
from slavery. Quite naturally many slaves attempted to escape by boat.
Sometimes this was on river steamboats, other times on coasting vessels,
as in the case of the sloop *Pearl* in 1848, when one mariner attempted to
carry away seventy-six fugitive slaves.

Another aspect of the slavery debate before the Civil War was the continued but illegal importation of African slaves after 1807. From 1820 until
1861 the U.S. Navy patrolled the African coast to suppress the slave trade
and seized about one hundred slave ships in that time. But convictions were
few and penalties light: between 1837 and 1860, seventy-four cases were
tried in the United States. The first—and only—American slave trader that
faced the full penalty of the law for slave trading was a Portland, Maine,
sea captain named Nathaniel Gordon. Federal authorities hanged him in
1862.

Frederick Douglass, "Escape from Slavery" (1838)

Frederick Douglass (1818–1895) was one of the foremost black abolitionists. An escaped slave himself, his experiences and formidable speaking and
writing skills made him a powerful presence in the abolition movement.
Less well known was Douglass's participation in the maritime industry. As
a slave in Baltimore, his master hired him out to work as a caulker in shipyards; on his escape from slavery, he worked on the docks of New Bedford
yet was denied work as a caulker because of his race. The following is ex-
cerpted from the chapter entitled "Escape from Slavery" in his 1882 autobiography, *The Life and Times of Frederick Douglass*.

In the first narrative of my experience in slavery, written nearly
forty years ago, and in various writings since, I have given the public
what I considered very good reasons for withholding the manner of
my escape. In substance these reasons were, first, that such publication at any time during the existence of slavery might be used by the
master against the slave, and prevent the future escape of any who
might adopt the same means that I did. The second reason was, if possible, still more binding to silence—for publication of details would
certainly have put in peril the persons and property of those who assisted. Murder itself was not more sternly and certainly punished in
the State of Maryland, than that of aiding and abetting the escape of a
slave. Many colored men, for no other crime than that of giving aid to

a fugitive slave, have, like Charles T. Torrey,[1] perished in prison. The abolition of slavery in my native state and throughout the country, and the lapse of time, render the caution hitherto observed no longer necessary. But even since the abolition of slavery, I have sometimes thought it well enough to baffle curiosity, by saying that while slavery existed there were good reasons for not telling the manner of my escape, and since slavery had ceased to exist, there was no reason for telling it. I shall now, however, cease to avail myself of this formula, and as far as I can, endeavor to satisfy this very natural curiosity. I should perhaps have yielded to that feeling sooner, had there been anything very heroic or thrilling in the incidents connected with my escape, but I am sorry to say I have nothing of that sort to tell; and yet, the courage that could risk betrayal, and the bravery which was ready to encounter death, if need be, in pursuit of freedom, were essential features in the undertaking. My success was due to address rather than courage; to good luck rather than bravery.

My means of escape were provided for me by the very men who were making laws to hold and bind me more securely in slavery. It was the custom in the State of Maryland to require the free colored people to have what were called free papers. This instrument they were required to renew very often, and by charging a fee for this writing, considerable sums, from time to time, were collected by the State. In these papers the name, age, color, height, and form of the free man were described, together with any scars or other marks upon his person, which could assist in his identification. This device of slaveholding ingenuity, like other devices of wickedness, in some measure defeated itself—since more than one man could be found to answer the same general description. Hence many slaves could escape by personating the owner of one set of papers; and this was often done as follows: A slave nearly or sufficiently answering the description set forth in papers, would borrow or hire them till he could by their means escape to a free State, and then, by mail or otherwise, return them to the owner. The operation was a hazardous one for the lender as well as the borrower. A failure on the part of the fugitive to send back the papers would imperil his benefactor, and the discovery of the papers in possession of the wrong man, would imperil both the fugitive and

---

1   Charles T. Torrey (1813–1846), a Massachusetts minister and abolitionist who was convicted of attempting to free a slave family and died in prison from disease.

his friend. It was, therefore, an act of supreme trust on the part of a freeman of color thus to put in jeopardy his own liberty, that another might be free. It was, however, not unfrequently bravely done, and was seldom discovered. I was not so fortunate to sufficiently resemble any of my free acquaintances as to answer the description of their papers. But I had one friend—a sailor—who owned a sailor's protection,[1] which answered somewhat the purpose of free papers—describing his person, and certifying to the fact that he was a free American sailor. The instrument had at its head the American eagle, which gave it the appearance at once of an authorized document. This protection did not, when in my hands, describe its bearer very accurately. Indeed, it called for a man much darker than myself, and close examination of it would have caused my arrest at the start. In order to avoid this fatal scrutiny on the part of the railroad official, I had arranged with Isaac Eolls, a hackman,[2] to bring my baggage to the train just on the moment of its starting, and I jumped upon the car myself when the train was already in motion. Had I gone into the station and offered to purchase a ticket, I should have been instantly and carefully examined, and undoubtedly arrested. In choosing this plan upon which to act, I considered the jostle of the train, and the natural haste of the conductor, in a train crowded with passengers, and relied upon my skill and address in playing the sailor as described in my protection, to do the rest.

One element in my favor, was the kind feeling which prevailed in Baltimore and other seaports at the time, towards "those who go down to the sea in ships." "Free trade and sailors' rights" expressed the sentiment of the country just then. In my clothing, I was rigged out in sailor style. I had on a red shirt and a tarpaulin hat and black cravat, tied in sailor fashion, carelessly and loosely about my neck. My knowledge of ships and sailor's talk came much to my assistance, for I knew a ship from stem to stern, and from keelson to cross-trees, and could talk sailor like an "old salt."

On sped the train, and I was well on the way to Havre de Grace before the conductor came into the negro car[3] to collect tickets and

---

1   Sailor's protection: a document issued by the federal government to prove the identity of seamen.

2   Hackman: somebody who drove a horse-drawn carriage for hire, analogous to a cab driver today.

3   Negro car: blacks were not permitted to ride with other passengers.

examine the papers of his black passengers. This was a critical moment in the drama. My whole future depended upon the decision of this conductor. Agitated I was while this ceremony was proceeding, but still externally, at least, I was apparently calm and self-possessed. He went on with his duty—examining several colored passengers before reaching me. He was somewhat harsh in tone, and peremptory in manner until he reached me, when, strangely enough, and to my surprise and relief, his whole manner changed. Seeing that I did not readily produce my free papers, as the other colored persons in the car had done, he said to me, in a friendly contrast with that observed towards the others: "I suppose you have your free papers?" To which I answered: "No, sir; I never carry my free papers to sea with me." "But you have something to show that you are a free man, have you not?" "Yes, sir," I answered; "I have a paper with the American eagle on it, and that will carry me round the world." With this I drew from my deep sailor's pocket my seaman's protection, as before described.

The merest glance at the paper satisfied him, and he took my fare and went on about his business. This moment of time was one of the most anxious I ever experienced. Had the conductor looked closely at the paper, he could not have failed to discover that it called for a very different looking person from myself, and in that case, it would have been his duty to arrest me on that instant, and send me back to Baltimore from the first station. When he left me with the assurance that I was all right, though much relieved, I realized that I was still in great danger. I was still in Maryland, and subject to arrest at any moment. I saw on the train several persons who would have known me in any other clothes, and I feared they might recognize me, even in my sailor "rig," and report me to the conductor, who would then subject me to a closer examination, which I knew well would be fatal to me.

Though I was not a murderer fleeing from justice, I felt perhaps quite as miserable as such a criminal. The train was moving at a very high rate of speed for that time of railroad travel, but to my anxious mind, it was moving far too slowly. Minutes were hours, and hours were days, during this part of my flight. After Maryland, I was to pass through Delaware—another slave State, where slave-catchers generally awaited their prey, for it was not in the interior of the State, but on its borders, that these human hounds were most vigilant and active. The border lines between slavery and freedom were the dangerous ones, for the fugitives. The heart of no fox or deer, with hungry hounds on his trail in full chase, could have beaten more anxiously or noisily than did mine, from the time I left Baltimore till I reached Philadelphia. The passage of the Susquehanna river at Havre de Grace was made by ferry boat at that time, on board of which I met a young colored man by the name of Nichols, who came very near betraying me. He was a "hand"[1] on the boat, but instead of minding his business, he insisted upon knowing me, and asking me dangerous questions as to where I was going, and when I was coming back, &c. I got away from my old and inconvenient acquaintance as soon as I could decently do so, and went to another part of the boat.

Once across the river I encountered a new danger. Only a few days before, I had been at work on a revenue-cutter,[2] in Mr. Price's shipyard, under the care of Captain McGowan. On the meeting at this point of the two trains, the one going South stopped on the track just opposite to the one going North, and it so happened that this Captain McGowan sat at a window where he could see me very distinctly, and would certainly have recognized me had he looked at me but for a second. Fortunately, in the hurry of the moment, he did not see me; and the trains soon passed each other on their respective ways. But this was not my only hair-breadth escape.

A German blacksmith whom I knew well, was on the train with me, and looked at me very intently, as if he thought he had seen me somewhere before in his travels. I really believe he knew me, but had no heart to betray me. At any rate he saw me escaping and held his peace.

The last point of imminent danger, and the one I dreaded most, was Wilmington. Here we left the train, and took the steamboat for Philadelphia. In making the change here I again apprehended arrest, but no one disturbed me, and I was soon on the broad and beautiful Delaware, speeding away to the Quaker City. On reaching Philadelphia in the afternoon, I inquired of a colored man how I could get on to New York. He directed me to the William Street depot, and thither I went, taking the train that night. I reached New York on Tuesday morning, having completed the journey in less than twenty-four hours. Such is briefly the manner of my escape from slavery—and the end of my experience as a slave.

---

1   Hand: short for deckhand.
2   Revenue-cutter: a patrol vessel belonging to the U.S. Revenue Cutter Service.

Questions for Discussion:

1. What does this document reveal about racial relations in antebellum America?

2. What does this document reveal about African American seafarers in the 1830s?

3. What posed the greatest danger to Douglass in his escape?

Frederick Douglass, *The Life and Times of Frederick Douglass* (London: Christian Age Office, 1882), 165–69.

New London Gazette, "The Suspicious Looking Schooner" (1839)

The *Amistad* incident was one of several that galvanized abolitionist activity in the antebellum period. In the summer of 1839, the Navy brig *Washington* discovered a suspicious looking schooner off Montauk Point. Lieutenant Richard W. Meade, on boarding the vessel, found it was the Spanish schooner *Amistad*, which had been carrying a cargo of enslaved Africans from Havana, Cuba, to Puerto Principe, Cuba, when the black captives rose and overpowered the white crew, killing the captain and one of the crew. The Africans spared the lives of two Spanish men to navigate the schooner back to Africa. The Spanish, however, tricked the Africans by sailing the vessel northward and westward by night in hopes that a passing vessel might rescue them.

For two months the vessel sailed aimlessly, running low on both food and water, until the crew of USS *Washington* took possession of it. The Navy took *Amistad* to nearby New London, Connecticut, where federal officials charged them with piracy and murder. Abolitionists stepped forward to defend the Africans, while the Spanish government pressured the U.S. government to restore them to the Cubans who claimed to own them. Their trial aroused great public interest and helped to rouse the abolitionist movement in America.

Abolitionists such as Lewis Tappan (1788–1863) paid for the legal defense of the enslaved Africans, arguing that they had been illegally brought to Cuba and therefore were free men and women who had been kidnapped and were acting in self-defense when they killed the captain and crew of the Spanish vessel. Eventually the case went before the Supreme Court, where former President John Quincy Adams (1767–1848) gave an eight-and-a-half-hour-long speech advocating for the freedom of the Africans. Ultimately the Supreme Court agreed with Adams and acquitted the Africans.

Below is an account from the *New London Gazette*, apparently based in

part on Lt. Meade's account of what he saw and partly on the editor's tour
of *Amistad* after its capture by the Navy.

"The suspicious looking schooner"
captured and brought into this port.

Much excitement has been created in New York for the past week,
from the report of several Pilot Boats having seen a clipper-built
schooner off the Hook, full of negroes, and in such condition as to
lead to the suspicion that she was a pirate. Several Cutters and naval
vessels are said to have been dispatched in pursuit of her, but she has
been most providentially captured in the Sound, by Capt. Gedney, of
the surveying Brig *Washington*. We will no longer detain the reader,
but subjoin the official account of the capture, very politely furnished
to us by one of the officers.

U. S. Brig *Washington*,
NEW LONDON, AUG. 26th, 1839.

While this vessel was sounding this day between Gardner's and
Montauk Points, a schooner was seen lying in shore off Culloden
Point, under circumstances so suspicious as to authorize Lt. Com.
Gedney to stand in to see what was her character—seeing a number of
people on the beach with carts and horses, and a boat passing to and
fro a boat was armed and dispatched with an officer to board her.

On coming along side a number of negroes were discovered on her
deck, and twenty or thirty more were on the beach—two white men
came forward and claimed the protection of the officer. The schooner proved to be the *"Amistad,"* Capt. Ramonflues, from the Havana
bound to Guanaja, Port Principe, with 54 blacks and two passengers
on board; the former, four nights after they were out, rose and murdered the captain and three of the crew; they then took possession of
the vessel with the intention of returning to the coast of Africa. Pedro
Montes, passenger, and Jose Rues owner of the slaves and part of the
cargo, were only saved to navigate the vessel.

After boxing about for four days in the Bahama Channel the vessel
was steered for the Island of St. Andrews, near New Providence; from
thence she went to Green Key, where the blacks laid in a supply of
water. After leaving this place the vessel was steered by Pedro Montes
for New Providence, the negroes being under the impression that she
was steering for the coast of Africa—they would not, however, permit
her to enter the port but anchored every night off the coast.

The situation of the two whites was all this time truly deplorable, being treated with the greatest severity, and Pedro Montes, who had charge of the navigation, was suffering from two severe wounds, one in the head and one in the arm, their lives threatened every instant. He was ordered to change the course again for the coast of Africa, the negroes themselves steering by the sun in the day time, while at night he would alter their course so as to bring them back to their original place of destination.—They remained three days off Long Island, to the Eastward of Providence, after which time they were two months on the ocean, sometimes steering to the Eastward, and whenever an occasion would permit the whites would alter the course to the Northward and Westward, always in hopes of falling in with some vessel of war, or being enabled to run into some port, when they would be relieved from their horrid situation. Several times they were boarded by vessels; once by an American schooner from Kingston. On these occasions the whites were ordered below, while the negroes communicated and traded with the vessel; the schooner from Kingston supplied them with a demijohn of water, for the moderate sum of one doubloon—this schooner, whose name was not ascertained, finding that the negroes had plenty of money, remained lashed alongside the *Amistad* for twenty-four hours, though they must have been aware that all was not right on board, and probably suspected the character of the vessel—that was on the 18th of the present month; the vessel was steered to the northward and westward, and on the 20th instant, distant from N.Y. 25 miles, the pilot boat *No. 3* came alongside and gave the negroes some apples. She was also hailed by *No. 4*; when the latter boat came near, the negroes armed themselves and would not permit her to board them; they were so exasperated with the two whites for bringing them so much out of their way that they expected every moment to be murdered.

On the 24th they made Montauk Light and steered for it in the hope of running the vessel ashore, but the tide drifted them up the bay and they anchored where they were found by the brig *Washington*, off Culloden point. The negroes were found in communication with shore, where they laid in a fresh supply of water, and were on the point of sailing again for the coast of Africa. They had a good supply of money with them, some of which it is likely was taken by the people on the beach.—After they were disarmed, and sent on board from the beach, the ringleader jumped overboard with three hundred doubloons about him, the property of the captain, all of which he succeeded in loosing from his person and then permitted himself to be captured. The schooner was taken in tow by the brig and carried into New London.

TUESDAY, 12 o'clock, M.[1]

We have just returned from a visit to the *Washington* and her prize, which are riding at anchor in the bay, near the fort. On board the former we saw and conversed with the two Spanish gentlemen who were passengers on board the schooner, as well as owners of the negroes and most of the cargo.

One of them, Jose Rues, is very gentlemanly and intelligent young man, and speaks English fluently. He was the owner of most of the slaves and cargo, which he was conveying to his estate on the Island of Cuba.

The other, Pedro Montes, is about fifty years of age, and is the owner of three slaves. He was formerly a ship-master, and has navigated the vessel since her seizure by the blacks. Both of them, as may be naturally supposed are most unfeignedly thankful for their deliverance. Signor Pedro is the most striking instance of complacency and unalloyed delight we ever have seen, and it is not strange, since only yesterday his sentence was pronounced by the chief of the buccaneers, and his death song chanted by the grim crew, who gathered with uplifted sabres around his devoted head, which, as well as his arms, bear the scars of several wounds inflicted at the time of the murder of the ill-fated captain and crew.

He sat smoking his Havana on the deck, and, to judge from the martyr-like serenity of his countenance, his emotions are such as rarely stir the heart of man. When Mr. Porter, the prize-master, assured him of his safety, he threw his arms around his neck, while gushing tears coursing down his furrowed cheek, bespoke the overflowing transport of his soul. Every now and then he clasps his hands, and with uplifted eyes gives thanks to "the Holy Virgin" who had led him out of all his troubles.

Senor Rues has given us two letters for his agents. Messrs. Shelton, Brothers & Co., of Boston, and Peter A. Harmony & Co., of New York. It appears that the slaves, the greater portion of whom were his, were very much attached to him, and had determined, after reaching the

---

1 M: Meridian, or noon.

coast of Africa, to allow him to seek his home what way he could, while his poor companion was to be sacrificed.

On board the brig we also saw Cingues,[1] the master-spirit and hero of this bloody tragedy, in irons. He is about five feet eight inches in height, 25 or 26 years of age, of erect figure, well built, and very active. He is said to be a match for any two men on board the schooner. His countenance, for a native African, is unusually intelligent, evincing uncommon decision and coolness, with a composure characteristic of true courage and nothing to mark him as a malicious man. He is a negro who would command, in New Orleans, under the hammer, at least $1,500.

He is said to have killed the captain and crew with his own hand, by cutting their throats. He also has several times attempted to take the life of Senor Montes, and the backs of several poor negroes are scored with the scars of blows inflicted by his lash to keep them in submission. He expects to be executed, but nevertheless manifests a sang froid[2] worthy of a Stone under similar circumstances.

With Capt. Gedney,[3] the surgeon of the port, and others, we visited the schooner, which is anchored within musket shot of the *Washington*, and there we saw such a sight as we never saw before, and never wish to see again. The bottom and sides of this vessel are covered with barnacles and sea-grass, while her rigging and sails present a scene worthy of the *Flying Dutchman*, after her fabled cruise. She is a Baltimore built vessel of matchless model for speed, about 120 tons burthen and about six years old.

On her deck were grouped, amid various goods and arms, the remnant of her Ethiop crew, some decked in the most fantastic manner in the silks and finery pilfered from the cargo while others, in a state of nudity, emaciated to mere skeletons, lay coiled upon the decks. Here could be seen a negro with white pantaloons and the sable shirt which nature gave him, and a planter's broad-brimmed hat upon his head, with a string of gewgaws around his neck; and another with a linen cambric shirt, whose bosom was worked by the hand of some dark-eyed daughter of Spain, while his nether proportions were enveloped in a shawl of gauze and Canton crape. Around the windlass

---

1 Cingues: today usually spelled *Cinqué*.
2 Sang froid: from the French; it literally means cold blood, but in this case means a cool or deliberate manner.
3 Gedney: Lieutenant Thomas R. Gedney, commander of the *Washington*.

were gathered the three little girls, from eight to thirteen years of age, the very images of health and gladness.

Over the deck were scattered, in the most wanton and disorderly profusion, raisins, vermicelli, bread, rice, silk, and cotton goods. In the cabin and hold were the marks of the same wasteful destruction.—Her cargo appears to consist of silks, crapes, calicoes, cotton and fancy goods of various descriptions, glass and hardware, bridles, saddles, holsters, pictures, looking-glasses, books, fruits, olives, and olive oil, and "other things too numerous to mention," which are now all mixed up in a strange and fantastic medley.

On the forward hatch we unconsciously rested our hand on a cold object, which we soon discovered to be a naked corpse enveloped in a pall of black bombazine. On removing its folds we beheld the rigid countenance and glazed eye of a poor negro who died last night. His mouth was unclosed, and still wore the ghastly expression of his last struggle. Near by him, like some watching fiend, sat the most horrible creature we ever saw in human shape, an object of terror to the very blacks, who said that he was a cannibal. His teeth projected at almost right angles from his mouth, while his eyes had a most savage and demoniac expression.

We were glad to leave this vessel, as the exhalations from her hold and deck were like anything but "gales wafted over the gardens of Gul."[1] Capt. Gedney has dispatched an express to the U.S. marshal, at New Haven, while he has made the most humane arrangements for the health and comfort of the prisoners, and the purification of the prize. There are now alive 44 negroes, three of whom are girls; about 10 have died. They have been at sea 63 days.

The vessel and cargo were worth $40,000 when they left Havana, exclusive of the negroes, which cost from 20 to $30,000. Vessel and cargo were insured in Havana. Capt. Gedney, when he first espied the *Amistad*, was running a line of sounding toward Montauk Point. He had heard nothing of this vessel being on the coast till after his arrival in this port.

Questions for Discussion:
1. What does this document reveal about race relations in America circa 1839?

---

1   gardens of Gul: a fabled sweet-smelling flower garden in the Middle East; the author is saying the *Amistad* stank.

2. What does this document reveal about conditions on board the *Amistad* before the crew of USS *Washington* captured it?

3. What assumptions do the observers in this article make about the Spanish and African persons they encountered on the deck of *Amistad*?

"'The suspicious looking schooner' captured and brought into this port," *New London Gazette*, August 26, 1839, in *A History of the Amistad Captives: Being a Circumstantial Account of the Capture of the Spanish Schooner Amistad* by John W. Barber (New Haven, Conn., E. L. & J. W. Barber, 1840), 3–5.

Daniel Drayton, "Escape on the *Pearl*" (1848)

Slaves seeking to escape bondage frequently chose to escape by boat or ship, or in the case of Frederick Douglass, simply by dressing as a sailor. Mariners who assisted escaping slaves risked more than jail time; if caught, they could be subjected to lynching.

In this instance, a coastal seaman named Daniel Drayton (1802–?) recounts his efforts to assist over seventy-five escaping slaves on the sloop *Pearl* and his subsequent capture, imprisonment, and near death at the hands of a mob. Unfortunately, there was not a happy ending to this story. Most of the slaves on the *Pearl* were sold to slave traders and transported to the Deep South to prevent further attempts at escape. Drayton and another man from the *Pearl* spent more than four years in the Washington, D.C., jail until President Millard Fillmore pardoned them in 1852.

My trading up and down the bay, in the way which I have described, of course brought me a good deal into contact with the slave population. No sooner, indeed, does a vessel, known to be from the north, anchor in any of these waters and the slaves are pretty adroit in ascertaining from what state a vessel comes than she is boarded, if she remains any length of time, and especially over night, by more or less of them, in hopes of obtaining a passage in her to a land of freedom.

During my earlier voyagings, several years before, in Chesapeake Bay, I had turned a deaf ear to all these requests. At that time, according to an idea still common enough, I had regarded the negroes as only fit to be slaves, and had not been inclined to pay much attention to the pitiful tales which they told me of ill-treatment by their masters and mistresses.

But my views upon this subject had undergone a gradual change. I knew it was asserted in the Declaration of Independence that all men

are born free and equal, and I had read in the Bible that God had made
of one flesh all the nations of the earth. I had found out, by intercourse
with the negroes, that they had the same desires, wishes and hopes,
as myself. I knew very well that I should not like to be a slave even to
the best of masters, and still less to such sort of masters as the greater
part of the slaves seemed to have. The idea of having first one child
and then another taken from me, as fast as they grew large enough,
and handed over to the slave-traders, to be carried I knew not where,
and sold, if they were girls, I knew not for what purposes, would have
been horrible enough; and, from instances which came to my notice,
I perceived that it was not less horrible and distressing to the parties
concerned in the case of black people than of white ones. I had never
read any abolition books, nor heard any abolition lectures. I had fre-
quented only Methodist meetings, and nothing was heard there about
slavery. But, for the life of me, I could not perceive why the golden
rule of doing to others as you would wish them to do to you did not
apply to this case. Had I been a slave myself, and it is not a great while
since the Algerines used to make slaves of our sailors, white as well
as black, I should have thought it very right and proper in anybody
who would have ventured to assist me in escaping out of bondage; and
the more dangerous it might have been to render such assistance, the
more meritorious I should have thought the act to be. Why had not
these black people, so anxious to escape from their masters, as good
a right to their liberty as I had to mine?

I know it is sometimes said, by those who defend slavery or apolo-
gize for it, that the slaves at the south are very happy and contented, if
left to themselves, and that this idea of running away is only put into
their heads by mischievous white people from the north. This will do
very well for those who know nothing of the matter personally, and
who are anxious to listen to any excuse. But there is not a waterman
who ever sailed in Chesapeake Bay who will not tell you that, so far
from the slaves needing any prompting to run away, the difficulty is,
when they ask you to assist them, to make them take no for an answer.
I have known instances where men have lain in the woods for a year
or two, waiting for an opportunity to escape on board some vessel. On
one of my voyages up the Potomac, an application was made to me on
behalf of such a runaway; and I was so much moved by his story, that,
had it been practicable for me at that time, I should certainly have
helped him off. One or two attempts I did make to assist the flight

of some of those who sought my assistance; but none with success, till the summer of 1847, which is the period to which I have brought down my narrative.

I was employed during that summer, as I have mentioned already in trading up and down the Chesapeake, in a hired boat, a small black boy being my only assistant. Among other trips, I went to Washington with a cargo of oysters. While I was lying there, at the same wharf, as it happened, from which the *Pearl* afterwards took her departure, a colored man came on board, and, observing that I seemed to be from the north, he said he supposed we were pretty much all abolitionists there. I don't know where he got this piece of information, but I think it likely from some southern member of Congress. As I did not check him, but rather encouraged him to go on, he finally told me that he wanted to get passage to the north for a woman and five children. The husband of the woman, and father of the children, was a free colored man; and the woman, under an agreement with her master, had already more than paid for her liberty; but, when she had asked him for a settlement, he had only answered by threatening to sell her. He begged me to see the woman, which I did; and finally I made an arrangement to take them away. Their bedding, and other things, were sent down on board the vessel in open days and at night the woman came on board with her five children and a niece. We were ten days in reaching Frenchtown, where the husband was in waiting for them. He took them under his charge, and I saw them no more; but, since my release from imprisonment in Washington, I have heard that the whole family are comfortably established in a free country, and doing well.

Having accomplished this exploit, and was it not something of an exploit to bestow the invaluable gift of liberty upon seven of one's fellow-creatures. The season being now far advanced, I gave up the boat to the owner, and returned to my family at Philadelphia. In the course of the following month of February, I received a note from a person whom I had never known or heard of before, desiring me to call at a certain place named in it. I did so, when it appeared that I had been heard of through the colored family which I had brought off from Washington. A letter from that city was read to me, relating the case of a family or two who expected daily and hourly to be sold, and desiring assistance to get them away. It was proposed to me to undertake this enterprise; but I declined it at this time, as I had no vessel, and because the season was too early for navigation through the canal. I saw the same person again about a fortnight later, and finally arranged to go on to Washington, to see what could be done. There I agreed to return again so soon as I could find a vessel fit for the enterprise. I spoke with several persons of my acquaintance, who had vessels under their control; but they declined, on account of the danger. They did not appear to have any other objection, and seemed to wish me success. Passing along the street, I met Captain Sayres, and knowing that he was sailing a small bay-craft, called the *Pearl*, and learning from him that business was dull with him, I proposed the enterprise to him, offering him one hundred dollars for the charter of his vessel to Washington and back to Frenchtown, where, according to the arrangement with the friends of the passengers, they were to be met and carried to Philadelphia.

This was considerably more than the vessel could earn in any ordinary trip of the like duration, and Sayres closed with the offer. He fully understood the nature of the enterprise. By our bargain, I was to have, as supercargo, the control of the vessel so far as related to her freight, and was to bring away from Washington such passengers as I chose to receive on board; but the control of the vessel in other respects remained with him. Captain Sayres engaged in this enterprise merely as a matter of business. I, too, was to be paid for my time and trouble, an offer which the low state of my pecuniary affairs, and the necessity of supporting my family, did not allow me to decline. But this was not, by any means, my sole or principal motive. I undertook it out of sympathy for the enslaved, and from my desire to do something to further the cause of universal liberty. Such being the different ground upon which Sayres and myself stood, I did not think it necessary or expedient to communicate to him the names of the persons with whom the expedition had originated; and, at my suggestion, those persons abstained from any direct communication with him, either at Philadelphia or Washington.

Sayres had, as cook and sailor, on board the *Pearl*, a young man named Chester English. He was married, and had a child or two, but was himself as inexperienced as a child, having never been more than thirty miles from the place where he was born. I remonstrated with Sayres against taking this young man with us. But English, pleased with the idea of seeing Washington, desired to go; and Sayres, who had engaged him for the season, did not like to part with him. He went with us, but was kept in total ignorance of the real object of the voyage. He had the idea that we were going to Washington for a load of ship-timber.

We proceeded down the Delaware, and by the canal into the Chesapeake, making for the mouth of the Potomac. As we ascended that river we stopped at a place called Machudock, where I purchased, by way of cargo and cover to the voyage, twenty cords of wood; and with that freight on board we proceeded to Washington, where we arrived on the evening of Thursday, the 13th of April, 1848. . . .

It was arranged that the passengers should come on board after dark on Saturday evening, and that we should sail about midnight. I had understood that the expedition had principally originated in the desire to help off a certain family, consisting of a woman, nine children and two grand-children, who were believed to be legally entitled to their liberty. Their case had been in litigation for some time; but, although they had a very good case, the lawyer whom they employed (Mr. Bradley, one of the most distinguished members of the bar of the district) testified, in the course of one of my trials, that he believed them to be legally free, yet, as their money was nearly exhausted, and as there seemed to be no end to the law's delay and the pertinacity of the woman who claimed them, it was deemed best by their friends that they should get away if they could, lest she might seize them unawares, and sell them to some trader. In speaking of this case, the person with whom I communicated at Washington informed me that there were also quite a number of others who wished to avail themselves of this opportunity of escaping, and that the number of passengers was likely to be larger than had at first been calculated upon. To which I replied, that I did not stand about the number; that all who were on board before eleven o'clock I should take: the others would have to remain behind.

Saturday evening, at supper, I let English a little into the secret of what I intended. I told him that the sort of ship-timber we were going to take would prove very easy to load and unload; that a number of colored people wished to take passage with us down the bay, and that, as Sayres and myself would be away the greater part of the evening, all he had to do was, as fast as they came on board, to lift up the hatch and let them pass into the hold, shutting the hatch down upon them. The vessel, which we had moved down the river since unloading the wood, lay at a rather lonely place, called White-house Wharf, from a whitish-colored building which stood upon it. The high bank of the river, under which a road passed, afforded a cover to the wharf, and there were only a few scattered buildings in the vicinity. Towards the town there stretched a wide extent of open fields. Anxious, as might naturally be expected, as to the result, I kept in the vicinity to watch the progress of events. There was another small vessel that lay across the head of the same wharf, but her crew were all black; and, going on board her just at dusk, I informed the skipper of my business, intimating to him, at the same time, that it would be a dangerous thing for him to betray me. He assured me that I need have no fears of him that the other men would soon leave the vessel, not to return again till Monday, and that, for himself, he should go below and to sleep, so as neither to hear nor to see anything.

Shortly after dark the expected passengers began to arrive, coming stealthily across the fields, and gliding silently on board the vessel. I observed a man near a neighboring brick-kiln, who seemed to be watching them. I went towards him, and found him to be black. He told me that he understood what was going on, but that I need have no apprehension of him. Two white men, who walked along the road past the vessel, and who presently returned back the same way, occasioned me some alarm; but they seemed to have no suspicions of what was on foot, as I saw no more of them. I went on board the vessel several times in the course of the evening, and learned from English that the hold was fast filling up. I had promised him, in consideration of the unusual nature of the business we were engaged in, ten dollars as a gratuity, in addition to his wages.

Something past ten o'clock, I went on board, and directed English to cast off the fastenings and to get ready to make sail. Pretty soon Sayres came on board. It was a dead calm, and we were obliged to get the boat out to get the vessel's head round. After dropping down a half a mile or so, we encountered the tide making up the river; and, as there was still no wind, we were obliged to anchor. Here we lay in a dead calm till about daylight. The wind then began to breeze up lightly from the northward, when we got up the anchor and made sail. As the sun rose, we passed Alexandria. I then went into the hold for the first time, and there found my passengers pretty thickly stowed. I distributed bread among them, and knocked down the bulkhead between the hold and the cabin, in order that they might get into the cabin to cook. They consisted of men and women, in pretty equal proportions, with a number of boys and girls, and two small children. The wind kept increasing and hauling to the westward. Off Fort Washington we had to make two stretches, but the rest of the way we run before the wind.

Shortly after dinner, we passed the steamer from Baltimore for Washington, bound up. I thought the passengers on board took particular notice of us; but the number of vessels met with in a passage up the Potomac at that season is so few, as to make one, at least for the idle passengers of a steamboat, an object of some curiosity. Just before sunset, we passed a schooner loaded with plaster, bound up. As we approached the mouth of the Potomac, the wind hauled to the north, and blew with such stiffness as would make it impossible for us to go up the bay, according to our original plan. Under these circumstances, apprehending a pursuit from Washington, I urged Sayres to go to sea, with the intention of reaching the Delaware by the outside passage. But he objected that the vessel was not fit to go outside (which was true enough), and that the bargain was to go to Frenchtown. Having reached Point Lookout, at the mouth of the river, and not being able to persuade Sayres to go to sea, and the wind being dead in our teeth, and too strong to allow any attempt to ascend the bay, we came to anchor in Cornfield harbor, just under Point Lookout, a shelter usually sought by baycraft encountering contrary winds when in that neighborhood.

We were all sleepy with being up all the night before, and, soon after dropping anchor, we all turned in. I knew nothing more till, waking suddenly, I heard the noise of a steamer blowing off steam alongside of us. I knew at once that we were taken. The black men came to the cabin, and asked if they should fight. I told them no; we had no arms, nor was there the least possibility of a successful resistance. The loud shouts and trampling of many feet overhead proved that our assailants were numerous. One of them lifted the hatch a little, and cried out, "Niggers, by God!" an exclamation to which the others responded with three cheers, and by banging the butts of their muskets against the deck. A lantern was called for, to read the name of the vessel; and it being ascertained to be the *Pearl*, a number of men came to the cabin-door, and called for Captain Drayton. I was in no great hurry to stir; but at length rose from my berth, saying that I considered myself their prisoner, and that I expected to be treated as such. While I was dressing, rather too slowly for the impatience of those outside, a sentinel, who had been stationed at the cabin-door, followed every motion of mine with his gun, which he kept pointed at me, in great apprehension, apparently, lest I should suddenly seize some dangerous weapon and make at him. As I came out of the cabin-door, two of them seized me, took me on board the steamer and tied me; and they did the same with Sayres and English, who were brought on board, one after the other. The black people were left on board the *Pearl*, which the steamer took in tow, and then proceeded up the river.

To explain this sudden change in our situation, it is necessary to go back to Washington. Great was the consternation in several families of that city, on Sunday morning, to find no breakfast, and, what was worse, their servants missing. Nor was this disaster confined to Washington only. Georgetown came in for a considerable share of it, and even Alexandria, on the opposite side of the river, had not entirely escaped. The persons who had taken passage on board the *Pearl* had been held in bondage by no less than forty-one different persons. Great was the wonder at the sudden and simultaneous disappearance of so many "prime hands," roughly estimated, though probably with considerable exaggeration, as worth in the market not less than a hundred thousand dollars, and all at "one fell swoop" too, as the District Attorney afterwards, in arguing the case against me, pathetically expressed it! There were a great many guesses and conjectures as to where these people had gone, and how they had gone; but it is very doubtful whether the losers would have got upon the right track, had it not been for the treachery of a colored hackman, who had been employed to carry down to the vessel two passengers who had been in hiding for some weeks previous, and who could not safely walk down, lest they might be met and recognized. Emulating the example of that large, and, in their own opinion at least, highly moral, religious and respectable class of white people, known as "dough-faces," this hackman thought it a fine opportunity to feather his nest by playing cat's-paw to the slave-holders. Seeing how much the information was in demand, and anticipating, no doubt, a large reward, he turned informer, and described the *Pearl* as the conveyance which the fugitives had taken; and, it being ascertained that the *Pearl* had actually sailed between Saturday night and Sunday morning, preparations were soon made to pursue her.

A Mr. Dodge, of Georgetown, a wealthy old gentleman, originally from New England, missed three or four slaves from his family, and a small steamboat, of which he was the proprietor, was readily obtained. Thirty-five men, including a son or two of old Dodge, and several of those whose slaves were missing, volunteered to man her; and they set out about Sunday noon, armed to the teeth with guns, pistols, bowie-knives, &c., and well provided with brandy and other liquors. They heard of us on the passage down, from the Baltimore steamer and the vessel loaded with plaster. They reached the mouth of the river, and, not having found the *Pearl*, were about to return, as the steamer could not proceed into the bay without forfeiting her insurance. As a last chance, they looked into Cornfield harbor, where they found us, as I have related. This was about two o'clock in the morning. The *Pearl* had come to anchor about nine o'clock the previous evening. It is a hundred and forty miles from Washington to Cornfield harbor.

The steamer, with the *Pearl* in tow, crossed over from Point Look-out to Piney Point, on the south shore of the Potomac, and here the *Pearl* was left at anchor, a part of the steamer's company remaining to guard her, while the steamer, having myself and the other white prisoners on board, proceeded up Coan river for a supply of wood,[1] having obtained which, she again, about noon of Monday, took the *Pearl* in tow and started for Washington.

The bearing, manner and aspect of the thirty-five armed persons by whom we had been thus seized and bound, without the slightest shadow of lawful authority, was sufficient to inspire a good deal of alarm. We had been lying quietly at anchor in a harbor of Maryland; and, although the owners of the slaves might have had a legal right to pursue and take them back, what warrant or authority had they for seizing us and our vessel? They could have brought none from the District of Columbia, whose officers had no jurisdiction or authority in Cornfield harbor; nor did they pretend to have any from the State of Maryland. Some of them showed a good deal of excitement, and evinced a disposition to proceed to lynch us at once. A man named Houver, who claimed as his property two of the boys passengers on board the *Pearl*, put me some questions in a very insolent tone; to which I replied, that I considered myself a prisoner, and did not wish to answer any questions; whereupon one of the bystanders, flourishing a dirk in my face, exclaimed, "If I was in his place, I'd put this through you!" At Piney Point, one of the company proposed to hang

---

1   Wood: the steamer needed to be refueled with wood.

me up to the yard-arm, and make me confess; but the more influential of those on board were not ready for any such violence, though all were exceedingly anxious to get out of me the history of the expedition, and who my employers were. That I had employers, and persons of note too, was taken for granted on all hands; nor did I think it worth my while to contradict it, though I declined steadily to give any information on that point. Sayres and English very readily told all that they knew. English, especially, was in a great state of alarm, and cried most bitterly. I pitied him much, besides feeling some compunctions at getting him thus into difficulty; and, upon the representations which I made, that he came to Washington in perfect ignorance of the object of the expedition, he was finally untied. As Sayres was obliged to admit that he came to Washington to take away colored passengers, he was not regarded with so much favor. But it was evidently me whom they looked upon as the chief culprit, alone possessing a knowledge of the history and origin of the expedition, which they were so anxious to unravel. They accordingly went to work very artfully to worm this secret out of me.

I was placed in charge of one Orme, a police-officer of Georgetown, whose manner towards me was such as to inspire me with a certain confidence in him; who, as it afterwards appeared from his testimony on the trial, carefully took minutes but, as it proved, very confused and incorrect ones—of all that I said, hoping thus to secure something that might turn out to my disadvantage. Another person, with whom I had a good deal of conversation, and who was afterwards produced as a witness against me, was William H. Craig, in my opinion a much more conscientious person than Orme, who seemed to think that it was part of his duty, as a police-officer, to testify to something, at all hazards, to help on a conviction. But this is a subject to which I shall have occasion to return presently.

In one particular, at least, the testimony of both these witnesses was correct enough. They both testified to my expressing pretty serious apprehensions of what the result to myself was likely to be. What the particular provisions were, in the District of Columbia, as to helping slaves to escape, I did not know; but I had heard that, in some of the slave-states, they were very severe; in fact, I was assured by Craig that I had committed the highest crime, next to murder, known in their laws. Under these circumstances, I made up my mind that the least penalty I should be apt to escape with was confinement in the penitentiary for life; and it is quite probable that I endeavored to console myself, as these witnesses testified, with the idea that, after all, it might, in a religious point of view, be all for the best, as I should thus be removed from temptation, and have ample time for reflection and repentance. But my apprehensions were by no means limited to what I might suffer under the forms of law. From the temper exhibited by some of my captors, and from the vindictive fury with which the idea of enabling the enslaved to regain their liberty was, I knew, generally regarded at the south, I apprehended more sudden and summary proceedings; and what happened afterwards at Washington proved that these apprehensions were not wholly unfounded. The idea of being torn in pieces by a furious mob was exceedingly disagreeable. Many men, who might not fear death, might yet not choose to meet it in that shape. I called to mind the apology of the Methodist minister, who, just after a declaration of his that he was not afraid to die, ran away from a furious bull that attacked him "that, though not fearing death, he did not like to be torn in pieces by a mad bull." I related this anecdote to Craig, and, as he testified on the trial, expressed my preference to be taken on the deck of the steamer and shot at once, rather than to be given up to a Washington mob to be baited and murdered. I talked pretty freely with Orme and Craig about myself, the circumstances under which I had undertaken this enterprise, my motives to it, my family, my past misfortunes, and the fate that probably awaited me; but they failed to extract from me, what they seemed chiefly to desire, any information which would implicate others. Orme told me, as he afterwards testified, that what the people in the District wanted was the principals; and that, if I would give information that would lead to them, the owners of the slaves would let me go, or sign a petition for my pardon. Craig also made various inquiries tending to the same point. Though I was firmly resolved not to yield in this particular, yet I was desirous to do all I could to soften the feeling against me; and it was doubtless this desire which led me to make the statements sworn to by Orme and Craig, that I had no connection with the persons called abolitionists, which was true enough; that I had formerly refused large offers made me by slaves to carry them away; and that, in the present instance, I was employed by others, and was to be paid for my services.

On arriving off Fort Washington, the steamer anchored for the night, as the captors preferred to make their triumphant entry into the city by daylight. Sayres and myself were watched during the night by a regular guard of two men, armed with muskets, who were relieved from time to time. Before getting under weigh again, which they did about seven o'clock in the morning of Tuesday, Feb. 18, Sayres and myself were tied together arm-and-arm, and the black people also, two-and-two, with the other arm bound behind their backs. As we passed Alexandria, we were all ordered on deck, and exhibited to the mob collected on the wharves to get a sight of us, who signified their satisfaction by three cheers. When we landed at the steamboat-wharf in Washington, which is a mile and more from Pennsylvania Avenue, and in a remote part of the city, but few people had yet assembled. We were marched up in a long procession, Sayres and myself being placed at the head of it, guarded by a man on each side; English following next, and then the negroes. As we went along the mob began to increase; and, as we passed Gannon's slave-pen, that slave-trader, armed with a knife, rushed out, and, with horrid imprecations, made a pass at me, which was very near finding its way through my body. Instead of being arrested, as he ought to have been, this slave-dealer was politely informed that I was in the hands of the law, to which he replied, "Damn the law! I have three negroes, and I will give them all for one thrust at this damned scoundrel!" and he followed along, waiting his opportunity to repeat the blow. The crowd, by this time, was greatly increased. We met an immense mob of several thousand persons coming down Four-and-a-half street, with the avowed intention of carrying us up before the capitol, and making an exhibition of us there. The noise and confusion was very great. It seemed as if the time for the lynching had come. When almost up to Pennsylvania Avenue, a rush was made upon us, "Lynch them! Lynch them! The damn villains!" and other such cries, resounded on all sides. Those who had us in charge were greatly alarmed; and, seeing no other way to keep us from the hands of the mob, they procured a hack, and put Sayres and myself into it. The hack drove to the jail, the mob continuing to follow, repeating their shouts and threats. Several thousand people surrounded the jail, filling up the enclosure about it.

Questions for Discussion:

1. What does this document reveal about the attitudes of slaveholders toward abolitionists?

2. What motives did Drayton have for trying to help slaves escape to freedom?

3. What advantages and disadvantages did an attempt to escape by boat offer southern slaves?

Daniel B. Drayton, *Personal Memoir of Daniel Drayton, for Four Years and Four Months a Prisoner (for Charity's Sake) in Washington Jail* (Boston, Bela Marsh, 1854), 20–40.

C.R.P. Rodgers, "A Suspected Slaver" (1853)

The United States banned the importation of slaves in 1807, but despite the law slavers continued to import African slaves. The consequences for engaging in the slave trade were serious: in 1819 Congress deemed slave trading piracy, and therefore it was punishable by death.

The U.S. Navy patrolled the African coast from 1820 to the start of the Civil War despite southern opposition. As recounted in naval historian Donald Canney's *Africa Squadron*,[1] patrolling African waters was unpopular duty in the Navy, and the effort was never very successful. Canney lays the blame not on the ships and personnel of the Navy, but on the various secretaries of the Navy who took little interest in antislavery patrols.

In fact, slavers proved adept at manipulating the legal system in their favor or eluding antislavery patrols altogether. In November 1853, the commander of the African Squadron found that "the Slave trade is reviving on this Southern Coast, and that the American flag is extensively used in its prosecution. Several cargoes of Slaves have been recently carried off in American Vessels." What follows is the report of Lieutenant C.R.P. Rodgers, who led the boarding party from USS *Constitution* that seized the American-flagged schooner *H. N. Gambrill* on suspicion of engaging in the slave trade, a rare success in the struggle to stop the slave trade.

Excerpt of Memoranda from Lieutenant C.R.P. Rogers, USS *Constitution*, detailing the seizure of the slave trader *H.N. Gambrill* on 3 November 1853.

US Ship *Constitution*

At Sea 3rd November, 1853

1   Donald L. Canney, *Africa Squadron: The U.S. Navy and the Slave Trade, 1842–1861* (Washington, D.C.: Potomac Books, 2006).

Memoranda relating to the seizure of
the American Schooner *H. N. Gambrill*

On boarding the American Schooner *H. N. Gambrill*, this morning, I found her papers apparently formal and correct, but I could find no list of her cargo, the Captain informing me that he had sent it to Ambriz. I then proceeded to examine the vessel and on going to the caboose house found it closed. The cook objected to my entering it, but on speaking to the Captain, he made no further objection and the door was opened. On taking away a tarpaulin, I found a very large copper boiler, recently set in brick work such a copper as would be required to cook the food for slaves.

On opening the hatches I found a deck of loose hemlock boards laid smoothly and carefully upon the tiers of casks, which upon examination were found to contain provisions and several thousand gallons of water. The fore-peak, usually occupied by the crew, had no bulkhead to separate it from the hold, but the crew's quarters were next to the cabin.

I found three persons on board whose names were not on the crew list, and the Captain informed me that they were persons he had found at Kabenda, to whom he had given a passage to Ambriz. Two of them told me that they had arrived at Kabenda a short time since, in the Amn. Schr. *Sarah Hope*, from New York, and were on their way to Loando. The other was a cabin passenger, and apparently a man of education. I had more than one conversation with him, in the course of which he told me that he was a native of Spain that a few months since he had been captured in a Portuguese vessel called the *San Domingo*, by an English cruiser, and had been sent on shore by her commander at Kabenda. He at first said that he was supercargo of the *San Domingo*, but some hours afterwards spoke of himself as a passenger. He said that being tired of the coast of Africa, he had asked the captain of the *H. N. Gambrill* to take him away from it, and that he had kindly permitted him to work his passage, and as he had been an officer took him into the cabin. He said he had paid no passage money in consequence of his poverty, but I afterwards found in his trunk a hundred dollars or more, chiefly in American gold; besides an ample stock of clothes and many articles proving him to be a man with a free command of money to purchase the superfluities of life.

He told me he had long commanded a vessel in the trade between Spain and Havana, and a steamer on the coast of Cuba. He said that

he had been about two months at Kabenda. On examining his papers I found his passport to go from Cuba to the United States in
June, his hotel bills in New York for the months of July and August
and a receipt four nautical instruments bought in New York at that
time. I also found letters directed to Rio Janerio, and a commission
for some masonic degree in the lodge of the place. The letters being
from his wife, were returned to him without examination. The captain and Mate stated that had landed a hundred barrels of provisions
at Kabenda, and showed the entries in the logbook to prove it. The
Captain asserted that he had delivered this portion of his cargo to one
Don Guillermo, a white man at Kabenda, who had shown him a letter
from the owner of the vessel, authorizing him to demand it but he said
that he had taken no receipt whatever for it although he admitted that
this Don Guillermo was personally unknown to him.

Upon privately examining the cook and the steward, they most
positively asserted that no provisions in any quantity and no cargo
had been landed at Kabenda. The cook at last told me the whole story
of the voyage, as far as he knew it, in substance as follows. He had
shipped to go in the schooner on an honest trading voyage to the coast
of Africa, but after going on board he was somewhat surprised to find
that she was detained six days, and that the crew were not allowed to
communicate with the shore. At length the Captain made his appearance accompanied by the Spanish passenger, and they went to sea. On
the passage the cargo excited his suspicion, and he asked the steward
what he thought of the strange quantity of water on board &c. At last
the Steward talked with the Captain about it, and the Captain admitted that he was going for slaves.

On their arrival at Kabenda the two passengers came on board who
said that they had come out in the *Sarah Hope*, and after remaining
there two days, they sailed for the River Congo. In the meantime they
had discovered that the water casks which had formerly been used
to contain brandy, had soured and injured the water, and as soon as
they got into the fresh water of the Congo, the casks were emptied,
and all hands busily employed in filling them with sweet water. While
doing this the Captain urged cook to assist, offering to pay him for
extra work, and the Spanish passenger also offered to pay him after
they got the slaves on board. While in the Congo a boat came off
and communicated in Spanish with the Captain and Spanish passenger and received a present of a ham and some other provisions. They

sailed from the Congo on the evening of the 1st, and yesterday they knocked down the bulkhead which separated the forecastle from the hold, broke up a part of the mens chests, threw overboard their old clothes, empty barrels, &c, in order to make room, and laid the slave deck, ready for the reception of the Negroes. The crew moved their quarters from forward, aft. They then got up a big box, took from it the copper for cooking, and set it in brickwork in the caboose house.

All doubt was then removed as to the object of the voyage.

When the *Constitution* was discovered from the masthead this morning, the Captain examined her with his glass, and declared that she was the brig he had seen in the Congo. When he found out that it was a frigate it was too late to run away. This is the story of the cook. The Steward admitted the refilling of the casks in the Congo, and that the copper had been put up within a couple of days, and that the slave deck had been carefully put its place, but he was evidently unwilling to tell all he knew. I found in the chest of the Spanish passenger a Quadrant or sextant and three charts of Cuba and the Bahama islands.[1] Two of the Kromen[2] on board the *Constitution*, declare that they know him well, and were employed by him within two years, at the Gallinas, on the north coast, and that they worked for some time on board a slaver which he commanded, and saw the slaves taken on board.

The Captain or some of his men also told me that while in the Congo they had seen a merchant Brig painted green. This was the English Brig *Coquette* of Liverpool which I boarded on the evening of the 1st. Her master told me that he had seen a very suspicious looking schooner, of American model, in the Congo, that afternoon. He was convinced that she was a slaver.

The captain of the *H. N. Gambrill* stated that the provisions found on board were consigned to a Mr. Walker, a merchant at Ambriz to whom he had sent the invoice by a launch, but the barrels showed no mark indicating any such consignment, nor had the captain any paper or letter of instructions to prove his assertion.

Every thing I saw and heard stamped her unequivocally as a slaver, on the very eve of receiving her cargo.

---

1   Cuba and the Bahama islands: typical places from which slaveships made entry into American waters.

2   Kromen: Krumen were Africans who lived near the coast. Many of them cooperated with slave traders in return for pay or trade goods.

The *H. N. Gambrill* was towed to sea on the 20th August by the steamer *Active*. It may be possible to prove that the Spanish passenger was on board by the testimony of the Captain of the steamer and by the Pilot. The logbook records that the 25th Oct. the Schooner arriver at Kabenda, that on the 26th she discharged 50 barrels of bread and 10 of beef, and on the 27th forty barrels of beef. The cook and the steward most explicitly declare that no cargo was discharged, nor could it have been discharged without their knowledge. The logbook also makes the following record in the remarks for October 29th, "at 4 p.m. one cabin passenger and two seamen, passengers came on board." The schooner sailed on the 29th. There is no mention of her filling up her water casks in the Congo, although it must have been a work of great labor. The only cabin passenger on board when I boarded her was Juan Baptista Arbaza, who came out in her from New York, and there is no doubt in my mind that the entry in the log book recording his coming on board at Kabenda, and that of the discharge of a hundred barrels of provisions, are both false entries.

Questions for Discussion:
1. What evidence did Lt. Rodgers find on board the *H. N. Gambrill* that made him suspicious?
2. How did the slavers try to fool Lt. Rodgers as to their true intentions?
3. What does this account reveal about how the slave trade operated?

National Archives and Records Administration, Record Group 45: "African Squadron Letters Received by the Secretary of the Navy from the Commanding Officers of Squadrons," 1853, no. 36.

CIVIL WAR

The Civil War's naval battles are less well-known than those on land, but the naval component was nonetheless vital to the war, with both sides seeking to disrupt the waterborne economy of the other. It was a conflict that saw action in the high latitudes of the Pacific, the English Channel, the Bahamas, the coastal waters of the United States from Texas to Maine, and on the nation's rivers, especially the Mississippi. Most famous of all was the battle of Hampton Roads, the first duel between armored steam vessels, the *Monitor* and the *Merrimack*. There were two enduring legacies of the Civil

War in maritime terms: the first was the advent of armored warships known as ironclads; the second was the decline of the U.S.-flagged merchant marine. Both can be traced to the Confederacy's attempt to deal with the vastly superior Union Navy.

The U.S. Navy's primary role throughout the war was to enforce the "Anaconda plan" by blockading the southern coastline and seizing control of the Mississippi, thereby denying external supplies to the Confederate military and dividing the western rebel states from the eastern. The Confederacy, which started with no navy of its own, was aware of the blockade plan and moved to nullify its effect by building armored warships that could easily overcome the wooden Union warships and defend the western rivers. The North countered with its own ironclad program, producing the revolutionary USS *Monitor*, which featured a rotating gun turret. Northern ironclads quashed the Confederate attempts to break the stranglehold the blockade had on the southern economy.

Faced with a continued blockade, southern leaders embarked on two efforts to reduce its impact. The first was to utilize swift blockade runners that carried supplies from Europe through the blockade at night or in reduced visibility. Many of these blockade runners based themselves in the Bahamas, then a British possession that lay within a hundred miles of the southern coastline. The other was to purchase swift, lightly armed ships in Britain and use them to hunt down and destroy the Union's large merchant fleet in an effort to distract the U.S. Navy from its blockade duties. Blockade runners did indeed ensure that a steady trickle of military supplies reached the South, and the commerce raiders heavily damaged the American merchant marine, but neither were sufficient to disrupt the Anaconda plan, which ultimately succeeded in crushing the Confederate economy.

Franklin Buchanan, "Battle of Hampton Roads" (1862)

The Battle of Hampton Roads, sometimes known as the duel between the *Monitor* and the *Merrimack*, occurred on March 8 and 9, 1862, in an open anchorage off Norfolk, Virginia, known as Hampton Roads. It was the first battle between self-propelled armored vessels. The Confederate vessel was CSS *Virginia*, formerly the USS *Merrimack* until its capture and partial destruction. Confederate engineers remade what had been a traditional wooden warship into an armored ship boasting ten cannon arranged in the traditional broadside and a lethal ram projecting from its bow. Its purpose was to raise the blockade the Union fleet had imposed on the southern coastline. On its first day in action, it and its attendant vessels either destroyed or sank three powerful Union wooden warships, and CSS *Virginia* returned to its base to repair the minor damage it had received.

The next day was not to be so easy, for the Union's first ironclad, the little USS *Monitor*, arrived on the scene. Unlike *Virginia*, the *Monitor* was made completely of iron and had but two cannon, but these were extremely powerful and positioned in an armored revolving turret. The two vessels fought all day March 9, but neither gained an advantage, and the battle was proclaimed a draw. However, the Union blockade remained in place, giving the North the strategic advantage. Readers wanting to understand the technological implications of ironclads may want to read William H. Roberts's *Civil War Ironclads*,[1] a study of how the U.S. Navy coped with the enormous engineering challenges of a largely experimental technology.

Below is a report by the *Virginia*'s captain, Captain Franklin Buchanan (1800–1874), CSN, who was wounded during the battle.

NAVAL HOSPITAL,

Norfolk, March 27, 1862.

SIR:

Having been confined to my bed in this building since the 9th instant, in consequence of a wound received in the action of the previous day, I have not had it in my power at an earlier date to prepare the official report, which I now have the honor to submit, of the proceedings on the 8th and 9th instant, of the James River Squadron under my command, composed of the following-named vessels: Steamer *Virginia*, flagship, 10 guns; steamer *Patrick Henry*, 12 guns, Commander John R. Tucker; steamer *Jamestown*, Lieutenant Commanding J. N. Barney, 2 guns; and gunboats *Teaser*, Lieutenant Commanding W. A. Webb, *Beaufort*, Lieutenant Commanding W. H. Parker, and *Raleigh*, Lieutenant Commanding J. W. Alexander, each 1 gun; total, 27 guns.

On the 8th instant, at 11 a.m., the *Virginia* left navy yard, Norfolk, accompanied by the *Raleigh* and *Beaufort*, and proceeded to Newport News to engage the enemy's frigates *Cumberland* and *Congress*, gunboats, and shore batteries. When within less than a mile of the *Cumberland*, the *Virginia* commenced the engagement with that ship with her bow gun, and the action soon became general, the *Cumberland*, *Congress*, gunboats, and shore batteries concentrating upon us

---

1   William H. Roberts, *Civil War Ironclads: The U.S. Navy and Industrial Mobilization* (Baltimore: Johns Hopkins University Press, 2002).

their heavy fire, which was returned with great spirit and determination. The *Virginia* stood rapidly on toward the *Cumberland*, which ship I had determined to sink with our prow, if possible. In about fifteen minutes after the action commenced we ran into her on starboard bow; the crash below the water was distinctly heard, and she commenced sinking, gallantly fighting her guns as long as they were above water. She went down with her colors flying. During this time the shore batteries, *Congress*, and gunboats kept up their heavy concentrated fire upon us, doing us some injury. Our guns, however, were not idle; their fire was very destructive to the shore batteries and vessels, and we were gallantly sustained by the rest of the squadron.

Just after the *Cumberland* sunk, that gallant officer, Commander John R. Tucker, was seen standing down James River under full steam, accompanied by the *Jamestown* and *Teaser*. They all came nobly into action, and were soon exposed to the heavy fire of shore batteries. Their escape was miraculous, as they were under a galling fire of solid shot, shell, grape, and canister, a number of which passed through the vessels without doing any serious injury, except to the *Patrick Henry*, through whose boiler a shot passed, scalding to death four persons and wounding others. Lieutenant Commanding Barney promptly obeyed a signal to tow her out of the action. As soon as damages were repaired, the *Patrick Henry* returned to her station and continued to perform good service during the remainder of that day and the following.

Having sunk the *Cumberland*, I turned our attention to the *Congress*. We were some time in getting our proper position, in consequence of the shoalness of the water and the great difficulty of managing the ship when in or near the mud. To succeed in my object I was obliged to run the ship a short distance above the batteries on the James River, in order to wind her. During all the time her keel was in the mud; of course she moved slowly. Thus we were subjected twice to the heavy guns of all the batteries in passing up and down the river, but it could not be avoided. We silenced several of the batteries and did much injury on shore. A large transport steamer alongside of the wharf was blown up, one schooner sunk, and another captured and sent to Norfolk. The loss of life on shore we have no means of ascertaining.

While the *Virginia* was thus engaged in getting her position for attacking the *Congress*, the prisoners state it was believed on board that ship that we had hauled off; the men left their guns and gave three cheers. They were soon sadly undeceived, for a few minutes after we opened on her again, she having run on shore in shoal water. The carnage, havoc, and dismay caused by our fire compelled them to haul down their colors and to hoist a white flag at their gaff and half-mast another at the main. The crew instantly took to their boats and landed. Our fire immediately ceased, and a signal was made for the *Beaufort* to come within hail. I then ordered Lieutenant Commanding Parker to take possession of the *Congress*, secure the officers as prisoners, allow the crew to land, and burn the ship. He ran alongside, received her flag and surrender from Commander William Smith and Lieutenant Pendergrast, with the side arms of those officers. They delivered themselves as prisoners of war on board the *Beaufort*, and afterward were permitted, at their own request, to return to the *Congress* to assist in removing the wounded to the *Beaufort*. They never returned, and I submit to the decision of the Department whether they are not our prisoners. While the *Beaufort* and *Raleigh* were alongside the *Congress*, and the surrender of that vessel had been received from the commander, she having two white flags flying hoisted by her own people, a heavy fire was opened on them from the shore and from the *Congress*, killing some valuable officers and men. Under this fire the steamers left the *Congress*, but as I was not informed that any injury had been sustained by those vessels at that time, Lieutenant Commanding Parker having failed to report to me, I took it for granted that my order to him to burn her had been executed, and waited some minutes to see the smoke ascending her hatches. During this delay we were still subjected to the heavy fire from the batteries, which was always promptly returned.

The steam frigates *Minnesota* and *Roanoke* and the sailing frigate *St. Lawrence* had previously been reported as coming from Old Point, but as I was determined that the *Congress* should not again fall into the hands of the enemy, I remarked to that gallant officer Flag-Lieutenant Minor, "That ship must be burned." He promptly volunteered to take a boat and burn her, and the *Teaser*, Lieutenant Commanding Webb, was ordered to cover the boat. Lieutenant Minor had scarcely reached within 50 yards of the *Congress* when a deadly fire was opened upon him, wounding him severely and several of his men. On witnessing this vile treachery, I instantly recalled the boat and ordered the *Congress* destroyed by hot shot and incendiary shell. About this period I was disabled and transferred the command of the ship to that gallant, intelligent officer, Lieutenant Catesby Jones, with orders to fight her as long as the men could stand to their guns.

The ships from Old Point opened their fire upon us. The *Minnesota* grounded in the north channel, where, unfortunately, the shoalness of the channel prevented our near approach. We continued, however, to fire upon her until the pilots declared that it was no longer safe to remain in that position, and we accordingly returned by the south channel (the middle ground being necessarily between the *Virginia* and *Minnesota*, and *St. Lawrence* and the *Roanoke* having retreated under the guns of Old Point), and again had an opportunity of opening upon the *Minnesota*, receiving her heavy fire in return, and shortly afterwards upon the *St. Lawrence*, from which vessel we also received several broadsides. It had by this time become dark and we soon after anchored off Sewell's Point. The rest of the squadron followed our movements, with the exception of the *Beaufort*, Lieutenant Commanding Parker, who proceeded to Norfolk with the wounded and prisoners as soon as he had left the *Congress*, without reporting to me. The *Congress*, having been set on fire by our hot shot and incendiary shell, continued to burn, her loaded guns being successively discharged as the flames reached them, until a few minutes past midnight, when her magazine exploded with a tremendous report.

The facts above stated as having occurred after I had placed the ship in charge of Lieutenant Jones were reported to me by that officer.

At an early hour next morning (the 9th), upon the urgent solicitations of the surgeons, Lieutenant Minot and myself were very reluctantly taken on shore. The accommodations for the proper treatment of wounded persons on board the *Virginia* are exceedingly limited, Lieutenant Minor and myself occupying the only space that could be used for that purpose, which was in my cabin. I therefore consented to our being landed on Sewell's Point, thinking that the room on board vacated by us could be used for those who might be wounded in the renewal of the action. In the course of the day Lieutenant Minor and myself were sent in a steamer to the hospital at Norfolk.

The following is an extract from the report of Lieutenant Jones of the proceedings of the *Virginia* on the 9th:

At daylight on the 9th we saw that the *Minnesota* was still ashore, and that there was an iron battery near her. At 8 [o'clock] we ran down to engage them (having previously sent the killed and wounded out of the ship), firing at the *Minnesota* and occasionally at the iron battery. The pilots did not place us as near as they expected. The great length and draft of the ship rendered it exceedingly difficult to work her. We ran ashore about a mile from the frigate and were backing fifteen minutes before we got off. We continued to fire at the *Minnesota*, and blew up a steamer alongside of her, and we also engaged the *Monitor*, sometimes at very close quarters. We once succeeded in running into her, and twice silenced her fire. The pilots declaring that we could get no nearer the *Minnesota*, and believing her to be entirely disabled, and the *Monitor* having to run into shoal water, which prevented our doing her any further injury, we ceased firing at 12 [o'clock] and proceeded to Norfolk.

Our loss is 2 killed and 19 wounded. The stem is twisted and the ship leaks. We have lost the prow, starboard anchor, and all the boats. The armor is somewhat damaged; the steampipe and smokestack both riddled; the muzzles of two of the guns shot away. It was not easy to keep a flag flying. The flagstaffs were repeatedly shot away. The colors were hoisted to the smokestack and several times cut down from it.

The bearing of the men was all that could be desired; their enthusiasm could scarcely be restrained. During the action they cheered again and again. Their coolness and skill were the more remarkable from the fact that the great majority of them were under fire for the first time. They were strangers to each other and to the officers, and had but a few days' instruction in the management of the great guns. To the skill and example of the officers is this result in no small degree attributable.

Questions for Discussion:

1. According to this account, what role did technology play in the Battle of Hampton Roads?

2. What shortcomings or weaknesses did CSS *Virginia* display in this battle?

3. How did Buchanan distinguish the conduct of his own crew from that of the Union Navy?

Edward K. Rawson and Robert H. Woods, eds., *Official Records of the Union and Confederate Navies in the War of the Rebellion, Series I, Volume 7: North Atlantic Blockading Squadron (March 8, 1862–September 4, 1862)*, (Washington, D.C.: Government Printing Office, 1898) 44–49.

J. E. Montgomery and S. L. Phelps, "Battle at Plum Point Bend" (1862)

Some of the fiercest naval battles of the Civil War took place on the western rivers, especially the Mississippi. Union naval forces, based in Cairo, Illinois, moved down the Mississippi in the spring of 1862, but while shelling Confederate-held Fort Pillow, Tennessee, on May 10th, found themselves under attack by eight southern rams. During the battle at Plum Point Bend, the Confederate fleet sank the Union ironclad *Cincinnati* and badly damaged the *Mound City*, though both were raised within days and later repaired. This was a rare victory for Confederate naval forces, but the Union Navy was soon able to proceed down river and attacked Memphis in June. The vessels involved in these battles were either timberclads, essentially civilian riverboats sheathed in wood twelve inches thick or more, or ironclads, which were occasionally purpose-built naval vessels but usually had wooden hulls and frames covered with iron plating above the waterline. The Union, with its far greater industrial capabilities, generally produced superior vessels in terms of firepower, armor, and engines. Both sides referred to these vessels as *rams*, and ramming was indeed practiced in these battles.

The following reports of the battle, one Confederate and one Union, give different versions of the same event. J. E. Montgomery's report from the Confederate side is that of a squadron commander who has just inflicted a defeat on a superior enemy force. S. L. Phelps's report is that of a Union ironclad commander to his wounded superior who was not present at the battle.

Flag-Boat *Little Rebel*,

Fort Pillow, Tenn., May 12, 1862.

SIR:

I have the honor to report an engagement with the Federal gunboats at Plum Point Bend, 4 miles above Fort Pillow, May 10:

Having previously arranged with my officers the order of attack, our boats left their moorings at 6 a.m., and proceeding up the river passed round a sharp point, which brought us in full view of the enemy's fleet, numbering eight gunboats and twelve mortar boats.

The Federal boat *Carondelet* was lying nearest us, guarding a mortar boat, that was shelling the fort. The *General Bragg*, Capt. W.H.H. Leonard, dashed at her; the *Carondelet*, firing her heavy guns, retreated toward a bar where the depth of water would not be sufficient for our boats to follow. The *Bragg* continued boldly on under fire of nearly the whole fleet, and struck her a violent blow that stopped her farther flight, then rounded down the river under a broadside fire and drifted until her tiller rope, that had got out of order, could be readjusted. A few moments after the *Bragg* struck her blow the *General Sterling Price*, First Officer J. E. Henthorne, ran into the same boat a little aft of her starboard midship, carrying away her rudder, sternpost, and a large piece of her stern. This threw the *Carondelet*'s stern to the *Sumter*, Capt. W. W. Lamb, who struck her, running at the utmost speed of his boat.

The *General Earl Van Dorn*, Capt. Isaac D. Fulkerson, running, according to orders, in the rear of the *Price* and *Sumter*, directed his attention to the *Mound City*, at the time pouring broadsides into the *Price* and *Sumter*. As the *Van Dorn* proceeded, by skillful shots from her 32-pounder, W. G. Kendall, gunner, silenced a mortar boat that was filling the air with its terrible missiles. The *Van Dorn*, still holding on the *Mound City*'s midship, in the act of striking, the *Mound City* sheered, and the *Van Dorn* struck her a glancing blow, making a hole 4 feet deep in her starboard forward quarter, evidenced by splinters left on the iron bow of the *Van Dorn*. At this juncture the *Van Dorn* was above four of the enemy's boats.

As our remaining boats, the *General M. Jeff. Thompson*, Capt. J. H. Burke; the *Colonel Lovell*, Capt. J. C. Delancy, and the *General Beauregard*, Capt. J. H. Hurt, were entering boldly into the contest in their prescribed order, I perceived from the flag-boat that the enemy's boats were taking positions where the water was too shallow for our boats to follow them, and, as our cannon were far inferior to theirs, both in number and size, I signaled our boats to fall back, which was accomplished with a coolness that deserves the highest commendation.

I am happy to inform you, while exposed to close quarters to a most terrific fire for thirty minutes, our boats, although struck repeatedly, sustained no serious injuries.

Our casualties were 2 killed and 1 wounded arm broken.

General M. Jeff. Thompson was on the *General Bragg*; his officers and men were divided among the boats. They were all at their posts, ready to do good service should an occasion offer.

To my officers and men I am highly indebted for their courage and promptness in executing all orders.

On the 11th instant I went on the *Little Rebel* in full view of the enemy's fleet. Saw the *Carondelet* sunk near the shore and the *Mound City* sunk on the bar.

The position occupied by the enemy's gunboats above Fort Pillow offers more obstacles to our mode of attack than any other between Cairo and New Orleans. But of this you may rest assured, if we can get fuel, unless the enemy greatly increase their force, they will never penetrate farther down the Mississippi.

I am, with great respect, your obedient servant,
J. E. MONTGOMERY,

Senior Captain, Commanding River Defense Service.

General G. T. BEAUREGARD, Comdg. C. S. Army of the West.

Robert N. Scott, ed., *The War of the Rebellion: A Compilation of the Official Records of the Union and Confederate Armies, Series I, Volume 10 (Part I)* (Washington, D.C.: Government Printing Office, 1884), 888–89.

U.S. Gunboat *Benton*,

Off Fort Pillow, May 11, 1862.

MY DEAR SIR: You will have heard of the fight yesterday morning. Eight rebel gunboats came up to the point, and four or five of them proceeded at once toward the *Cincinnati*, then covering the mortar boat, one of the rebel boats, with masts, being considerably in advance. Captain Stembel, in the most gallant manner, steamed up, rounded to, and opening fire, stood down for the rebels. As he approached the fire was withheld, the ram striking Stembel's vessel in the quarter and swinging both broadsides to, when, the muzzles absolutely against the rebel boat, a broadside was poured into her, making a terrible crashing in her timbers. The rebel swinging clear made downstream, with parting salute of other guns, in a helpless condition. By this time the *Benton*, *Mound City*, and *Carondelet* were far enough down, half way at least, to Stembel's assistance to open an effective fire; the *Pittsburg* not yet clear of the bank and the *Cairo* just sending a boat out to cast off her hawsers. The *St. Louis* came down pretty well; two rams were making for the *Cincinnati* and one again hit her in the stern, receiving the fire of the stern guns. That boat struck Stembel twice doing little damage, but using sharpshooters to such effect as to dangerously wound Stembel and the fourth master, Mr. Reynolds, and one man in the leg. By this time we were in their midst and I had the satisfaction to blow up the boilers of the ram that last hit the *Cincinnati* by a shot from our port bow 42 rifle.[1] I fired it deliberately with that view, and when the ram was trying to make another hit. Another ram had now hit the *Mound City* in the bows, and had received the fire of every gun of that vessel in the swinging that followed the contact. We interposed between another and the *Mound City* and the rascal, afraid to hit us, backed off, when he also blew up from a shot I fired from the same rifle, hitting only a steam pipe or cylinder. All their rams drifted off disabled and the first one that blew up could not have had a soul remaining alive on board, for the explosion was terrific. We could have secured two or three of them had we had steam power to do so, but as it was, saw them drift down helpless under the fort, and one is said to have sunk in deep water. The mortar boatmen acted with great gallantry, firing away to the end. The rebels fired two 32-pounder shots through the mortar boat and two volleys of musketry into her, without hurting a man.

The *Mound City* had her bow pretty much wrenched off and was run onto the shoal opposite where we had been lying. The *Cincinnati* ran to the bank below where we laid when you left, and sunk in 11 feet water.

The *Champion*, steamer, fortunately arrived, having on board a 20-inch steam pump, and the *Mound City* is now afloat, but greatly damaged. The *Cincinnati* will be raised in twenty-four hours. My plan of logs suspended is immediately to be tried. The wounded of the squadron are 5; killed, none. Stembel we hope will recover. He did splendidly; so all did, saving as above stated. The loss of the rebels must be very heavy; their vessels were literally torn to pieces, and some had holes in their sides through which a man could walk. Those that blew up—it makes me shudder to think of them.

I have written very hastily, knowing that you would be anxious to hear and would find excuses for my style and writing, in remembering with what busy circumstances we must be surrounded just now, and I am very nervous from an unwonted amount of exertion and movement. I count off the days, anxious for them to roll around, when you

---

1   42 rifle: a rifled cannon that fired a forty-two-pound shot.

will return, and the *Eastport*, with some power, come to the squadron with your flag flying.

All hands went into the fight with a will. We have no news from below. Colonel Fitch will land his force in the morning.

This I believe is the first purely naval fight of the war.

May heaven bless you, my dear sir, and restore you to us in health very soon.

Respectfully and very truly, yours,

S. L. PHELPS.

Flag-Officer A. H. FOOTE, U. S. Navy,
Cleveland, Ohio.

Questions for Discussion:

1. How do the above reports agree and disagree with one another?
2. Do these reports put greater emphasis on the weapons and technology involved, or on the heroism of the officers and men of the respective fleets?
3. What do these reports reveal about naval warfare on the western rivers?

Charles W. Stewart, ed., *Official Records of the Union and Confederate Navies in the War of the Rebellion, Series I, Volume 23: Naval Forces on Western Waters (April 12, 1862–December 31, 1862)* (Washington, D.C.: Government Printing Office, 1910), 18–19.

S. C. Hawley, "Blockade Runners" (1863)

With the failure to raise the Union blockade, the Confederacy found itself cut off from trade with the rest of the world, especially Europe, on which it relied for shipments of arms and munitions. To remedy this situation, the Confederacy resorted to fast unarmed cargo vessels that attempted to get cargoes through the blockade by a combination of stealth and speed. The Bahamas, then British territory, proved an ideal base for blockade runners because of its proximity to southern shores. Historian Robert Browning's meticulously researched *Success Is All That Was Expected*[1] is a fine example of the growing literature on the Civil War's naval elements.

In this piece, the U.S. consul (a sort of junior diplomatic officer usually involved in overseeing shipping matters) reports on the economics of blockade running and how difficult it will be to stop the practice.

---

1 Robert M. Browning Jr., *Success Is All That Was Expected: The South Atlantic Blockading Squadron During the Civil War* (Washington, D.C.: Brassey's, 2002).

U. S. CONSULATE,

Nassau,[1] *New Providence, June 1, 1863.*

SIR: I beg leave to state, after careful enquiry into the business of blockade running, that the opinion which I expressed in my dispatch No. 23, that "blockade running since I have been here has been on the whole unprofitable," was founded in error. I therefore write to lay before you such data and estimates as I have been able to collect, after careful enquiry and conference with intelligent persons here.

Since the 10th of March last steam vessels have made, or attempted to make, voyages to the States in rebellion, viz: *Wave Queen, Granite City, Stonewall Jackson, Victory, Flora, Beauregard, Emma, Ruby, St. John, Margaret and Jessie, Eagle, Calypso, Cherokee* (late *Florida*), *Nicolai I, Gertrude, Douro, Georgiana, Antonica, Pet, Britannia, Ella and Annie, Charleston, Banshee, Dolphin, Sirius, Orion, Norseman, Minna* 28 in all. Of these vessels the following have been lost and destroyed or captured, to wit: *Wave Queen, Granite City, Stonewall Jackson, St. John, Eagle, Cherokee, Nicolai I, Gertrude, Douro, Georgianna, Dolphin, Minna,* and *Norseman,* or 13 of 28. Eight of the 13 were captured, 5 were driven on shore and destroyed or otherwise wrecked. This proportion of loss seems too large to allow the business to be profitable, but this view is deceptive. The number of successful and unsuccessful voyages must be compared to make a sound conclusion.

Access can not be had to the custom-house record, and there is no other certain means of ascertaining the number of voyages made by these 28 steamers since the 10th of March last. Careful enquiry, however, has satisfied me that the voyages will average two to each steamer, making 56 voyages, counting a trip to Dixie[2] and back as a voyage. This gives us one capture to 4{1/3} voyages, about. To arrive at the probable profits of the business, I made an estimate in the case of the *Ella and Annie.* She came into the business in April, has made two successful voyages, and is now absent on the third venture.

One voyage outward cargo, say 100,000
One voyage expense, etc *15,000*
115,000

---

1   Nassau: the largest port on New Providence Island in the Bahamas.
2   Dixie: a nickname for the Confederacy.

She returns with 1,300 bales of cotton, weighing an average of 400 pounds per bale, equal to 45 cents per pound, or

234,000
From which deduct the cost *115,000*
    Leaves profit *119,000*

Assume that she makes the average four voyages and is lost on the fifth with her cargo the account would stand thus: Four voyages, profit at $119,000 each, is $476,000; deduct cost of steamer, $100,000, and cargo, $100,000, equal $200,000, leaves as profit on four voyages, $276,000. This estimate of profits is far less; it is not half as great as the figures made by those engaged in the business. Such profits are sure to command a large fleet of steamers to engage in the business. Notwithstanding the number of steamers lost within the last eighty days, the number engaged is as great as ever, and I do not expect to see it reduced until our blockade is made more effective, or the cities of Charleston and Fort Fisher (Wilmington)[1] are taken.

Since my dispatch No. 23, there have arrived from England and entered upon the business the *Orion, Sirius, Norseman, Gladiator,* and *Warrior.* The two last named have not yet sailed on the contraband trade, but are preparing for it. We are now in the midst of moonlight nights, and for the week past there has been less movement than ever before since I have been here. The fall in the price of cotton materially interferes with the margin of profits. The holders at Charleston are slow to concede a corresponding reduction in price, which would be from five to six times as much as the fall here, as transactions there are at the standard of Confederate paper.[2] The new wheat crop has come in in the Confederate States, and the demand for breadstuff is not now considerable. The number of persons in that unfortunate country who have nothing to pay with (whatever may be their wants) is rapidly increasing and proportionately reducing the demand for goods furnished by blockade runners.

I beg leave to direct attention to another view of the subject. In making the 56 voyages above referred to the "runners" have passed

---

1   Charleston and Fort Fisher (Wilmington): Both Charleston, South Carolina, and Wilmington, North Carolina, were major blockade-running ports that did not fall until late in the war. Fort Fisher defended Wilmington.
2   Confederate paper: Confederate paper money quickly lost its face value.

our blockading squadron, say, 42 times in less than ninety days. Our squadron has captured and destroyed but 10 or 11, others having been casually wrecked. Suppose a foreign power should allege that our blockade is null and void for want of force or vigilance, would a reply that our blockade had defeated or captured 1 in 10 or 12 of the ventures satisfy the requirements of the law of blockade?

I have the honor to remain, sir, very respectfully,

your obedient servant,

S. C. HAWLEY,

U. S. Consul.

Hon. WILLIAM H. SEWARD,
Secretary of State, Washington, D. C.

Questions for Discussion:
1. What does this document reveal about the economic aspects of the Civil War?
2. What sort of calculations and plans did blockade runners make in conducting their business?
3. According to Hawley, what did the Union need to do to reduce the effectiveness of blockade runners?

Edward K. Rawson and Charles W. Stewart, eds., *Official Records of the Union and Confederate Navies in the War of Rebellion, Series I, Volume 9: North Atlantic Blockading Squadron (May 5, 1863–May 5, 1864)* (Washington, D.C.: Government Printing Office, 1899), 80–81.

James Iredell Waddell, "CSS *Shenandoah* Logbook" (1864–1865)

The most successful Confederate naval efforts were made by the handful of oceangoing commerce raiders that together destroyed some 110,000 tons of Union merchant shipping. Unlike privateers, which were privately owned vessels that captured enemy merchant ships and carried them into port, commerce raiders were naval vessels that destroyed enemy ships, usually by burning them. The threat was so great that many Northern shipowners sold overseas or reregistered their vessels under a foreign flag, usually British, an effect known as *flight from the flag*. By the end of the Civil War, the American merchant fleet was a million tons smaller than it had been in 1861, and peace did not bring recovery.

The following document is from the logbook of the CSS *Shenandoah*. Like many other commerce raiders, *Shenandoah* was built in the United